Introduction to
Counselling and
Psychotherapy

Introduction to Counselling and Psychotherapy

the essential guide

edited by
Stephen Palmer

Los Angeles | London | New Delhi
Singapore | Washington DC

ISBN: 978-0-7619-5543-6
ISBN: 978-0-7619-5544-3 (pbk)

SAGE Publications Ltd
1 Oliver's Yard, 55 City Road
London EC1Y 1SP

SAGE Publications Inc
2455 Teller Road
Thousand Oaks, California 91320

SAGE Publications India Pvt Ltd
B1/I 1 Mohan Cooperative Industrial Area
Mathura Road, New Delhi 110 044
India

SAGE Publications Asia-Pacific Pte Ltd
33 Pekin Street #02-01
Far East Square
Singapore 048763

British Library Cataloguing in Publication data
A catalogue record for this book is available from the British Library

Typeset by Mayhew Typesetting, Rhayader, Powys
Printed and bound in Great Britain by the MPG Books Group

To Maggie and also the future generations:
Kate, Tom, Emma, Leonora, Rebecca and Laura

CONTENTS

ABOUT THE EDITOR

Stephen Palmer PhD is Founder Director of the Centre for Stress Management, London, and Director of the Centre for Multimodal Therapy. He is currently an Honorary Visiting Professor at City University, an Honorary Senior Research Fellow at the University of Manchester, and a Consultant Director of the New Zealand Centre for Rational Emotive Behaviour Therapy.

His current interests are in stress counselling, brief therapy, multicultural counselling, technical eclecticism and integration. He has written and edited over fifteen books including *Counselling for Stress Problems* (1995, with W. Dryden), *Stress Management: a Quick Guide* (1996, with L. Strickland), *Dealing with People Problems at Work* (1996, with T. Burton), *Counselling: The BAC Course Reader* (1996, with S. Dainow and P. Milner), *Client Assessment* (1997, with G. McMahon), *Stress Counselling: a Rational Emotive Behaviour Approach* (1997, with A. Ellis, J. Gordon and M. Neenan), *Handbook of Counselling* (1997, with G. McMahon), *The Future of Counselling and Psychotherapy* (1997, with V. Varma), *Integrative Stress Counselling* (1998, with P. Milner), and *Counselling in a Multicultural Society* (1999 with P. Laungani). He is editor of a number of book series including *Brief Therapies* (Sage).

He co-edits *The Rational Emotive Behaviour Therapist* and is Associate Editor of the *British Journal of Medical Psychology*. During 1999, he launched a new practitioner journal on the internet, *The Online Journal of Multimodal and Rational Emotive Behaviour Therapy*. He was Managing Editor of *Counselling, The Journal of The British Association for Counselling* from 1990 to 1995.

He is President of the Institute of Health Promotion and Education and Honorary Vice President of the International Stress Management Association (UK). He is a Chartered Counselling Psychologist, a United Kingdom Council for Psychotherapy registered psychotherapist, and a Fellow of the British Association for Counselling. He appears occasionally on radio and television in Britain and abroad discussing counselling, stress management and health related issues.

CONTRIBUTORS

Gerhard Baumer studied psychology and trained as an Adlerian Psychotherapist in Berlin. He has been working in private practice for 25 years and writes articles, gives lectures and runs workshops regularly in Germany and England. He is an international Adlerian trainer.

John Brickell is the Director of the Centre For Reality Therapy (UK). He is a senior faculty member of the William Glasser Institute (based in the USA) and is also Director of Training for the Reality Therapy Association (UK). John has taught Reality Therapy in both the USA and the Middle East, as well as throughout the UK.

Michael Burton is a counselling psychologist, psychotherapist (Guild of Psychotherapists) and counsellor (Brighton). As Director of the Psychological Counselling Services Unit at the University of Sussex he teaches on the Unit's Diplomas in Counselling and Supervision as well as pursuing a clinical practice.

Jenny Clifford has worked in the National Health Service for 30 years as a speech and language therapist. She has a psychology degree and is an Adlerian therapist, family counsellor, supervisor, trainer, author and co-director of the Institute of Adlerian Psychology.

David Crossley gained his first degree in theology and religious studies, before qualifying in medicine. He worked first as a GP and subsequently in psychiatry and psychotherapy and has several publications in the field of psychiatry. He has also worked as a teacher and medical officer in Africa. Currently he is Senior Registrar in Psychotherapy in Liverpool.

Berni Curwen is a cognitive-behavioural psychotherapist accredited by the British Association of Behavioural and Cognitive Psychotherapies (BABCP) and registered with the United Kingdom Council for Psychotherapy. She has a psychiatric nurse background and has worked in both the NHS and private practice. She contributed two chapters to *Client Assessment* (Sage, 1997).

Ken Evans is Director of the Sherwood Psychotherapy Training Institute, Nottingham, where he is also the Programme Leader for the MA in Gestalt Psychotherapy. He is a past President of the European Association for Psychotherapy and currently Training Standards Officer for the United Kingdom Council for Psychotherapy.

Colin Feltham is Head of the Counselling Development Unit, School of Education, Sheffield Hallam University, a Fellow of BAC, and author or editor of many books, including *Time-Limited Counselling* (Sage, 1997), *Which Psychotherapy?* (Sage, 1997) and *Controversies in Psychotherapy and Counselling* (Sage, 1999). He jointly edits the *British Journal of Guidance and Counselling*.

Fay Fransella is a clinical psychologist and a registered psychotherapist with the United Kingdom Council for Psychotherapy. On taking early retirement from the University of London to found the Centre for Personal Construct Psychology, she was awarded an Emeritus Readership by the University. She is currently director of the Centre for Personal Construct Psychology. She is known internationally for her writings and work on personal construct psychology and repertory grid methods, particularly in the areas of counselling and psychotherapy. In 1997 she gave papers at the International Congress on Personal Construct Psychology in Seattle, USA and, at the invitation of the British Council, in Belgrade, Serbia and Skopje, Macedonia.

Maria C. Gilbert is a Teaching Member of both the Gestalt Psychotherapy Training Institute in the United Kingdom and of the International Transactional Analysis Association. Currently she is head of the Integrative Psychotherapy and the Supervision trainings at the Metanoia Institute in West London.

Michael Göpfert has worked in general nursing, neurology, adult psychiatry, child psychiatry and psychotherapy in England, Canada and Germany. He has co-edited a book on *Parental Psychiatric Disorder* (Cambridge, 1996) and is the author of papers in neurolinguistics, psychosomatics and psychotherapy. He has been a Consultant Psychotherapist in Liverpool since 1987. His therapeutic orientation is integrative (systemic bias).

Juliet Grayson is a UKCP Registered NLP Psychotherapist. She has a Master Practitioner NLP Certificate, a Diploma in Professional Counselling, and a Diploma in Relationship and Sexual Therapy. Based in Kingston, Surrey, she sees individuals and couples for therapy, and also offers training and consultancy.

Jean Hardy worked for 25 years in universities teaching sociology and political philosophy. She discovered psychosynthesis in the early 1980s, writing *A Psychology with a Soul* (Woodgrange, 1996) out of curiosity about the ideas underlying transpersonal psychology. She teaches now on the Psychosynthesis and Education Trust M.A. in London, and at Synthesis in Bristol. She is Editor of *Green Spirit*.

Peter J. Hawkins is Reader in Health Psychology at the University of Sunderland. He has published numerous papers and book chapters in the field of counselling psychology and hypnosis, as well as giving workshops in many European countries, including Russia.

Sarah Hawtin works as a part-time educational counsellor at the University of East Anglia (UEA) and as a General Practice counsellor in Norwich. She is also a trainer with the UEA Person-centred Diploma in Counselling.

John McLeod is Professor of Counselling at the University of Abertay Dundee. His interests are in experiential and narrative approaches to counselling and psychotherapy, and in developing ways of making therapy research more relevant for practice.

Gladeana McMahon is a BAC Fellow, Accredited Counsellor and Counselling Supervisor and a BABCP Accredited Cognitive-Behavioural Psychotherapist. She tutors on the Post-Graduate Diploma in Therapeutic Counselling (Integrative) at the University of East London and is External Assessor to the Diploma in Therapeutic Counselling (Integrative) at Bromley College. She is also a published author and occasional broadcaster.

Michael Neenan is Associate Director of the Centre for Stress Management in Hayes, Kent. He is an accredited therapist in cognitive-behaviour therapy (CBT) and rational emotive behaviour therapy (REBT) and is co-chair of the Association of Rational Emotive Behaviour Therapists. He is on the editorial boards of *Counselling*, the Journal of the British Association for Counselling and *Stress News*, the Journal of the International Stress Management Association (UK). He has co-authored six books on REBT including *A Dictionary of Rational Emotive Behaviour Therapy* (Whurr, 1995) and *Dealing with Difficulties in Rational Emotive Behaviour Therapy* (Whurr, 1996).

Richard Nelson-Jones, a Fellow of both British and Australian Psychological Societies and the British Association for Counselling, has been a university counselling trainer, author of numerous books and articles, and counselled in educational, occupational, medical and private practice settings. He now lives in Chiang Mai, Thailand, where he directs the Lifeskills Centre.

Bill O'Connell is a senior Lecturer at the University of Birmingham, Westhill. He is a BAC Accredited counsellor and author of *Solution Focused Therapy* (Sage, 1998).

Brigid Proctor is a Fellow and Accredited Supervisor of the British Association for Counselling, and a Founder member of CASCADE Associates. She has NLP Practitioner training from ITS and uses NLP presuppositions and techniques in her freelance counselling, training, supervisor development and writing.

John Rowan has been involved in primal work since 1977. He has given the keynote speech at two conferences of the International Primal Association. He is a Fellow of the British Psychological Society, and has been active in the field of research and in the field of the theory of subpersonalities. He is in private practice in London and also teaches at the Minster Centre.

Peter Ruddell is a cognitive-behavioural psychotherapist accredited by the BABCP and registered with the United Kingdom Council for Psychotherapy. He has worked in both the private and voluntary sectors. He contributed two chapters to *Client Assessment* (Sage, 1997). He is on the editorial board of *The Rational Emotive Behaviour Therapist*.

Julia Segal is Senior Counsellor at the CMH Multiple Sclerosis Unit, Central Middlesex Hospital, London. Since training with Relate in 1979–83 she has published work on disability, illness, children with ill parents and the ideas of the psychoanalyst Melanie Klein.

Ian Stewart is Co-Director of The Berne Institute, Nottingham. He is a Teaching and Supervising Transactional Analyst and UKCP Registered Psychotherapist. He is co-author of *TA Today* (Lifespace, 1987), and author of three books on TA published by Sage: *TA Counselling in Action* (1989), *Eric Berne* (1992) and *Developing TA Counselling* (1996).

Jean Stokes is a UKCP registered Jungian Analytical Psychologist with a private practice in South West London. She trained with the Association of Jungian Analysts (AJA) and is also a member of the International Association of Analytical Psychologists (IAAP) and a Psychotherapy Member of FPC/WPF. She teaches on the AJA training and at the Westminster Pastoral Foundation where she is also a Training Supervisor.

Lawrence Suss works in private practice, and part-time in Psychological and Counselling Services at Sussex University where he convenes the Diploma in Counselling. He is BAC accredited and UKRC registered, has trained in CAT at Guy's Hospital, London, and in psychoanalytic psychotherapy training with the Association for Group and Individual Psychotherapy.

Kasia Szymanska is a Chartered Counselling Psychologist, a BABCP accredited psychotherapist and is also UKCP registered. She works in private practice, for a Stress Unit in the City of London and as a lecturer in counselling psychology. She also works as a trainer and is the editor of *Counselling Psychology Review*, published by the British Psychological Division of Counselling Psychology. She is an Associate Director of the Centre for Stress Management, London.

Tony Tilney came into counselling after careers in the pharmaceutical industry and teaching. He is the director of a transactional analysis training institute, Thanet Centre for Psychotherapeutic Studies, and is the author of *Dictionary of Transactional Analysis* (Whurr, 1998).

Diana Whitmore is Chairperson of the Psychosynthesis and Education Trust which offers a Postgraduate Diploma in Psychosynthesis Counselling (BAC accredited) and an MA in Psychosynthesis Psychotherapy (UKCP Member) validated by the University of East London. She trained in Psychosynthesis with Roberto Assagioli and has trained professionals in Psychosynthesis for over 25 years. She has published *Psychosynthesis in Education; a Guide to the Joy of Learning and Psychosynthesis Counselling in Action* (Sage, 1991).

Robert Wubbolding is the Director of Training for the William Glasser Institute (USA) and is Professor of Counselling at Xavier University, in Cincinnati, Ohio. He has served as a consultant for the drug and alcohol programmes for the US Army and Air Force and is the author of over 100 publications and nine books on Reality Therapy.

Sarah Young originally trained as an Orthopist and worked in the NHS for 15 years. She is now a UKCP registered Psychotherapist and a Chartered Counselling Psychologist working in private practice. She is a visiting lecturer and supervisor at the School of Psychotherapy and Counselling at Regent's College and also at the New School of Psychotherapy and Counselling, Royal Waterloo House. As a member of the Executive Committee of the Society for Existential Analysis, she was responsible for organizing five of their annual conferences. She is a volunteer helpliner for Breast Cancer Care.

PREFACE

This book is a guide to 23 different approaches to counselling and psycho-therapy. It is written for beginner counsellors, counselling psychologists and psychotherapists in training or those more experienced who wish to have one text that covers the main approaches practised in Britain. The book has also been written for the layperson or casual reader who would like to increase their understanding of the different forms of therapy.

Stephen Palmer

ACKNOWLEDGEMENTS

I would like to thank all the contributors involved with this book. This venture was a large task which needed everyone's ongoing cooperation. The support and encouragement received from the publishers, in particular Seth Edwards, Alison Poyner and Susan Worsey at Sage, was invaluable.

INTRODUCTION

Stephen Palmer

W hy an introductory book focusing on different counselling and psychotherapy approaches? Over the years I have trained many counsellors,
psychotherapists and psychologists in a range of therapeutic approaches. So
often, the questions, 'What exactly is multimodal therapy?' or 'What is rational
emotive behaviour therapy?' are asked by prospective trainees before they attend
a course at the training centre at which I work. On other occasions, trainees
have admitted that they attended their first training course elsewhere without
even realizing that different approaches of counselling existed. For beginner
counsellors, counselling psychologists and psychotherapists entering into this
profession it can appear similar to walking into unknown and possibly hostile
terrain. If they refer to a counselling textbook then prior knowledge of the
subject may be expected. Considering the number of approaches to counselling
and psychotherapy available, how many counsellors and psychotherapists have
trained in an approach that either clashes with their personality or is unsuited to
the client group with which they wish to work?

Let us now consider those who are thinking about entering into therapy.
Where can they obtain information or guidance about the different approaches
to counselling that does not require prior knowledge? How easy is it for them to
compare and contrast the different therapies available and read case studies
illustrating how each theory is applied to the practice of the particular
approach? What help can they receive in choosing an appropriate approach that
would suit their temperaments and be relevant to the particular presenting
problem(s)?

In the light of some of the difficulties often encountered by beginner counsellors (as well as their potential clients) this book provides information about
the theory and practice of 23 different approaches to counselling and psychotherapy. It will help potential trainees and clients to enter training or counselling
with informed consent. The chapters reflect what is currently practised in many
counselling rooms across Britain. Therefore where earlier forms of psychotherapy have been included the contents have a pinch of post-modernism. I have not
included the most recent forms of therapy or those that are based on body work
which are less associated with the field of counselling.

In Chapter 1 Colin Feltham introduces the subject of counselling and psychotherapy and provides a useful overview to the models covered in this book. For
beginner counsellors this is probably a good place to start reading this book.
For convenience, he has divided the different approaches into psychoanalytic,

cognitive-behavioural, humanistic and 'other' approaches. Apart from the last title, these are the main groupings that are normally applied within the field of counselling and psychotherapy.

Chapters 2–24 cover the different therapeutic approaches which have been listed for the reader's ease in alphabetical order. In these chapters, to help the reader compare and contrast each approach the contributors were asked to maintain an identical format as below:

Introduction
Development of the therapy
Theory and basic concepts
Practice
Which clients benefit most?
Case study
References
Suggested reading
Discussion issues

However, within each section the contributors were given some flexibility to include factors that were relevant to their particular approach. All 25 chapters include suggested reading material and discussion issues, the latter to stimulate further reflection or deliberation. Some of the discussion issues are also suitable as essay titles.

In Chapter 25 John McLeod introduces the importance of research in counselling and psychotherapy. A glossary of key terms and concepts used in this book has been provided. Appendix 1 comprises an extended list of therapies to highlight the wide range of approaches practised although not necessarily easily available in Britain. Appendix 2 is a client checklist for potential clients uncertain about what to ask the counsellor when attending their first counselling session. The Afterword includes details of the three main British professional bodies that either accredit practitioners or recognise particular training programmes.

Every attempt has been made to convey ideas in readily understandable language, but readers may find that certain approaches are less immediately accessible than others. This is probably because they rest on rather complex concepts or chains of ideas not easily conveyed in brief chapters. It simply *is* the case that some approaches are theoretically more complex than others. In such cases, interested readers are advised to consult the glossary where necessary and also to follow up on recommended further reading. It should, moreover, be acknowledged that individual readers may find more of an affinity with some approaches than with others, so that certain chapters seem easier to absorb.

Although it is usual practice to read books starting at the beginning and reading through to the end, this book has been written to allow readers to dip into any chapter that gets their attention or is necessary for study if they are attending a training course.

1

AN INTRODUCTION TO COUNSELLING AND PSYCHOTHERAPY

Colin Feltham

Most people today probably have at least some hazy notion of what counselling is, since the term is now used so widely. However, misunderstandings and disagreements still abound about what the differences are between advice giving, counselling, psychotherapy and similar terms. Although I cannot go into it all here, it is true to say that a whole host of activities, professions and relationships, from befriending, co-counselling and mutual aid groups, to clinical psychology, counselling psychology, psychiatry and social work, in some ways resemble and overlap with each other. In this chapter I will focus on understandings of counselling skills, counselling and psychotherapy, before going on to look succinctly at different approaches.

COUNSELLING SKILLS

Terms such as counselling skills, communication skills, interpersonal or relationship skills, are often but not always used interchangeably. It is sometimes thought that there are certain communication and relationship-building skills that all or most approaches have in common, and these tend to be skills used intentionally in conversation towards certain helpful ends. Counselling skills may be said to differ from everyday, casual conversation in the following ways.

- While much ordinary conversation is characterized by rather casual, perhaps somewhat inattentive listening, a key counselling skill is active listening which involves the conscious discipline of setting aside one's own preoccupations in order to concentrate as fully as possible on what the other person is expressing. This may involve a high level of awareness of one's own prejudices and idiosyncrasies.

- While ordinary conversation may contain a great deal of interaction, anecdotes, sharing thoughts and ideas and changing the subject aimlessly, another key counselling skill involves the discipline of responding mainly to the other person, in a purposeful, non-judgemental and often rather serious way, which tends to mean that such conversation usually has a somewhat one-way character.

- While ordinary conversation is not usually constrained by any agreements about confidentiality, counselling skills are usually backed up by either an implicit or explicit understanding about confidentiality.

- While ordinary conversation is often thought to be 'natural' and to have no particular rules governing it, counselling skills may often feel or be experienced as somewhat unnatural. For example, the person using counselling skills may strive to understand very accurately and demonstrate this striving by sometimes repeating parts of the other's statements in order to clarify or deepen understanding.

- Finally, while much ordinary conversation wanders across many subjects with no necessary goal, counselling skills are generally associated with some sort of goal, be it helping with decision-making, offering an opportunity to discharge emotions, offering alternative interpretations or suggesting strategies for making desired changes.

Although there is some disagreement about the extent to which counselling skills may be possessed naturally by many people, it is widely (although not universally) believed that the skills have to be identified, understood, learned and practised repeatedly if one is to be able to be a consistently good listener and effective helper. Also, it is important to remember that while skills of this kind may be learned by many professionals, sometimes for their own ends (for example, salespeople intending to win customers over), the use of counselling skills is properly associated with therapeutic, helping or healing ends and not with self-centred agendas.

Counselling skills may be used in all sorts of situations – in the classroom, at a hospital bedside, in training settings, or at bus stops or parties! In other words they may be used within professional contexts, in voluntary work, or simply in everyday social and domestic settings, when someone is trying to listen in a disciplined manner, to be as helpful, constructive or interested as possible. Fairly typically, students on counselling skills courses may be nurses, teachers, ministers of religion, residential social workers and similar professionals, as well as those engaged in voluntary work. Typical too on counselling skills courses is some sort of (three or five stages of the helping process) model drawn from the ideas of Gerard Egan (Professor of Psychology and Organizational Studies), Richard Nelson-Jones (Counselling Psychologist), Sue Culley (Counsellor) and others, usually advocating systematic practice in basic and advanced empathy, paraphrasing, summarizing, open questioning, challenging, and so on.

COUNSELLING

Counselling differs in its formality from interactions where counselling skills are used. Counselling is generally characterized by an explicit agreement between a counsellor and client to meet in a certain, private setting, at agreed times and under disciplined conditions of confidentiality, with ethical parameters, protected time and specified aims. Usually (although not always) the counsellor will have had a certain level of training (beyond the level of a certificate in counselling skills, typically a diploma or above), will belong to a professional body with a published code of ethics, and will receive confidential supervision for her or his counselling.

It is widely accepted that counselling may be a suitable form of help for a variety of personal problems or concerns, the most common being depression, anxiety, bereavement, relationship difficulties, life crises and traumas, addictions, self-defeating behaviour and thwarted ambitions. It can help with issues of loss, confusion and other negative conditions or it may also be used more proactively and educationally to learn for example how to relax, be more assertive, deal with stress and lead a more fulfilling life.

It is not essential to know where counselling comes from etymologically, historically, and so on, but it probably does help to consider a few facts. The term itself does of course stem from the verb 'to counsel', which has always meant to advise, so it is not surprising that some people still have this misconception about counselling. Although some forms of counselling contain some advice-giving components, counselling is mostly dedicated to enhancing or restoring clients' own self-understanding, decision-making resources, risk-taking and personal growth. Telling people what to do is therefore usually eschewed as a short-term and often counterproductive remedy.

A great deal of counselling in Britain is associated with the non-directive, client-centred approach of the psychologist and psychotherapist Carl Rogers, and indeed we have to thank Rogers as one of the most active promoters of counselling in the USA. Many early British counsellors, too, took their ideas and training from Rogers' approach which, as we shall see later in this book, rests heavily and optimistically on belief in the innate resourcefulness and goodness of human beings. But it is important to know that hundreds of different theoretical approaches to counselling now exist, many of which do not share Rogers' views, and some of which may be almost diametrically opposed to Rogers. Theoretically, then, counselling is a very broad and potentially confusing field of learning itself.

It may help when you come to consider differing approaches to counselling and psychotherapy to remember that each is necessarily an imperfect product of a certain time and place, which in its own way strives to make sense of distress and to promote methods of effective help. While each approach emphasizes certain aspects of human functioning and therapeutic skills, it has been argued that most depend on common factors such as a healing (second chance) relationship, a good fit between client and counsellor, the readiness of clients to be helped, the belief of clients and counsellors in the efficacy of counselling and the plausibility of espoused theories.

PSYCHOTHERAPY

Do not despair or blame yourself if you are confused by the differences between counselling and psychotherapy; the alleged differences are indeed confusing and even many of the most prominent practitioners disagree. Psychotherapy originally referred to a less intense form of psychoanalysis and is still understood by some professionals as being, properly speaking, psychoanalytic psychotherapy only. However, the client-centred or person-centred approach is referred to as both counselling and psychotherapy, usually without distinction. Various forms of brief psychotherapy challenge the simplistic claim that psychotherapy is long-term and counselling is brief. It is now common to see the term 'behavioural psychotherapy' (which is regarded as a contradiction in terms by some because 'psyche' refers to the mind, even the deep mind, rather than to superficial behaviour), but this only demonstrates that as yet no one owns the term psychotherapy and that what is carried out under that name is a very wide range of activities. It is probably advisable to ask anyone who uses the term psychotherapy exactly how they are using it, and with what justification!

Most psychotherapy, like counselling, is fundamentally talking-based therapy resting on psychological contact, theories and techniques. My own view is that you cannot ultimately distinguish between counselling and psychotherapy, and indeed other similar practices.[1] None the less it is important to accept that some practitioners (mainly those trained as psychotherapists) strongly believe in significant differences. Since clients or potential clients sometimes ask about such matters, it is important in the long run to become informed about them. I now outline what I think are the basic differences as claimed by many psychotherapists.

- Psychotherapy (and its psychoanalytic variants in particular) involves lengthy training (three to four years and sometimes more) which usually includes ongoing mandatory personal therapy for all trainees, exposing them to the subtle, unconscious layers of conflicts and defences they inevitably have. Working through one's own unconscious conflicts lessens them, makes it unlikely that clients' and therapists' issues will become confused or that clients will be intentionally or unintentionally exploited or abused, and is the best way of experientially understanding the theory and enhancing the practice of psychotherapy. In counselling training, personal/training therapy has recently become mandatory, with counselling psychologists and counsellors having to complete at least 40 hours as partial fulfilment of requirements for chartered and accredited status respectively.

- Psychotherapy addresses the deep, unconscious, long-standing personality and behaviour problems and patterns of clients (frequently referred to as patients), rather than focusing on and superficially resolving only their presenting symptoms. Psychotherapy is about radical, far-reaching personality change which is likely to be much more robust than the symptomatic and temporary changes effected by counselling.

- Psychotherapy, originally closely associated with the medical profession, takes very seriously clients' psychopathology, or entrenched psychological distress patterns, usually thought to derive from very early relationships in childhood and/or from partly innate drives. Psychotherapy holds out hope of making real differences to the lives of some very disturbed or damaged people who could not benefit from once-weekly, symptom-oriented or crisis-related counselling.

- Psychotherapy requires a substantial time commitment, sometimes demanding that patients attend several times a week for several years. Counselling, by contrast, is often very short-term and usually once-weekly.

It is important to state that such a brief summary risks caricaturing both psychotherapy and counselling. Also, it is true to say that many practitioners do not adopt antagonistic positions such as these, instead agreeing that valuable work is carried on under different names or that different kinds of work are being usefully carried on by two (or more) different professional groups. By examining the literature of the British Association for Counselling (BAC), United Kingdom Council for Psychotherapy (UKCP), British Psychological Society (BPS), British Confederation of Psychotherapists (BCP) and the Independent Practitioners' Network (IPN), you may become acquainted with such issues in greater depth if you so choose. It is also worth watching the Lead Body for Counselling, Advice, Mediation, Psychotherapy Advocacy and Guidance for developments in National Vocational Qualifications (NVQs), about which there are many lively debates in the counselling and psychotherapy world.

APPROACHES TO COUNSELLING

There follows a condensed overview of the main approaches to counselling to be found in this book. The purpose of this admittedly whirlwind tour is to encourage readers to:

- get an overall sense of the field, some of its complexity, its historical and theoretical breadth

- begin thinking about the key differences between approaches – why they differ, how the differences are of interest and use, and how they are perhaps not so useful

- begin to consider what the main, common effective ingredients of the approaches may be

- ask themselves why they may be especially attracted to some approaches more than to others, and on what grounds

Given that this is a highly complex and controversial field, you are cautioned that I, like all practitioners, am likely to have my own biases and limitations in understanding. The positive value of a book such as this is that it condenses and represents multiple theories and practices in a manageable format. If you intend to look more deeply into the intricacies of particular approaches and the debates between counsellors, it is usually advisable to refer both to traditional literature (original sources) and to the latest editions of specialist texts by those representing their own theoretical orientation. I have arranged this overview according to the convention of psychoanalytic, humanistic and cognitive-behavioural traditions (kinds of umbrella groupings), with a broad category of 'others' for those not necessarily belonging to those three traditions or whose affiliation is disputed.

PSYCHOANALYTIC APPROACHES

Psychoanalysis was the creation of the physician Sigmund Freud at the end of the nineteenth century. Many of Freud's early adherents split from him for theoretical and personality reasons, and many psychoanalytic approaches have evolved from Freud's in recent decades. The terms psychoanalytic, analytic, dynamic, psychodynamic and depth psychological may be said to share a stake in belief in the existence and power of the unconscious dimension of the mind, with its complex conflicts, symbolisms and defence mechanisms; in the importance of early childhood development and its long-standing effects; and in the replay of unconscious forces in the therapeutic relationship in various kinds of transference phenomena. Critics suggest that these approaches may be too long-winded, elitist, expensive, ineffective and based on very far-fetched, implausible theories.

Freudian

Sigmund Freud is probably regarded by a majority of counsellors as the single most significant founding figure in the development of counselling and psychotherapy. Although some now argue that there is no truly current *Freudian* therapy (because other variants have incorporated and bettered Freud), we must credit Freud with a particular view of a complex unconscious system made up of innate drives as well as early developmental vulnerabilities. Freud's concepts of ego, id and superego, his identification of defence mechanisms, insistence on the unconscious significance of dreams, jokes and slips of the tongue, on the importance of working through transference material in therapy, and other contributions have had an enormous influence on counselling and on popular culture.

Jungian

At one time very close to Freud, the psychiatrist Carl Jung established his own 'analytical psychology' or Jungian analysis (although he was not happy with the latter term) from the early part of the twentieth century. Jung disagreed with Freud's stress on childhood as the seat of all later ills, gave due weight to adulthood and old age and the complexity of the psyche, and focused on a lifelong process of individuation. Jung was influenced by mythology, anthropology, theology, astrology, alchemy and other disciplines, advocated a collective as well as an individual unconscious, and introduced many non-Freudian techniques. Modern Jungian therapy has its own schools of developmental, archetypal and classical therapy and is sometimes considered a transpersonal (spiritually oriented) approach.

Adlerian

Alfred Adler, a physician, had also been a colleague of Freud before launching his own 'individual psychology' around 1912. Adler disputed Freud's emphasis on psychosexual development and instead stressed the importance of a holistic view, incorporating the social and educational dimensions. Adler examined issues of power in families, particularly in sibling relationships, faulty private logic leading to mistaken life goals, and many other phenomena. Sometimes criticized for being too akin to common sense (and therefore arguably not psychoanalytic), Adlerian therapy or counselling has also been claimed by some (for example Albert Ellis) as influential in the development of cognitive-behavioural therapy.

Kleinian

Melanie Klein, psychoanalyst, represents a second or possibly third wave of psychoanalytic development, dating from around the 1920s and 1930s. Klein was more interested than Sigmund Freud in infant observation, in inferences about the long-standing influence of early relationships ('object relations') and in formulating developmental stages aligned with vulnerable early relationships with primary caregivers. She also developed methods of child psychotherapy and theory and practice relating to psychoses. Klein, who developed much of her work in Britain, was affiliated with the object relations school whose therapeutic work is characterized by a belief in the inevitable replay of powerful, damaged early states as unconsciously driven reactions towards the therapist.

COGNITIVE-BEHAVIOURAL APPROACHES

Historically, behaviour therapy pre-dates the cognitive therapies and these may be seen as quite distinct from each other. However in the last few years a kind of merger has been tacitly acknowledged. Behaviour therapy, stemming from psychological science in the 1920s and clinical psychology in the 1950s (in the UK), is based on an attempt to produce scientific therapy by observing problematic behaviour accurately, generating testable theories and robust and effective remedies. Broadly speaking, it is about eliminating or reducing distressing behaviour and is not concerned with alleged causes or global personality changes. With the cognitive dimension comes the recognition of certain mediating thought processes between behaviour and distress. The cognitive-behavioural approaches seek to assess and treat identified symptoms and concerns in an efficient, largely here-and-now, verifiable manner, using precise assessment techniques, and a range of in-session and homework-based tasks. Critics suggest that these approaches deal short-sightedly with mere symptoms, not with the whole person, and that they miss out the entire area of feelings, human potential and spirituality, for example.

Behaviour therapy

Stemming from a number of countries and pioneers, behaviour therapy set out to promote a scientific theory of behaviour, behavioural problems and their remedies, without recourse to gratuitous and unprovable concepts. We learn unhelpful behaviours (by using faulty ways of dealing with stress, by always responding with panic to certain situations, for example) and proceed to reinforce our unhelpful behaviour. Behaviour therapists identify precise situational factors associated with problem behaviours and teach coping and social skills, systematic desensitization (gradual exposure to what we fear, while learning to relax) and response prevention (learning not to keep checking electrical appliances, for example, as in obsessive-compulsive disorder). It is said to be especially successful with phobias, obsessive-compulsive problems and other well-specified conditions.

Rational emotive behaviour therapy (REBT)

Albert Ellis, a clinical psychologist, created REBT (originally called rational therapy, then rational emotive therapy) from the 1950s as an attempt to provide a more efficient approach than the psychoanalytic methods he had been trained in. REBT is an active-directive, here-and-now, cognitively affiliated therapy (that is, based primarily on *thinking*), drawing from stoical philosophy and arguing that we are not upset directly by events in our lives but by the irrational beliefs we hold about ourselves and about life. REBT aims to help overcome situational problems (for example exam anxiety) and self-rating problems (for example low self-esteem) among others, using a range of educational, confrontational and other techniques.

Cognitive therapy

Aaron Beck, psychiatrist and psychotherapist, developed cognitive therapy from the 1950s, in an attempt to improve upon psychoanalytic methods. Noting that we frequently appear to have automatic thoughts about our circumstances and that we make many incorrect inferences about our situation that may both create and worsen negative moods, Beck successfully applied his findings initially to depression. Cognitive therapy is now an elaborate and thriving method of therapy, based on collaboratively helping clients to understand how their own cognitions (thinking) affect their moods and behaviour, and how certain common lifelong belief patterns can be overthrown methodically. Similar to REBT, but perhaps less confrontational, cognitive therapy is becoming widely available in Britain, especially in the NHS.

Reality therapy

Reality therapy, introduced by another disaffected analytic practitioner, the clinical psychologist and psychiatrist William Glasser, in the 1960s, is not necessarily always considered cognitive-behavioural. I place it here because it has an emphasis on people gaining self-respect through a somewhat no-nonsense, common-sense therapeutic process involving direct behaviour change. Clients are helped to become morally responsible for their own actions by identifying their needs, their actual behaviour and discrepancies between these, and making desired changes. Reality therapy has had considerable successes with offenders, troubled young people, and those involved in drug and alcohol misuse, but has not yet taken hold widely in the UK.

Personal construct therapy (PCT)

Again, personal construct practitioners (more likely to be psychologists than counsellors or psychotherapists) may disagree with the view that theirs is a cognitive-behavioural approach. The psychologist George Kelly formulated PCT in the 1950s as a theory of personality and therapy, also known as constructive alternativism, which demonstrates among other things that we usually (and inaccurately and unhelpfully) construe our experiences in extreme polar opposites, with which we become stuck (for example if I am not brilliant I must be stupid). PCT is a complex approach, utilizing specialist concepts and, sometimes, tabulated exercises. It has been very influential in the development of the so-called 'narrative-constructivist' approaches and of cognitive analytic therapy.

Multimodal therapy

Arnold Lazarus, originally a prominent behaviour therapist, sought greater breadth and techniques tailored to individual clients and devised this systematically eclectic form of therapy based on identifying the primary modalities in which people function, acquire and correct their problems: behaviour, affect, sensation, imagery, cognition, interpersonal and drugs/biological and lifestyle factors (BASIC ID). Assessment allows counsellors to apply the techniques (borrowed from any other approach) most likely to be helpful in each case, which may include assertiveness training, anxiety management, visualization and so on.

Lifeskills counselling

Associated with Richard Nelson-Jones and others, this essentially psycho-educational approach focuses on identifying and coaching people in the acquisition, refinement and maintenance of skills they need to learn to overcome problems in everyday living and to establish more successful coping styles. Most problematic areas of functioning, for example those including intimate relationships and job seeking, can be broken down into units amenable to concrete improvement and can be addressed successfully by such an approach.

HUMANISTIC APPROACHES

What the humanistic approaches share broadly speaking is an optimistic belief in the self-determination of the person. Thus, the emphasis is more on the present and future than on the past, more on trusting feelings and their expression than on limited rational thinking and traditional science, more on looking hopefully at holistic potential than at psychopathology and symptoms for behavioural change, more on shared human growth than on professional expertise, more on radical social change than on adapting to a sick society. Many of the humanistic schools emerged from or found their natural home in California in the 1960s and 1970s. 'Humanistic' is not used in its atheistic sense but in contrast to alienating, scientistic, medically and expert-oriented approaches. Critics suggest that the humanistic approaches are romantic, self-indulgent, not necessarily concerned with ordinary people's everyday pressing worries and are often hostile to attempts at scientific verification.

Person-centred counselling

Carl Rogers, rejecting the traditions of psychoanalytic and behavioural approaches and the powerful profession of psychiatry that claimed to have the answers, developed his non-directive (later called client-centred, and now person-centred) therapy from around the 1940s on the basis of experience and research suggesting that therapeutic conditions such as unconditional positive regard, empathy and congruence were the key to successful personal growth. This optimistic philosophy and practice, championing the view that human beings are essentially and positively self-actualizing, has informed much training in the UK and Europe especially.

Gestalt therapy

Fritz Perls, originally a neuropsychiatrist, with his wife Laura and others, devised Gestalt therapy (Gestalt is German for 'whole' and suggests looking at all aspects of being and behaviour) partly as a reaction against psychoanalysis and intellectualizing systems, placing much more emphasis on non-verbal and bodily language, here-and-now behaviour and potential, and the client's conscious responsibility for his or her actions, decisions, thoughts, feelings and awareness. Perls was influenced by, among other things, Zen Buddhism, existentialism and psychodrama. Modern Gestalt uses a range of powerful techniques such as chairwork and is not necessarily the confrontational approach it is often caricatured as.

Existential counselling

A number of therapists who became disillusioned with analytic approaches, or regarded them as insufficient, drew inspiration from ancient and modern philosophers. Instead of dwelling on individuals' psychopathology, existentialists argue that the human condition confronts us all with challenges of life and death, freedom, meaning, values, choice and commitment. Counselling is an intensely specific, relatively atheoretical and technique-free process guiding clients to identify their own responsibility for life values and choices.

Transactional analysis (TA)

Eric Berne, psychiatrist and psychoanalyst, departed from the psychoanalytic tradition by focusing on observable interpersonal interaction as well as private, inner, unconscious states. He roughly converted the analytic idea of superego,

ego and id into the now well-known Parent, Adult and Child ego states of TA. People can be helped consciously to recognize how and why they move between states, and how they can change or harness lifelong or current self-defeating scripts, rackets, games and drivers. Modern TA requires a great deal of theoretical mastery. There are some disagreements about how truly humanistic, or psychoanalytic or even cognitive-behavioural TA is.

Psychosynthesis counselling

Originally a psychoanalyst, Roberto Assagioli started formulating psychosynthesis in the early part of the twentieth century, drawing on various religious traditions, yoga, humanistic psychology and adding many of his own ideas and techniques (for example mental imagery, inner dialogue, ideal model). Psychosynthesis is a transpersonal approach which seeks to include but go beyond a focus on personal problems stemming from the past, and everyday problems, into questions about the purpose of life, the superconscious, higher self and collective unconscious.

Primal integration

The 1970s spawned many heavily feelings-based therapies, one of the most sensational being the psychologist Arthur Janov's primal therapy (a variety of which, incidentally, is now espoused by Alice Miller). Primal integration, related to this, dwells on the uncovering and expression of deep feelings, often suppressed for decades. These feelings may relate to painful birth (or pre-birth) experiences, childhood or later abuse (physical, sexual or emotional) or deprivation, but they may also relate to joyful and spiritual experiences and can result in profound psychological and bodily changes.

OTHER APPROACHES

Here I include approaches which do not fall naturally under the three other broad umbrellas. This may be due to their being very recently developed, or very novel, or (as is often the case) to their drawing eclectically from various other approaches or attempting to formulate their own integrative approach based on the theories of others. While the transpersonal has been sometimes hailed as the 'fourth force' (after psychoanalytic, cognitive-behavioural and humanistic), some writers are predicting that multicultural counselling, for example, will become the major new fourth force. Perhaps this shows that counselling is indeed a dynamic, ever-changing field.

Hypnosis

Forms of hypnosis have existed for centuries and Freud experimented with and later discarded hypnotic techniques. Hypnotherapy has sometimes attracted misplaced interest, being caricatured as an almost magical process conducted by mysterious, master practitioners, and associated sometimes with unscrupulous, exploitative and superficially trained practitioners. It is adaptable for use with other approaches such as REBT, is often successful for pain control (for example in dentistry) and some habit disorders (for example smoking), and is often preferred by clients seeking rapid results or who have not found predominantly talking approaches helpful.

Neuro-linguistic programming (NLP)

Developed by John Grinder, Assistant Professor of Linguistics, and Richard Bandler, psychologist, from the 1970s, NLP draws on certain Gestalt, hypno-therapeutic, cybernetic and other ideas and techniques and is concerned not only with counselling but with accelerated learning and management development. We can re-programme our minds by means of reframing, visualization and substituting constructive for self-defeating beliefs and inner dialogue. NLP is replete with techniques and strategies, including some that aim to produce rapid and complete cure of phobias, for example.

Cognitive analytic therapy (CAT)

CAT is commonly presented as an integrative approach because it is in fact an integration of elements of psychoanalytic (particularly object relations) therapy, personal construct psychology, and cognitive and behavioural approaches. It is one of the few British-grown approaches, devised by Anthony Ryle (originally a doctor), in the 1980s to fit NHS needs for realistically short-term treatment for a relatively wide variety of problems including eating disorders, borderline personality disorders and suicide attempts. Many diagrams and paperwork exercises are used.

Solution focused therapy

Also known simply as brief therapy, originated by Steve de Shazer and other American strategic family therapists from the 1970s (and influenced by Gregory Bateson, Jay Haley and Milton Erickson), the solution focused approach challenges several cherished assumptions and proposes new methods. Instead of searching for putative causes of problems in clients' pasts, instances of effective coping are sought, clients' imaginations are enlisted by using techniques which encourage them to visualize themselves producing solutions, and in effect questioning their own tendency to psychopathologize themselves.

Problem focused counselling

This term can be used to describe any of the approaches used, often by psychologists, to help increase clients' coping skills. Problem focused counselling aims to identify exactly what clients' problems really are, what change goals arise from these, what steps can be taken towards these goals, what decisions and actions are required, and what action and evaluation. To this extent the approach has much in common with Egan, Nelson-Jones, Glasser and others. The form of problem focused counselling presented in this book adds the important dimension of separating out the emotional from the practical aspects of clients' problems, by first using rational emotive behaviour therapy to dispel emotional obstacles to problem-solving strategies.

Integrative

This term has many competing meanings. Here it is used to refer to the work and approach of Gerard Egan, Sue Culley and others, stemming from around the 1970s. Egan's work has been and probably still is enormously influential in Britain. This approach recognizes the importance of building a good therapeutic relationship with clients (using Rogerian core conditions), enabling them to open up and unfold their 'story' in the early stages of counselling, but also of establishing goal-oriented expectations. The rather person-centred beginning stage feeds into a middle stage of working towards concrete identification of goals and subgoals, and the ending stage encourages specific actions towards real change in the everyday world. The approach may thus be seen as an integration of aspects of the Rogerian/person-centred approach with aspects of approaches such as the cognitive-behavioural.

CONCLUSIONS

Hopefully by now you have begun to get an impression of the breadth, complexity, fascination and problems of the field of counselling and psychotherapy. As a field that is now over 100 years old, that is represented by numerous and competing traditions, theories and techniques as well as by several similar professions, that is continuously being developed, no individual can hope to ever 'know it all', nor does anyone need to know it all or to feel demoralized by any relative ignorance. Researchers are busily trying to identify exactly what is most effective in the field, and some forecasters attempt to pinpoint trends, such as the apparent decline of certain approaches and the growth and success of others. Critics from outside and inside counselling note some clients' claims of abuse, exploitation and ineffectiveness. It is important, I believe, if you are persisting with learning in this field, that you find questions and frameworks to guide your learning and to help you become selective in a manner that is as free from prejudice as possible and as committed as possible to the shared understanding and pursuit of better mental health.

REFERENCE

1 Feltham, C. (1995) *What is Counselling?* London: Sage.

SUGGESTED READING

Feltham, C. (1995) *What is Counselling?* London: Sage. Examines definitions of counselling, distinctions between counselling, psychotherapy and similar professions in some depth, and also looks succinctly at the historical background of counselling, and its religious, philosophical and political dimensions.

Feltham, C. and Dryden, W. (1993) *Dictionary of Counselling*. London: Whurr. The first specialized dictionary of counselling, this contains well over 1,000 terms of relevance to counsellors.

Palmer, S., Dainow, S. and Milner, P. (eds) (1996) *Counselling: The BAC Counselling Reader*. Contains sections on different approaches to counselling, techniques, contexts, research issues and critical themes; and helps to set the development of counselling in historical context.

Palmer, S. and McMahon, G. (eds) (1997) *Handbook of Counselling* (2nd edn). London: Routledge. Authoritative collection of chapters on counselling themes, agencies, typical presenting problems, ethics and also on important topical issues such as the rise of brief and time-limited counselling.

DISCUSSION ISSUES

You may apply these questions both to what you have read in this chapter and to the chapters following.

1 How important is it to decide on the real differences between counselling and psychotherapy (and similar professions), and what will guide your decision?

2 To what extent do the summarized approaches seem to belong reasonably cohesively to the groups to which they are allocated, as opposed to seeming like unrelated endeavours? Why does this matter?

3 Which of the approaches seem to rely most on the relationship between client and counsellor, which on the expertise, theory and techniques of the counsellor?

4 Which of the approaches do you personally find most compelling, and why? How would you go about finding objective evidence that any approach is superior to another?

2

ADLERIAN COUNSELLING AND PSYCHOTHERAPY

Jenny Clifford and Gerhard Baumer

A dlerian therapy is a cognitive approach which means that clients are encouraged to look at and understand and possibly change the ideas and beliefs that they hold about themselves, the world and how they will behave in that world. In addition, Adlerian therapists set assignments with their clients that challenge existing ideas and beliefs and which represent changes in their habitual pattern of behaviour. The Adlerian approach has an optimistic view that people have created their own personalities and therefore can choose to change. Clients are encouraged to value their strengths and to acknowledge that they are equal members of society who can make a worthwhile contribution.

DEVELOPMENT OF THE THERAPY

Alfred Adler, who was a medical doctor, developed a new school of psychology called Individual Psychology in 1911 in Vienna. He had previously been part of Sigmund Freud's Psychoanalytical Society but broke away from him when the two men's approaches became too divergent. Adler wanted to show his holistic approach to personality – the word *individual* really means indivisible. Adler was a medical doctor who became interested in patients who were suffering from physical ailments that did not have a physical cause; we call these functional disorders or hysterical conditions. Adler himself was a brilliant, insightful practitioner who did not formalize his therapy approach but talked about patients in his lectures to show how they demonstrated his theory of personality and his philosophy of society. After the First World War he changed his focus from working with neurotic patients to working with people who could change society; he considered that teachers who were able to influence children should be the focus of his attention and he held open teacher–child counselling sessions. Adler reluctantly left Vienna in 1934 and settled in America, as did many of his followers; some Adlerians went to Europe and practised and taught Individual

Psychology to medical and educational professionals, and several Institutes and Adlerian Societies were set up. During the Second World War Adlerian activity ceased in Europe but later revived and is now active in many Western and Eastern European countries, in Japan, Scandinavia, Australia, USA and many other countries. Nowadays the approach is called Adlerian and the term Individual Psychology is used less. The Adlerian Society and Institute for Individual Psychology has counselling training courses in London and there are training courses in Buckinghamshire and Cambridge.

THEORY AND BASIC CONCEPTS

Holistic

Adler's view was that people's actions, thoughts and feelings had to be seen as one consistent whole. People choose to be the sort of people they are through trial and error as children and consistently remain those sorts of people throughout their lives. Adler called this consistency their style of life, pattern of life or lifestyle; people form views of themselves and of the world and the people in it and how they will behave in that world. The ideas and beliefs in the lifestyle are generalizations – for example, I always have to be better than others or I always have to be liked by everyone. Adler was not so concerned with what people inherited from their parents as with what they did with their genetic inheritance and how they responded in their own unique way to their environment; he considered they were responsible for the sort of people they were.

Social

Adler suggested that, as people were social in nature, their behaviour had to be interpreted in a social context, so he was interested in how they behaved in the first group to which they belonged, their family of origin, and how they behaved in their school groups as children and their work groups as adults, how they behaved within their friendship groups and within intimate relationships. The human baby is born in an inferior position, quite helpless and dependent on others for survival; this dependence lasts well into teenage years in Western society. Wise parenting will enable children to grow to feel that they are social equals in their families; social equals have equal rights, equal respect and share equal responsibilities. Children who belong as equals expect their views to be taken into account whenever decisions are being made that affect the whole family; an example would be family holidays or moving house. They expect to be spoken to with respect and treated with respect. They are willing to take their share of chores and responsibilities to enable family life to run smoothly. The parents will have the same expectations of the children. The parents will not pamper the child; that is, they will not do anything for the child that the child can do for him or herself. Pampering is the most disabling form of parenting and perpetuates the child's initial feelings of inferiority. Spoiled children who are used to getting their own way from doting parents find school and adult life rather hostile; fellow pupils and teachers and work colleagues are not willing to give in to them. Children who are made to feel special and superior to others will also find school and adult life difficult. Peer groups may not want to give that person special status and will be irritated by their attention-seeking behaviour. Children who act in a superior way will find themselves isolated and their peers will feel put down by them.

Teleological

This word comes from the Greek word *teleo*, meaning goal. Adler thought that all behaviour had a purpose. In order to understand someone's behaviour we must know what goal they are unconsciously seeking by behaving in this way. What is the purpose, for example, of always being late? People will give all sorts of excuses but the Adlerian psychologist will want to know that person's goal; are they putting other people's affection for them to the test – wanting to know whether people will still like them even if they are always late? Or are they late to show people how busy they are? The underpinning belief is that people will only know how busy I am if I am consistently late for all my appointments. Or perhaps they need to show that they will always do what they want to do – that they are in control and no one can make them be on time. Lateness could serve some other purpose. The goals are unconscious so the person will be unaware of the goal of his or her chronic lateness and the underlying belief that supports the behaviour. Adlerians call the beliefs that underpin people's goals of behaviour, *private logic*; this is because the belief makes sense to the person and is logical, but in fact to everyone else it is neither logical nor common sense. Not everyone would consider it necessary to be late for all appointments in order to show people how busy they were.

Psychological disturbance

As described already, some children are ill-prepared for the demands of life. The pampered child might find learning at school difficult, making decisions impossible, and gaining independence unattainable. The pampered child will have been used to parents doing things for him and guiding and protecting him; the consequence of this is that as the child grows older he will become less and less confident about his ability to face challenges and make decisions. He will not have had the learning experience of making independent decisions and living through the consequences of those decisions; he will not have experienced learning through his mistakes, and discovering that mistakes are okay. It could happen that a child such as this starts to make decisions as a teenager when his parents can no longer exert total control over him and these decisions are unwise; this merely confirms the parents' and the child's belief that the child needs help and is incapable of being wise. There are many pampered adults who rely on others stronger than themselves to make their decisions for them; they may not have done well at school and may not be able to get a job. They will feel alienated from society and could be led into crime, develop chronic illness, avoid social relationships and, most testing of all, be unable to maintain an intimate relationship. They have a sense that they are not realizing their potential but they have not had the experience of doing things for themselves and have a great fear of the unknown which keeps them just where they are. Spoilt children will find that the world does not give them what they want; this makes them resentful as they were always made to feel very special and powerful by their families and unbelievably the world just treats them as one of the crowd. They find ways to feel powerful and, if they are really angry, to get even. Crime is one activity which these people find satisfying; they might see something they want, so they take it; this makes them feel powerful. They might also want to feel that they are getting their own back on a society that has let them down and has not acknowledged how special they are. They may have difficulties making relationships with others because they want to be in a position of power; they will expect that the temper tantrums that they had as children which terrorized their doting parents into giving into them should work with their friends; as a result friends could drift away and intimate partners leave them; they would then experience a sense of loss of their special place. They might take alcohol or drugs excessively in order to avoid feeling the pain of their loss. These people feel inferior because they have never experienced social equality; they only know about competition and acting as superior to, or feeling inferior to others. Adler described a person's sense of equality as *gemeinschaftsgefuhl*, which does not translate easily into English. It means that a person feels he or she has an equal place in society and a sense of belonging to the community – Adler preferred the translation of 'social interest'. Each child is born with the potential to develop social interest and with the appropriate upbringing this will develop. Those children who grew up to feel inferior may need therapy to become aware of the beliefs and ideas they have about themselves which are causing them discouragement. They need to understand their lifestyle and their private logic and the mistaken goals and hidden purposes of their behaviour. They then have the opportunity to change their beliefs and their behaviour. Adler considered that each person has chosen to be the person that he or she is; we are the authors of our own creations of ourselves. This approach is very optimistic because it gives people the opportunity to change themselves if they wish. However, change is not easy for an adult; we are all expert at being our old selves and will be clumsy beginners at being a different version of ourselves.

The goals of the Adlerian approach are:

- to uncover with clients their mistaken goals and underlying ideas so that they understand their own unique lifestyle
- to encourage clients to acknowledge that they are social equals

This is achieved in four phases of therapy:

- establishing a relationship
- gathering information in order to understand the client
- giving insight
- encouraging reorientation

Establishing a relationship

The first phase is to establish a relationship of social equals in which the partners have equal respect, equal rights and equal responsibilities. Most clients have never experienced such a relationship before and the relationship with their therapist may be their first democratic relationship. The therapist acts as a good parent, accepting the client unconditionally, developing with the client an understanding of who she is and encouraging the client by pointing out her strengths and abilities and believing that the client can make changes if she wishes. The client needs to feel safe to explore her innermost thoughts and express deep feelings with the therapist. The therapist will also expect respectful behaviour from the client so that agreements about appointments and payments are kept. The client and therapist will need to be sure that they share common goals for the therapy. The therapist must not play games with the client, for example by getting into power games and fighting with the client, or by being controlled or pleased by the client.

Gathering information

The second phase, of understanding the person, will start as soon as the client enters the room. Adler was reported to be expert at gathering information about the client by observing the way the client entered the room and how he sat down and how he spoke and behaved in the sessions. Direct questions are asked by the therapist, not only about why the person has come for therapy but also about himself generally; a great deal can be learned about a client by what he tells and does not tell, as well as by the content of his answers. The therapist will be interested in his participation in the workplace, his friends and social life and if he has an intimate relationship and how it is going on. The therapist will also want to know about the person's family of origin. It was in this family that the client developed his lifestyle containing his thoughts, goals and feelings. The therapist will ask him to describe his siblings and parents when he was a child. He chose to be a particular child in his family through trial and error. His siblings were also making choices about the sort of children they would be. The therapist and the client will be beginning to develop hypotheses about the personality that the child developed. Was this client an eldest child who was threatened by a younger brother or sister who had decided to strive to be better than his or her siblings and in the process lost no time in putting the other siblings down? Or was this client a pampered youngest child who had two parents and older siblings doing things for him and over-protecting him? It is now necessary for the therapist to gather information from another source. The client will be asked to give a few early memories: Adler discovered that people remember things that reinforce the beliefs and ideas in their private logic; the memories are symbolic representations of these ideas and beliefs. The memory may be of an insignificant occurrence in the client's childhood and yet out of all the things that have happened to him, he produces that memory; that memory is produced because it has particular significance to him and symbolizes a belief maybe about himself or about the world or about how he should behave in his perceived world. Dreams are also used for interpretation as they too contain symbolic representations of a person's private logic. Together the therapist and the client interpret the early memories and dreams.

Giving insight

The third phase is giving insight. The therapist will have formed some hypotheses about the clients' view of themselves, their view of the world and their unconscious decisions about how to move through life. These guesses need to be checked out with the client. The client can agree or disagree. Very often the therapist will know that she has guessed correctly when the client shows recognition either verbally or through a non-verbal response such as a smile. The client needs to own the insight and the therapist would not impose her suggestions, as this is a working partnership. The feelings, beliefs and ideas are recognized by the client who also has an understanding as to how he came to have these so that there is no mystery. The client may recognize how his private logic has restricted him and may want to change his ideas and goals; the therapist may have to challenge the client's goals and ideas so that the client can align his goals with common sense and not with his private logic. The therapist will help the client see how his presenting problems fit in with his lifestyle – for example, if you are a person who believes that life is dangerous then you will be very frightened of new and demanding situations and may have presented with a problem of feeling stuck. If you are a person who likes to be better than everyone else then it is likely you will end up lonely and without real friends.

The reorientation phase then starts and this is where the client has the hardest work. The therapist will be there guiding and encouraging as the client finds a way to change. The therapist will encourage the client by pointing out the client's strengths and by believing that the client will find a way to move on. Progress can be sporadic and the therapist is there to point out when the mistaken ideas are still holding the client back. Attainable assignments are set with the client; these challenge the private logic and break through blocks that the client may have had in his life. They are new behaviours for the client and the therapist will be able to hear how the client experienced a new behaviour and will congratulate the client on achieving such a change. There is no set format for a session. Adlerian therapy respects the individual and so clients can lead the session at the beginning if they wish, bringing to the session what they want to talk about. The therapist may refer to previous sessions if there are issues that are common; in fact there usually are recurrent themes running through all the sessions because they are looking at the consistent lifestyle. The therapist may end the session in order to finish on time and to set assignments if appropriate.

WHICH CLIENTS BENEFIT MOST?

The Adlerian approach uses verbal descriptions from the client, and therapist and client explore interpretations with the therapist wanting recognition from the client to confirm that they are on the right track. This requires from the client a certain level of language ability. We once described the Adlerian approach to a member of the public at a conference, and when I had finished she said, 'Oh so you do it with words' – other stalls were using crystals, colours or were looking into people's eyes, etc. Adlerians do not always use words – psychodrama, art therapy and non-verbal exercises are also used. However, the client needs to talk about and understand what they discover about themselves during their art or drama. When the Adlerian family counsellor works with children she meets the whole family and may only need to speak to the children to check their goals; the rest of the work is done with the parents or carers. This can also be done with the families and carers of adults who do not understand language. The Adlerian approach is based on a distinct philosophy of human life – that people want to belong as equals and a society of equals allows each person to develop to their full potential. If a person agrees with this goal for society and for its members then they will be able to work with an Adlerian therapist. Clients who are able to accept responsibility for their behaviour and who are willing to take risks and make changes will benefit from the approach.

Case study

THE CLIENT

Mary was 28 when she was referred by a psychiatrist with depression and suicidal tendencies.

Understanding the client

Mary told me that she felt very low and exhausted and had a sense of emptiness. She worried a lot, her negative thoughts going round in vicious circles; one of these thoughts was of committing suicide. She had vague guilt feelings. She had lost her appetite, slept badly and had no interest in sex. She added that she was no longer able to concentrate and found it difficult to follow the lessons at the adult education centre where she had just started doing some A levels. In class Mary believed she had nothing to contribute and when she was asked a question she would blush and stammer or just remain silent. She felt stupid and inferior to the other students so she avoided contact with them and as a result felt very lonely. She had thought about leaving the course.

I wanted to find out more about her situation now. I looked at her strengths; what things made her an attractive, useful or at least tolerable person? After some hours of exploration it was obvious she liked to please people; she also looked after people and felt responsible. I acknowledged these strengths. For Adlerians, encouragement is quite important; I used it to stabilize her low self-esteem and to start her thinking that she could make a useful contribution. Looking at Mary's positive side gave me an idea of her potential growth areas. During a long period of therapy this would give both of us positive goals to work towards and would constantly reaffirm to Mary that she had value as a person.

During further sessions I learned that she had been in a relationship with a man for five years; when they first met he used to be very active and sociable, studying Social Science and working in a night-club. Over the past few years he had given up his studies, played strange music with strange friends, enjoyed alcohol and cannabis, and earned money at a pub nearby, helping in the kitchen. Mary was very unhappy about the way he was living his life and about their situation and felt they no longer had much in common. She had trained as a pharmacy assistant and worked part-time in a pharmacy; she complained about the poor wages and the amount of work she had to do because of staff shortages, but she could not leave her job because she did not want to disappoint her boss.

Here is her family constellation: Mary was brought up on a farm; it was a working farm that her mother had inherited. Mother was described as quiet and very caring. Father was seen as authoritarian; he got cross easily, shouted and punished the children; he was moody and unpredictable. Mary tried to avoid him. He liked spending money on his own pleasures and bought big cars, bred horses and dogs, was a member of the local hunting club and threw parties for its members. After some years the farm was run down financially and it was sold, with her father carrying on as tenant for a while.

Mary had four siblings – a sister five years older, a brother eighteen months older, a sister two years younger and a brother ten years younger. Her older sister Susan was a bully, stood up to her father, and dominated the younger siblings. Mary saw her as very selfish. This was Susan's reaction to being dethroned; she had been an only child for three-and-a-half years and had lost her special place. Susan left home when she was eighteen, married, and was rarely seen at home from then on. The older brother was described as very sensitive and he and Mary were very close. As a teenager he committed suicide. His death was still an unresolved problem for Mary when she came for therapy.

Mary used to like looking after her younger sister Lizzie. Lizzie had been the youngest for eight years and was very sociable. The baby brother, Nick, was very pampered by his father and had become dependent on him. Mary was very angry with her father and tried to influence him but she did not succeed. It appeared from the family constellation that Mary had chosen to be the good child, the responsible one.

I asked Mary for three early recollections in order to learn more about her lifestyle.

This was the first memory given: 'I was about 5 years old and I was sitting on the back of a pony and was very proud. All of a sudden there was a loud noise; the pony startled and I fell off. My sister laughed at me. I felt very ashamed and incompetent.'

The second memory was thus: 'I was about 8 years old. The family was all in the living room. All of a sudden my older sister stood up, walked over to my father, who had nodded off behind his newspaper, and demanded her pocket money. He refused – she insisted and there was a terrible row. I was sitting next to mother clinging on to her arm in despair. My sister left the room, slamming the door after my father had tried to kick her. I think my sister was a troublemaker and I hated her for that. It was a spoilt Sunday afternoon.'

The third memory was: 'I was about 8 years old and I was helping mother in the kitchen. It was a really bright day and I looked out of the window and saw my brothers and sisters playing out there. I felt very excluded and sad; I felt envious and thought life is unfair.' And she added: 'I always helped mother. Helping in the kitchen was my job. It was a safe place. I used to dream a lot while I was doing my chores.'

We have seen that in Mary's family constellation she chose to be the good child and from these early recollections we can also see her belief system giving more information about her view of herself, what she expects from others and how she moves through life. The first early recollection shows the whole tragedy. When I am active and try to have fun something might happen that will spoil it. The message is: life is dangerous, expect the unexpected to happen and do not trust people. The second memory confirms this view of people and events and shows Mary inactive and frightened. It also shows how powerful men are and may indicate that Mary sees herself (or women) as a victim. The third memory shows Mary withdrawing from real life and living in a fantasy world. It is important for her to feel safe and she lacks courage to join in. The price she has to pay is sadness. She sees her life as a burden and her frustration and anger are a consequence of this. She is not talking in that early recollection; Mary has not learned how to express herself.

During the first phase of therapy we worked a lot on practical problems that she was experiencing at the time – how to make contact with other people and how to react in certain situations. We discussed her self-image, her expectations and how she behaved in her lessons. She developed a more realistic view of her situation and was more connected with reality. She got rid of the anger she had been keeping in for years. I was empathetic, supportive and encouraging whenever possible. She felt better and three times during the first year she stopped coming. Each time she came back, depressed again. It was not easy for her to trust but we had some serious discussions about the fact that she still had a lot to do in therapy, so she finally agreed to make a full commitment. After our relationship became stable I offered her a place in a group in addition to one-to-one therapy. This was quite a challenge for her. Her social interest or feeling of belonging was limited and it was not easy for her to talk with others about herself. At first she was very quiet, then she gave others good advice. She had to learn that it is not always appropriate to give advice – at least not before people have reached a certain level of awareness. She slowly gained insight and learned how to share her experiences with others. She became more sociable. She was also more active and her self-confidence grew. We were now able to work on her past, her childhood and her family experiences; this was painful for her.

At the end of the second year we went through a difficult phase. She was able to cope with her mother's death but it was too much that her father started to spend the children's inheritance. He even sold most of their antique furniture. At the same time she learned that her boyfriend was in love with somebody else, and the friendship with her best friend became unstable. Mary had a very serious setback. I acted in the next group meeting, expressed my fears and asked her to promise not to commit suicide for the next six months. It took the whole evening for her to agree. I knew she would not let anybody down once she had given her word. We could now go on to solve her problems. She was really angry with me; she felt I had forced her and that caused a strong father transference where she reacted to me as though I was her father. It took more than six months for her to be able to accept my intervention. Mary made progress again. She did well in her exams and made some new friends. She left her partner and found a new boyfriend. She saw that her mother merely had limitations and was not a victim. She discovered aspects of herself which reminded her of her father. It became obvious that she was seeking power and she also needed to improve her tolerance. In the fourth year of therapy she became more and more confident. Her social life improved and her mood became stable. At the same time she decided to study agriculture and education. We both agreed at that point that we could finish the therapy. The last thing I heard was that she had started teaching at an agricultural college and that she was living a busy and fulfilled life.

SUGGESTED READING

Two recent translations of books by Alder are:

Adler, A. (1992) *Understanding Human Nature*, trans. Colin Brett. Oxford: Oneworld Publications. This book is based on a series of lectures that Adler gave at the People's Institute in Vienna. The aim of the book is to enable people to understand themselves and each other better. This is a new translation from the original by Colin Brett.

Adler, A. (1992) *What Life Could Mean to You*, trans. Colin Brett. Oxford: Oneworld Publications. Once again, Colin Brett, in translating Adler's original text, has produced what is probably the most readable book available on Adler's theory and practice.

DISCUSSION ISSUES

1　Many contemporary psychological and psychotherapeutic approaches have adopted Adler's ideas without acknowledgement. Describe three examples and discuss.
2　The Adlerian counsellor will want to explore the client's childhood with the client. Why?
3　All experience is subjective. How does this idea affect the way Adlerian practitioners think about people and work with them?
4　Early memories provide a window onto the personality. Discuss with an example.

3

BEHAVIOUR COUNSELLING AND PSYCHOTHERAPY

Berni Curwen and Peter Ruddell

B ehaviour therapy is aimed at changing observable and measurable human
behaviour. These changes are chosen by the therapist and the client
together. As this approach is aimed at behaviour change, some problems are
better suited to behaviour therapy than others. The therapist is directive, giving
the client clear guidelines about what to do in order to bring about such changes.
This direction is guided by the therapist's detailed assessment. The assessment
considers three main areas: the factors immediately preceding the problem, the
problem behaviour itself and the consequences of the behaviour for the client (as
well as those people around him or her).

Behaviour therapy covers a range of approaches. At one end, the focus is
entirely upon behaviour; thoughts (cognitions) are not denied but are considered
to be peripheral to therapeutic work. At the other end, thoughts are considered
to be a central and mediating factor of behaviour, and are therefore taken fully
into account in bringing about behaviour change. The range of approaches
therefore merges into cognitive behaviour therapy which is discussed elsewhere
in this book.

DEVELOPMENT OF THE THERAPY

In the early 1900s, Ivan Pavlov, a physiologist, demonstrated classical conditioning.[1] A dog will salivate when it is shown food. As this happens naturally
and automatically it is called an *unconditioned response*. The unconditioned
response is triggered by something, in this case food. This trigger is known as the
unconditioned stimulus. If showing the food to the dog is paired with ringing a
bell at about the same time, the dog will eventually salivate at the sound of the
bell alone. As the bell, not the food, now triggers the dog salivating, the ringing
of the bell is now known as the *conditioned stimulus*. This new response of
salivating to the sound of the bell alone is known as a *conditioned response*. If

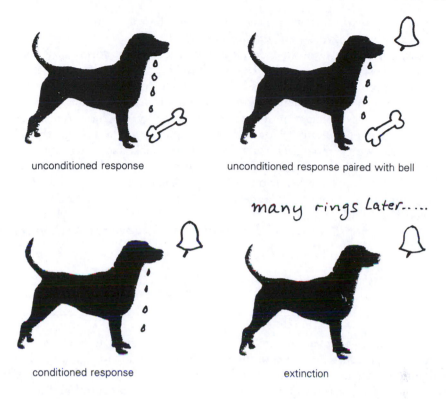

unconditioned response

unconditioned response paired with bell

many rings Later.....

conditioned response

extinction

FIGURE 3.1 Classical conditioning

the conditioned stimulus (bell) is presented too many times without the unconditioned stimulus (food), the conditioned response (salivation) will fail to occur
when the bell is rung. This process is known as *extinction* (see Figure 3.1).

John Watson, a psychologist, and his associates, in 1920, proposed that
phobias were just this process.[2] A conditioned emotional response (fear) had
been paired with a previously neutral stimulus, such as a spider. Joseph Wolpe,
in 1958, outlined a practical treatment procedure, called systematic desensitization, where relaxation training is paired with the conditioned stimulus. The
confrontation of the feared stimulus, in this example, a spider, is a central part
of behaviour therapy, known as *exposure treatment*. There are a variety of ways
in which this exposure may be carried out and these will be described more fully
later.

Prior to the development of classical conditioning, Edward Thorndike, a
psychologist, had demonstrated that behaviour was mainly determined by its
consequences;[3] if a particular behaviour is rewarded by a favourable outcome, it
tends to be reinforced and repeated. This reward learning became known as
operant conditioning or instrumental conditioning. For example, if a cat is in a
box and accidentally touches a lever which opens a door allowing the cat to
escape (the reward), the action of touching the lever becomes reinforced: the
lever-touching behaviour is therefore mainly determined by the consequence of

escape. This work was formalized in one of the most influential works in American psychology, *Animal Intelligence*, 1911.

Behaviour therapy was first developed in a consistent form by Burrhus F. Skinner, a psychologist, in the 1950s. Skinner proposed that all behaviour, whether helpful or unhelpful, was brought about by operant conditioning and that changing behaviour merely required the appropriate operant conditioning. Another key psychologist in behaviour therapy was Arnold Lazarus who popularized it in the late 1950s and who emphasized the role of thought in behaviour. Two psychologists, Hans Eysenck and Jack Rachman, and two psychiatrists, Isaac Marks and Michael Gelder, were important figures in Britain for developing and applying behavioural therapy. They were part of the Maudsley group (operating from the Maudsley Hospital in south-east London) which formed the British Association for Behavioural Psychotherapy which is now known as the British Association for Behavioural and Cognitive Psychotherapies.

THEORY AND BASIC CONCEPTS

We mentioned at the end of the introduction that behaviour therapy covers a range of approaches. At one end, the focus is entirely upon behaviour; thoughts (cognitions) are not denied but are considered to be peripheral to therapeutic work. At the other end, thoughts are considered to be a central and mediating factor of behaviour, and are taken fully into account in bringing about behaviour change. The range of approaches merges into cognitive behaviour therapy which is covered elsewhere in this book. We shall therefore focus entirely on the behavioural end of the range.

Therapists from many different orientations now generally accept that thoughts (cognitions), feelings (emotions) and actions (behaviour) all go hand in hand. A change to one will usually lead to change in the other two. For example, if a person moves from feelings of depression to feelings of happiness, she will tend to think about herself, the world and the future more optimistically and to adopt behaviour which she had previously neglected. Behaviour therapists focus their work on bringing about changed behaviour. They takes the view that changed feelings and thoughts will follow automatically as a result of changed behaviour.

You may wish to remind yourself at this point of the terms *classical* and *operant conditioning*, and *exposure treatment* introduced on pp. 30–1, as these are basic elements of behaviour therapy.

Behaviour therapy takes the view that all behaviour, whether helpful or unhelpful, normal or abnormal, is learned through classical or operant conditioning. Symptoms are seen as unwanted behaviours. For example, a person bitten by a dog may become fearful of dogs: through classical conditioning, he may associate the conditioned response of fear with the previously neutral stimulus of dog. Oliver Twist's thieving behaviour was rewarded and reinforced by his peers through the process of operant conditioning.

Once psychological disturbance has been acquired, it is perpetuated either through failure to learn new behaviour or through avoiding feared objects/ situations which results in a conditioned response failing to be extinguished. For example, the dog phobic avoids the feared stimulus – dog. The conditioned emotional response – fear – fails to be extinguished as exposure to the dog without adverse consequences has not taken place. Therapy is seen as changing such behaviour through new learning, or unlearning old behaviour through exposure treatment. This is where the skill of the behaviour therapist is essential.

First, it is very frightening to confront your fear. If you simply tell a dog-phobic to go and stroke dogs, or an agoraphobic to enter a busy supermarket, they will be unlikely to do so and will consider your suggestion as unhelpful or even ridiculous. Therefore the therapist employs a range of strategies and techniques which are designed to bring the client into contact with the feared situation in a planned fashion that is acceptable to the client. These will be described later.

Second, the person with symptoms in need of help, will often be unaware of all the occasions when the problem behaviour is present. For example, a person with social anxiety may be aware that they experience anxiety with groups of people but not be aware of the specific features of social situations which trouble them, such as making eye-contact, being the focus of others' attention, or making requests. As we shall see in the next section, the therapist conducts a detailed assessment called a *behavioural analysis*.

Third, unless a new behaviour is practised frequently, over a sufficient period of time, therapy will usually fail. Often, clients do not persist in their new behaviours for long enough. The therapist therefore takes appropriate steps to build a therapeutic relationship through which the client's motivation is encouraged and maintained in the face of difficulties. Motivation is aided by negotiating clear goals with the client and providing a detailed explanation of how this may be accomplished. This will include discussing with the client the way in which the proposed programme differs from the client's own (failed) attempts at overcoming the problem. The client is encouraged to adopt the role of a 'scientist', in which role tasks are carried out. These tasks are viewed as experiments where the client gains valuable insight into her problem. Where a client is unable to perform a task, this will not be viewed as a failure, but as important new information about her problem. This approach is helpful in maintaining motivation.

PRACTICE

The general goals of behaviour therapy are to bring about desired and realistic changes in behaviour through a planned and consistent approach. Specific goals will be negotiated with the individual client and a treatment programme tailored to fit the goals. For the reasons outlined above, the approach focuses directly on behaviour and not on non-conscious processes – compare this with *psychodynamic therapy*. Instead, behaviour therapy assumes that changed emotions and thoughts will follow on automatically from changed behaviour. When anxiety and fears are involved, the aim is not to rid the person completely of these (an aim which is unlikely to succeed in any case), but to bring them to a point where they are in perspective and manageable rather than incapacitating.

The main tools of behaviour therapy are *exposure therapy* and *skills and self-control training* which are consistent with the principles of classical and operant conditioning respectively, described earlier.

Assessment

A person with her particular problems will usually have been assessed and referred on for behaviour therapy if appropriate (see p. 38). If the person and her problems are suitable for behaviour therapy, a full *behavioural assessment* of the problem would be carried out. This is also known as a *behavioural analysis*. The therapist takes a problem-oriented and directive approach, asking the client direct questions about the nature of the problem. Typical questions would be as follows.

Can you tell me about your problem?
When did it begin?
Can you give me a recent example?
Returning to your example, can you tell me what was going on immediately
    before it happened?
Is it constant or fluctuating?
When is it at its worst?
When is it least of a problem?
Do any factors help it?
Does anything make it worse?
Why have you come for help *now*?
In what way(s), if any, does it stop you getting on with your life?
Is there anything the problem leads you to avoid?
In what way(s) would your life be different if you no longer had the problem?

These types of questions would be used with a range of problems, such as phobias, anxiety, sexual dysfunctions, compulsive behaviour and so on. They would not be asked mechanically and are not in a specific order. They are designed to discover the full extent of the problem and to find out what behaviours are present before, during and after the problem. This would include seeking information about behaviours, both helpful and unhelpful, which the client currently uses to cope with the situation. An example of helpful behaviour may be the person who talks about her fears with her spouse. Unhelpful behaviour might be the person who dulls her anxieties by drinking alcohol or taking illicit drugs. Often, much of the information being sought would be volunteered in response to relatively few questions: for example, the question, 'Can you tell me about your problem?' might well lead a client to give a detailed description about when it began, a recent example, the context in which it occurred, etc.

Once the problem has been described generally using this approach, further information then needs to be gained which is specific to a particular type of problem. For example, a person experiencing difficulty in taking part in social situations (social phobia) might be asked whether this applies to going into shops, pubs, restaurants, work, meeting people she does not know, starting friendships, making eye-contact. Many, many more enquiries would be made about other specific situations. If you imagine about 40 such situations, a person might experience no discomfort in some of these situations, great discomfort or avoidance for other situations and moderate discomfort in yet other situations. A more scientific way of assessing and evaluating the scope of the problem is to use a questionnaire. The situations would be listed individually and the client would be asked to rate the discomfort she experiences in the situation on, say, a five-point scale where 1 is no discomfort, 2 is a little discomfort, 3 is moderate discomfort, 4 is great discomfort and 5 maximum discomfort/avoidance.

Apart from finding out about the scope and detail of the problem, this type of questionnaire has other advantages. First, it helps the client to appreciate the problem in context, and to understand better where it begins and ends and in which particular situations it occurs. Second, it helps the therapy by showing which areas need most work, which need least and where best to begin; some areas will need no work at all. Third, the rating of each item enables the client and the therapist to gauge the degree of change taking place in therapy. This is particularly helpful when setbacks occur, as they often do, for they act as reminders of the progress that has been made by the client. Fourth, the individual items of the questionnaire can be used to design tasks for the client to carry out in between sessions. We will describe some of these tasks later, but it is important to emphasize that tasks carried out by the client between sessions form the bedrock of behaviour therapy.

The process of therapy

Once the target problem has been fully assessed, theraeputic work can begin. This will include some form of exposure therapy and may or may not include self-control or skills training. These terms are explained later. Progress in therapy is achieved by clearly explaining to the client what is involved in therapy, how the process works, what is expected of her and the part she will play in her own progress. Any pitfalls she anticipates will be openly discussed and solutions generated. Such an open exchange can only take place if a good therapeutic relationship, initiated by the therapist, has been developed between client and therapist early on. Client drop-out from therapy is highest at the start of therapy, and if a good working relationship is not quickly established, the chances of drop-out are heightened. The therapist develops this relationship by being warm towards the client, attempts to understand her by being empathic, and shows respect and support throughout the therapeutic process.

Exposure therapy

We previously gave an example of exposure therapy in which a person afraid of dogs was exposed to them. The principle of exposure is always the same. By continued exposure to the feared object or situation, anxiety will initially rise, but eventually fade to a tolerable level. This requires consistent and continued practice. Longer exposure leads to better and quicker results. You may have thought that this is no different from the call to 'pull yourself together'. The difference is that exposure is carried out in a structured and manageable fashion, always with the client's understanding and consent but also with a clear rationale being given. How long the exposure needs to be, so as to be effective, and how quickly the client should face her worst fears, depend upon the client, the amount of discomfort she can tolerate, the nature of the focal problem and how long it has been established. The exposure programme is individually tailored to fit the client, but outlined below are some broad forms this may take.

To describe exposure techniques, we will use as an example a person with spider phobia (arachnophobia). The range of the problem may be slight anxiety if imagining a money spider but extreme fear and panic if suddenly handed a large hairy spider. The most rapid form of exposure is *flooding*. This is where the person is exposed to the worst feared situation for a prolonged period, remaining with it until her fear subsides. In this example, this would mean handling the large hairy spider. Many people would not be willing to do this, and one of the other approaches described below would be used. However, some people (but not usually arachnophobics!) are willing to face their worst fear in this way.

Another flooding technique, using the worst feared situation, but in imagination only, is called *implosion*. All types of exposure can be carried out either in reality (*in vivo*), or in imagination (*in fantasy*).

Where a client is not willing to confront the most feared situation, either in reality or in imagination, or where there are medical reasons for not doing so (such as a person with asthma or heart disease), a more gradual form of exposure is required. Such an approach is graded exposure. Here, the client lists all the situations, from the least (money spider) to the most (large hairy spider) anxiety-provoking, in ascending order of difficulty. The therapist then helps the client to expose herself systematically to the range of anxiety-provoking situations on the list, starting with a manageable item and gradually working up to the most difficult.

The client may be able to enter the feared situation alone (self-exposure), or accompanied by the therapist (therapist-aided exposure). Sometimes, family members or friends are called upon to act as *co-therapists* or *aides*.

Exposure is often made difficult because the client engages in *avoidance*. As behaviour is mainly determined by its consequences, a particular behaviour if rewarded by a favourable outcome, tends to be reinforced and repeated. If a person with dog phobia runs away from a dog (avoidance), he will experience a lowering of anxiety at the time. This leads to the avoidance being *reinforced* and strengthens the phobia. *Avoidance* is therefore a key area to be worked on in therapy.

A specific form of avoidance is ritualistic behaviour. For example, a client with *obsessive-compulsive disorder* may wash compulsively after contact with dirt (real or imagined). She will be encouraged to refrain from carrying out the rituals so that she is exposed to the fear-evoking cue (dirt on hands). The client will be encouraged to find something else to occupy herself initially until the urge to perform the washing ritual lessens. This is known as *response prevention*.

Skills training

Much human behaviour is learned. Many people learn a wide range of skills in many different areas but may lack skills in other areas. Part of the behaviour therapist's work is therefore involved with *skills training*. This is carried out step by step. Common areas in which the therapist engages are assertion skills training, social skills training and sexual skills training. A range of techniques is used for all types of skills training. In *modelling* the therapist demonstrates appropriate behaviour, component by component, and encourages the client to follow the example, giving feedback and praise for good performance. For example, assertion skills training might include verbal and non-verbal behaviour such as eye-contact, facial expression and posture. *Role play*, in which the client and therapist enact problem scenarios is also commonly used and may take place within a group setting. For example, the client might role play changing goods in a shop, asking a favour of a friend or refusing a request. In these cases, the therapist models the behaviour at an appropriate level for the client.

Self-control training

Self-control training is aimed at helping the client to control their own behaviour and feelings. Often a problem behaviour is immediately preceded by events which trigger the problem behaviour. But these triggers or cues may be unrecognized by the client. She will often be asked to keep a daily record of the problem behaviour and the circumstances in which it happens. This form of self-monitoring is used widely in behaviour therapy. For example, a problem drinker would record what she drinks, when she drinks it and associations between drinking and either stressful events or unwanted emotions. From self-monitoring, the client may be able to identify specific cues which trigger the drinking behaviour and encouraged to exercise self-control when these occur. The client is encouraged to reward herself in some way for doing so. This is called self-reinforcement.

Format of a typical session

The main assessment session is different from ongoing sessions as it is designed to find out a great deal of information about the client and his problem.

Subsequent sessions will to some extent be determined by the nature of the client's particular problem but will follow a general plan. The therapist will welcome the client and negotiate an agenda for the session. If any questionnaires need to be completed, these will often follow next. Assignments outside of therapy sessions are central to behaviour therapy and this homework is reviewed and discussed in some detail. Further and ongoing treatment aims will be considered, with any in-session work such as role play, exposure therapy and so on, being focused on a target problem for the session. Homework will be negotiated for further therapeutic work needing to be carried out before the next session. The session will then be reviewed with the client. Feedback is encouraged and the client given due praise for work done and progress made.

WHICH CLIENTS BENEFIT MOST?

Behaviour therapy has been applied to a wide range of people with a variety of problems. It may take an experienced therapist to recognize certain behaviours to be problematic! People who are able (with help if necessary) to decide upon clear behavioural goals are most likely to benefit from behaviour therapy provided they are willing to cooperate and to do homework assignments outside of sessions. Motivation, or the ability to be motivated by the therapist is also an important factor. People with some major physical or mental complications which would make the exposure and skills training work too difficult, even with therapist assistance, are least likely to benefit. Others least likely to benefit are those who take in excess of two units of alcohol or 10 milligrams of diazepam (medication prescribed for anxiety), or similar, daily. If they are willing and able to reduce this to a suitable level beforehand, with help if necessary, they may be suitable.

We will now outline the types of problems most suitable for behaviour therapy. Most phobias, such as spider, height or blood phobia, agoraphobias or social phobias are suitable. Obsessive-compulsive disorders, especially where pronounced habits are involved, have been successfully treated. It is also beneficial for a range of sexual problems such as premature ejaculation, painful intercourse in women (vaginismus) and masochism. Habit disorders, such as stammering and bed-wetting are well suited to behaviour therapy. People with social skills problems respond well to training.

Case study

THE CLIENT

Penny was referred for therapy by her General Practitioner. She is 32 years old and lives with her only son, aged 6, in a ground-floor maisonette. She has never been married, and separated from her last partner shortly after the birth of their child. She works part-time as a laboratory assistant in a local university.

The referral letter from the General Practitioner stated that she had a five-year history of anxiety. She had been prescribed tranquillisers on a number of occasions but was not currently taking any. On assessment, she was found to be experiencing social anxiety where she feared a wide range of social situations and avoided many of these. She said that in these situations she became very shaky, experienced palpitations and a tight feeling in her chest, breathlessness, sweating and tingling of her fingers. Her concentration was severely affected at these times. Assessment did not show her to be suffering from panic disorder. These symptoms had progressively worsened over a five-year period and Penny was visibly distressed at this in the session. She had developed a pattern of drinking alcohol to control her anxiety in social situations. This problem had intensified in the last two years and she was now consuming alcohol prior to attending work, and had also started to show signs of depression, although this was not pronounced. She said this was since her new line manager had been in post and was more attentive of her work and required her to take part in staff meetings. She said that she was on the verge of not being able to go to work because of the problem and this is why she came for help now.

THE THERAPY

The first session explored Penny's problems as outlined above. She was asked to complete a *social situations questionnaire* to establish which aspects of the problem caused her most concern. This enabled goals for treatment to be negotiated. From these goals, tasks would gradually be identified throughout the course of therapy. One such task which it was important for Penny to achieve, was to reduce her consumption of alcohol to a maximum of one to two units daily. This is important in behaviour therapy, because alcohol cancels out the benefits of exposure therapy and has other negative effects, such as being a depressant. The principles of behaviour therapy were fully explained to Penny and the difficulties regarding alcohol were included. She seemed to be very diligent in her employment and maintained her sense of humour despite her difficulties. The therapist made a note of these as being positive attributes in the therapeutic process.

From the assessment and the social situations questionnaire the following goals for therapy were negotiated:

- to mix with people in groups, both in social settings and at work
- to attend and actively participate in staff meetings
- to go into restaurants, pubs, cafes and discos
- to start and maintain conversations with people she does not know very well

- to start a friendship with someone of the opposite sex
- to give own opinions which conflict with those of others
- to talk about self and feelings in conversation with others

With these goals as the focus for therapy, tasks would be set at each session to achieve them. The main work would be *exposure therapy* to a range of social situations. The therapist thought that some *assertion training* might be necessary later on in therapy.

The tasks set at the end of the first session were:

- to read the sections on social phobia, and bodily changes during anxiety, in *Living with Fear*[4]
- to practise relaxation skills daily, using the tape provided
- to contact her friend, Ann, and to go to a chosen pasta restaurant, and remain there until her anxiety reduces
- to monitor her anxiety in staff meetings and social situations on a 0–5 scale

Progress was reviewed at the start of each session, and at the second session, the client had successfully carried out all of the tasks except for relaxation training. Praise was given for her diligent work in the other areas. Penny said that she was surprised at enjoying herself in the restaurant, although feeling anxious initially. She had completely stopped taking alcohol in the mornings and had committed herself to be alcohol-free for the sessions. She felt very pleased with herself for doing this. Tasks continued to be set for subsequent sessions consistent with the goals outlined above. Practice is very important in behaviour therapy.

By the sixth session Penny had firmly grasped that in order to make progress, it was essential for her to face up to her fears. She recognized that avoiding them was easier at the time, but led to long-term difficulties. Facing her fears was only possible in practice by a structured programme of self-exposure. She persevered with self-exposure in many social situations which she had previously avoided, until her level of anxiety in each was much lower and acceptable to her. These social situations were all in relation to the goals stated above. Penny had done some work towards achieving all of her goals except for the last two:

- to give own opinions which conflict with those of others
- to talk about self and feelings in conversation with others

She had worked hard up to this stage. It would still be important for her to continue with self-exposure towards the goals already partly achieved until the process became 'natural' to her.

However, Penny did encounter a setback which prompted her to deal with the goals she had not yet worked upon. She said that she had been unfairly criticized by her boss at work. Although angry, she felt unable to tell him that she found his criticism unjust. This led to her feeling 'low' and drinking up to ten units daily. Within the session, Penny was encouraged to role play an assertive response towards her boss's unfair criticism and employed her humour to good effect in this! Her task at the end of this session was to speak to her boss assertively on this matter and to share her feelings about it with her friend Ann. In the following session, she said she had been surprised at her performance with her boss, and the positive comments she had received from colleagues!

She continued to make good progress in therapy and found exposure to the feared situations caused her some discomfort but she was able to endure this. She said that the benefits of taking part in these social activities far outweighed the discomfort.

In a follow-up session three months after counselling had ended, Penny continued to maintain her progress. She completed some self-evaluation questionnaires which showed her anxiety to be minimal in most of the social situations identified. Although she still found it difficult to give her own opinions when they conflicted with those of others, she had taken positive action by enrolling in an assertiveness class at her local adult education centre. She no longer had symptoms of depression and she now only drank socially and not to excess. Her humour was no longer suppressed by her feelings of social anxiety.

REFERENCES

1 Pavlov, I.P. (1927) *Conditioned Reflexes*. London: Oxford University Press.
2 Watson, J.B. and Rayner, R. (1920) 'Conditioned emotional reactions', *Journal of Experimental Psychology*, 3: 1–14.
3 Thorndike, E.L. (1911) *Animal Intelligence*. New York: Macmillan.
4 Marks, I.M. (1978) *Living with Fear*. New York: McGraw Hill.

SUGGESTED READING

Crowe, M. and Ridley, J. (1990) *Therapy with Couples*. Oxford: Blackwell. This is a practical book based on firm theory, research and experience, about working with couples and sexual problems. It gives clear guidelines for effective therapy.

Marks, I.M. (1978) *Living with Fear*. New York: McGraw Hill. This popular self-help book is very easy to read and gives a wide range of information which is still relevant today. It combines a deep knowledge of the subject with some interesting anecdotes.

Marks, I.M. (1986) *Behavioural Psychotherapy*. Bristol: Wright. *Behavioural Psychotherapy* is a brief but highly condensed handbook providing clinicians with information necessary to assess and treat clients and to communicate with referral agents.

Richards, D. and McDonald, B. (1990) *Behavioural Psychotherapy*. London: Heineman Nursing. This book is subtitled 'A Handbook for Nurses'. It is a clear and practical guide to behavioural psychotherapy and will be useful reading for a range of practitioners other than nurses.

DISCUSSION ISSUES

1 To what extent is it necessary to focus on client's thoughts in bringing about client change in therapy?
2 Behaviour therapy considers symptoms and behaviour but leaves underlying psychological problems unresolved. Discuss.
3 Do thoughts determine behaviour and feelings or does changed behaviour bring about changes in client's feelings and thoughts?
4 Exposure therapy is no more than telling a person to 'pull themselves together'. Discuss.

4

COGNITIVE ANALYTIC COUNSELLING AND PSYCHOTHERAPY

David Crossley and Michael Göpfert

Cognitive Analytic Therapy (CAT) is a brief, collaborative therapy which integrates at a theoretical and pragmatic level psychoanalytic and cognitive approaches. The therapy developed both within and outside of the NHS to meet the psychotherapy demands of a very wide variety of people with minimum selectivity.

CAT is cognitive in the sense that it is problem focused and aims to describe accurately and explicitly the difficulties people face as a process involving links between their aims, beliefs, thoughts and actions. It is psychoanalytic in its emphasis on relationship and in its expectation that early relationships are likely to help explain current difficulties and influence the therapy. CAT therefore uses the conscious and unconscious aspects of the therapeutic relationship as a way of promoting change, as well as having recourse to a wide variety of techniques that cognitive behaviour therapists may use. CAT is not indiscriminate but works from a specific unified model of how emotional problems develop and are maintained.

CAT was developed by Anthony Ryle in the UK in the late 1970s and 1980s. It now has a professional association (Association of Cognitive Analytic Therapists) with its own accreditation procedures and is part of the United Kingdom Council of Psychotherapists.

The development of CAT has reflected the demands of a needs-led system like the NHS for a clinically effective, auditable, flexible and teachable form of psychotherapy. The development was in some ways a pragmatic response to this but is also a reflection of the professional biography of Ryle in his desire to create a common language for the psychotherapies. Ryle's career was initially in General Practice, then in student health, and ultimately as Consultant Psychotherapist at Guy's and St Thomas' Hospitals in London servicing an inner city area where accessibility is important.

CAT has been used across a range of problems including eating disorders, deliberate self-harm and personality disorders. Several research projects, outcome research (for example in borderline personality disorder) and published audits are based on the CAT model.

CAT aims to combine what is most useful in psychoanalytic and cognitive therapy theories within a single framework, especially for the many people whose difficulties are not easily understood in other models of psychotherapy and have thereby often been excluded. This framework can claim to be a child of these two traditions (the cognitive and the analytic) but like any child is also different from either parent. To start with, it has a different name which is a bit of a mouthful: the procedural sequence object relations model (PSORM). Beneath the jargon there is much intuitive common sense, but before presenting this child in depth the parents will be introduced to illustrate how problems are seen in CAT and how the therapist sets up an active collaborative relationship to promote change.

CAT inherits its analytic perspective from the 'object-relations' school. We not only need relationships but relationships are also the making of us. Thus the desire for relationships not only is a prime motivation, but also determines who we are, our 'selves' as it were. This takes us back to our childhood. In line with object-relation theorists CAT proposes that we develop our sense of who we are from those early experiences of being a child-in-relationship-to-important-others (usually parents). We start off physically and emotionally connected to our mothers; we end up as separate persons, but still connected. How is this separation achieved so that I become confident of where the subject (I) stops and the object (you) begins? We may bring into ourselves (as it were) aspects of others – caring aspects of our parents for example – and also disown aspects of ourselves preferring to 'see' them as a part of others as if they are problematic in some way. For example I may consider myself not to be an angry person but I see it in you. Often this takes the form of an internal dialogue, for example between the voice of 'me' (the inner child) and the voice of 'I' (the parent). CAT differs from orthodox object-relations theory in its emphasis on the historical experience of an individual over and against a view that emotional difficulties are the result of constitutionally conflict-prone inner drives and impulses warring with each other.

For a CAT therapist this theoretical background will mean that a major focus is on relationships – past and present, external and internal. We learn to do to ourselves and for ourselves what others in the past have done to/for us. This is what we come to expect. So the therapist's relationship with the client is the opportunity for re-education in the deepest sense, not only because it can show us anew how other people care for and control us but also how we care for and control ourselves. This is a perspective CAT derives from the Russian psychologist Lev Vygotsky.

The other major 'parental' influence on CAT is from cognitive psychology. Here CAT picks up the assumption – from personal construct theory – that people actively 'construct' their realities. We are, as it were, always in dialogue with our world. The dialogue and questioning may only become active when change is afoot – for example when the old system of assumptions ('constructs') is starting to fail because of overwhelming life events. Or it may have never been put together very well, for example in people with personality problems. The realities we construct may sometimes limit our ability to learn from experience depending on the framework we have made (or been given) to frame the questions in. If I am being cared for by someone in some way – say in my marriage, or by my therapist – I will expect the other person to be in a certain role. For example, if I am to be cared for I may implicitly expect you to be parental whereas I adopt a child-like role. You must play along with whom I expect my parent to be or else conflict arises. But consciously I may be unaware of my expectation. Therapy is, in part, about making the expectations explicit and therefore open to change.

These roles do not just happen on the outside but on the inside too. As I care for and control myself, the roles get enacted internally together with the expectations and the feelings that go with them. Thus I may have an angry demanding part that relates to a resentfully submissive aspect of myself. The former may be derived from the experience of my mother, the latter from myself as her child. These aspects of me are not my entire self but important parts of me (especially the feelings bit). CAT terms these 'self-states'. They may get split off from other parts – for example the parts where I can nurture and look after myself. Therapy is then about integrating the parts into a whole, putting all the self-states on the same map.

The CAT therapist is always going to try and provide in a collaborative explicit way an 'overview' function and anticipate how she and the client will get drawn into the client's pattern of relating. CAT does this at a theoretical and practical level. So now we come to the way CAT brings together its analytic and cognitive inheritance into something new. This is the PSORM. Behind the jargon is merely the attempt to describe how we go about things. Intentional behaviour is part of a process which begins with an aim and may then involve appraisal of the situation in some way, then the action itself and any evaluation after the action. CAT uses the term 'procedure' to describe this. It is important to note that procedures are cyclical – behaviours beget consequences that beget behaviour. They are also hierarchical. Maybe you are reading this book as part of your training, so reading is an aim within the wider aim of becoming a counsellor. CAT would say that reading the book is a subprocedure. So there are procedures within procedures.

Thinking about what the steps are in training for the job of counsellor is one thing but procedures to do with relationship are different. How do I go about relating to another person? Relating is not possible without role behaviour. A particular situation or perception may determine this. If you are my mother – or just seem to be a bit like her – I will have certain expectations about my role and yours. The jargon here is 'reciprocal role procedure'. I will have to have an idea about two roles – yours and mine – and I will establish a reciprocal role procedure, or complementarity. If I am six months old I may play the 'hungry infant' role to your 'providing mother'. This is where object-relations theory is embedded at a cognitive level within CAT and how the therapist understands his or her relationship with the client. The client expects a certain role from the therapist and indeed may elicit it (for example a 'needy' client to a 'providing' therapist) but not always, because the therapist may choose to not play the role if the role exemplifies the client's difficulties – for example a needy, victim-like client to an all-knowing perpetrator-like therapist. This requires comment and understanding, not enactment, on the part of the therapist. Empathy on its own may not facilitate progress, and may even hinder it.

CAT understands our activity (including thinking) in 'procedure' terms and our relating activity in 'reciprocal role procedure' terms. Procedures that are faulty may follow recognizable patterns – patterns of thought, feeling and behaviour linked in some recurrent sequence that end up in some emotional difficulty. CAT describes this psychological disturbance in terms of three patterns called traps, dilemmas and snags. Therapy is about first learning to recognize and then to change these patterns, and so move towards psychological health.

A trap is a vicious circle in which an action reinforces the problem. For example my problem may be a fear of leaving my house. In not leaving the house I never give myself the opportunity to discover how it might not be frightening and my avoidance feeds my fear. A dilemma is a false or narrow choice. Past experience may suggest to us we have no real choices – as if neither option is correct by itself. For example, either I stick up for myself but nobody loves me, or I give in but get put upon. A snag is when an action or a choice seems unavailable, as if forbidden. For example, we may sabotage our success as if success is a problem to ourselves (eliciting guilt) or to others (I feel their envy). So a child may feel disloyal and guilty if she does better than her parents, and therefore she does not.

This framework – the PSORM – gives an interpersonal focus to CAT but the therapist does not proceed by making interpretations about the client's unconscious. The emphasis is cognitive in the sense of making accurate descriptions to allow clients to observe themselves in a new way.

PRACTICE

The goal of therapy is to enhance clients' ability to recognize their unhelpful procedures and then to enable them to adopt an active problem-solving stance. CAT is time-limited, commonly to 16 weekly sessions of 50/60 minutes each. Therapy consists of three phases. Three introductory sessions are primarily concerned with assessing the client's problems and their background and laying down the foundations of a shared understanding that cements the therapeutic relationship. The fourth session is the point at which the therapist gathers all the strands together and offers their understanding of the client's distress in a written form, called the 'reformulation' letter. This is aimed at establishing a mutual understanding of and agreement about the major issues with which therapy will concern itself. The remaining sessions are devoted to improving the recognition of how these issues (the target problem procedures) operate in the client's daily life, and subsequently working towards change. The ending of therapy and its meaning for the individual client is also a crucial consideration of CAT which has to be addressed in good time.

There is no one style of therapeutic relationship 'prescribed' for the therapist in CAT but because of its collaborative ethos it is unlikely that the therapist will remain too 'hidden' or inactive. From early on the client is encouraged to be active in relation to their problems – as active enquirer, active learner, active experimenter.

The therapist's assessment will be oriented towards the writing of the reformulation letter. To this end information is harvested from many sources, through the unstructured interview process, through the therapist's critical evaluation of the client–therapist relationship and from pen and paper self–report tasks.

A therapist's focus of attention during the unstructured interview will be to help identify the sequences of assumptions, predictions, actions and evaluations that the client uses repeatedly despite having negative outcomes, that is, the possible range of 'target problem procedures'. This process involves hearing the client's account of their early years, key relationships and significant life events. It may also be highly relevant for the therapist to observe their own responses to the account given as this may give valuable insight into how the client looks after him or herself.

The therapist will try and get a sense of the chronically endured distress that the client brings and will try to understand their inability to discover effective escape routes from it. In addition to the unstructured interviewing and the therapist's self-reflection, the client is also asked to become an active observer by the use of pen and paper techniques. These can be used with a degree of flexibility although one questionnaire – the Psychotherapy File – is always given. This offers the client examples of patterns of thoughts, feelings and behaviour that are failing to help the client yet are hard to break, characterized in the form of 'traps', 'dilemmas' and 'snags' (see above). This file is generally given in the first session so that clients will be able to recognize aspects of themselves in a non-judgemental way. Ideally clients may be able to find their own words for these patterns (the problem procedures) and some may come to see how they may be unwittingly contributing to their own difficulties. Self-monitoring in the form of a diary of mood shifts and symptoms can be used for 'diagnostic' purposes (for example by getting clients to keep a diary of event–thought–feeling links) but it also can promote confidence in the client's ability to solve problems and be targeted at specific problem procedures. Other methods of self-observation can also be used in the assessment phase, such as writing a self-portrait as if by a friend.

Reformulation

This is a key task in CAT. By the third or fourth session the therapist should come to a provisional view about the origins and central features of the client's core problems as defined in procedural terms as traps, dilemmas and snags. This is committed to paper and shared and revised with the client. The style of the reformulation is usually a letter from therapist to client but other approaches may be used. For example it may be possible to use the client's own voice if this is not overly intrusive. The reformulation should validate the client's experience and propose what problems should be worked on. The therapist will need to gather together all the strands of information available and weave them into a coherent narrative to make sense of the client's specific emotional difficulties and the reasons for seeking help now. The account is likely to identify areas of emotional resilience as well as vulnerability. It may go on to predict the course of therapy on the basis of the client's previous experience of 'helping' relationships. Commonly a brief summary and validation of the client's experience leads to a detailed description of target problem procedures. These are succinctly and positively framed and understood as having developed through the client's attempts to cope with and master life.

The reformulation is read out and the response actively sought. Inaccuracies – factual or emotional – are corrected and agreement looked for about the focus of therapy and the target procedures. The overall aim of therapy is related to these procedures. For example, a target problem procedure may be 'it seems that if I feel I must, then I won't.' The aim may be 'to be able to choose'.

The reformulation letter is given to the patient and a copy kept by the therapist and the remaining number of sessions are agreed upon.

Subsequent sessions

The therapeutic focus can now be directed at the mutually agreed target problems and the procedures that lead to those problems. There is no prescribed way in which a session goes but any homework or diaries will be reviewed. Diaries are aimed at improving the recognition of procedures and their subsequent revision (for example, a 'snag' diary). The client should be made aware of the session number so that the end point is always kept in view. Progress is rated at the end of each session on a simple visual analogue scale. There are many techniques to promote change that can be used flexibly and are not specific to CAT. For example, planned and graded exposure to feared situations may enable people to overcome avoidance and gain a sense of self-mastery; role play may enable clients to become aware of hidden feelings; and a disciplined attempt to think about the client's thinking may enable them to challenge negative ideas and assumptions. The therapist may reflect on the way the client's procedures affect the relationship with the therapist, helping them to move between the here-and-now and the there-and-then. CAT does have one technique that promotes self-observation that it may call its own. This is the use of a diagram which relates all the major target problem procedures together. A core self-state or states is named in the middle of it all (the dominant reciprocal role pattern) as the place of deep long-standing distress out of which there are failed escape attempts (the 'target problem procedures'). Using a diagram can help clients view themselves more coherently and is particularly valuable for those who have very unstable changes of mood, thoughts and behaviour. It can be used in sessions to plot minute-by-minute changes.

Ending therapy

Being time-limited helps CAT to remain problem focused and minimize the risk of excessive dependency on the therapist. The ending of therapy may resonate with the client's own difficulties, such as unresolved loss, and provide an opportunity for therapeutic work.

Finally, the therapist writes a 'goodbye letter' and invites the client to do likewise. These letters review what has been achieved and reflect on difficulties ahead (for example, sustaining change). Usually they are read out in the last session. A follow-up at about three months is arranged for a review of therapeutic gains. Occasionally, further follow-up or more therapy will then be arranged.

WHICH CLIENTS BENEFIT MOST?

Since CAT was largely developed within a public health system it is necessarily versatile within general limitations. Clients need to be able to make the commitment to attend and their lives should not be too disorganized by alcohol or drugs. Clients cannot remain entirely passive in relation to their difficulties if therapy is to succeed. Social class and ethnic backgrounds are no obstacle as long as therapists acknowledge and are alert to differences between themselves and clients.

Broadly speaking clients may come to therapy in three ways. Some may come after a personal crisis has thrown into doubt their ability to cope using their 'procedural system'. These may make rapid use of new procedures. Others may come because of their difficulties in maintaining their current system – it is overly restrictive, or symptomatic in some way. These clients need to be simultaneously supported and challenged so that they can be helped to revise their approach. Clients with eating disorders and various patterns of anxiety may be included here, although clients with marked phobias or obsessional behaviours may benefit from behaviour therapy first. A third group shows considerable emotional instability with poorly integrated procedures. The problem here may be at the level of personality. Therapy may promote a greater sense of integration. Clients who have a psychiatric history or who self-harm are not excluded from CAT. Clients who are psychotic usually are.

In conclusion: CAT is a recent therapy usable for a wide range of problems. The evaluative data from the research to date looks promising. CAT's popularity as reflected in the demand for training indicates that it will become a mainstream therapeutic modality.

Case study

THE CLIENT

This is an unusual therapy in that the client is a counsellor, a competent colleague, on social terms with her GP who referred her, and also in that her response to the idea of therapy was different. She illustrates how important it is to adapt the therapy format to make it meaningful and to avoid rigidly prescriptive attitudes.

Maria, a 41-year-old single mother of two boys aged 11 and 15, worked in a building society and as a part-time counsellor. She was referred because of mood swings and severe recurrent depression. She believed that suicide would be inevitable and had a tendency to 'lose' herself in other people's reality, inevitably making her feel bad and reinforcing her critical self-image. She had had an affair with the children's father for 17 years until his wife found out and stopped it. His marriage eventually ended and he wanted to re-unite with Maria. He was very unreliable in his contact with the children but Maria could never confront him because of her belief that children need fathering, especially adolescent boys. This was additionally complicated by the fact that this man had a slight physical handicap and the children's difficulties with this also compounded her misery. Maria herself would get caught up in long phone calls with him where he would alternately say she was wonderful or a totally useless mother.

She would dwell on this and feel totally brainwashed by him. The pattern of idealization and denigration had been inadvertently repeated in a previous course of therapy. This left her feeling worse, apart from gaining some insight into how much she was persecuted by her mother's critical voice. This was activated whenever she wanted to take care of her own needs. Maria needed to excel at work and at home which consumed enormous energies. She found her children difficult, and felt guilty for having had children as a single parent.

The therapy

At first Maria was fearful of a repeat of therapy because (in her words): 'Therapy becomes a bottomless pit.' Hence the main focus initially was on avoiding a repeat. A hopeful sign was that, in a confident moment, she had started legal proceedings against her ex-partner. A series of only eight sessions was negotiated as more seemed too risky. It became clear that as soon as any empathy was expressed her mood nose-dived; once she came back saying that if this happened again she would have to stop. After session four the reformulation was agreed following intense discussion and alterations. Maria expressed a curious sense of being understood without empathy which puzzled her because it ran counter to her counselling training. However she was pleased that she had avoided any tears apart from on one occasion. She felt cautiously optimistic though still very sceptical.

Maria's reformulation

Dear Maria,

You wanted more therapy because you find it difficult 'to stay with your own wisdom'. At the same time you are very good with words, but at critical moments you tend to lose yourself in them, be it with your ex-partner, your sons or yourself.

You said that you knew all the facts about your family but we both puzzled over the question why feelings about your past were virtually non-existent. Your mother's verdict was very clear: 'We don't do things like that', meaning any expression of emotion. Emotional communication tended to be channelled through other family members, often you, but was never directly expressed. However this did not mean a licence to be emotional. It is as if the rule in your family was that nobody could express any emotional needs, or have them met. Relationships were only possible within strictly defined limits which for you seem to have been determined by your mother, like the rule that you should not be emotional. If current patterns tell us anything about what was going on when you were little it is as if you could safely join your mother in her criticism of the world ('we are not like that') but your own views would be crushed.

Thus, whenever you feel needy you experience a sense of vulnerability. It is as if a spotlight turns on you. You have to run away from this, feeling contemptible and worthless. For instance, when you feel critical of your ex-partner you might want me to join in the criticism. But as soon as we start looking at your side of the relationship you begin to feel vulnerable, which rapidly turns into a sense of hopelessness, and therapy becomes 'a bottomless pit'. This powerfully reinforces that you must never be needy. You have never been shown how to take care of your vulnerable feelings other than by denial and bottling up. Hence they are overwhelming and trigger contempt for yourself.

If you feel needy and others respond it makes one part of you feel undeserving. Therefore you cannot engage, but you feel as if there are always more hidden unmet needs. If by any chance somebody says anything good about you, you feel uncertain and either expect this to be followed by a contemptuous attack or begin to attack yourself (or the other person).

A part of you will hear this as if this is all your fault. To me it seems that there is confusion between guilt and responsibility. This makes it difficult to reflect on any bad feelings as they are intertwined with guilt. Your first response is to make them go away instantly. Hence, therapeutic dilemmas abound: frequently, you may turn my attention on you into criticism, reinforced by feeling as if you should not have any emotions. Therefore you might feel as if you cannot have anything but difficult experiences in therapy. Therapy will not work as long as its limits are imposed by the very problems you wish to tackle: namely, that you are caught in the dilemma either of having utterly overwhelming feelings of being needy and demanding, or of cutting yourself off from any need altogether. Therefore I suggest that we focus on the following issues:

1   As soon as you have an opportunity to feel close to someone you either feel needy and undeserving, overwhelmed by those needs. Or you adopt a distant and rational attitude. This is very much alive in our therapeutic relationship where emotional understanding causes distress.

2   You often end up being contemptuous of others or yourself, in which case you also feel contemptible. Because you strongly disapprove of being contemptuous, you invariably end up being critically dismissive of yourself.

Your Therapist.

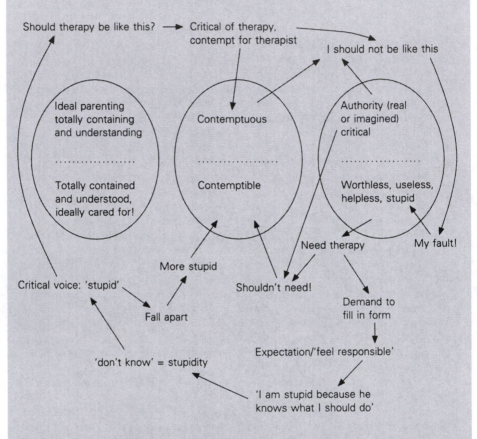

FIGURE 4.1   Sequential diagrammatic reformulation

When I read this out to Maria she was very attentive and nodded at the point where it said that she would probably feel criticized. We agreed corrections that were incorporated in the above text. An attempt at agreeing a formulation in her own words of a target problem procedure for the rating sheet ran aground. She took the form home but returned empty-handed, feeling miserable and a failure. I had made her feel worse. I dealt with this by drawing a simple diagram. This helped us understand why it was so important to her to keep me in an idealized position because otherwise I would be either useless or abusive, with her feeling both totally critical of me and superior, or completely crushed by my criticism.

Figure 4.1 illustrates how Maria rapidly moves from one 'self-state' where she feels helpless in the face of a perceived authority to another where she feels contemptible.

The therapist and his perceived demands represented the authority here. Maria acknowledged how important it was to protect the therapist from this. Therefore, she had to ensure that therapy remained in the domain of 'ideal care' and so take responsibility for all that was wrong. This drawing resulted in a degree of satisfaction in Maria not encountered before.

The formulation for the rating sheet focused on her inability to say 'no' to people who appeared to express an expectation of her. Her aim was to have the choice and the ability to say no without guilt. Afterwards it was as if she felt that the work had now been done. When this was pursued she felt criticized but for the first time challenged me because I had potentially made her feel worse. The following session she could not remember anything about this, which helped her understand her powerful capacity for denial.

She acknowledged that I could do nothing that would make her feel better. Two sessions later she reported – reluctantly! – some improvement in her relationships with her sons. She had also obtained an injunction against their father forbidding him to phone her any more, and she had changed her phone number. Visiting arrangements were conditional on him being on time. We discussed a bye-bye letter, and as before the dilemma was the certain anticipation that she would fail my expectations. Hence she 'succeeded' in not writing a bye-bye letter.

Excerpts from the therapist's bye-bye letter:

Dear Maria,

When you came for another attempt at therapy you had already taken a major step to change your situation; you had started legal proceedings against J. to stop him harassing you with telephone calls. Amongst other things, this had the effect of creating more space for therapy. The main aim of the work to date was to find ways for you of not being overwhelmed by your despair. Furthermore, you managed to consider alternatives to the ways of thinking and feeling which have been dragging you down over the years.

Your helplessness and your need to fend it off were centre stage for most of our 8 sessions. When I was trying to be understanding and empathic you became helpless. When I was trying to engage you in doing tasks at home you became helpless. In essence your helplessness then triggered contempt (for yourself) which in turn made the helplessness intolerable. Now you have begun to be able to think about it and accept that it is just you who has these expectations of yourself.

But you changed even further: your mother, for instance, often gave you unwanted plants which you then neglected. This illustrates how people's intention to care for you can turn into a demand/expectation. When your mother visited she would invariably comment on the drooping plant she had given you but now you accept this behaviour of your mother as a fact of life and it does not trigger despair or contempt any more.

The clearest example of the shift in your thinking is when you talked about being addicted to this state of mind of yours, where helplessness turns into contempt of yourself or others. You acknowledged that it was difficult to let go of this just yet. This might be partly because if you stop feeling helpless it might leave you feeling lonely and isolated, and you then cannot call on help since you are not helpless.

This is also where a sense of 'so what' and disappointment is lingering on: the sense of helplessness is not gone because the task is to learn to live with it. This task will remain with you after this, our last session. I am confident that you can handle it with success.

With very best wishes,

Your Therapist.

She liked the letter and commented how previously it would have been impossible for her not to write a bye-bye letter once I had suggested it. She produced a whole list of improvements and emphasized that she was pleased with the outcome of therapy.

At the follow-up session she said she was astounded at how these eight sessions had made such a big difference. She could recognize her patterns and take care of herself. She still found the idea of having to depend on other people (including therapists) aversive but could recognize it for what it was. She said she now knew how to use therapy if necessary.

SUGGESTED READING

Ryle, A. (1991) *Cognitive Analytic Therapy: Active Participation in Change* Chichester: Wiley. Offers theoretical background, how-to-do-it chapters and early research data.

Ryle, A. (1995) *Cognitive-Analytic Therapy: Developments in Theory and Practice.* Chichester: Wiley. Less of Tony Ryle, more from other practitioners. Broader in scope than the earlier book by Ryle. A couple of chapters offer a succinct summary of the theory to date.

Ryle, A. (1997) *Cognitive-Analytic Therapy and Borderline Personality Disorder: The Model and the Method.* Chichester: Wiley. A more collaborative book which offers a good summary of the theory, but with a focus on more difficult patients. Excellent in placing CAT in the context of the literature on the treatment of borderline personality disorders.

Wilde–McCormack, E. (1990) *Change for the Better*. London: Thorson & Unwin. A well-tried self-help manual based on CAT concepts. Very user-friendly and easy to understand.

DISCUSSION ISSUES

1   CAT comes to a 'reformulation' by the fourth session in therapy. How difficult might this be to achieve for you as therapist? And what advantages might there be for the therapy in so doing?

2 When is empathy useful and when could it be counterproductive in therapy?

3 CAT is an active and collaborative therapy by trying to make explicit what is implicit. What strengths and weaknesses may there be to this approach?

4 What 'reciprocal roles' of your own do you think are involved in your interest in counselling/therapy?

5

COGNITIVE COUNSELLING AND PSYCHOTHERAPY

Kasia Szymanska and Stephen Palmer

C ognitive therapy is an approach which combines the use of cognitive and behavioural techniques to help individuals modify their moods and behaviour by changing their self-defeating thinking. The therapist acts like a trainer, teaching clients techniques and strategies which they can use to overcome their problems. It is used in the treatment of a number of psychological problems such as anxiety, phobias and depression, in a variety of settings. These include the NHS, doctors' surgeries and within the corporate training field, specifically with reference to stress management.

DEVELOPMENT OF THE THERAPY

Historically, cognitive therapy can be traced back to the work of the philosopher Epictetus, who, in the first century AD, suggested that people, 'are not disturbed by things but by the view they take of them'. More recently its roots lie in the work of John Broadus Watson,[1] a behavioural psychologist who is known as the 'father' of the behavioural approach, and the work of the Russian physiologist, Ivan Petrovich Pavlov who, on the basis of his animal research, derived the principle of classical conditioning. Later influences include psychiatrist Alfred Adler, who in his book entitled *What Life Should Mean to You*[2] wrote, 'Meanings are not determined by situations, but we determine ourselves by the meaning we give to situations' (p. 14). Also in the 1950s George Kelly,[3] the originator of personal construct therapy, argued that individuals are scientists who develop ideas and then test them out by acting on them. His work paved the way for the development of cognitive therapy. Subsequently the work of psychologists such as Albert Ellis,[4] the founder of rational emotive behaviour therapy and Donald Miechenbaum[5] emphasized the importance of cognitive processes. In the 1960s cognitive therapy came into its own through the work of psychiatrist Aaron Beck, who, dissatisfied with the lack of scientific basis for psychoanalytic theories, brought cognitive therapy into the forefront of the profession. The journal *Cognitive Therapy and Research* was first established in 1977 and one of Beck's best known books in this field, *Cognitive Therapy for Depression*[6] was published by Beck and his colleagues in 1979.

Since then cognitive therapy has flourished, initial'y within the United States and more recently within the United Kingdom. The accrediting body in the UK for cognitive and behavioural psychotherapists is the British Association for Behavioural and Cognitive Psychotherapies (BABCP), which is registered in the Behavioural and Cognitive Section of the United Kingdom Council for Psycho-therapy (UKCP). The number of therapists using this approach is also increasing for, in a survey conducted by the British Association for Counselling in 1993, 19 per cent of members were found to be adhering to a cognitive or cognitive-behavioural model.[7]

THEORY AND BASIC CONCEPTS

Basic assumptions

The basic premise of cognitive therapy is that the way an individual feels or behaves is largely determined by their appraisal of events. These evaluations are referred to as cognitions, and cognitive therapists are concerned in particular with self-defeating thoughts which contribute to low moods. Also of importance are physiological responses, for example, a racing heart, sweating, and behav-iour – specifically avoidant behaviour. The relationship between these modalities is illustrated in Figure 5.1.

The ABC format, in which 'A' stands for the activating event, 'B' for beliefs about the event and 'C' the consequences, is a common framework used to understand the inter-relationship between these modalities. The example below illustrates the application of the ABC to a specific problem, fear of flying.

A Activating event
David is on a plane which is flying through severe turbulence.

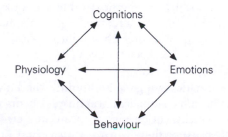

FIGURE 5.1   The relationship between the modalities

B **Beliefs about the event: self-defeating/automatic thoughts**
  - this plane is going to crash
  - I'll never see my family again
  - this is it
  - I can't bear this

C **Emotional consequence**
  - anxiety/panic

Behavioural response
  - asks the air steward for reassurance
  - tries to read his newspaper

Physiological response
  - racing heart, shaking, sweating

Diagrammatic illustration of the problem using the ABC can serve to strengthen a client's conceptual understanding of cognitive therapy. In the above example, David's anxiety at C is not due to the turbulence but rather to his *appraisal* of the turbulence at B. In cognitive behavioural literature, self-defeating beliefs are also known as automatic thoughts, so called because they occur very quickly and may appear to be both plausible and realistic to the person. They can also be present in the form of images or pictures. For example, someone may become very anxious before a meeting at work. This is because they have just had an image go through their mind of the last meeting when they experienced difficulty answering some of the questions.

Becoming aware of automatic thoughts can be a difficult task as individuals are not usually accustomed to focusing on the content of their thoughts. Therefore, clients may need help in identifying their self-defeating thoughts, particularly during the beginning stages of the counselling. One method is to keep a record of situations in which the client feels depressed or anxious and the accompanying self-defeating thoughts and feelings. An example of a record/diary is shown below:

Date	*Situation (A)*	*Thoughts (B)*	*Feelings (C)*
12 April	Eating a curry with accompanying side dishes in the local restaurant.	Oh, God, this is so fattening, I'll never lose weight, the people at the next table are looking at me and thinking 'she's huge'. I'm such a failure I can't even keep to my diet.	shame depression

Having identified automatic thoughts and understood their interaction with emotions and behavioural/physiological responses, clients are then encouraged to view automatic thoughts in terms of 'thinking errors' (also known as 'cognitive distortions' because they lead to a distortion of reality). Commonly used categories of thinking errors are listed below:

- all-or-nothing thinking – evaluating experiences using extremes such as 'excellent' or 'awful'
'If I don't get this job, I'll never work again.'

- mind reading/jumping to conclusions – assuming a negative response without the relevant information
'As he didn't say "good morning" to me, that means he is annoyed with me.'

- personalization – blaming yourself for an event
'It's totally my fault the relationship ended.'

- over-generalization – drawing sweeping negative conclusions on the basis of one or more events
'Because my report had a mistake in it, my appraisal will be awful and I won't get my payrise.'

- fortune-telling – assuming you know what the future holds
'Now I've had one panic attack, I'm always going to have them.'

- emotional reasoning – confusing feelings with facts
'I feel so anxious, driving on motorways must be dangerous.'

- labelling – using unhelpful labels to describe yourself or others
'I'm so stupid.'

- magnification – blowing things out of proportion
'Forgetting to phone my client today was probably the worst possible thing I've done.'

A client who is anxious about public speaking, for example, may have the following thoughts: 'I know I'm going to mess this speech up' (fortune-telling) or 'Everyone will laugh at me' (jumping to conclusions). A client suffering from depression, on the other hand, may think: 'I'm a useless, worthless human being' (labelling) or 'Life is awful' (all-or-nothing thinking and magnification). While everyone has unhelpful thoughts from time to time, individuals with emotional problems such as depression or anxiety, tend to experience self-defeating thoughts on a more frequent basis.

How psychological problems are acquired

A number of factors contribute to the acquisition of psychological problems. They include:

- life events such as marital problems, bereavement, job loss and physical illness
- social factors such as poor housing, stress at work and loneliness
- poor coping strategies, for example increased alcohol consumption to alleviate the symptoms of stress

Childhood experiences can also be informative. As part of their early development individuals learn a number of unspoken rules or assumptions which help them to make sense of the world and other people. Known as schemas, these underlying beliefs influence a person's automatic thoughts and behaviour in specific situations. Two psychologists, Ivy Blackburn and Kate Davidson[8] cite three ways in which schema differ from automatic thoughts: 'They are abstract and, therefore, the patient is largely unaware of them, hence the term "silent assumptions". They are influenced by an individual's social and cultural background and differ from more adaptive attitudes only in their form, that is they are too general, too rigid and undifferentiated' (p. 83). In the example used at the start of this section, it is possible that as a child David was told by his parents to be careful, avoid risks and be on his guard, and so developed two schemas – 'The world is a dangerous place' and 'I need to be in control all the time.' These schemas were activated as a result of his negative automatic thoughts about the severe turbulence the plane was experiencing.

How psychological problems are perpetuated

Psychological problems are perpetuated by the maintenance of thinking errors and unhelpful schema. For example, a person who became highly anxious while giving a lecture at work, may have held the following beliefs: 'Everyone must have noticed my hands were shaking, how embarrassing' (jumping to conclusions) and 'My boss will probably sack me' (fortune-telling). If the person continues to hold these unhelpful beliefs he or she is likely to avoid giving future presentations (avoidance behaviour) in order not to experience the anxiety again, and so the problem is perpetuated.

How an individual moves from psychological disturbance to psychological health

The move to psychological health involves the systematic application of specific cognitive and behavioural techniques by both the counsellor and client to the problem(s). In certain cases where the emotional disturbance is very strong (for example, suicidal ideation as part of depression) this may be coupled with medication, as prescribed by the client's doctor. In addition, a decrease in the influence of external, non-psychological pressures can contribute to increased well-being (for example, a new job with better pay and flexibility). It is important to note, however, that the reduction of external pressures alone is unlikely to result in good psychological health. The person who is anxious about giving presentations may receive temporary relief from the symptoms of anxiety on leaving the job, but if in the future he or she is asked to give any presentations the symptoms may return. Therefore technique-application with the aim of helping the client to cope with problems in a constructive manner and modify their thinking is viewed as central to the acquisition of psychological health.

Cognitive therapy is an educative and problem-orientated approach, the goals of which are:

- to ameliorate and resolve difficulties or problems
- to help the client acquire constructive coping strategies
- to help the client modify thinking errors and/or schema
- to help the client become their own 'personal therapist'

Since the counselling is goal orientated, at the start both client and counsellor discuss what the client would like to achieve by the end of the counselling. The client's goals are often written down and examined to see whether they are realistic and achievable within the time limit available. For example, if a client came to see a cognitive therapist for a phobia about travelling in tube trains, it would be unrealistic for the counsellor and client to predict that by the end of the first session the client would be 'cured'. Counsellors work in the 'here and now', helping clients become aware of their unhelpful beliefs and then modify these beliefs using cognitive and behavioural strategies. The aim is that clients should use these strategies to deal with any future problems, without therapeutic support, and thus become their own personal therapist.

Case conceptualization

Assessment of the client's problems, also known as case conceptualization or formulation, is an important component of cognitive therapy. Over the first and often second sessions, the counsellor, with the information the client has provided and using appropriate questioning, can gain an in-depth picture of the client's problems. This tentative formulation can then guide the counsellor in understanding how they arose and how they are perpetuated and which techniques would need to be adopted by the client to overcome their problems. Some of the main features of the case conceptualization include:

- a detailed description of the client's problem(s), specifically in relation to the modalities of behaviour, feelings, physiology and cognitions (see 'basic assumptions', pp. 57–9)
- an understanding of the problems in terms of development and course, that is, whether the problem(s) developed suddenly or slowly, and whether they get better at certain times and worse at others.
- identification of any factors which exacerbate the problem – for example clients who experience anxiety when speaking to people they don't know, may make the problem worse by drinking three vodkas to gain courage before speaking to others

- compiling of a problem list by the counsellor and client, for those clients with more than one problem
- discussing and setting achievable and realistic goals
- if appropriate, request that the client fill out a questionnaire to supplement the counsellor's knowledge of the client's problem(s), for example the 'Multi-modal Life History Inventory' by Arnold Lazarus and Clifford Lazarus[9]

Session structure

A key characteristic of this therapy is structured sessions; a typical format is outlined below:

1 Review client's current psychological state (how does the client feel emotionally?).
2 Negotiate the agenda for the session (what is it that the counsellor and client would like to focus on in this session?).
3 Review homework assignments, carried out since the last session (for example, did the client complete the recommended reading?). If a client does not do the negotiated homework assignment, this issue is discussed.
4 Work on specific session targets, which have been agreed on when negotiating the agenda (for example, how to cope with being lonely at weekends).
5 New homework assignments are negotiated that relate to the session's agenda (the client with a phobia of trains may be asked by the counsellor to use the train for a specified period and, while on it, to practise the techniques discussed in the session to reduce their anxiety).
6 The counsellor obtains feedback from the client as to how they found the session (that is, did they understand everything that was discussed in the session, and are they clear about the homework?).

In addition to structured sessions, other characteristics of cognitive therapy include:

- A collaborative or team approach to counselling. The counsellor and client work together to solve the client's problems. The client is encouraged to ask questions when appropriate, the emphasis being on an open relationship.
- The counsellor and client work towards goals which are specific, measured, achievable, realistic and time-limited (SMART).
- Sessions last 50 minutes or an hour.
- Counselling is normally short-term (between six and twenty sessions), although long-term counselling is often more appropriate with clients who have more difficult problems.
- Negative automatic thoughts and thinking errors are the focus of the beginning part of the therapy, whereas the middle and ending part tend to focus on modifying schema. (Schema may not be explored in brief therapy.)

Cognitive counsellors employ a number of cognitive and behavioural techniques, a selection of which are outlined below. Cognitive techniques are used to help clients identify, evaluate and modify negative automatic thoughts and schema, while behavioural techniques serve to help clients test their negative automatic thoughts. It is important to remember that these techniques are not applied on a random basis. The information gathered during the initial assessment enables the counsellor to make a tentative case formulation, thereby informing technique selection.

Cognitive techniques
Questioning   Direct questioning, also known as Socratic questioning, is used to help clients become aware of their negative thoughts/images and to modify unhelpful beliefs. To identify negative thoughts, clients are asked to think of situations in which they experienced strong negative emotions such as anxiety or depression and then ask themselves what was going through their minds at that moment. Having identified negative beliefs, the next step is to examine the validity of them by using Socratic questions which include:[10]

Where is this way of thinking getting you?
Is there any evidence for this belief?
Are there any alternative ways of looking at the situation?
What is the effect of thinking this way?
What are the advantages and disadvantages of thinking this way?
Are you jumping to conclusions?
Is this an example of mind-reading or fortune-telling by you?
Are you taking things personally which have little or nothing to do with you?

Automatic thought forms   These forms are usually divided into four sections: a) the situation or activating event; b) negative automatic thoughts (NATs); c) emotional and behavioural consequences; and d) a self-helping response. Clients use these forms to record their NATs, feelings and actions regarding events they are upset about and the subsequent self-helping responses that they have developed to deal with the situation.

Distraction   Distraction exercises may help clients to stop thinking negatively. Examples include: counting back from 100 in threes; reading an interesting book; remembering a pleasant image in detail, for example a day from your last holiday, what you were doing, the conversation, the colours, any smells etc.

Double standard method   Often people are much harsher on themselves than on friends or colleagues, so clients are asked to treat themselves as they would a friend in the same situation.

Advantages and disadvantages   Initially with the counsellor's assistance, clients are asked to make a list of the advantages and disadvantages of holding their negative beliefs.

Looking for other explanations   In some situations people often draw incorrect conclusions where other more rational explanations may be possible. If a client holds the belief 'When I got home tonight my husband didn't say hello, therefore he must be angry with me', she is asked to consider alternative explanations – for example was her husband annoyed with her in the morning; if not, is it possible that he was preoccupied in thinking about work?

Dealing with emotional reasoning   Clients are encouraged not to confuse feelings with facts; for example, if a person *feels* out of control, is there evidence that they *are* out of control?

Testing out the validity of their automatic thoughts   Having examined their beliefs and developed more helpful ones, clients are asked to test out their new beliefs using behavioural experiments. For example, to test out the belief, 'I can stand travelling on buses', the behavioural exercise would be to take a bus journey.

Eliciting schema and underlying assumptions   The process for identifying schemas and underlying assumptions is known as the downward arrow and it focuses on the personal meaning of events:

> *Client*: I know the customer hated the presentation because I didn't get the contract.
> *Counsellor*: Let's suppose that's true, what does that mean to you?
> *Client*: That I'm useless at giving presentations.
> *Counsellor*: And if that was the case, what does that mean to you?
> *Client*: If I can't do my job well, then I'm useless.

In the above example, the hypothesized underlying assumption is, 'If I can't do my job well, I'm useless' and the schema is 'I'm useless'. This is shared with the client and if they are in agreement with it, the counsellor and client then go on to modify it.

Modifying schema   A three-step process is adopted by Padesky and Greenberger,[11] which involves:

1   Writing down the belief, then underneath listing experiences that indicate that this belief is not 100 per cent true.
2   Writing down a new, more realistic belief and then underneath it recording experiences which support this belief.
3   Rating confidence in the new belief on a regular basis.

Behavioural techniques

Relaxation   There are a number of different techniques available which can be used to help clients control their physiological responses to stress, such as a racing heart, headaches and knots in the stomach. Relaxation is a form of cognitive distraction which helps to relax the mind and body.

Graded exposure   This technique can be used to help clients face their fears, step by step, starting with the least anxiety-provoking step. For example, if the goal of a client who is scared of spiders is to hold one in their hand, the first step could be to read a magazine with photographs of spiders in it, the second to sit in the same room with a spider in a jar, and so on, until the client is able to hold the spider in their hand without feeling anxious.

Scheduling activities   Often clients who are depressed, who lack motivation and who hold the belief, 'I can't be bothered to do anything', may benefit from planning their activities on a hourly and daily basis. This enables them to be active and to recognize that by doing things they can become more motivated and less depressed.

Behavioural experiments   These are used by clients to test out their new self-helping beliefs. For example, a client who has a fear of public speaking may be asked by the counsellor to practise repeating their new beliefs before a speech, with the aim of reducing anxiety.

WHICH CLIENTS BENEFIT MOST?

Cognitive therapy is practised in various settings and applied to a number of different client problems, such as anxiety; phobias; depression; eating disorders; obsessive-compulsive disorder; psychosomatic problems; sexual dysfunctions; chronic fatigue; schizophrenia; Post Traumatic Stress Disorder; substance abuse problems; and personality disorders. Over recent years, the number of therapists using this approach has grown and the demand for it continues to increase. Being research-based and short-term, cognitive therapy is widely used within medical settings where the need for a cost-effective treatment is vital. The techniques are also used in the growing industry of stress-management training.[10]

This approach may not benefit clients who want to explore their past in great depth, as the emphasis is largely on the here-and-now, or clients who are not motivated to make changes in their lives. Acceptance of the cognitive model and willingness to undertake homework assignments are crucial factors when considering suitability for cognitive therapy.

Case Study

THE CLIENT

David is a 42-year-old deputy director of a large geological company, who came for therapy after having experienced severe anxiety on a number of airline flights over the previous two years. His anxiety was triggered after a flight which involved severe turbulence. Since then he found himself starting to worry about any flight a few days before he was due to fly out. On arriving at the airport he follows a set pattern; he checks in and then heads straight for the bar to have a drink to 'calm his nerves'. He then continues to drink on the flight, arriving at his destination tired and at times quite drunk. On several occasions the stewards on the plane refused to serve him more alcohol because he appeared very drunk, causing him severe embarrassment. In addition, the previous month he had arrived intoxicated for a meeting in Germany. The meeting had to be cancelled as a result and on his return to the UK his director had warned him that his job was in jeopardy unless he 'sorted out' his drinking. This triggered his request for help.

David is married with two young children and his wife is supportive of his endeavour to seek counselling.

THE THERAPY

Session 1

This session involved the assessment of the client's problems, taking into account David's background. David had no history of anxiety and his anxiety was confined to the few days before the flight and during it. He noticed that five days before the flight he would start to feel restless and have trouble sleeping, and he would be 'extra nice' to his wife and children in case his worst fear happened, the plane crashed and he would never see them again. David was an intelligent client who recognized that his fear was irrational but when on the plane he 'felt certain that he was going to die'.

In this assessment session the therapist explained to David the rationale behind cognitive therapy and the importance of structured sessions (in particular homework assignments), and together the counsellor and David identified his goal, namely to reduce his level of anxiety while flying and to stop drinking while on the flight. The therapist explained to David that using alcohol to reduce his anxiety was unhelpful as it was a depressant and only prevented him from getting used to flying. Finally the therapist and David agreed to meet for six weekly sessions of 50 minutes. The therapist set David his first homework assignment – to buy a book on the fear of flying which focused on the use of cognitive-behavioural techniques. The counsellor developed a tentative case conceptualization which outlined David's problem and indicated which interventions might be beneficial to help him overcome his irrational fear of flying.

At the start of the session the agenda was negotiated and the therapist asked David about the homework assignment (this process was repeated at the start of every session). He had purchased the book and had started to read it. He was comforted by learning that he was not the only person who suffered from a fear of flying. The focus of this session was to identify David's automatic thoughts which contributed to his anxiety.

To help this process the therapist asked David to describe the last flight he was on. As he talked about the flight David began to feel anxious. He experienced knots in his stomach, tension in his shoulders and his heart began to race. He identified a number of associated negative automatic thoughts:

'This pilot doesn't know what he is doing.'
'This plane is going to crash.'
'My heart is going to stop.'
'I can't bear it.'

The therapist then asked David to link his automatic thoughts to thinking errors; for example, 'This plane is going to crash' involves fortune-telling. Finally, the therapist showed David how to fill out the automatic thought form, inserting the negative beliefs described above. For homework David decided to continue with the reading, and the counsellor suggested adding negative automatic beliefs about the flight to the automatic thought form.

The focus of these sessions was on examining David's automatic thoughts and modifying them with more realistic and helpful beliefs. An example of the dialogue pertaining to his last flight went as follows:

Therapist: [refers to automatic thought form] You have written here, 'this plane is going to crash'.
David: Yes, that's right. On the plane I know it's going to crash.
Therapist: David, how many times have you had this thought while flying?
David: In total at least 100 times.
Therapist: And what has happened?
David: Nothing.
Therapist: What does that suggest to you?
David: That it's only a thought and thoughts don't equal facts.
Therapist: That's right and in your book what does it say about the chance of crashing?
David: That to be sure to be in a major disaster you need to fly every day for 26,000 years.
Therapist: So based on this fact what is the likelihood of your next flight crashing?
David: I think I've got more chance of winning the lottery [laughing].

The counsellor and David worked on examining his automatic thoughts and writing down alternative realistic thoughts, such as 'My heart is not going to stop because I feel anxious, that is not possible' on the automatic thought form. For homework David was asked to continue reading his book and to read through the session notes, focusing on the alternative thoughts.

Sessions 5 and 6

In these two sessions the counsellor and David went over the realistic thoughts that David had been writing down both in sessions and as part of his homework. The counsellor encouraged David to copy down some of the more 'powerful' thoughts in the form of statements on to a small card which he could read on a regular basis to remind himself of the realistic, more helpful thoughts; for example, 'I've got more chances of winning the lottery than the plane crashing.' The counsellor also recommended that David buy a relaxation tape which he could use to reduce his tension. David agreed to use the tape every other day and to take it on the plane, if he needed to control his anxiety while flying.

Coping imagery was also introduced. The client was asked to picture himself coping on the flight using the techniques previously mentioned. For homework he was asked to keep practising using the coping imagery and the relaxation tape on a daily basis. The counsellor and client also negotiated a date for a follow-up session which was scheduled for after David's next flight. During the follow-up session David reported that his anxiety had greatly reduced, and that in particular he found the using the coping statements and imagery very helpful. However, if he had remained very anxious whilst flying, the counsellor may have negotiated additional counselling sessions to focus on David's underlying schema (see p. 60).

REFERENCES

1 Watson, J.B. and Rayner, R. (1920) 'Conditioned emotional reactions', *Journal of Experimental Psychology*, 3: 1–4.
2 Adler, A. (1958) *What Life Should Mean to You* (ed. A. Porter). New York: Capricorn. (Originally published, 1931.)
3 Kelly, G. (1955) *The Psychology of Personal Constructs*, vols 1 and 2. New York: Norton.
4 Ellis, A. (1962) *Reason and Emotion in Psychotherapy*. New York: Lyle Stuart.
5 Miechenbaum, D. (1997) *Cognitive Behaviour Modification: An Integrative Approach*. New York: Plenum Press.
6 Beck, A.T., Rush, A.J., Shaw, B.F. and Emery, G. (1979) *Cognitive Therapy of Depression*. New York: Guilford Press.
7 British Association for Counselling (1993) *Membership Survey*. Keele: Mountain and Associates, Marketing Services Ltd.
8 Blackburn, I.V. and Davidson, K.M. (1990) *Cognitive Therapy for Depression and Anxiety*. Oxford: Blackwell Scientific Publications.

9 Lazarus, A.A. and Lazarus, C.N. (1991) *Multimodal Life History Inventory*. Champaign, IL: Research Press.
10 Palmer, S. and Dryden, W. (1995) *Counselling for Stress Problems*. London: Sage Publications.
11 Greenberger, D. and Padesky, C. (1995) *Clinicians' Guide to Mind over Mood*. New York: Guilford Press.

SUGGESTED READING

Burns, D. (1990) *The Feeling Good Handbook*. New York: Plume. This book provides an excellent introduction to this therapy and it is full of examples and exercises.

Kennerley, H. (1991) *Managing Anxiety: A Training Manual*. Oxford: Oxford University Press. This book provides all the information needed to work with clients who experience anxiety, it contains case examples and information sheets which can be photocopied for clients.

Greenberger, D. and Padesky, C. (1995) *Clinicians' Guide to Mind over Mood*. New York: Guilford Press. Another good book which serves to introduce readers to this approach, it is best read in conjunction with client's guide below.

Greenberger, D. and Padesky, C. (1995) *Mind over Mood: A Cognitive Therapy Treatment Manual for Clients*. New York: Guilford Press. This book is aimed at clients providing step-by-step information on how to overcome a number of problems such as anxiety.

DISCUSSION ISSUES

1 What part do automatic thoughts play in the perpetuation of clients' psychological problems?
2 How would you explain the rationale behind cognitive therapy to a client?
3 In what ways does cognitive therapy differ from other therapies?
4 What homework tasks would you negotiate with a client who is suffering from stress due to work pressures?

6

EXISTENTIAL COUNSELLING AND PSYCHOTHERAPY

Sarah Young

Existential therapy is an approach to counselling and psychotherapy that is based on a philosophical understanding of what it is to be a human being, what it means to exist. This understanding draws on the work of many philosophers, and therapists vary in the emphasis they give to particular philosophers. The existential approach does not involve simply learning a way of thinking about existence and applying it to others in a detached manner. Instead the therapist's involvement with this philosophy becomes meaningful in a highly personal way – in short it becomes a way of being.

Counsellors who espouse this approach draw on their own experience of life and living as well as on centuries of philosophical thought. Essentially we are talking about an attitude, a 'world view' that informs both the counselling work and the way the counsellor lives his or her life. Since every individual's philosophy of life is unique to them it is misleading to discuss the existential approach in very general terms. Any informed discussion of this approach will always be personal and will reveal the particular life experiences brought to it by the therapist. Nevertheless, in this chapter I will attempt to provide an outline of the approach that will, I hope, meet with the approval of most of those who practise existential counselling.

DEVELOPMENT OF THE THERAPY

Existential therapy has its roots in existential philosophy. There is no one school of existential therapy any more than there is one school of existential philosophy. Any philosopher who has concerned him or herself with the understanding of human existence could be described as existential. Therefore a list of relevant existential philosophers might include some of the earliest Greek philosophers as well as the more commonly accepted European existential philosophers of this century. Søren Kierkegaard (1813–55) and Friedrich Nietzsche (1844–1900), the so-called philosophers of freedom, are often described as the forerunners of existential philosophy. Their disgust with the 'sheeplike' mentality of people drove them to call for a radical rethinking of religion and to stress our responsibility for how we lead our lives. It could be argued that Martin Heidegger (1889–1976) – the founding father of existentialism – has had the greatest influence on existential psychotherapy and counselling. Though Heidegger was not himself directly concerned with psychotherapy, his philosophy of existence was taken up by two Swiss psychiatrists, Ludwig Binswanger (1881–1966) and Medard Boss (1903–90), and used by them in their understanding of their patients' difficulties. Their method of psychotherapy marked the starting point for the existential approach.

In this country R.D. Laing (1927–89), the 'anti-psychiatry' psychiatrist, also used some existential ideas to increase his understanding of his patients' problems. The most important contribution to the development of existential psychotherapy and counselling in this country has been made by the philosopher and psychotherapist Emmy van Deurzen. She was responsible for setting up the first courses in existential psychotherapy and counselling and in 1988 published the first book dealing solely with this approach.[1] In the same year Emmy van Deurzen founded the Society for Existential Analysis. This society is now chaired by Ernesto Spinelli, a practising psychotherapist and counselling psychologist, who has also made an influential contribution to the field of existential psychotherapy and counselling, in particular to the phenomenological aspects of this approach. No description of more recent developments would be complete without mention of the psychotherapist Hans W. Cohn, whose numerous papers and recently published book[2] have given us an extremely clear and thorough exposition of the existential approach. The psychologist Rollo May (1909–94), with his editorship of *Existence*,[3] was responsible for taking existential ideas to America, and the psychiatrist Irvin Yalom[4] has given further prominence to existential concerns in that country.

THEORY AND BASIC CONCEPTS

Existential thinking makes several basic assumptions about what is true for all of us as human beings, assumptions about what it means to exist. These fundamental assumptions are often referred to as the 'givens' of existence.

Human nature

Jean-Paul Sartre (1905–80), perhaps the most popularized existential philosopher, argues that there is really no such thing as 'human nature', unless it is our nature to be essentially nothing. At the core of our being is a nothingness.[5] We become something through the choices we make – in this way we fill ourselves up. The something we become is never fixed, it is never once and for all. Rather what we are is always in process, always changing. So to talk of personality types or even to ask 'Who am I?' is a nonsense for we are never one thing but are forever involved in a process of becoming. Many existentialists regard the 'self' as a construction, a convenient fiction. From the existentialist perspective the self is not a thing, not a discrete entity that can be delineated and described. From moment to moment a new self emerges, each new experience leaves us in a different place and we can never be precisely what we were before.

Choice

Many find this idea difficult to grasp as most of us have a sense of continuity and a strong sense of self. We feel we are the same person we were this morning, yesterday, 20 years ago. We appear to need this sense of sameness because without it we feel intolerably insecure. At the same time existentialists argue that we limit ourselves by seeing ourselves in this fixed and unchangeable way. How often have we heard ourselves or others say, 'I'm just like that', 'That's how I am'? We talk as if nothing can change and as if we are not responsible for the way we are – 'I'm made that way' we say. Sartre argued that we have far more choice than we for the most part allow ourselves and he believed that within the limits of our 'facticity' we can be whatever we choose. 'Facticity' refers to the facts of our existence, those aspects over which we have no choice – for example, the circumstances of our birth, our parents, the place, time and culture we are born into, our genetic endowment, the environment we grow up in. Where we do have a choice is in our response to these limitations: this is our freedom.

Freedom

We often find it difficult to accept this measure of freedom and instead we 'pass the buck' and allow others to take responsibility for who we are. We look to others to make the rules rather than choose for ourselves. Sartre argues that there are no certainties (aside from the certainty of death), no absolutes, it is for us to decide how we wish to lead our lives, to make our own rules, find our own meaning. In other words we carry a huge burden of responsibility. To acknowledge that we are responsible for ourselves in this way provokes enormous anxiety, and yet at the same time this awareness of our freedom can be experienced as extremely liberating. Nevertheless it often feels easier to 'play it safe' and do what we have always done, follow the rules and pretend that we have no choice. In so doing we deny ourselves a more passionate and exhilarating experience of living.

Anxiety and guilt

Existentialists argue that because we have this measure of freedom and are 'condemned' to choose, this inevitably involves us in being anxious. Existential anxiety is regarded as an aspect of existence, an existential 'given' that none of us can avoid however hard we try. Ultimately our lives are our responsibility and this makes us anxious. At the same time existentialists argue that we cannot fulfil our responsibility to ourselves, we can only attempt to do so. Since we can never fulfil our potentiality, since we inevitably fall short of what we might be, we cannot avoid being existentially guilty. We are always in debt to ourselves, we owe it to ourselves to be more than we are, hence our guilt. Like existential anxiety, existential guilt is regarded as an inevitable aspect of human existence.

Being-in-the-world

Existential philosophers have come to certain conclusions about the individual. Heidegger describes existence as 'Being-in-the-world'.[6] He uses this phrase to emphasize our inevitable relationship, our 'built-in' connection to all that we encounter. We can get out of a car, but as long as we are alive we can never get out of our world. We are always *in* the world and that world is ours. When I die, *my* world, the world I know dies with me.

With-world

Not only do we always carry our world with us but we also always live in connection with others, we live in a 'with-world'.[7] We are always in relationship, even if we choose to live in isolation from others, we do so in relation to others. It is only through others that we gain a sense of ourselves, in relation to others we become what we are. At the same time, what we are is always in a state of flux. The person I am with my friend, with my sister, with my boss, with whomever, is a different person in each of these relationships. Just as each person's response to me is different, no one sees me in exactly the same way as another person sees me. It is perhaps true to say 'I have as many personalities as I have friends.'

Interpreted world

The emphasis on our inevitable relationship to all there is suggests that in a sense we are not separate individuals, but rather are mutually involved with those we meet. At the same time existentialists also stress that we are all unique, no one's experience is exactly like mine. I can never really know what it is like to be you. We all stand in our own unique place and each one of us views the world from our own particular perspective. Paradoxically, we are both connected to others and at the same time ultimately isolated from them. However similar our experiences may be, each one of us experiences things somewhat differently. The meaning I give to something belongs to me; someone else may give the same thing a very different meaning. Thus the meaning of any object, situation or experience belongs with the person giving the meaning – it does not reside in the object, situation or experience itself. In other, more succinct, words, we live in an 'interpreted world'.[8] Through our responses to whatever we encounter we, in a sense, create our world.

We are forever interpreting and ascribing meaning to all we experience. The meaning we give things can change over time; something that once meant a great deal may now mean very little. We often limit ourselves by believing that the meaning we give things is fixed and cannot be changed, we become rigid and inflexible. The recognition that it is within our power to change, both in relation to our view of ourselves and in terms of the meaning we give things, is for many a profoundly liberating experience.

Death

One thing we cannot change is the inevitability of our own death, the one certainty we all have. Though, of course, the time and place of our death is unknown and the meaning we give to death will vary. Rather than regarding death as a calamity, Heidegger suggests that the awareness of death is freeing. Death is a dimension of living and in denying death we may limit our experience of living. Try to imagine that you are going to live forever. Life loses some of its urgency and some of its intensity. If we have in mind that we are mortal, that life is finite, then we will, it is argued, live more fully in the present.

Acquiring and perpetuating psychological disturbance

Existential therapists do not concern themselves with diagnostic categories, with labelling people and pathologizing their difficulties. In other words they do not regard those they see in therapy as suffering from some definable illness. Instead they would regard their clients' concerns and difficulties as 'problems in living' to which we are all subjected, client and therapist alike. We do not 'acquire psychological disturbance', but rather human existence, living itself, is regarded as disturbing. As discussed earlier, human existence inevitably involves certain givens: the experience of anxiety and guilt; living towards death; the responsibility for finding our own meaning in life; living in a with-world and at the same time being ultimately isolated.

It may be that we have chosen to ignore the 'call of conscience' – the call to take up on the challenge of living life more fully – and therefore feel our lives are lacking in some way. We may find decision-making and responsibility too much for us. Previous experiences may have influenced us in such a way that our self-esteem is low and our relationships poor. Our lives may lack meaning or purpose. Our difficulties continue because we are not aware of the ways in which we perpetuate them. We find all sorts of ways of avoiding the givens of existence. By continually avoiding our responsibility, by denying our freedom and ignoring the possibilities available to us we limit ourselves. In our constant striving towards an unattainable level of security we restrict ourselves and perpetuate our problems.

The move to psychological health

So called 'psychological health' from the existential perspective is not a possibility. Our striving for a worry-free, non-stressful and balanced life can perpetuate our difficulties. Through facing up to our problems and taking responsibility for our choices we experience a greater sense of control. At the same time we may become more anxious, though perhaps anxious in a different way from when we thought it was possible to make life certain and safe. If we are prepared to take the risk and allow for insecurity and uncertainty, we are better able to deal with what life brings us. It requires great courage and determination to take your life into your own hands but some would argue that the rewards are incalculable.

PRACTICE

Goals

The existential therapist is not concerned with setting specific goals for therapy. The opening up of possibilities could be described as a general goal of existential therapy. Clients often arrive in therapy feeling their lives are restricted or lacking in purpose. They may have unsatisfactory relationships, or perhaps feel they are the victim of circumstances or others, they may wish to change the way they lead their lives but see no way of doing so. Clients may describe themselves as feeling stuck and unable to change. Hopefully, through the process of therapy clients come to realize that they have more freedom than they previously thought they had and that there is the possibility of a change in outlook. Despite the many limitations we are subject to, we still have a choice in how we respond to those limitations. During therapy clients come to realize their responsibility in the choices they make in the present, have made in the past and will make in the future. This involves the recognition that choice is often difficult – in choosing we say yes to one thing and no to another and, of course, in not choosing we are making a choice.

This being the case, existential therapists will not work towards ridding their clients of their existential anxiety, for to do so would be to deny their freedom and responsibility. Instead, existential therapists will encourage their clients to confront their difficulties and face up to the anxiety this entails. The same goes for existential guilt. Rather than attempt to remove feelings of guilt, existential therapists will facilitate their clients' ability to recognize when they avoid taking on the responsibility of fulfilling their potential. This will be done in the knowledge that we can never fulfil ourselves, we always fall short. In other words we cannot not fail to fail.

Authenticity has been described as the goal of existential therapy, but it is a frequently misunderstood concept. Heidegger discussed authenticity as a way of being that is true to existence. It is not about being true to some mythical core self. When we are authentic we are aware of the givens of existence – freedom, responsibility, death etc. We are mindful of Being, aware of what it means to exist. This mindfulness is not a permanent state but rather it is something that occurs momentarily, for example when our life or the life of someone close to us is threatened through illness. Once the threat is removed we revert to inauthenticity. For the most part we are forgetful of Being, we follow the crowd and ignore our mortality. It may be that through the process of therapy clients become more aware of the possibility of authenticity, however fleeting, but ultimately it will always be the client who decides the goal of therapy.[9]

Method

In their efforts to gain an understanding of existence existential philosophers adopted the phenomenological method first described by Edmund Husserl (1859–1938). Simply put, this method involves taking nothing for granted and questioning everything. We are asked to become naive, to adopt an open, almost childlike attitude which does not assume we know or understand anything. The so-called 'phenomenological reduction' asks us to set aside prior knowledge, to drop our prejudices and biases and to show an attitude of wonder to all that we encounter. By reducing our assumptions about whatever it is we are investigating we can then gain a better understanding and get closer to the thing itself. In so doing we increase our knowledge of the phenomenon (the object of our investigation) rather than simply staying with our ideas about it.

Existential therapists also adopt the phenomenological method in their approach to counselling and psychotherapy. They will attempt to set aside their prejudices and theories about their fellow human beings, about what makes them troubled and about what is best for them. In so doing they will remain available to their client in such a way that they are able to hear the client's concerns from the client's perspective rather than from their own. By simply staying with whatever the client presents, with the phenomena, and not looking for causes or explanations, the therapist and client will gradually gain a better understanding of the client's experience. The therapist will attempt to describe what he or she has understood so that a greater clarity on the client's way of being can be achieved.

Therapeutic relationship

As discussed above, a fundamental proposition of existential thinking is that we are always in relationship, we live in a 'with-world'. In other words all that we do, say and feel occurs in relationship to others. This understanding leads us to the recognition that in any interaction we are constantly influencing each other. When therapist and client meet they become what they are in relation to each other. What the client discloses to one therapist will not necessarily be the same as their disclosures to another therapist. Equally the therapist's responses are in relation to a particular client. This stress on the mutuality of any relationship means we are not seen as having fixed internal worlds inside our heads but rather we become what we are in interaction with another. In other words, what we are at any given moment does not reside in either individual but in the 'in-between', between us and the other, this is where the relationship occurs.

Therapist's attitude

Existential therapists do not regard themselves as in any way superior to their clients and they have a respect for their client as a fellow human being. We are all equal in that each of us faces the same givens. Therapists are not without their own difficulties in the present nor do they consider themselves immune from them in the future. It perhaps makes more sense to talk of 'persons-in-therapy' rather than therapist and client. Both client and therapist will be changed by the relationship they form. At the same time it would be foolish to suggest that there are not inequalities inherent in the relationship. The focus is on the client's concerns and the client is coming to the therapist for help. The therapist's concerns remain, for the most part, undisclosed. Nevertheless therapists will work towards an equal relationship in which they and the client are co-explorers of the client's experience.

Interventions

Silence is perhaps the most important intervention a therapist can make in that it is only when we are silent ourselves that we can hear what the other is saying. At the same time an existential therapist is not averse to questioning their client or to challenging their client's assumptions. The phenomenological attitude means that the therapist takes nothing for granted and does not assume that they or the client have understood what is being described. The client will be asked to clarify exactly what it is they are saying and experiencing. The therapist will attempt to tease out any assumptions embedded in what the client is discussing in order to allow the client's world view to emerge. Through this process it is hoped that what really matters for the client will be revealed.

The therapist will not interpret what the client is saying so that something comes to mean something else. Rather they will attempt to describe what they have understood from the client. Interpretations remain strictly descriptive. An object that appears in a dream, say a box, will not become something else such as a womb, but rather the box will be investigated on its own terms so that its meaning for the client can be revealed more fully.

The change process

The existential therapist provides the client with the space in which to explore their experience. The therapist will work towards developing a trusting and caring relationship in which the client feels safe enough to reveal him or herself. The therapist's endeavour is to discover something of what life is like for the client, to gain an approximation of the client's experience. Through this process clients will begin to question their firmly held assumptions about themselves and what is possible for them. They may begin to realize they have more choice than they previously thought and will start to recognize their responsibility for themselves. The therapist sets aside whatever ideas they might have about what is good for their clients, for it is always for the client to decide on any changes.

Format of a typical session

Existential therapists would agree that it is not possible to describe the format of a typical session as every therapeutic encounter is different. Since both therapist and client are unique individuals they respond to the therapeutic setting in their own particular way. There are no clearly defined rules for existential therapy. Within the framework of existential philosophy each therapist is responsible for developing his or her own particular style of working. Having said that, existential therapists would always leave it for the client to set the agenda for the session.

WHICH CLIENTS BENEFIT MOST?

It seems excessive to suggest that anyone can benefit from existential therapy, but it could be argued that all of us are suited to this approach since we all face the same givens of existence. Because the concern is always with the client's *particular situation* the existential approach is potentially useful to anyone. Some might argue that those who wish to re-evaluate themselves, to look at the way they lead their lives, to explore what choices are available to them and to ask themselves what they want for the future may find the existential approach particularly helpful.

Clients who are looking for advice or for a highly structured and technique-oriented approach to therapy may find the existential approach too open and unstructured. Existentialists accept that living life as fully as possible involves anxiety and uncertainty, a message that those hoping for security and an easy life will not wish to hear. Taking responsibility for oneself is not easy and many will find the challenge too great and prefer others to order their lives for them.

Case study

THE CLIENT

When I first met Jane she described herself as a very private person who did not like talking about herself. She had no real desire to be in therapy as she considered her life quite satisfactory and was concerned that nothing should change, particularly in terms of her close family relationships. Jane had enrolled in a counselling course, hence her search for a therapist. I was the third she had seen. Jane's son had left home and while she involved herself in local church matters, charity work, occasionally helping out in her husband's business and looking after her home and garden, she wished to do something more. A friend had suggested that Jane might become a counsellor. Jane was attracted to the idea as she wished to do something for others but when she discovered it would involve her in her own process of self-exploration she began to have serious doubts.

Jane described something of her family background. Her mother had died when she was 8 years old and two years later her father had left home. She had been brought up by her eldest sister (there were three other siblings) and her aunt who was guardian to the five children. Despite losing both her parents at a young age Jane described her childhood as reasonably happy.

THE THERAPY

We agreed to meet on a weekly basis for a trial period of six weeks so that Jane could decide if she wished to continue. In this short case study I will discuss one particular theme which was the focus of much of our work, namely Jane's guarded attitude in relation to others, her wish to remain private and her reluctance to involve herself more fully with others. We were able to make links between her behaviour in several different contexts – again and again this theme emerged.

Initially Jane found coming to therapy difficult and it was extremely hard for her to talk about herself. She was also reluctant to talk about her relationships to others, particularly those close to her, as this felt disloyal. I left it for Jane to begin the sessions and although she found this hard and we sometimes sat in silence, she usually found something to discuss. I intervened to reflect back to her what I had understood, to clarify further what she was describing and sometimes to question her more fully on her experience. During the early stages of our relationship I withheld from questioning Jane too closely or from challenging her too directly. In other words, as she described it, I was gentle with her. I constantly struggled with myself. Should I be more forthright in my approach to her? Was I 'colluding' with her? When we discussed her experience of coming to therapy and of our relationship she acknowledged that if I had pushed her at this early stage she would have stopped coming.

Jane decided to continue coming to see me, but no decision was made as to how long this would be for. Gradually, as the trust between us developed she became more willing to focus on herself and she began to own her feelings of vulnerability. At the same time I became less tentative in my approach to her. Jane frequently described how often she refrained from letting others know what was going on for her and how she never allowed anyone to get too close. She feared not being in control, not knowing what might happen. I asked her what this meant for her in the context of coming to see me. By exploring this further she was able to look at her difficulties and question the assumptions she was making about herself and other people's perceptions. In saying something about what she experienced in relation to me she was doing what she so often refrained from, namely, she risked directly communicating her personal experience.

Slowly she took it upon herself to speak more openly about herself. She had always taken the line of falling in with others and of never making any demands on anyone. She began to ask herself if she had been missing out, if by becoming more involved she might get more out of life. Jane often said she would like to be less guarded and more relaxed but at the same time she had no liking for those she described as loud and extrovert. When we explored this conflict further Jane acknowledged that there were times that she envied those on her counselling course who appeared to find it easy to speak in the large group. On the one hand she wished she could speak out, on the other hand she did not want strangers to know anything about her, or her life. We explored her fears further and she discovered how important it was for her to remain in control and not to allow others in any way to have the upper hand.

As a child Jane had always kept 'herself to herself' and tried not to make any difficulties. On one occasion when she talked about her mother's death she described how she had decided after her mother had died not to 'let anyone in'. From an early age she had built barriers around herself in order not to get hurt again. Jane recognized how often she had played it safe and avoided taking the risk of exposing herself to any kind of uncertainty. We explored her assumptions and expectations around what might occur if she adopted a less rigid stance and became more open with people. She began to have doubts as to whether the strategies she had once employed were really necessary now and if by becoming more involved the rewards might be worth the risk.

Eventually Jane began to describe occasions when she 'emerged from her shell' and revealed something of herself – for example, in the group at college, during a talk at a conference, with a relative at a family function. She found that when she did involve herself more fully, despite the anxiety, the experience was rewarding. She started to take risks and to offer her opinion more readily, to say what she wanted in particular situations, to be less rigid about her running of the home, allowing others to have a say. She described herself as being easier with people, more open and relaxed. Jane often surprised herself and was gratified to find that these changes brought unexpected rewards.

Jane often wanted to discuss with me her work with clients as this was something that concerned her and provoked a great deal of anxiety. There were times when I found this problematic in that there was a tendency for therapy to become supervision. I often had to restrain myself from becoming the supervisor. Nevertheless this provided opportunities for us to talk about our relationship and her experience of therapy. We began to investigate further her difficulties with uncertainty and at the same time she came to accept its inevitability.

There was obviously a great deal that was not addressed in therapy. Clearly any changes that did occur were as much due to Jane's experiences on the course, in supervision and as a counsellor as they were to the work she did with me. At the end of our work together (50 sessions over a period of 16 months) Jane agreed to being included in this chapter. She acknowledged that if I had asked her a year earlier she would definitely have said no. I admired her courage in saying yes.

From the existential perspective being-with-others is a given. One way of being-with-others is communicating with them personally and it was here that Jane had difficulty. She was being inauthentic to the extent that she was denying this aspect of relating. At the same time she was ill at ease with this position and wanted to overcome her guarded approach to others. Gradually Jane began to make different choices, she revealed more of herself to others and despite the anxiety involved she felt rewarded for her efforts.

REFERENCES

1 Deurzen-Smith, E. van (1988) *Existential Counselling in Practice*. London: Sage.
2 Cohn, H.W. (1997) *Existential Thought and Therapeutic Practice*. London: Sage.
3 May, R. (ed.) (1958) *Existence*. New York: Basic Books.
4 Yalom, I. (1980) *Existential Psychotherapy*. New York: Basic Books.
5 Sartre, J.-P. (1958) *Being and Nothingness* (trans. H. Barnes). London: Methuen.
6 Heidegger, M. (1962) *Being and Time* (trans. J. Macquarrie and E. Robinson). Oxford: Blackwell.
7 Heidegger, M. (1962) ibid.
8 Spinelli, E. (1989) *The Interpreted World*. London: Sage.
9 Cohn, H.W. (1993) 'Authenticity and the aims of psychotherapy', *Journal of the Society for Existential Analysis*, 4: 48–55.

SUGGESTED READING

Cohn, H.W. (1997) *Existential Thought and Therapeutic Practice. An Introduction to Existential Psychotherapy*. London: Sage. This book presents an overall framework for an existential-phenomenological approach to psychotherapy and shows how this affects the practice of psychotherapy. Throughout, existential ideas are compared with the assumptions of psychoanalysis. An extremely concise and clear account.

Deurzen-Smith, E. van (1996) *Everyday Mysteries. Existential Dimensions of Psychotherapy*. London: Routledge. A comprehensive book which covers the full spectrum of philosophical ideas that underpin existential psychotherapy. A systematic method of psychotherapy is also described and illustrated with detailed case material. An important book for anyone wishing to gain an understanding of the existential approach from the perspective of one of its best known practitioners.

Spinelli, E. (1994) *Demystifying Therapy*. London: Constable. Dr Spinelli provides a thorough examination of the fundamental assumptions of counselling and psychotherapy and demonstrates the philosophical naiveté of many of these assumptions. The psychoanalytic, cognitive-behavioural and humanistic models are criticized and the existential-phenomenological approach is presented as an alternative. Well argued and provocative.

Spinelli, E. (1997) *Tales of Un-Knowing: Therapeutic Encounters from an Existential Perspective*. London: Duckworth. Through the discussion of eight highly dramatic case studies several important and diverse therapeutic issues are covered from an existential perspective. Written in an extremely clear and accessible style.

DISCUSSION ISSUES

1 What does the concept of freedom mean for you? Are we as free as some existential philosophers suggest?
2 To what extent do you believe it is possible to set aside your assumptions and prejudices when you first meet someone?
3 What is your understanding of the so-called existential 'givens'? Are they meaningful in terms of your own experience?
4 From the existential perspective what is meant by authenticity? Can we achieve it?

7

GESTALT COUNSELLING AND PSYCHOTHERAPY

Maria Gilbert and Ken Evans

G estalt therapy is a humanistic/existential approach to counselling and psychotherapy which has been in use for over 50 years. Humanism stresses the importance of a person's own inborn capacity for growth and change. Existentialism stresses the responsibility people have for their own lives and their choices. The primary focus of existentialism is on heightening awareness of our being in the world.

We distinguish between *classical* Gestalt developed by Perls and his immediate followers[1] and *contemporary* Gestalt. Whereas the goal and method of classical Gestalt is on developing self-awareness, contemporary Gestalt is focused more on contact, that is, an awareness of the person's relationship to self, to others and to the world. Consequently there is a greater emphasis on the nature of the therapeutic relationship in current Gestalt theory and practice. In this chapter we will focus on classical Gestalt and refer the reader to appropriate sources on contemporary Gestalt.

DEVELOPMENT OF THE THERAPY

Gestalt therapy was founded in the 1940s by the psychoanalysts and creative psychotherapists Frederick (Fritz) and Laura Perls, and subsequently developed by others. It requires both the therapist and the client to focus on their immediate perceptual and sensory experience. What is directly perceived and experienced is considered most significant in therapy and in life. This is the *phenomenological basis* of Gestalt therapy which emphasizes that subjective human experience is more reliable than explanations and interpretations. The goal is for the client to become aware of *what* he is doing and *how* he is doing it, rather than concentrating on the *why*. Focusing on *why* people do things encourages endless questioning and speculation. This search for explanations often removes the person from the immediacy of his 'here-and-now' experience. In this process of focusing on his immediate experience the client can learn how to value and accept himself and trust his own experience. In short, Gestalt therapy is more interested in what is happening (process) than what is being discussed (content). We, therefore, describe it as a process-orientated therapy. What is being experienced at the moment is given more emphasis than what was, might be or should be happening.[2]

Gestalt therapy started with a focus on the internal world of the client as well as on the interpersonal. However, what tended to develop in the early years was the focus on the client's awareness of their own process rather than on the relationship between client and therapist. In contemporary Gestalt there is more of a balance between the intrapsychic (the client's internal process of awareness) and the interpersonal (the therapeutic relationship). What is happening between the client and the therapist is frequently the material of therapy. Client and therapist both share their own experience (phenomenological perspectives) in the course of a session. Differences in how they perceive the process between them leads to further dialogue. For recent developments in Dialogical psychotherapy, you are referred to the work of Richard Hycner, psychotherapist and clinical psychologist,[3] and Gary Yontef, psychotherapist, psychologist and clinical social worker.

THEORY AND BASIC CONCEPTS

Creative adjustment in childhood results in habitual blocks to awareness

Human beings resist change because in the course of childhood we make a creative adjustment to particular circumstances in our families and surroundings which then becomes our habitual way of being in the world (organizing the field of our experience). This creative adjustment was the best possible adaptation to the situation in the family. Such rigid and habitual patterns of behaviour may even have been life-preserving in our family of origin but now in adulthood impede organismic self-regulation (the ability to take in what is nurturing from the environment and reject what is toxic). The problem can take two possible forms. Either the person's inner awareness is blocked so a clear figure does not emerge into awareness, for example, physical sensations are ignored and feelings of anger to another are denied. Alternatively, the person's perception of the environment may be coloured by beliefs and attitudes taken from others which have not been thought through and are taken for granted as the 'truth' of experience. These assumptions may be outdated and very restrictive. A frequent example: 'people in authority always know best' may inhibit a person's independent thinking. These two processes may then lead to blocks to awareness which form a particular characteristic pattern in each person.

Blocks to awareness

Leading on from the above, we consider that the process of internalizing the beliefs and attitudes of significant others (introjection) forms the basis for the principal block to awareness. Introjection influences the person's perception in all aspects and underpins her way of being in the world (creative adjustment). Some introjected beliefs may prove helpful to a person; but any beliefs held rigidly and without careful consideration can block the person's awareness. Introjection shows as the 'musts', 'shoulds' and 'oughts' of everyday life. These undermine free choice and so interfere with self-responsibility – for example, 'I must not question what I have been taught . . .' Introjection is maintained by secondary blocks to awareness (interruptions to contact), the chief of these being projection, retroflection and confluence.

Projection, retroflection and confluence

In *projection*, we attribute to others thoughts, feelings and attitudes that we deny in ourselves. To continue the example above, we may say of others: 'You know better than me.' *Retroflection* involves turning back on oneself certain thoughts, feelings and behaviours that would be more appropriately expressed to others. In the above example: 'I am so stupid', said angrily to oneself leads to feelings of low self-esteem and self-deprecation and possibly shame. In *confluence*, we blur the boundary between self and other. For example, we may stay in a relationship with a partner who can only feel important at the cost of putting someone else down, because this feels familiar and 'true' to us. In confluence, the person merges with the other and does not acknowledge his own needs. Difference is experienced as threatening to the introjected beliefs that support the confluent relationship.

Self-responsibility

Gestalt philosophy stresses the central importance of self-responsibility. This is well expressed by the psychologist and psychotherapist Eleanor O'Leary:

> Being responsible for oneself is at the core of Gestalt therapy. Clients are assisted to move from a position of dependence on others, including the therapist, to a state of being self-supporting. They are encouraged to do many things independently. Initially they see their feelings, emotions and problems as somehow outside themselves: they use phrases such as 'he makes me feel so stupid'. They assume no responsibility for what they are, and it seems to them that there is nothing they can do about their situation other than accept it. They do not see themselves as having input into or control of their lives. Clients are helped to realise that they are responsible for what happens to them. It is they who must decide whether to change their life situation or allow it to remain unaltered.[5]

Organismic self-regulation

Psychological health refers to the person's capacity for self-regulation. The Gestalt therapist facilitates the person's capacity for self-regulation in helping her to become aware of her needs and to take effective action to meet those needs, by undoing retroflections, re-assessing introjects, owning projections and dealing with confluence in the process of acknowledging a more separate sense of self.

PRACTICE OF GESTALT THERAPY

The goals of Gestalt therapy

The goal of Gestalt therapy is awareness and the primary methodology is awareness. Awareness of how one is in the world enables free choices. This position also requires that the person take responsibility for how they are in the world, which is usually both a painful and an exciting process. This process is threefold: the client needs to acknowledge (a) how they respond (creative adjustment); (b) what contributes (past and present) to the response in the here-and-now; and (c) that they can take responsibility to do things differently (self-responsibility). These steps require the awareness of how the person behaves, what led her to behave this way and that she has the power to do things differently.

In the process of normal development and of becoming socialized, there are inevitably obstacles to a person's self-regulation. This process is in part a necessary aspect of the socialization process and for the maintenance of the community. This constant dilemma of balancing the needs of the individual and the needs of the community results in greater or lesser blocks to awareness for any particular individual.

Theory of change

Gestalt therapy is based on *a paradoxical theory of change:*[6] the more one respects where someone is, the more the person will feel supported to change. The Gestalt theory of change maintains that change occurs when a person becomes who they are, not when they try to become who they are not. Change does not take place through coercion by the individual or by another person such as a partner or the therapist. Change takes place if the person takes the time and effort to become who they are. When an awareness of what *is* does not readily emerge for a person, then Gestalt therapy is one way of increasing awareness and so choice and responsibility by highlighting the person's blocks to awareness. By acknowledging what *is*, you may then become who you want to be.

This respect for the person's being and immediate experience, for the person's capacity for growth and change, places Gestalt firmly in the humanistic tradition. So, paradoxically, by accepting and staying with a person's present experience, the Gestalt therapist may help create the atmosphere in which change is possible. This combination of existentialism and humanism means that Gestalt has an optimistic approach to change based on the reality of human existence.

Dealing with unfinished business

In Gestalt therapy, experience is valued as more important than simply acquiring intellectual understanding. If a person focuses on his here-and-now lived experience, he will become more in contact with his own needs. Blocks to awareness as discussed above and *unfinished business* may interfere with the person's full contact with self, others and the world around her. The term 'unfinished business' was derived by Perls, Hefferline and Goodman[7] from the Gestalt psychology principle of closure. When we perceive a figure that is incomplete, the mind acts to perfect it and complete or end it. Perls extended this principle to therapy. We all exhibit a tendency to want to complete unfinished business. In fact, the unfinished business 'pushes for completion' and we may be preoccupied, get into compulsive behaviour or feel oppressed by such incomplete experiences. If we ignore the unpleasant feelings associated with an event and do not express or experience them, these unresolved feelings or unfulfilled needs constitute the unfinished business of our lives. Such unfinished business may then interfere with our ability to 'form clear figures' and be aware of our needs in the present.

Employing techniques in the service of awareness

The therapeutic core of Gestalt therapy is increasing awareness. Techniques in Gestalt therapy are in the service of greater awareness. The learning of technical skills is *not* Gestalt therapy. Technique needs to be grounded in the ongoing therapeutic relationship and in the process of therapy. Without that, technique becomes a way of manipulating people to change in a particular way desired by the therapist or the current conventions of society. The sole purpose of a technique is to facilitate awareness to enable clients to find their own direction. Therefore, the technique is in the service of the client rather than imposed upon him. The creativity and spontaneity of the therapist leads to infinite variety and is intended to empower the client, not lead her in any particular direction.

Arising out of the here-and-how process of the therapy session, the client is supported to experiment with experiences that may facilitate awareness and remove blocks to self-regulation. Often in the process of experiencing in the here-and-now, the person becomes aware of unfinished business from the past. From a Gestalt perspective, the past is always present in the ground but becomes figure when the person becomes aware of the past in the form of unfinished business.

People use language to distance themselves from the fullness of their experience. We shall give several examples to illustrate the process of raising awareness of personal experience.

By using qualifiers such as 'perhaps', 'just', 'maybe' or 'possibly'

Client: I am probably a bit upset about what my boss said to me.
Therapist: What was it that your boss said to you?
Client: He said: 'You're stupid . . . you've forgotten again.'
Therapist: And you are 'probably a bit upset'?
Client: I am a bit upset.
Therapist: A bit?
Client: I am upset – hurt more like it.

By converting 'it' to 'I'

Individual clients are encouraged to convert impersonal language to personal language, for example, 'we' to 'I', 'it' to 'I' and 'one' to 'I'. Inviting them to repeat a sentence can lead to a heightened awareness of their own experience and acknowledge responsibility for themselves.

Client: One felt a little irritated by his put down.
Therapist: I invite you to say 'I felt irritated when he put me down.'
Client: I feel really angry, actually.

By changing questions to statements

Clients frequently ask questions rather than make statements, and thereby avoid taking ownership of their thoughts.

Client: But expressing anger is wrong, isn't it?
Therapist: Turn that question into a statement.
Client: I believe it's wrong to be angry.
Therapist: Really?
Client: I'm not sure I agree with that statement any more!

By taking ownership of action

Clients sometimes avoid responsibility by discounting their own capacity to take effective action and/or solve problems. Through changing 'can't' to 'won't', clients become aware of their resistance to taking more control over their actions. In this way, they take responsibility rather than blaming others or attempting to manipulate them to take control.

Client: I can't stand up to my boss.
Therapist: I invite you to experiment with saying: 'I won't stand up to my boss.'
Client: I won't stand up to my boss. Maybe he's right and I am too stupid?

In a similar vein, the therapist may invite the client to change 'I should' or 'I ought' or 'I have to' to 'I choose to'.

Bodily awareness

Perls was influenced by the work of the psychoanalyst Wilhelm Reich who believed that unconscious processes are somatized in the body through the body armour. So Gestalt therapists pay attention to body posture, breathing, tight and slack muscles, to emphasize, for example, apparent incongruence between what someone says and how they look.

Client: I'm feeling okay.
Therapist: I'm noticing that your fists are clenched. I can see the white of your knuckles and **your** jaw looks very clenched too.

Gestalt therapists also facilitate clients to become aware of their body sensations and name the associated feelings. Following on from our example above . . .

Client: Yes, I am feeling a little tense.
Therapist: Stay with that and increase the tension in your fists and in your jaw. [*The client responds by doing this for a few moments.*]
Therapist: Now be aware of what you are feeling.

Experimentation

Experimentation forms an important part of classical Gestalt. The therapist may suggest that the client 'experiment' with a new way of approaching a situation or experience with a view to increasing her awareness of a wider range of possibilities and choices. Sometimes experiments are fruitful and increase the person's awareness of alternative choices; others may not be productive. A Gestalt therapist will not push for any particular outcome but rather work with whatever emerges from the experiment, including resistance to doing an experiment! Joseph Zinker[8] states: 'An experiment . . . transforms talking into doing, stale reminiscing and theorising into being fully here with all one's imagination, energy and excitement.'

Experiments should be graded as to the level of challenge according to certain criteria, for example the strength of the therapeutic alliance, the level of self-support, the length of time in therapy. For an example of a two-chair experiment, see the case study.

Working with dreams

Dreams are an important focus in Gestalt therapy. Sigmund Freud said that dreams were the royal road to the unconscious; Perls said dreams were the royal road to integration. For Perls, every aspect of a dream represents a disowned part of one's personality. Drawing on a wide range of techniques, he would encourage clients to work on a dream until the meaning became apparent to them.

A typical session

It is not possible to describe a typical session in Gestalt therapy. By the very nature of Gestalt therapy, there is no set format to a session. The sessions will flow according to what is figural for the client. The therapist's creativity and spontaneity will mean that there is no predetermined shape, no set direction nor any fixed outcome to a session. The aim is purely to increase the client's awareness of their process.

WHICH CLIENTS BENEFIT MOST?

Gestalt therapy is potentially suitable for a wide range of client groups, depending on the experience, the level of training and the knowledge of the therapist. Gestalt therapy, like most in-depth therapies, helps clients to re-assess their way of being in the world. To be able to manage the process, clients need to draw on their own resources (self-support) without undue personality fragmentation. Even so, the process of therapy can at times be destabilizing and provoke strong feelings and challenge long-standing beliefs. There is inevitably pain involved in such a process and it is important to warn the client that therapy can be both exciting and exacting.

Given these parameters, Gestalt can and has been used with a wide variety of clients and client problems, ranging from mild to severe, but engagement with more deep-rooted problems requires a full assessment of the therapist's experience and available resources. Gestalt therapists have responsibility to practise only in those areas where they have experience and knowledge. Generally speaking, Gestalt therapists would not work with more seriously disturbed clients unless they have had an appropriate mental health background and experience.

Gestalt therapy has suffered, not only because Gestalt therapists have used Gestalt techniques divorced from the theory and values of the approach, but also because other therapists are attracted to the techniques and use them out of context and without fully appreciating their impact. We would therefore counsel that techniques derived from the Gestalt approach are not used out of context or without a fuller understanding of the underlying philosophy, methods and goals.

Case study

THE CLIENT

The client is a 33-year-old woman who works as a senior clerk in an accounts office. Her reasons for coming into therapy were the breakdown of her relationship, a general sense of being unfulfilled with her life, and a belief that she is continually passed over for promotion at work.

THE THERAPY

During the first few months of therapy a story unfolds of a bullying and aggressive father who could not tolerate disagreement. Her mother appears to be a quiet and ineffectual woman who responded to her husband's harassment with compliance. Gradually the client has begun to recognize that her father was a tyrant at home and that this has had consequences for her, particularly in her apparent inability to express anger or disagreement. The client has an increasing awareness of her characteristic ways of being in the world and has also begun to translate this growing understanding to the workplace. She is beginning to appreciate that her self-effacing demeanour provides encouragement for her boss, another apparent bully, to humiliate her. In this particular session the client has acknowledged that she felt hurt after her boss had publicly called her stupid in front of two of her work colleagues. She acknowledges that she feels angry but immediately blocks this awareness by questioning the appropriateness of this emotion and also justifying his behaviour on the ground that she is indeed stupid and maybe he has a right to be angry with her. While the client is speaking, I draw her attention to her body and particularly to her clenched fists and the tension in her jaw. The session continues thus:

> *Therapist*: Be aware of what you're feeling.
> *Client*: I'm not feeling anything! [*said with an angry startled tone*] I'm sorry I . . .
> *Therapist*: I feel excited by how angry you sounded just then.
> *Client*: Really?
> *Therapist*: Yes.

The therapist is deliberately offering support to the client for her new-found expression of anger. Given the therapist's previous experience of this client he anticipates that she is likely to close down on her emotion and retroflect her energy and eventually discount her behaviour and thus retain the status quo. In the therapist's opinion the therapeutic alliance is now sufficiently strong to support an experiment. The intention is to explore at a deeper level the power of the introjected messages concerning the inappropriateness of anger which appear to be major blocks in her ability to self-regulate.

> *Therapist*: I would like to suggest an experiment.
> *Client*: [*looks interested*]

Therapist: There seems to be one part of you that strongly believes that it's wrong to be angry.

Client: Yes.

Therapist: And yet, you were angry with me?

Client: Yes I was, wasn't I?

Therapist: I suggest that we separate out these two parts and on this cushion put the part of you that believes it's wrong to be angry and on this other cushion, put the part of you that was angry with me and let them have a conversation.

Client: How would I do that?

Therapist: You choose which one you'd like to sit on first.

Client: [*a little hesitant*] Okay. [*Gets up and sits on a cushion.*]

Therapist: Just remind me which cushion you're sitting on.

Client: I'm the part that doesn't believe that it's right to be angry.

Therapist: I suggest that you talk to the other part and tell her all the reasons why it's not okay to be angry.

Client: I don't know what to say.

Therapist: Well, say to that other part, 'I don't know what to say to you.'

Client: I don't know what to say but . . . it is wrong to be angry you know. I mean, it won't get you anywhere . . . for one thing it's not safe you know . . . you'll just pay for it later.

Therapist: Is there anything more you want to say from that place?

Client: I don't think so.

Therapist: Then I suggest you switch to the other cushion and reply.

Client: [*Moves across to the other cushion and after a few moments' silence she looks across at the first cushion.*] But I was just angry with him. [*Looks towards therapist, gets up and switches to the first cushion and continues to speak.*] You don't trust him do you? He's probably not telling you the truth, he doesn't really like you being angry with him. [*Client then switches back to the other cushion and looks at therapist.*] I know who that is.

Therapist: Who?

Client: My mum, that's exactly what she'd say, that it's not safe to be angry, that you pay for it in the end and that it's best to be quiet and wait for it to blow over, that's the way she was with him. [*I assume she means father.*] She tiptoed around him all his life . . . a doormat.

Therapist: I'm sorry I didn't quite hear that?

Client: She was a doormat. When my father beat my brothers she used to just leave the room. And I used to think how good she was for not wanting to see what was happening. She should have said something really.

Therapist: You sound sad?

Client: Yeah, sad for my mum and sad for me.

The rest of the session was taken up with continued exploration of her mother's subservient relationship to her father and the realization on the part of the client of the degree to which she had internalized her mother's modelling of subservience in her own way of being in the world.

In the following session the client looks unusually energized and somewhat younger.

Therapist: I notice there's something different about you today.

Client: [*Looks a little startled and curious.*] What?

Therapist: You look different.

Client: [*With a slight grin*] On Tuesday [two days earlier] my boss raised his voice to me and demanded to know where some letters were that I should have typed. He hadn't even given the letters to me for typing, he'd given them to my colleague, Josie. I told him that and I asked him not to speak to me like this as it was unfair and rude.

Therapist: What happened then?

Client: He just muttered something and walked away [*client grins.*]

Therapist: I notice you have a huge grin on your face.

Client: Yes, I felt so scared after I'd said it but then he just walked away. He's not shouted at me since and the two other girls in the office, Josie and Pat, came up to me in the tea break and said it was about time that I'd stood up to him.

Therapist: And how do you feel?

Client: Well I still can't believe it really, well I do but it's like it was happening to somebody else.

Therapist: Somebody else?

Client: It's not the kind of thing I say [*breaks into a giggle*].

Therapist: Congratulations!

Client: You really are pleased for me aren't you?

Therapist: Yes

Client: Can we do some more work like we did last week?

Therapist: I suggest you turn that question into a statement and take responsibility for what you want.

Client: I want to do some more work like last week.

Therapist: Okay, have you some idea of what it is you want to work on?

Client: Anger. I want to talk to my father but I feel very scared.

Therapist: I suggest that we put your father on a cushion and that you talk to me about him rather than speak to him directly.

Client: [*Looks surprised and a little pleased*] So I can tell you some of the things about him and I don't have to tell him directly to his face?

Therapist: If you would prefer to speak to him face to face that's fine [*client begins to look frightened*] but I'm suggesting that we begin with you talking to me about him and then perhaps later on in our work together, you can speak to him face to face if you want to.

Client: That sounds okay, I'll put him over here. [*Client gets up immediately and picks up a very large cushion and puts it over at the far end of the room. She returns and sits on her cushion.*]

It is customary practice in Gestalt therapy to invite a client to speak directly to a person in the present tense, thereby offering more immediacy to the resulting experiment. However, it is important to grade an experiment according to the level of challenge that a client is able to support. Clearly this client was wanting to begin to explore anger with regard to her father but she also looked terrified. The danger of a direct confrontation is that the client would regress to an early age of development and relive the experience, be re-traumatized and end up disempowered once again. In this experiment I invite the client to speak in the third person, that is to speak to me about her father. In this way she is less likely to regress to a place of retraumatization and she will have the opportunity of telling her story to another person whom she has experienced as supportive. I am at the same time providing a developmentally needed response from an adult. The client's reality is confirmed and affirmed.

Client: I think the worst times were on weekends, specially on Sunday afternoons. My father wasn't particularly religious or anything like that but he had been brought up to believe that Sundays were family days and that we were supposed to be together. I hated it. He just sat there reading a newspaper and we had to sit around and be quiet. I remember this old clock on the mantelpiece that had a very loud tick tock sound. It was so quiet that the sound of the clock seemed to get louder and louder. I wanted to scream and scream and scream and go running out of the room. My older brother, Kevin, found it hard to be still; if he moved at all my father would look at him with a cold stare and eventually he would get a smack across the head. It must have hurt him but he didn't cry. His eyes would tear up and he would grit his teeth and just sit silently. It was horrible.

Therapist: What about your mum?

Client: She would leave the room, make a cup of tea or something.

And so the client went on to describe the starkness and coldness of home life and the terror that her father instilled in all the family.

Client: The worst thing was he always seemed to be angry. It's like he bristled with it, breathed it in from the air and breathed it back out on to the world. He had this furrowed brow and very black, bushy eyebrows, a bit like Stalin. Oh that's a good one, yeah I never thought of that before, my dad was just like Stalin! I hate him.

Therapist: We've got about 10 minutes before the end of our session today so I suggest we finish this experiment now and spend a little time reflecting on the session, if that's okay with you?

Client: Yes, erm, can I just try one thing?

Therapist: Are you still asking my permission?

Client: [*Looks at me and grins, turns to look at her father and says in a voice just above a whisper.*] You shouldn't have frightened me like that. I was only little. That was wrong of you.

It is important when a client has been engaged in experiential work of this nature to alert them to the impending end of the session so that there is time for reflection and for the client to let go of the experience sufficiently to re-enter the world.

Over subsequent weeks the client continued to work on the theme of anger and on several occasions talked directly to her father on a cushion, including several very strong expressions of anger towards him for his mistreatment of her and her brothers and her mother. As she became more assertive with her father in therapy so the client reported a growing assertiveness outside of therapy, particularly at work. She relinquished the role of 'doormat'! The client began to wear brighter and more attractive clothing, adopted a modern hairstyle and began to walk with a more erect and confident posture so very different from the client who initially gave the appearance of apologizing for walking through space.

One of the strengths of Gestalt therapy is its willingness to engage clients in experimentation through which they may practise new ways of being, first in the therapy room and then in the world outside.

REFERENCES

1 Perls, F., Hefferline, R.F. and Goodman, P. (1951) *Gestalt Therapy*. New York: Julian Press.
2 Yontef, G.M. (1993) *Awareness, Dialogue and Process*. New York: The Gestalt Journal Press.
3 Hycner, R. (1993) *Between Person and Person*. New York: The Gestalt Journal Press.
4 Yontef, G.M. (1993) op. cit.
5 O'Leary, E. (1992) *Gestalt Therapy, Theory, Practice and Research*. London: Chapman & Hall.
6 Beisser, A. (1970) 'The paradoxical theory of change', in J. Fagan and I. Shepherd (eds), *Gestalt Therapy Now*. Palo Alto: Science and Behavior Books.
7 Perls *et al.* (1951) op. cit.
8 Zinker, J. (1977) *Creative Process in Gestalt Therapy*. New York: Vintage Books, Random House.

SUGGESTED READING

Latner, J. (1986) *The Gestalt Therapy Book*. New York: The Gestalt Journal Press. An outstanding introduction to the principles of Gestalt therapy, it has something to offer both beginners and experienced clinicians. This is a very readable book enhanced by the manner in which Latner encapsulates the spirit of Gestalt in his style of writing.

Mackewn, J. (1997) *Developing Gestalt Counselling*. London: Sage. This book focuses on recent developments in Gestalt therapy with a particular emphasis on the dialogical relational' perspective of contemporary Gestalt. It will be of help to both students and teachers of Gestalt by providing an overview of the evolution of Gestalt therapy.

O'Leary, E. (1992) *Gestalt Therapy: Theory, Practice and Research*. London: Champman and Hall. This book covers Gestalt theory from its origins to the present day and suggests new directions for Gestalt. It includes a valuable chapter on research in Gestalt therapy. It is well written and gives a comprehensive overview of Gestalt in a short book.

Sills, C., Fish, S. and Lapworth, P. (1997) *Gestalt Counselling*. London: Winslow Press. This book is a comprehensive and enjoyable introduction to Gestalt, spanning its development from Perls to the present day. The book is written in an involving and reader-friendly way. It emphasizes the phenomenological method of Gestalt and the dialogic relationship. The authors suggest exercises to further the reader's understanding of Gestalt at a personal level as well as with clients.

Zinker, J. (1997) *Creative Process in Gestalt Therapy*. New York: Vintage Books, Random House. This book is written for Gestalt therapists. Zinker encourages the Gestalt therapist to be spontaneous and creative with the emphasis on the development of individual style. In addition, he focuses on the importance of grading experiments. This work stands out because of the space Zinker accords to experimentation in Gestalt.

DISCUSSION ISSUES

1 Awareness is both the goal and the method of Gestalt therapy. Discuss.
2 Provide an example of unfinished business from your own experience and consider ways in which this may have hampered you.
3 Introjection is the primary interruption to contact (block to awareness). Discuss.
4 Technique divorced from theory is potentially abusive. Discuss.

8

HYPNOSIS IN COUNSELLING AND PSYCHOTHERAPY

Peter J. Hawkins

Hypnosis (*hypnos* is the Greek word for sleep) is not sleep but rather a shift in attention that can occur in a matter of seconds, either with guidance or spontaneously. The popular view of hypnosis is that it is a specially induced 'trance' state in which the individual loses, to a greater or lesser degree, his or her logical faculty and experiences changes in sensations, perceptions, thoughts or behaviour. This state can occur naturally or may be formally induced by the therapist, in cooperation with the client, or by clients themselves (as in self-hypnosis). Although there are many different hypnotic inductions, most include suggestions for relaxation, calmness, and well-being. Instructions to imagine or think about pleasant experiences are also commonly included in hypnotic inductions. Although people respond to hypnosis in different ways and to different degrees, most describe their experience as very pleasant. A person's ability to experience hypnotic suggestions can be inhibited by fears and concerns often arising from some common misconceptions obtained from the media. They typically remain aware of who they are and where they are and they usually remember what happened during the hypnosis.

It is important to note that hypnosis is a secondary strategy, or an adjunctive procedure, with respect to the primary intervention strategy, for example behaviour therapy, cognitive therapy, transactional analysis, counselling, etc. In other words those practising hypnosis are first trained counsellors or psychotherapists for whom the utilization of hypnosis can enhance their intervention skills. The relationship between hypnosis (secondary strategy) and the psychotherapeutic interventions (primary strategy) is shown in Figure 8.1, along with other contextual factors such as core conditions.

The view of human nature of therapists who practise hypnosis will of course depend on the type of therapy that they practise, that is whether it is based on behavioural, psychodynamic or humanistic principles. However, many hypnotherapists believe that individuals have an unconscious mind which has resources for healing and self-realization, and that they are able to engage in a process known as 'unconscious search' to 'recover' these unconscious resources in order to find solutions to their problems.

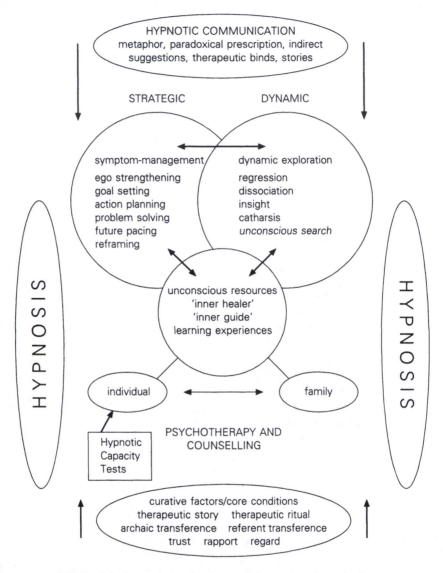

FIGURE 8.1 The relationship between hypnosis and psychotherapy

DEVELOPMENT OF HYPNOSIS

Hypnosis has always been part of the medical culture, influencing it at a covert level although its popularity has waxed and waned. The 'father' of hypnotism is usually acknowledged to be Franz Anton Mesmer (1733–1815), a medical doctor, who spoke of the importance of bodily stroking ('passes') in order to 'magnetize' the client. Mesmer argued that animal magnetism produced a crisis which effected a 'cure' in the client. Later, in the nineteenth century, John Elliotson, a physician, and James Esdaile, a surgeon, amongst others, popularized the anaesthetic properties of magnetism, rather than the 'crises' induced by Mesmer.

However, James Braid, a surgeon, rejected the idea of magnetism and developed his own theories of increased susceptibility and suggestibility. In his later writings he abandoned much of his earlier physiological theories and dealt more with the psychological aspects of hypnotism, demonstrating that the observed phenomena are the product of the imagination of the client powerfully influenced by the suggestions of the therapist, given either deliberately or accidentally.

During the 1880s controversy raged between two schools of hypnotism represented by Jean-Martin Charcot, an eminent French neurologist at the Saltpêtrière in Paris, and Hippolyte Bernheim, a physician, at the University of Nancy. Bernheim argued that hypnosis was the result of suggestion and insisted that normal people could be hypnotized. He introduced the concept of degrees of hypnosis: a subject could be lightly, moderately or deeply hypnotized. Charcot, on the other hand, developed a pathological theory and suggested that hypnosis was similar to hysteria, both being products of a diseased nervous system.

Charcot pioneered the uncovering of forgotten memories under hypnosis. His work exerted a profound influence on Sigmund Freud, a physician, who established with Joseph Breuer, another physician, the ideas of hypnotic regression and dynamic psychotherapy. Later Freud rejected hypnosis in favour of the new school of psychoanalysis, a development which had a profound negative effect on the development of hypnosis. However, a temporary revival of interest was brought about by the occurrence of a large number of functional disorders (that is, mental problems which are primarily psychological in origin) in the First World War. J.A. Hadfield, a physician with a particular interest in psychopathology, used hypnosis to allow soldiers to relive their battle experiences, an approach which he labelled 'hypnoanalysis'. In clinical hypnosis there was a gradual move away from direct methods of inducing hypnosis to the use of indirect suggestions (for example stories and metaphors). These approaches were pioneered by Milton Erickson, a medical doctor, and were aimed at 'utilising the client's own belief system and inner resources.' Erickson explained that his approach was naturalistic in the sense that he very carefully observed his clients' natural behavior and continually utilized their own language, world view and inner resources to help them solve their own problems in their own way. In this regard, an Ericksonian approach is strategic (that is, where the focus of the therapy is on 'solutions') and the therapist is actively responsible for setting goals, planning treatment and delivering interventions designed to accomplish those goals. Erickson believed that people have all the necessary resources within themselves to solve their problems.

THEORY AND BASIC CONCEPTS

There are two opposing schools of thought regarding the nature of hypnosis, the 'state' and the 'non-state'. Ernest Hilgard[1] proposes a neo-dissociation model in which there is a central executive which controls activity and behaviour. In hypnosis a dissociation between thinking and behaviour occurs so that 'involuntary' behaviours (such as arm rigidity, amnesia, automatic writing, positive and negative hallucinations) may occur. In this case the hypnotist becomes the central executive, controlling and directing an individual's actions. In contrast, the social psychological perspective (non-state) argues that there is no 'involuntariness' or by-passing of cognitive executive function.[2] Rather, the person is enacting a set of behaviours because of the strong influence of expectation and belief about hypnosis. Recently, it has been argued that this division is no longer appropriate.[3]

Because hypnosis is a secondary strategy within the context of counselling and psychotherapy (Figure 8.1), it follows that any view of human nature alluded to in the clinical situation must be attributed to the primary approach (person-centred, Gestalt therapy and so on). However, many hypnotherapists accept the following assumptions in their clinical practice:

1 The hypnosis state, or 'trance' state is natural and occurs without formal induction by a 'hypnotherapist'.
2 All hypnosis is self-hypnosis.
3 Individuals have an unconscious mind which has resources for healing and self-realization.
4 Clients are able to engage in the process known as 'unconscious search' to 'recover' these unconscious resources in order to find solutions to their problems.

These assumptions are similar to those postulated by Erickson in his utilization approach to hypnosis and psychosomatic problems. Erickson used the term 'unconscious' to represent the core of the person. For him, the therapeutic task was to arrange the conditions that would encourage and facilitate the emergence of the unconscious as a positive force so that all the resources necessary to transform the client's experience were made available.

The hypnotherapeutic approach helps the individual to modify experiences by utilizing 'hypnotic phenomena', for example regression (greater access to childhood memories), time distortion, amnesia, spontaneous movements (for example ideomotor behaviours such as finger movements or arm levitation), changes in bodily sensations (ideosensory behaviours), and an opportunity to create, develop and control dissociative experiences, if these facilitate the therapeutic process. One of the most important is the heightened susceptibility to accept therapeutic suggestions, both at overt (direct suggestions) and covert levels (indirect suggestions presented in metaphors and stories). For example, someone with chronic and intractable pain whose normal state of reason and logic would prevent them from believing that the pain could be resolved (in whatever way), could in the trance state accept a therapeutic suggestion (provided by the therapist) that the pain could be given away to a friendly animal. The latter action is not logical or reasonable but given a well-motivated client can be accepted during 'trance' with good therapeutic outcomes.

It is well known that people have different capacities to enter into hypnosis although this may be more to do with motivation and collaboration with the therapist than with any biological difference. Tests such as the Hypnotic Induction Profile (HIP) developed by psychiatrists Herbert and David Spiegel[4] measure this capacity level. Children are generally more susceptible to hypnosis than adults, with the peak of susceptibility occurring between 9 and 12 years, the level afterwards declining steadily with age. It is reasonable to assume that individuals who have a rich fantasy life and compulsively comply with external signals would more easily give up a rational and critical way of functioning. On the other hand, individuals who emphasize rationality and are relatively non-compliant, valuing reason above all, would exhibit a low capacity of hypnosis experience (that is, it is a much harder task to induce them to 'give up' their critical faculty and go into 'trance').

PRACTICE

Before inducing the 'trance' state it is essential to prepare the client for hypnosis. This involves a number of factors:

* dealing with any resistance
* providing the client with information concerning the procedures
* clearing up any misunderstandings concerning the nature of hypnosis.

As a consequence both motivation and the client–therapist relationship is improved, and the probability of the client resisting the procedure diminished.

Taking the case history

This is more than just finding out about the problems that the client is experiencing – it is an important part of the treatment. Some of the more important questions are listed below:

* Who referred the client?
* What are the motivations for the client to seek help for the current symptoms?
* Are the current symptoms/difficulties being used to get needs met by others?
* Why is the client seeking treatment at this particular time?
* How long has the client been experiencing the problem?
* Are there times when the problem is better? (The answer to this is usually 'yes', in which case the therapist can respond by pointing out to clients that they therefore have the resources to help alleviate the problem although they may not know how to do this consciously at this moment in time, the implication being that they have the resources which they can find at some time in the future.) At this point it is useful to ask the client to imagine the

time when the problem was being experienced the least by using a visual analogue scale (VAS), for example: '*When you are experiencing the problem now that it is much better* [ask them to imagine the time when this occurred] *tell me where the pointer rests on a 10-point scale somewhere between 0 and 10, where 10 is the most uncomfortable (distressful) and 0 the most comfortable and relaxing.*' This introduces them to the idea of regression, the use of the imagination to recall and evaluate their experiences. It also provides the therapist with a useful device to monitor the progress of the therapy during the session or over the course of treatment.

- Are there any specific events/experiences related to the problems being better (or worse)?
- Does the client have a story that explains the problem? It should be emphasized to the client that this is their own personal story and doesn't have to be based on absolute facts or evidence. The clients' stories are extremely important and can provide the therapist with valuable information and indications for therapeutic strategies. It should always be remembered in this context that the client always knows more than the therapist about their problem.

Information concerning the nature of the presenting symptoms and difficulties, family background, health and medical history (including current medical treatment), employment and educational situation, current lifestyle and personal interests, and previous experiences and beliefs about therapy and hypnosis, should also be obtained. Another important aspect is an examination of the client's beliefs and misconceptions about hypnosis. Any previous experiences with hypnosis should be thoroughly explored, as well as the following myths:

- hypnosis is the same as sleep
- that the hypnotist has complete control over the client
- that hypnosis is an unusual and abnormal experience and therefore may be harmful
- that the client may begin talking spontaneously and divulge personal and confidential information
- that the client will lose all conscious awareness of surroundings and have no memory of the hypnotic experience
- that the client will not be able to exit from the hypnotic experience
- that the client may engage in strange behaviours suggested by the hypnotherapist

Of course none of the above is true!

The hypnotherapeutic relationship

The most powerful hypnotic tool in the treatment of any individual is the relationship. Because hypnosis is a collaborative experience rather than something that is done to an individual, it is crucial to devote time and effort to developing a positive relationship rather than concentrating solely on developing technical expertise with hypnosis. Building a good hypnotherapeutic relationship is basically no different from building a therapeutic alliance when any other form of therapeutic approach is to be used.

Induction methods

Induction methods can be broadly divided into two categories: formal methods of induction, and 'naturalistic' or Ericksonian methods, although it should be stressed that these approaches are not discrete and many clinicians will use both approaches. There are numerous techniques for hypnotizing but most include three main components:

- relaxation (suggestions of relaxation, peace, calmness, etc.)
- imagination (use of guided imagery, for example favourite place, pleasant scenes)
- enactment (for example eye fixation, hand levitation)

Formal methods of induction

Formal induction techniques generally involve the client in focusing on something external to themselves. This may be visual (for example an object such as the tip of a pen); auditory (music, stories, which may have 'hidden' therapeutic meanings, a metaphor); olfactory (smelling a flower); tactile (being touched, as in massage). Focusing may also be internal where the client focuses on an image suggested by the therapist, such as being in a quiet, relaxing place; or becoming aware of bodily sensations. As the client engages in these activities the therapist usually makes suggestions concerning relaxation, tiredness and heaviness of the eyes. Quicker formal methods include, amongst others, Spiegel's Eye Roll.[5] In this method the client is asked to 'roll up your eyes and close your eyelids to a point where you feel they just will not work'. There are many more traditional techniques and the reader is referred to Hellmut Karle and Jennifer Boys,[6] both clinical psychologists, and John Hartland,[7] a psychiatrist, for comprehensive accounts of such induction methods. The focusing techniques described above occur 'naturally', for example when absorbed in a book, watching a film, listening to music and so on.

As an example, here is a 'traditional' script ('Eye Fixation with Distraction') for inducing hypnosis. First of all tell the client what you are going to do and what you expect them to do.

In a moment I am going to ask you to find something (an object, spot on the wall, etc.) that is slightly above the level of your eye-gaze so that you will have to turn your eyes upwards in order to look at it. I want you to focus on that and at the same time count backwards from 300 in threes. When your eyes have closed then you should stop counting. While you are doing this I will be talking to you about relaxation. You will hear this but it won't interfere with your task. Any questions? Then we'll begin. Focus on the spot and start counting backwards. [The therapist then begins the following.] Your feet are becoming warm and heavy and relaxed as you continue to breathe slowly and effortlessly . . . with every exhalation your feet becoming warm and heavy . . . allowing the warmth and heaviness to spread up into your legs massaging away all of the residual tension . . . nothing you need do to make that happen . . . it can happen effortlessly all by itself . . . your legs are warm and heavy and totally relaxed as these sensations spread up into your thighs allowing them to become warm and heavy and relaxed . . . etc. [It is most probable that at some time in the progressive relaxation the client will blink their eyelids which may also show a cataleptic 'flutter'. Such behaviour can be utilized by saying:] And the next time your eye-lids close just allow them to stay closed and you will find that experience very relaxing and comfortable . . . allowing that feeling of relaxation to flow down to the tips of your toes just letting your body float . . .

It is important that clients continue with their 'hypno' therapy between sessions by using 'self-hypnosis', during which they can engage in therapeutic tasks such as positive thinking and ego-strengthening, for example imaging successful outcomes to the therapy. Self-hypnosis can be taught by adding the following to the above script:

. . . and you can do this for yourself at any convenient time just as you have done now. All you need do is to find a relaxing place and become aware of your breathing . . . as you breathe in roll up your eyes and as you breathe out closing your eyelids to a point where you feel they just will not work . . . allowing that feeling to spread right down to your toes, letting your body float just as it is doing now.

An audio-tape can be made of the session and given to clients to use on their own between sessions.

Ericksonian techniques

'Naturalistic' methods (or 'Ericksonian techniques') are informal because there is no apparent induction. The induction occurs as part of natural conversation or behaviour and therefore cannot be discerned by the client in the same way as the formal 'ritual' of hypnosis. Because the approach is natural and the client is not consciously aware of what is happening there cannot (*ipso facto*) be any resistance as might be the case when more direct techniques are being used. Erickson emphasized the importance of giving suggestions in a permissive, flexible manner that allows clients to respond in their own unique way so as to activate the client's own internal resources for psychosomatic healing ('the implied directive'). The implied directive is a way of facilitating an intense state of internal learning or problem solving.[8]

Once the client is hypnotized then the therapy can proceed often with some form of ego-strengthening.[9] An example is the so-called photograph album or scrapbook containing past positive experiences and events. The client is asked, while in 'trance', to imagine their photograph album into which is pasted all of their positive experiences, and to turn to a page near the beginning ('regression') and review the contents, feeling the positive emotions connected to those events. The client is then encouraged to bring these positive feelings of control and achievements into 'present time' and find solutions to a current problem. The positive feelings can then be 'taken' into the future and pasted into the photograph album along with the client's personal and therapeutic goals. This approach introduces the client to the idea that it is possible to review experiences from the past and also to allow the feelings associated with these positive events to be experienced. Introducing the client to the idea that regression can be positive as well as negative is an effective way of teaching them that the process provides for valuable learning experiences which can be utilized in resolving their problems. Later on in the context of psychodynamic approaches the therapist can then introduce the idea of regressing to (possible) traumatic memories without too many problems.

The role of hypnosis in psychodynamic therapy is to 'facilitate access to the unconscious' (hypnoanalysis). There are a number of standard techniques available which have been summarized by Karle and Boys[10] and psychologists Tony Gibson and Michael Heap.[11]

In the context of the psychodynamic approach the client is encouraged to 'find' the origin of the conflict or problem. This 'insight' into a traumatic event or experience will often lead the client into experiencing associated distressed feelings, for example sadness, anger, guilt and so on. The therapist can encourage the client to express the feelings motorically (by hitting a cushion, for example) or cognitively, as 'silent abreaction'. Silent abreactive methods (cognitive catharsis) are used extensively by therapists who utilize formal techniques of hypnosis in their clinical work. In these approaches the therapist suggests that, for example, the client imagines being angry with the protagonist, or imagines him or herself sobbing at a funeral. Alternatively, 'metaphorical' approaches may be used – for example the client is asked to imagine hitting a large rock with a stick in order to clear a pathway. Ideodynamic exploration can provide a systematic way to access, review and transform past experiences in a safe and creative manner. Because this approach works at the level of unconscious integration and psychosomatic problem resolution there is less chance of reopening traumatic wounds.

WHICH CLIENTS BENEFIT MOST?

Hypnosis has been used effectively for the treatment of many clinical and medical problems both in children and adults. These have included those which may be deemed psychological, such as phobias, habit disorders (in particular smoking), anxiety, psychosexual, eating problems, dissociative states, tinnitus, hypertension, burns, as well as those referred to as psychosomatic, such as skin disorder, irritable bowel syndrome, duodenal ulceration, asthma, migraine and pain. Hypnosis has also been used in medical and surgical procedures including obstetrics, rehabilitative work with clients with neurological disorders, dentistry, as well as the modification of immune responses to stress. In most cases hypnosis would be used as an adjunctive procedure alongside more traditional orthodox treatments; for example in the treatment of cancer hypnosis may be used as a procedure in the relief of pain and in the management of chemotherapy side effects.[12] Research has also demonstrated that the addition of hypnosis to cognitive-behavioural and psychodynamic treatments substantially enhances their efficacy. Caution must be exercised with clients who exhibit active suicidal symptoms, psychotic conditions, impairment with alcohol or other drugs, borderline personality disorder, and other conditions that present with extreme dependency and emotional liability. It is advisable for the beginning therapist to avoid these problems. Although many such clients can benefit from the use of direct and indirect hypnosis, the therapist must decide how hypnosis can best be introduced in these cases. However, the clinical utility and role of hypnosis in the treatment of various psychological and medical conditions remains to be established with greater specificity. For further discussion of the applications of hypnosis the reader is referred to Karle and Boys,[13] and Gibson and Heap.[14]

Hypnosis has been reported to be successful with a wide range of sexual dysfunctions. It can increase the effectiveness of a range of psychotherapeutic approaches used in sex therapy, for example insight oriented psychotherapy, rational-emotive cognitive restructuring, desensitization and so on.

The advantages of hypnosis in sex therapy have been summarized by a counselling psychologist, Peter Hawkins,[15] and include the following:

- may be used effectively with the individual client
- offers techniques that allow rapid exploration and identification of under-lying conflicts, unresolved feelings about past events, and factors beyond conscious awareness
- provides clients with a sense of self-control and mastery
- provides an easily learned technique (self-hypnosis) for stress and anxiety management
- helps develop feelings of hope and optimism and increases feelings of self-efficacy and confidence
- can facilitate the positive handling and utilization of negative emotional responses
- can help to revivify positive feelings connected to previous satisfactory sexual relationships
- can help to focus attention and increase sensory awareness, thereby facili-tating increased arousal and pleasure

However, it should be stressed that clinical hypnosis is not a panacea for the treatment of sexual problems, nor indeed any other problem.

Case study

THE CLIENT

The client (John) was aged 34, and had been married for eight years. At the beginning of his marriage sexual relations were satisfactory and enjoyable for both partners but gradually the frequency of sexual activity diminished markedly. When it did occur it was nearly always initiated by the wife but generally resulted in failure and frustration for both partners. The husband often experienced erectile failure, and on the occasions when this was not a problem delayed (or no) orgasm resulted.

John had a very close relationship with his mother although there was no evidence that this had been sexual in any way. His initiation into genital activity had been a homosexual one at the age of 14. Heterosexual intercourse occurred for the first time with his wife at the age of 26, which was the occasion of the consummation of his marriage.

THE THERAPY

John was a good hypnotic subject with high scores measured by the HIP.

Session 1

John was taught how to increase sensory awareness by accessing the times early on in his marriage when he was able to become aroused quickly and achieve a good erection followed (appropriately) by orgasm. He was asked to:

> look at your hand and allow it to become lighter and lighter and float into the air . . . just allowing your mind to go back to the time when you were first married and enjoyed having sex with your wife . . . an activity that you both enjoyed . . . be aware of the sensations all over your body. You can feel the same sensations and pleasure, and function just as you did then . . . just allowing that to happen . . . knowing that you have the resources to allow that to occur when it is appropriate in the future, maybe even later today or tomorrow or sometime soon. Just allowing those sensations in your body to increase in intensity and enjoying those feelings as they flow into your penis . . . noticing how enjoyable that is. Just as it happened then so it can happen again now . . . nothing has changed. The only important thing is the sensations you experience . . . Experience the texture, temperature, pressure and movement . . . Immersed in feeling and sensation . . . Nothing to do but to feel and experience the pleasure.
>
> You can feel the same feelings, experience the same sensations and pleasure, and function just as you did then. Everything can be just as it was when you first married . . . Just as much pleasure, just as much fun. Everything exactly the same.

A time progression was then used.

> Now that these sensations are very strong take them into the future . . . experiencing yourself making love with your wife . . . engaging in foreplay . . . achieving a good erection and inserting your penis into her vagina . . . both enjoying this and then reaching an orgasm. Be aware of how you are now feeling

... knowing that this can happen if you and your wife allow this to occur ... feeling more confident and excited about this prospect and wondering whether this will happen later today or tomorrow ...

John was reminded of the technique after the hypnosis session, and requested to practise the exercise at least twice a day. This technique accesses the positive 'psychosomatic' memories which the client has and allows him to become more confident, expectant and optimistic.

Session 2

In hypnosis arm rigidity was suggested in order to demonstrate the control that the client has over his own somatic functioning, that he has the (unconscious) resources to allow his arm to become rigid and hard 'without doing anything to make that happen'.

... and if you can allow your arm to become rigid and hard then you can allow other parts of your body to become rigid and hard in appropriate situations, including your penis ... and equally when it is appropriate you can allow your arm to totally relax ... to let go of all the tension and rigidity ... to become relaxed and comfortable. You have complete control over every part of your body and you can and you will control the erection in your penis.

Session 3

The first two sessions were primarily concerned with ego-strengthening, that is, building up a sense of control and mastery, of confidence, hope and optimism with respect to the future, as well as improving the symptomatology. There was no attempt to uncover the reasons why the client developed the problem. The third session was concerned with a dynamic investigation using an ideodynamic approach. John accessed past experiences that were related to the problem. Some conscious awareness of these events was attained, for example early relationship with mother, and later homosexual experience. After reviewing three past experiences related to the problem he hallucinated a date by which time he would be functioning well. He was 'progressed' to this date and experienced intense positive responses. In hypnosis he was told that

you have the resources to allow this to happen and you already know that you can change your bodily responses in an appropriate way to allow you to respond sexually when you are with your wife ... and your unconscious mind is utilizing the learnings that you have experienced here today concerning the origins of the problem to help you find solutions by the date that you have experienced or even earlier if it is appropriate for you ... and you may experience these pleasant sensations and experiences when you are dreaming later tonight ... and wake to find that you have a strong erection . . . and you may be wondering when and whether this can really happen . . . although part of you knows that it really can.

A review of the previous three sessions was carried out. John then entered 'self-hypnosis' and was given a garden metaphor (he was a keen gardener) including references to green shoots, development beneath the soil, the seasons of the year and so on. What is important in the use of metaphors and stories is the way in which the therapist creatively uses images and words that appropriately match the client's interests, experiences, aspirations, as well as the presenting symptomatology. The session concluded by utilizing creative dreaming as a way of involving unconscious search processes in problem resolution:

You already know how to experience stimulating dreams. And it's perfectly natural, following the kind of work we're doing, to have some pleasurable dreams. And your unconscious mind has the ability to continue to work on increasing your sexual desire towards your wife . . . and you may find that your dreams can be very creative and enjoyable . . . and you may be already wondering what you can dream later tonight . . . And because your goal is to increase your sexual desire, in all probability you will have an interesting experience tonight, or it may be tomorrow night or even the night after . . . and you may be surprised when it actually happens but I would be surprised if you have to wait until the weekend. And those desires will be carried with you into your day, where they will appropriately influence your thoughts and behaviour. And even though you won't remember all your erotic and sexy dreams in the mornings, you can still sense and know that something is different. And even if you don't believe that this can really happen you will be even more surprised when it does, knowing that you have this resource to allow you to find solutions even whilst you are asleep.

John reported that on the night following the session he had a very erotic dream in which he awoke and 'discovered' that he had an erection. He was extremely pleased with this 'discovery' and the fact that he still had this ability.

This was a conjoint session which included John's wife. It has been demonstrated that hypnosis can be used with couples or even families.

In this session both John and his wife were regressed to a positive sexual experience early on in their marriage (see Session 1). Afterwards they were encouraged to describe this experience including the sensations and feelings they experienced in their bodies. They were told that they could experience these feelings again, that they had the resources to allow that to happen if this is what they wanted to happen. Both partners were then progressed (in hypnosis) to some time in the future when this could happen '. . . knowing that your unconscious minds are already searching for the solutions even though you are not aware that this is happening.' The emphasis was on the development of hope and optimism, of personal control and positive feelings of mastery.

Follow-up and review

A follow-up six months later revealed that the couple were functioning sexually in ways that were appropriate for both of them. This improvement in intimacy also extended to other aspects of their life together. Significantly, they also enjoyed love-making without penetrative sex to a much greater degree than previously. The time spent in sexual activity decreased although the times when this happened was more intimate, enjoyable and fulfilling. Neither partner was concerned about the struggle to obtain 'good sex' any more and consequently a major stressor in their lives had been removed.

SUMMARY

Hypnosis can increase the effectiveness of a range of psychotherapeutic approaches that are utilized in psychotherapy. As with all other aspects of psychotherapy and counselling, though, the practitioner has to develop a creative approach to the treatment of problems that recognizes the uniqueness of individual clients as well as the problems that they present. The case study clearly demonstrates how clinical hypnosis can support cognitive, behavioural and psychodynamic interventions in dealing with psychological problems. It should be stressed, however, that hypnosis is not a panacea and a great deal more research is required to demonstrate its efficacy for certain problems and for certain clients.

REFERENCES

1 Hilgard, E.J. (1991) 'A neodissociation intepretation of hypnosis', in S.J. Lynn and J.W. Rhue (eds), *Theories of Hypnosis: Current Models and Perspectives*. London: Guilford Press.

2 Spanos, N.P. (1991) 'A sociocognitive approach to hypnosis', in S.J. Lynn and J.W. Rhue (eds), *Theories of Hypnosis: Current Models and Perspectives*. London: Guilford Press.

3 Kirsch, I. and Lynn, S.J. (1995) 'The altered state of hypnosis: changes in the theoretical landscape', *American Psychologist*, 50 (10): 846–58.

4 Spiegel, H. and Spiegel, D. (1978) *Trance and Treatment: Clinical Uses of Hypnosis*. New York: Basic Books.

5 Spiegel, H. and Spiegel, D. (1978) op. cit.

6 Karle, H. and Boys, J.H. (1987) *Hypnotherapy: A Practical Handbook*. London: Free Association Books.

7 Hartland, J. (1971) *Medical and Dental Hypnosis and its Clinical Applications*. Eastbourne: Baillière Tindall.

8 Rossi, E.L. (1996) *The Symptom Path to Enlightenment*. Palisades, CA: Palisades Gateway.

9 Karle, H. and Boys, J.H. (1978) op. cit., and Hartland, J. (1971), op. cit.

10 Karle, H. and Boys, J.H. (1978) op. cit.

11 Gibson, H.B. and Heap, M. (1991) *Hypnosis in Therapy*. Hove: Lawrence Erlbaum.

12 Hawkins, P.J., Liossi, C., Ewart, B.E., Hatira, P., Kosmidis, V.H. and Varvutsi, M. (1995) 'Hypnotherapy for control of anticipatory nausea and vomiting in children with cancer: preliminary findings', *Psycho-Oncology*, 4: 101–6.

13 Karle, H. and Boys, J.H. (1978) op. cit.

14 Gibson, H.B. and Heap, M. (1991) op. cit.

15 Hawkins, P.J. (1996) 'Hypnosis in sex therapy', *European Journal of Clinical Hypnosis*, 10: 2–8.

SUGGESTED READING

Gibson, H.B. and Heap, M. (1991) *Hypnosis in Therapy*. Hove: Lawrence Erlbaum. A good basic introduction to clinical hypnosis and its applications, including reference to research work.

Hartland, J. (1971) *Medical and Dental Hypnosis and its Clinical Applications*. Eastbourne: Baillière Tindall. A thoroughly good text for the beginning hypnotherapist. Full of traditional scripts for induction and deepening. Valuable for its description of ego-strengthening techniques.

Karle, H. and Boys, J.H. (1987) *Hypnotherapy: A Practical Handbook*. London: Free Association Books. Has become a standard text for basic courses in hypnosis. Includes many scripts for the beginner.

Rossi, E.L. (1996) *The Symptom Path to Enlightenment*. Palisades, CA: Palisades Gateway. The most recent text by Ernest Rossi providing a straightforward and exciting account of the 'hypnotherapeutic approach' that was originally developed by Erickson.

Spiegel, H. and Spiegel, D. (1978) *Trance and Treatment: Clinical Uses of Hypnosis*. New York: Basic Books. A very readable book that approaches hypnosis from a fairly traditional standpoint. Reasonably comprehensive in scope.

DISCUSSION ISSUES

1 What is the difference between direct and indirect suggestions? What are their respective advantages and disadvantages?

2 It is often argued that hypnosis can present real dangers for the client. Is there any truth in this statement?

3 In what ways does the 'trance state' facilitate the secondary strategy (for example cognitive therapy)?

4 What research evidence is there for the efficacy of hypnosis with specific clinical problems?

9

INTEGRATIVE COUNSELLING

Gladeana McMahon

I ntegrative counselling is a term used to describe either an integration of two or more therapies or an integration of counselling techniques (the latter may also be called technical eclecticism), or an integration of both therapies and techniques. Integrative counselling is not tied to any single therapy since its practitioners take the view that no one single approach works for every client in every situation.

While integrative counselling is usually pragmatic in content and has no qualms about borrowing useful concepts, skills or techniques from any source, provided the application of these benefits the client, this does not mean the approach is *ad hoc* or piecemeal in practice. Each client problem is tackled systematically, typically in three or more stages, and the counsellor is obliged to be disciplined and thorough, but still flexible, in her interactions with the client.

An overall structure is essential but is not slavishly followed since counselling is not a mechanical process. The therapy must fit the client, not vice versa. Research indicates that the most probable factors determining a successful outcome to therapy are the personal qualities of both therapist and client and the relationship between them, rather than the particular approach used.

DEVELOPMENT OF THE THERAPY

While it is not possible to pinpoint one person who 'invented' integrative counselling at a particular time, it is possible to view a number of developmental strands which merged or combined over a period of time and are still doing so.

In the early 1950s, as psychologist Carl Rogers was pioneering his client-centred approach, psychologist Harry Stack Sullivan was introducing the concept of a staged approach in psychiatric therapy. The concept of the counsellor as a skilled 'helper' operating within a structured framework also owes much to the work of psychologist Robert Carkhuff in the late 1960s and early 1970s. But perhaps it was not until 1975 that a full-blown comprehensive 'helping' model was developed by Gerard Egan, a psychologist, with the publication of *The*

Skilled Helper. This book has since been significantly revised and published in its fifth edition in 1994.

Although integrative counselling has tended to keep a humanistic client-centred flavour, it has continued to use ideas, concepts and skills from other sources, particularly from cognitive-behavioural approaches. The contribution of Albert Ellis, a clinical psychologist, to the understanding of the importance of thinking skills is widely acknowledged, as is his development of Rational Emotive Behaviour Therapy (REBT). The multimodal approach to therapy of psychologist Arnold Lazarus has provided yet another useful therapeutic methodology.

In more recent times, Richard Nelson-Jones, a counselling psychologist, has developed his practical down-to-earth approach of the Lifeskills Helping Model, and at the other end of the spectrum Petruska Clarkson has attempted to integrate traditional therapies with transpersonal, spiritual and philosophical concepts. Psychologist Sue Culley has also put together a practical model of integrative counselling which focuses on the use of counselling skills which can be used by counsellors regardless of theoretical orientation.

Mathematician Albert Einstein spent most of his later years attempting to develop a theory unifying a number of fundamental concepts which he and others had established. Integrative counselling is following a similar path with regard to human thinking, feeling and behaviour and how these might be changed to the benefit of the individual and, consequently, to society itself.

THEORY AND BASIC CONCEPTS

In the rest of this chapter I will focus on Sue Culley's integrative model.

One rarely stated basic concept in integrative counselling is that the counsellor does not and can never fully understand exactly how or why a client has acquired dysfunctional attitudes or behaviour nor what would be the optimum therapy to follow for this particular person. Humility on the part of the counsellor is what motivates the search for greater understanding of the human condition and for effective methods of helping clients to achieve desirable goals.

In common with many other approaches it is accepted that some less desirable human emotions, particularly depression, excessive pain, fear and guilt, can possibly be traced to inherited characteristics, inadequate or abusive parenting, unfortunate circumstances or environment or to misguided or unrealistic thinking, however acquired. The emphasis the counsellor places on the particular perceived source of the client's problems and the means of neutralizing the associated pain, fear or guilt largely determines whether the counsellor or the approach is described as psychodynamic, person-centred, cognitive-behavioural, or whatever.

Humility on the part of the counsellor leads to the concept of helping, a mutual exploration of problems, a partnership in establishing desirable goals and outcomes and agreed strategies for reaching them. A second but related concept is that clients can find themselves 'locked in' to particular forms of behaviour or particular attitudes, sometimes through ignorance or genuine misunderstandings (comparatively straightforward to deal with) but more commonly through a self-reinforcing process over a significant period of time. Although the intent is defensive or protective to ensure the survival of the outer or inner self, the effect is frequently over-inhibiting, leading to frustration or despair, an unwillingness to take reasonable risks, a lack of self-confidence, or perhaps to overt aggression, unsociability and a failure to relate to other people in mutually beneficial ways – what psychologist Daniel Goleman refers to as 'emotional intelligence' or the lack of it.

In moving to a position of psychological health, that is, to be able to cope successfully with a variety of real-life situations and achieve a desired degree of self-fulfilment, a person has to undergo a form of re-programing since in many cases the original program was badly written, contained bugs, was botched together or has since been subjected to undesirable amendment or interference. As a result of this, some would say that the person has written a life script for herself which is negative and non-fulfilling but one which she feels obliged to live out regardless.

Many computer programers will tell you that it is easier to write a good workable program from scratch rather than have to debug and rewrite a faulty program (the inability of many computer programs to cope with the year 2000 is costing billions of pounds). It may be that psychoanalytic practitioners take a similar view. However, this is of necessity a long, arduous and difficult process. A cognitive-behavioural practitioner might take the view that the program is workable provided one or two faulty modules or sub-programs are replaced. A person-centred practitioner might take a similar view but concentrate on the emotional elements within the program.

The integrative counsellor is obliged to keep an open mind on these matters, and it is thus preferable to recognize the validity of different approaches to particular problems – at the same time accepting the limitations of different therapies and her own abilities. Because the understanding of human functioning and behaviour is incomplete and, perhaps, may never be complete, the integrative counsellor may accept that there will be some clients, hopefully a small proportion, for whom all forms of therapy will fail. In an interview with psychologist Windy Dryden, psychologist Arnold Lazarus[1] describes in detail two such cases of clients who had undergone many different forms of therapy over periods of ten years or more with no noticeable improvement, and attributed this to ignorance on his and others' parts. He was modest enough to admit that there were also cases where considerable improvements had been made, but where he was unable to detect exactly what mechanism had brought about the improvement. Notwithstanding any reservations concerning lack of in-depth accurate knowledge of human thinking, emotions and behaviour, it is a fact that the great majority of clients can be helped through a process of learning and re-learning with the assistance of a counsellor.

One well known form of an integrative counselling process outlined by Sue Culley may be described in the following terms:

A Beginning stage

Counsellor aims

1 To establish a working relationship:
   • providing the core conditions of empathy, respect and genuineness first outlined by Carl Rogers to help form a working alliance with the client
2 To clarify and define problems:
   • which issues are you and the client addressing?
3 To make an assessment:
   • using a consistent theoretical framework to make sense of the information gathered. For example, using the three areas of work, relationships and identity to provide a structure for considering the client's situation and related problems
4 To negotiate a contract:
   • to outline clearly the terms of the counselling contract, for example, frequency/length of meetings, boundaries of confidentiality, and cost

Counsellor strategies for meeting these aims

1 Exploration of concerns
2 Prioritizing and focusing on specific issues
3 Communicating core values (typically the Carl Rogers' values of empathy, respect and genuineness)

Counsellor skills required

1 Attending and active listening:
   • attention to body language such as posture, eye contact
2 Reflective skills:
   • restating, paraphrasing, summarizing
3 Probing skills:
   • use of questions, making statements
4 Being concrete:
   • asking for concrete examples of a client's problem(s)

B Middle stage

Counsellor aims

1 To reassess problems:
   • to help the client consider their problem(s) from a new perspective
2 To maintain the working relationship:
   • the importance of ensuring that clients continue to experience the counsellor as helpful, accepting and understanding even if the counsellor is having to challenge some of the client's views of the world

3 To work to the contract:
  • to check that the work being undertaken is in line with the agreed therapeutic contract.

Counsellor strategies

1 Communicating core values (as before)
2 Challenging unhelpful or misguided client thinking

Counsellor skills required

As before

C Ending stage

Counsellor aims

1 To decide on appropriate change:
  • identify changes that need to take place and whether such changes will help the client attain their desired outcome
2 To transfer learning:
  • this may relate to aspects of self that the client has learnt about during the counselling relationship which are applicable to the client's interactions in the world generally
3 To implement change:
  • the client changes their behaviour in some way to reach their desired outcome
4 To end the counselling relationship:
  • ending the relationship and acknowledging what has been learnt and any feelings the client and counsellor may have about the work carried out and the ending itself.

Counsellor strategies

1 Goal setting:
  • helping the client devise SMART (Specific, Measurable, Achievable, Relevant, Time) goals
2 Action planning:
  • this involves planning what action is to be taken to achieve the client's stated aim, including consideration of what might hinder the process
3 Evaluating:
  • the progress the client is making and what amendment/further action is required by the client to achieve their desired outcome
4 Ending:
  • the client and the counsellor consider the work undertaken, the client's progress, what is needed to maintain change, the counselling relationship and the client's and counsellor's feelings regarding the ending itself

Counsellor skills required

As before

There are, of course, as many variations on this simplified model as there are counsellors and clients. Different clients with different problems will require different emphases within each stage. With some clients short-cuts may be taken; with others backtracking may be needed. Significant variations in approach exist: Egan sees the process as a client-centred problem-management process; Nelson-Jones sees it as people-centred with the objective of 'teaching' clients how to develop their own 'life skills' so that future problems can be dealt with without counsellor help. There is much to be said for this latter approach but it does call for extra skills on the part of the counsellor and probably a longer period of counselling.

A final note of caution is necessary to end this section. While it is widely recognized that the personal qualities and skills of the counsellor can largely determine the quality of the therapeutic relationship and whether outcomes are successful, relatively little attention is paid as to whether practising counsellors actually possess the required qualities and skills. Nelson-Jones lists helper anxiety, negative self-talk, unrealistic personal rules, lack of clarity on counsellor–client boundaries, the creation of client dependency, manipulation, misperception of clients who remind of significant others, difficulties in relating to clients with significant differences in age, sex, social class or culture, and inaccurate 'personifications' between counsellor and client as common potential problems. Egan similarly, at each stage of his problem-management model, lists what he calls the 'shadow' side of the helper/client relationship.

As individuals with a strong belief in and commitment to the efficacy of counselling perhaps counsellors should be first in line to take their own medicine?

PRACTICE

The goals of integrative counselling vary according to the stage in the counselling process.

Initially, the counsellor has to establish a working relationship with the client, building rapport and establishing core values. The client is helped to tell her story and to reveal, identify, describe and clarify her problems. Problems may need to be viewed from a different perspective; clients can have 'blind spots'. Throughout these early steps the counsellor will be looking for client skills, strengths and weaknesses. The client will be encouraged, in a multi-problem situation, to establish priorities. The counsellor will need to determine whether, after making an assessment, she is able to work with and help this particular client. A contract is negotiated determining the nature of the counsellor–client relationship, what is expected of both parties, numbers of sessions, fees, etc.

After this initial stage, which sets the scene for future work, goals tend to change or receive different emphasis. While maintaining the working relationship and keeping to the contract remain important goals, the emphasis changes to one of helping the client to develop a range of possibilities for a better future, to explore these and to make choices. Much work may need to be done in improving clients' thinking and action skills if realistic choices are to be made and desired scenarios achieved.

In a final stage the main goals are the encouragement of client self-help and independence and the formulation of action plans and strategies. Clients may be doing 'homework' to consolidate newly learned thinking and action skills. Progress can be reviewed and evaluated. Regular counselling may come to an end but with the option of *ad hoc* support sessions.

The integrative counsellor has no pre-determined theory that is applied regardless of the nature of the client's problems. The following three examples illustrate the possible variety in approach.

Jeff

Jeff was a highly intelligent computing services manager referred by his employer because of high staff turnover in Jeff's section and complaints that he was impossible to work with. His section was always short of staff and as a result important projects were seriously delayed. His director was concerned that, while Jeff was an excellent technician, a mistake might have been made in promoting him to manager.

Initially, Jeff was not happy at being referred to a counsellor but, realizing his job was on the line, he complied, though he remained critical and defensive. He complained that the staff he'd been given were 'rubbish' and he was forever having to re-do their work himself until it met his standards. Although he had undergone management training he referred to it as 'a waste of time'.

The counsellor quickly realized that Jeff was a not untypical example of a totally task-oriented person, continually seeking perfection and fearing the consequences if it was not achieved. He was oblivious to the effect he had on his staff by continually dabbling in their work and criticizing their mistakes. 'If you want a job done properly you've got to do it yourself' was his attitude.

The counsellor used a cognitive approach to help Jeff explore the basis and consequences of his attitudes and whether his thoughts and beliefs were helpful. He grudgingly admitted he was not able to do the work of six staff, however hard he worked. His relationship with his wife was becoming strained and his feelings of despair at not being able to cope were increasing in regularity.

The counsellor was able to build on Jeff's strengths of intelligence and his pride in and capacity for work, at the same time challenging his concept of what a manager should be and encouraging him to take risks with his staff. When, in one session, Jeff admitted that under a particular manager earlier in his career he had enjoyed a high degree of autonomy and had flourished as a result, the therapy was almost over. He started to relax, reduced his working hours and planned a long holiday with his wife.

Betty

Betty was on anti-depressants and had been referred by her GP. In the space of a year her father had died, she had miscarried and her partner had left her. In her first counselling sessions she spoke in a monotone and spent most of the time looking at the floor. These traumatic events had occurred some three years earlier.

Several sessions were spent exploring the details of Betty's relationship with her widowed father whom she had nursed through a terminal illness. Many boxes of tissues were consumed in the process. He had persuaded her to take a holiday and while she was away he had died. She was not able to forgive herself and she miscarried shortly afterwards. Her partner had been jealous of the time Betty had spent with her father and had formed an association with another woman. When she miscarried, he left her.

The counsellor made no attempt to change Betty but, using a person-centred approach, encouraged her to explore and express her feelings.

Somehow Betty had managed to hang on to her part-time job. After a while, as her interest in work returned, she decided to enrol on an evening course. Again, the main role of the counsellor was supportive and encouraging of Betty's development. Betty's father had always wanted her to improve her education and, in an almost transpersonal sense, she was still communicating with him, but without guilt and remorse.

Brian

Brian was a self-referral in his mid-twenties. His girlfriend, the latest in a long series, had left him. An attractive well-dressed young man with a certain boyish charm, Brian had no difficulty starting a relationship but could not sustain one for more than a few months. He had tired of being seen as a happy bachelor and was envious of his friends who had settled down to a stable family life. 'I just want to be normal', he declared.

Further probing revealed that Brian's girlfriends could not take his need to control them, even to the wearing of the smallest detail of clothing. His jealousy bordered on the obsessional. The counsellor sensed that she and Brian were in for a long haul. There were deep-seated problems which would need to be analysed and addressed. She shared her initial assessment with Brian who was happy to commit himself to longer-term counselling. Before embarking on a deeper analysis with Brian the counsellor first tried a cognitive approach which had the merit of revealing the full extent of Brian's need to manipulate and control but did not take him further forward. He had acquired strong survival techniques which were inhibiting his ability to enjoy a relaxed and trusting intimacy.

Using psychodynamic techniques, the counsellor took Brian back to his childhood. Raised by an alcoholic, promiscuous mother, Brian was often ignored and left alone. Moments of intimacy, which may have involved sexual abuse, were followed by the pain of separation and abandonment. During this process of discovery the counsellor had to deal with Brian's negative transference feelings towards her and her own annoyance (counter-transference) regarding Brian's need to control. Appointment times could not be changed. The consulting room and its contents had to remain the same for each session. Some eighteen months later, after a process of two steps forward and one step back. Brian was beginning to understand and deal with the results of a traumatic childhood. He had acquired a new girlfriend and they were still together after six months – a record.

There is no set format for a typical session in integrative counselling, which will vary according to the needs of the client, the stage in therapy and the particular approach or techniques being employed by the counsellor. Time will be devoted at the start of the session to the usual pleasantries, a brief review of progress, the outcome of any homework assignments and to deciding the agenda for the session. At the end, a summarization of the session may be undertaken, an indication of future work given and homework assignments agreed if appropriate.

WHICH CLIENTS BENEFIT MOST?

The question facing all counsellors with a new client is whether there are sufficient favourable factors present in the counsellor–client relationship to enable beneficial therapy to take place or whether negative factors will prevent this. Whole books can be devoted to this subject, for example Petruska Clarkson's *The Therapeutic Relationship*. Clearly the greater the knowledge and skills, particularly communication skills, of the counsellor the more extensive will be the range of clients who can be helped. The personal qualities which the counsellor and client bring to the therapeutic relationship are also key factors in developing the necessary rapport for successful work.

The first session or so will normally reveal whether client and counsellor are likely to be able to work together productively. Positive factors (or indications) include:

- genuine rapport
- sharing of common and core values
- good two-way communication and understanding
- ability of the counsellor to make accurate assessments and to choose appropriate approaches and techniques in the particular case
- positive motivations by both client and counsellor

Negative factors (or contra-indications) can include

- difficulty in establishing rapport
- differing values between client and counsellor
- inability to communicate through spoken language
- lack of knowledge and skills on the part of the counsellor

- significant differences in age, social class, religious belief, culture, etc., between counsellor and client
- mental illness, violence or psychopathic tendencies on the part of the client (or the counsellor!)

It is essential that a counsellor should recognize, at the earliest possible stage, a client with whom she is unlikely to be able to work successfully and to refer the client elsewhere. This is no more than sound professional practice.

Case study

THE CLIENT

Sharon, a 24-year-old computer programer referred herself for counselling with a presenting problem of obsessional checking. It could take her up to half an hour to leave the house as she had to check the cooker, taps and electric sockets a number of times before she felt able to leave. Although Sharon was 24 her manner and appearance gave the impression of a much younger woman of about 18.

Sharon's mother died unexpectedly when Sharon, an only child, was 18. Six months later her father then married a family acquaintance. Sharon's stepmother had been deserted by her husband many years previously and she had one son, David, who was two years younger than Sharon. At the time of her mother's death Sharon was about to move away from home to begin a degree in computing. The relationship between Sharon and her stepmother was hostile. Her stepmother found it hard to accept Sharon, a situation aggravated by the fact that Sharon's views and values (taken from her mother) appeared to be diametrically opposed to those held by her stepmother. Sharon's father would side with his new wife and her stepbrother also sided with his mother. While Sharon was away at college her stepmother rearranged the house, changed Sharon's bedroom to the smallest room and threw out much of her mother's furniture and ornaments without asking Sharon if she would like any of them.

Sharon had experienced a very close relationship with her mother and a rather distant one with her father. Her parents' marriage had not been a very happy one and Sharon had spent a disproportionate amount of time with her mother. Sharon felt the need to do well at school and was fearful of failure of any kind. She felt that she could never please her father. Sharon's relationships with men were difficult – the result of her apparent choice of emotionally unavailable men.

THE THERAPY

Although research has suggested that cognitive-behavioural techniques are the most successful in dealing with Obsessional Compulsive Disorders (OCD), the counsellor decided that attention needed to be given first to Sharon's long-term anxiety and sadness. In addition, it appeared that Sharon had not fully grieved for her mother, which the counsellor saw as an important piece of work within the counselling process. The counsellor shared her thoughts, ideas and proposed way of working with Sharon and an initial ten-session contract with a review on the tenth session was agreed.

By the second session it became clear that Sharon was benefiting from 'telling her story' (Egan Stage One) and the counsellor began to introduce the concept of the 'Wounded Inner Child' (Alice Miller). Sharon's feelings of loss came to the fore and a further three sessions were spent discussing her relationship with her mother. As Sharon grieved for her mother she was able to consider and accept the negative aspects of that relationship. Sharon came to understand that she had filled a gap in her mother's rather lacking relationship with her husband. Skills from the person-centred approach were used to aid the grieving process. By the end of the eighth session the counsellor began to help Sharon consider how she was still trying to please her father who it appeared was indifferent to her and impossible to please. The counsellor used skills derived from the psychodynamic school to aid this part of the work. During sessions nine and ten Sharon began to acknowledge her anger and disappointment towards her father and her deep dislike of her stepmother.

Part of session ten was turned over to review of the work undertaken and Sharon was asked to consider her progress. A framework of where she felt she started, where she was now and where she wanted to go was used. Sharon reported that her mood was lifted, she was checking less and was now able to cut down on her visits to her father and stepmother as their approval was less important than it had been. Sharon wanted to continue to work on her self-confidence and her relationships in general. A further ten sessions were agreed.

Sharon's relationships with men had always been difficult mainly because she sought intimacy with those unable or unwilling to give it. Sharon was able to see that she was simply acting out her own need to seek intimacy from her father, and the counsellor introduced her to the psychodynamic concept of 'repetition'. It was shortly after this session that Sharon ended an abusive relationship and found her own flat.

The counsellor was aware that Sharon's presenting problem had been one of obsessional checking, and although this had subsided the problem was still there. It was at this time that the counsellor discussed using a cognitive-behavioural approach to deal with the problem. Sharon was agreeable to this and the counsellor explained the theory behind the behavioural concept of exposure, teaching Sharon coping skills such as relaxation and thought-stopping techniques. Much to Sharon's delight the remainder of the obsessional checking problem was dealt with successfully over the next four weeks. In addition, attention was also given to considering Sharon's perfectionist tendencies and how, using cognitive-behavioural techniques, she could challenge these. At this point, the work of Albert Ellis was used with an REBT approach to challenge her core belief of 'I must succeed otherwise I am a failure.'

A second review took place at the end of the second set of ten sessions using the same format of considering where she had moved to since the last review, where she was now and what work she still had left to do. Sharon reported that she had begun to develop caring and supportive friendships, that her checking had totally ceased, that she had started a new relationship with an emotionally available man. Her perfectionism was also decreasing.

A further five sessions on a fortnightly basis were agreed during which time Sharon focused on her perfectionism and coping/problem-solving strategies. At the end of the fifth session a follow-up session was made for six months ahead. By the time Sharon ended her counselling she was able to form and sustain a rewarding network of friends, was capable of identifying supportive characteristics in partners and had accepted that her father and stepmother would never be any different and there was nothing that she could do to change them.

REFERENCE

1 Dryden, W. and Lazarus, A.A. (1991) *A Dialogue with Arnold Lazarus: 'It Depends'.* Buckingham: Open University Press.

SUGGESTED READING

Clarkson, P. (1995) *The Therapeutic Relationship.* London: Whurr. An interesting exploration of the therapist–client relationship using a number of historical, philosophical and spiritual contexts and identifying five different client–therapist relationships (humanistic/psychodynamic/transpersonal).

Culley, S. (1991) *Integrative Counselling Skills in Action.* London: Sage. This is a practical, easy-to-understand, three-stage approach.

Egan, G. (1994) *The Skilled Helper* (5th edn). Pacific Grove: Brooks/Cole. A comprehensive *tour-de-force* full of useful insights and analyses based on his three-stage problem-management approach to helping (client-centred/cognitive-behavioural).

Goleman, D. (1996) *Emotional Intelligence.* London: Bloomsbury Publishing. A stimulating approach to understanding the brain's architecture underlying emotion and rationality which argues that our view of human intelligence is far too narrow. Emotions play a far greater role in thought, decision-making and individual success than is commonly acknowledged.

Nelson-Jones, R. (1993) *Practical Counselling and Helping Skills* (3rd edn). London: Cassell. Excellent practical yet comprehensive approach with emphasis on development of client lifeskills based on his DASIE five-stage helping model (people-centred/cognitive-behavioural).

DISCUSSION ISSUES

1   To what extent are counsellors the 'victims' of the particular approach they are trained in? Do other professions encourage 'blinkered' approaches?

2 What personal qualities, knowledge and experience would make a successful counsellor? What role do training, counselling supervision and personal therapy play?
3 For every client there exists an ideal counsellor. Discuss.
4 What current developments in counselling and advances in scientific research are likely to influence the direction of counselling in the next twenty years?

10

LIFESKILLS COUNSELLING

Richard Nelson-Jones

L ifeskills counselling, otherwise known as lifeskills therapy or lifeskills help-ing, is an educational approach that has as its starting point the problems of living of ordinary people rather than those who have been seriously emotionally deprived or possess a psychiatric disorder. To live effectively and affirm their existences all people require lifeskills.

Lifeskills counselling's philosophical basis is humanistic-existential – human-istic in terms of the value placed on the individual, in a sense a leap of faith about the improvability of humans; existential in terms of its emphasis on choice and on creating one's existence within the challenges presented by death, suffering, change, meaning, isolation and freedom. On top of this, lifeskills counselling uses insights from 'cognitive-behavioural' approaches to counselling, those focusing on altering thoughts and actions, to sharpen the humanistic-existential message and provide clients with the skills they require to be more effective both now and in the future.

DEVELOPMENT OF THE APPROACH

In 1984, the origins of lifeskills counselling appeared in *Personal Responsibility Counselling and Therapy: An Integrative Approach*.[1] This book attempted to provide a framework for counselling, lifeskills training and self-helping that used personal responsibility as a central concept that integrated or put the different elements of theory and practice together. Right from the beginning I addressed the struggles and problems of ordinary people and tried to integrate the con-tributions of leading humanistic, existential, behavioural and cognitive ther-apists, for instance Carl Rogers, Irvin Yalom, Albert Ellis and Aaron Beck.

In 1988, the second edition of my book *Practical Counselling and Helping Skills*[2] presented the first version of my five-stage model of counselling practice. Then, in 1993, the third edition[3] presented the first full statement of the theory and practice of what was then called lifeskills helping. Here I introduced a simple super-language, called skills language, that frees counsellors to draw from different theoretical positions without becoming trapped in their separate languages. In 1997, both the theory and practice of the approach were updated in the book's fourth edition,[4] where the term lifeskills counselling replaced lifeskills helping. My emphasis on developing lifeskills in the wider community is reflected in my education and training books, *Relating Skills: A Practical Guide to Effective Personal Relationships*[5] and *Using your Mind: Creative Thinking Skills for Work and Business Success*.[6]

Lifeskills counselling still represents work in progress. Having moved to Thailand in mid-1997, I am increasingly interested in exploring the application of Eastern philosophy, religion and psychology to Western concerns and issues. In particular, I wish to develop the social, ethical and spiritual dimensions of lifeskills counselling's theory and practice.

THEORY AND BASIC CONCEPTS

Following are some central basic assumptions of lifeskills counselling. Fuller descriptions of lifeskills counselling's theory and basic concepts are provided elsewhere.[7,8]

Skills language

Most commonly life is regarded in terms of physical or biological life. However, the main concern of lifeskills counselling is with psychological rather than biological life. The primary focus of psychological life is the mind rather than the body and, correspondingly, the primary goal of psychological life is attaining human potential rather than physical health. Human psychological life goes beyond physical existence in that humans have a unique capacity for self-awareness and choice.

Apart from such obviously biological functions as breathing, virtually all human behaviour is viewed in terms of learned lifeskills. The term lifeskills in itself is neither positive nor negative. Lifeskills may be strengths or deficits depending on whether or not they help people both to survive and to maintain and develop potentials. A neutral definition of the term lifeskills is: *lifeskills are sequences of choices that people make in specific skills areas.* A positive definition of the term lifeskills is: *lifeskills are sequences of choices affirming psychological life that people make in specific skills areas.*

Skills language means consistently using skills to describe and analyse people's behaviour. In regard to counselling, skills language means thinking and talking about clients' problems in terms of lifeskills strengths and deficits. In particular, skills language involves identifying the specific thinking skills and action skills deficits that maintain clients' problems, and then translating them into counselling goals. Feelings too are important. However, feelings represent people's animal nature and are not skills in themselves. People can influence their feelings for good or ill through their use of thinking and action skills.

The inner and outer games of living

If people are to take charge of their lives, they need to think and act effectively. A simple way to highlight the distinction is to talk about the inner and outer games of living. The inner game refers to what goes on inside you, how you think and feel, or your thinking skills and feelings. The outer game refers to what goes on outside you, how you act, or your action skills. Thinking and feeling tend to be inner processes, whereas actions are out in the open.

Outer game: action skills

Action skills involve observable behaviours. Action skills refer to what you do and how you do it rather than what and how you feel and think. These skills vary by area of application: for instance, relating, studying, or working.

There are five main ways that you can send action skills messages:

- *Verbal messages*   Messages that you send with words. For example, saying 'I like you' or 'I hate you.'
- *Voice messages*   Messages that you send through your voice: for instance, through your volume, articulation, pitch, emphasis and speech rate.
- *Body messages*   Messages that you send with your body: for instance, through your gaze, eye contact, facial expression, posture, gestures, physical proximity and clothes and grooming.
- *Touch messages*   A special category of body messages. Messages that you send with your touch: for instance, through what part of the body you use, what part of another's body you touch, how gentle or firm you are, and whether or not you have permission.
- *Action messages*   Messages that you send when you are not face to face with others: for example, sending a memo.

Inner game: thinking skills

Though people are influenced by their genetic endowment, learning histories and social and cultural environments, lifeskills counselling assumes that, to a large extent, individuals create their thinking. Each of us possesses the potential to create unskilful as well as skilful thoughts, or a mixture of both.

Below are brief descriptions of twelve thinking skills areas derived from the work of leading psychiatrists and psychologists. The thinking skills are presented in 'you' language both to heighten readers' awareness of their meaning and to make the point that counsellors and clients require the same lifeskills.

- *Understanding the relationships between how you think, feel and act*   You possess insight into how you can influence how you feel, physically react and act, through how you think. You are aware that your feelings and actions in turn influence your thoughts.

- *Owning responsibility for choosing*   You assume personal responsibility for your life. You are aware that you are the author of your existence and that you can choose how you think, act and feel. You are aware of the limitations of existence, such as your death.

- *Getting in touch with your feelings*   You acknowledge the importance of getting in touch with how you feel. You are able to access significant feelings, for instance your wants and wishes, and accurately state them as thoughts.

- *Using coping self-talk*   Instead of talking to yourself negatively before, during and after specific situations, you can make coping self-statements that help you to stay calm and cool, coach you in what to do, and affirm the skills, strengths and support factors you possess.

- *Choosing realistic rules*   Your unrealistic rules make irrational demands on yourself, others, and the environment: for instance, 'I must be liked by everyone', 'Others must not make mistakes', and 'Life must be fair.' Instead you can develop realistic rules: for instance, 'I prefer to be liked, but it is unrealistic to expect this from everyone.'

- *Perceiving accurately*   You avoid labelling yourself and others either too negatively or too positively. You distinguish between fact and inference and make your inferences as accurate as possible.

- *Explaining cause accurately*   You explain the causes of events accurately. You avoid assuming too much responsibility by internalizing, 'It's all my fault', or externalizing, 'It's all your fault.'

- *Predicting realistically*   You are realistic about the risks and rewards of future actions. You assess threats and dangers accurately. You avoid distorting relevant evidence with unwarranted optimism or pessimism.

- *Setting realistic goals*   Your short-, medium- and long-term goals reflect your values, are realistic, are specific and have a time frame.

- *Using visualizing skills*   You use visual images in ways that calm you down, assist you in acting competently to attain your goals and help you to resist giving in to bad habits.

- *Realistic decision-making*   You confront rather than avoid decisions and then make up your mind by going through a systematic and realistic decision-making process.

- *Preventing and managing problems*   You anticipate and confront your problems. You assess the thinking and action skills you require to deal with them. You state working goals and plan how to implement them.

In reality, some of the skills overlap. For instance, all of the skills, even visualizing, involve self-talk. To distinguish the skill of coping self-talk I stipulate a definition by stating that it refers to self-statements relevant to coping with specific situations. Inter-relationships between skills can also be viewed on the dimension of depth. Arguably, owning responsibility for choosing is a more fundamental skill which is then exemplified in specific situations by using the skill of explaining cause accurately. Similarly, perceptions may represent underlying rules. Another example is that of explanations of cause underlying predictions. For instance, sales people making cold calls are more likely to be pessimistic if their tendency is to explain the cause of unsuccessful calls as permanent and pervasive rather than as transient and specific.

A deficit can be absence of a skills strength as well as presence of a skills deficit. For example, a person suffering from hypertension might just have the deficit of failing to use relaxing imagery rather than the added deficit of using anxiety-engendering imagery as well. Be careful about inappropriately stating deficits in all-or-nothing terms: for example, for many people *insufficient* use of relaxing imagery may be more accurate than failure to use any relaxing imagery at all.

Personal responsibility

Focusing on personal responsibility is almost like focusing on one's nose. Though right in front of the face, the concept is not always easy to observe. Lifeskills counselling adopts the existential notion of people as responsible for the authorship of their lives. Another metaphor is that people are responsible for inventing their lives. Authorship or invention requires a continuous process of choosing. Personal responsibility is an inner process in which people work from 'inside to outside'. This process starts with people's thoughts and feelings and leads to their observable actions. Furthermore, especially as people grow older, many if not most of the significant barriers to assuming responsibility are internal rather than external.

PRACTICE

Individual lifeskills counselling, the focus of this chapter, is one of a range of interventions for acquiring, maintaining and developing lifeskills in the wider community. Other interventions include couples and group lifeskills counselling, lifeskills education and training, self-helping, consultancy, and focusing on organizational change.

Goals

Lifeskills counselling goals encompass assisting clients both to manage problems and to alter the underlying problematic skills that sustain problems. Problem-management or problem-solving models are useful, since frequently clients require help to manage or solve immediate problems. However, a big drawback of such models is that they inadequately address the *repetition phenomenon*, the repetitive nature of many clients' problems. Clients require assistance in developing lifeskills strengths that last into the future and not just in managing or solving specific current problems. In reality, due to practical considerations, often counsellors and clients compromise on the amount of time and effort they take to address underlying patterns of skills deficits that predispose and position clients for further problems.

The elegant application of lifeskills counselling aims to develop the skilled person. Below, illustrative lifeskills required by the skilled person are grouped according to the five Rs of affirming psychological life.

- *Responsiveness* Responsiveness skills include existential awareness, awareness of feelings, awareness of inner motivation, and sensitivity to anxiety and guilt.
- *Realism* Realism refers to the thinking skills listed earlier, such as coping self-talk and visualizing.
- *Relating* Relating skills include: disclosing, listening, caring, companionship, sexual relating, assertion, managing anger and solving relationship problems.
- *Rewarding activity* Rewarding activity skills include identifying interests, work skills, study skills, leisure skills and looking after physical health skills.
- *Right-and-wrong* Right-and-wrong skills include social interest that transcends one's immediate environment, and ethical living.

DASIE: the five-stage model

The practice of lifeskills counselling is structured around DASIE, a systematic five-stage model. The model provides a framework or set of guidelines for counsellor choices. DASIE is a five-stage model not only for managing or solving problems but also for addressing underlying problematic skills. DASIE's five stages are:

D DEVELOP the relationship and clarify problems
A ASSESS and restate problems in skills terms
S STATE goals and plan interventions
I INTERVENE to develop lifeskills
E EMPHASIZE take-away and end

Stage 1 Develop the relationship and clarify problems
Stage 1 starts with pre-helping contact with clients and either ends sometime in the initial interview or may take longer. It has two main overlapping functions: developing supportive counselling relationships and working with clients to

identify and obtain fuller descriptions of problems. Supportive counselling relationships go beyond offering empathy, non-possessive warmth and genuineness to more actively fostering client self-support.

Many of the counsellor skills used in stage 1 are the same as those used in other approaches: for example, reflective responding, summarizing and confronting. Counsellors collaborate with clients to explore, clarify and understand problems. Together they act as detectives to 'sniff out' and discover what are clients' real problems and agendas. Then they break them down into their component parts.

Counsellors can use skills language when structuring initial sessions. One possibility is to start the session by giving clients an open-ended permission to tell their stories. After they respond, the following statement might structure the remainder of the session.

> You've given me some idea of why you've come. Now I'd like to ask some more questions to help us to clarify your problem(s) [specify]. Then, depending on what we find, I will suggest some skills to help you cope better. Once we agree on what skills might help you, then we can look at ways to develop them. Does this way of proceeding sound all right?

Homework in the form of 'take-away' assignments is a feature of lifeskills counselling. Between-session learning can be enhanced by clients listening at home to audio cassettes of counselling sessions. In addition, counsellors may negotiate other take-away assignments with clients, for instance completing monitoring logs.

Stage 2   Assess and restate problem(s) in skills terms
The object of this stage is to build a bridge between *describing* and *actively working* on problems and their underlying skills deficits. In stage 1, problems were described, amplified and clarified largely in everyday language. In stage 2, counsellors build upon information collected in stage 1 to generate and investigate propositions or hypotheses about how clients think and act that contributes to maintaining their difficulties. Stage 2 ends with a restatement of at least either the main or the most pressing problems in skills terms.

The emphasis in counsellors' questions differs in stage 2 from that in stage 1. In stage 1, counsellors ask questions to clarify clients' existing frames of reference. In stage 2 counsellors are likely to question as much from their own as from their clients' frames of reference. While the major focus is on pinpointing skills deficits, attention is also paid to identifying skills strengths and resources.

Counsellors need to develop good skills at restating problems in skills terms and communicating and negotiating these working definitions with clients. Restatements of problems in skills terms are essentially hypotheses, based on careful analysis of available information, about clients' thinking and action skills deficits. As hypotheses they are open to modification in light of further or better information.

I write restatements in skills terms on whiteboards. Visual presentation makes it easier for clients to retain what you say, if necessary suggest alterations, and make written records. I use a simple diagram to present thinking and action skills weaknesses for sustaining each problem. At the top of the diagram there are headings for 'Thinking skills deficits/goals' and 'Action skills deficits/goals'. These headings are divided by a long vertical line down the middle to allow specific deficits to be listed on either side.

Stage 3   State goals and plan interventions

Stage 3 consists of two phases: stating deficits as goals and planning interventions. Assuming counsellors succeed in restating problems in skills terms, stating goals becomes a relatively simple matter. Working goals are the flip-side of restatements: positive statements of skills strengths to replace existing skills deficits. Counsellors can easily change on the whiteboard statements of deficits into statements of goals. Counsellors should ensure that clients understand and agree with goals. Then client and counsellor record this statement as a basis for their future work.

Stating deficits as goals provides the bridge to choosing interventions. Counsellors not only hypothesize about goals, but also about ways to attain them. An important distinction exists between interventions and plans. Interventions are intentional behaviours, on the part of either counsellors or clients, designed to help clients attain problem management and problematic skills goals. Plans are statements of how to combine and sequence interventions to attain goals. Plans may be of varying degrees of structure. Most often I work with open plans that allow clients and myself flexibility to choose which interventions, to attain which goals, when. Clients may be more motivated to work on skills and material relevant at any given time than run through predetermined programmes independent of current considerations. Furthermore, owing to the frequently repetitive nature of clients' skills deficits, work done in one session may be highly relevant to work done on the same or different problems in other sessions.

Stage 4   Intervene to develop lifeskills

Lifeskills counsellors are developmental educators or, in more colloquial terms, user-friendly coaches. To intervene effectively they require good relating skills and good training skills. It is insufficient to know *what* interventions to offer without also being skilled at *how* to offer them. Skilled lifeskills counsellors strike appropriate balances between relationship and task orientations; less skilled helpers err in either direction.

Table 10.1 depicts methods of psychological education or training and methods of learning in lifeskills counselling. Counsellors work much of the time with the three training methods of 'tell', 'show' and 'do'. They require special training skills for each. 'Tell' entails giving clients clear instructions concerning the skills they wish to develop. 'Show' means providing demonstrations of how to implement skills. 'Do' means arranging for clients to perform structured activities and homework tasks.

Individual sessions in the intervention stage may be viewed in four, often overlapping, phases: preparatory, initial, working and ending. The preparatory phase entails counsellors thinking in advance how best to assist clients. Counsellors ensure that, if appropriate, they have available: session plans; training

TABLE 10.1 Methods of psychological education or training and of learning

Psychological education or training method	Learning method
Facilitate	Learning from self-exploring and from experiencing self more fully
Assess	Learning from monitoring and evaluating
Tell	Learning from hearing
Show	Learning from observing
Do	Learning from doing structured activities and take-away assignments
Consolidate	Learning from developing self-helping skills in all the above modes

materials, blank lifeskills counselling take-away sheets; and audio-visual aids, for instance whiteboards and audio cassette-recorders.

The initial phase consists of meeting, greeting and seating, then giving permission to talk. Though a skill not restricted to the initial phase, early on counsellors may wish to negotiate session agendas. For instance, counsellors may go from checking whether the client has any current pressing agendas, to reviewing the past week's homework, to focusing on one or more problematic skills and/or problems in clients' lives. As necessary, agendas may be altered during sessions.

Within a supportive relationship, the working phase focuses on specific thinking skills and action skills interventions designed to help clients manage problems and develop lifeskills strengths. Whenever appropriate, counsellors assist clients to use skills language. Frequently clients are asked to fill out 'take-away' sheets in which they record skills-focused work done on the whiteboard during sessions.

The ending phase lasts from toward the end of one session to the beginning of the next. This phase focuses on summarizing the major session learnings, negotiating take-away assignments, strengthening commitment to between-session work, and rehearsing and practising skills outside counselling.

Stage 5 Emphasize take-away and end

Most often either counsellors or clients bring up the topic of ending before the final session. This allows both parties to work through the various task and relationship issues connected with ending the contact. A useful option is to fade contact with some clients by seeing them progressively less often. Certain clients may appreciate the opportunity for booster sessions, say one, two, three or even six months later.

Lifeskills counselling seeks to avoid the 'train and hope' approach. Transfer and maintenance of skills is encouraged by such means as developing clients' self-instructional abilities, working with real-life situations during counselling, and using between-session time productively to listen to session cassettes and to rehearse and practise skills. Often counsellors make up short take-away cassettes focused on the use of specific skills in specific situations: for instance, the use of coping self-talk to handle anxiety when waiting to deliver a public speech. Counsellors can encourage clients to make up similar coping self-talk cassettes for other situations: for instance, participating in meetings. Thus, not only do clients possess cassettes they can use to maintain skills in future, they have also acquired the skills of making new cassettes, if needed.

In addition, counsellors work with clients to anticipate difficulties and set-backs to taking away and maintaining lifeskills. Then together they develop and rehearse coping strategies for preventing and managing lapses and relapses. Sometimes clients require help identifying people to support their efforts to maintain skills. Counsellors also provide information about further skills-building opportunities.

WHICH CLIENTS BENEFIT MOST?

Lifeskills counselling assumes that clienthood is ubiquitous. Its major emphasis is on the 'screwed-up-ness' of the majority. Illustrative problems for which it is appropriate include those pertaining to study, relationships, work, health and sport. I have successfully used lifeskills counselling with previously long-term, severely depressed redundant executives. Both work and home problems con-tributed to the severity of such clients' depression. Lifeskills counselling is not just an approach to remedying psychological pain. Counsellors, clients and others wishing to attain superior levels of psychological functioning can adopt the approach and create skilful thoughts in all areas of their lives.

Lifeskills counselling is also appropriate to non-Western cultures. I have run lifeskills counselling workshops in Hong Kong, Malaysia and Thailand. In each country, participants have indicated that, with some cultural adjustments, they can beneficially use the approach.

Case study

THE CLIENT

Louise Donovan, 43, was an accountant made redundant from a very senior posi-tion three years earlier. At the time of entering counselling, Louise worked for a relatively low salary in a position whose status was below where she was two moves ago. In the previous three years Louise had been for numerous interviews for very senior positions. However, she received consistent feedback that, while selec-tion panels evaluated her technical skills as excellent, they had serious reservations about her people skills and found her too pedantic. Louise was referred to me in my capacity as sessional counselling psychologist for an outplacement consulting firm. She had already been through the firm's standard interview training programme as well as participating in numerous discussions with one of the firm's outplacement advisers.

THE COUNSELLING PROCESS

In the initial session, I started by giving Louise permission to tell her story. As well as using empathic responding, I asked questions that clarified the history of Louise's problem, and her feelings, physical reactions, thoughts and actions in relation to it. All the time I was observing how Louise related to me, looking for clues as to why panels found her so off-putting. She was one of the brightest and most personally overwhelming clients I have ever come across. Stage 1 of the lifeskills counselling model, 'develop the relationship and clarify problems', merged into stage 2, 'assess and restate problems in skills terms', as I asked a series of further questions to confirm or negate hypotheses about how she might be sustaining her problems.

After about 40 minutes, I asked Louise if she would mind my looking at my notes and drawing together threads so that I could put some suggestions on the white-board about skills she might address, as the basis for establishing goals for our work together. I told Louise that we could discuss anything about which she was either unclear or unhappy. As appropriate, we could modify, rephrase or erase my suggestions. The groundwork for the restatement in skills terms was laid in the first 40 minutes of the session, so there were no real surprises for Louise. Table 10.2 shows the restatement in skills terms. Note that I have identified and illustrated skills deficits/goals. I use the term deficits/goals to indicate from the start that deficits are goals.

Toward the end of the initial session, I proceeded to stage 3, 'state goals and plan interventions'. I explained to Louise how deficits could be translated into goals.

> Louise, I'd just like to say again that areas shown on the whiteboard as deficits are really skills that we can work to develop. In other words, the deficits are our goals. For example, your thinking skills goals are developing a realistic rule, accurate perceptions and replacing negative with coping self-talk. Your action skills goals are developing good interview skills by focusing on improving your verbal, voice and body messages. I'll now reword each skills deficit on the whiteboard accordingly, but leave the illustrations of the deficits so that we can recall them later. Afterwards, if you agree, we can both write this down on a specially designed assessment of problem(s) form so that we can remember it for future sessions.

Louise and I decided to use an open plan to address her interview skills deficits. In reality her interview skills deficits were just the tip of the iceberg in a well-entrenched, cumbersome, pedantic and off-putting style of professional relating.

Stage 4, 'intervene to develop lifeskills', began in the second session. Throughout this stage, at the start of each session Louise and I would establish an agenda for that session's work. Early sessions focused mainly on building Louise's interview skills. As a take-away assignment Louise made a list of questions she was likely to be asked at interviews. In addition, I wrote up on the whiteboard some points about answering questions. Then Louise and I engaged in a series of cassette-recorded question-and-answer sessions. After each trial we played back the cassettes, looking for specific evidence to confirm or negate her using the skills entailed in the points written on the whiteboard. During her evaluation of the cassettes, Louise became aware of how altering her verbal, voice and body messages

TABLE 10.2   Restatement of Louise's problem in skills terms

Thinking skills deficits/goals	Action skills deficits/goals
Unrealistic rule • 'I must give the perfect answer.'	Poor interview skills • verbal: answers too long, perceiving unfocused and lecturing
Perceiving inaccurately • interviews for senior positions are knowledge exams • others' reactions to personal style not picked up adequately • own strengths insufficiently acknowledged	• voice: booming, overpowering • body: stiff posture, eyes glaring, unsmiling (not user-friendly)
Negative self-talk • 'I don't know how to improve.' • 'Things are going to go wrong again.'	

could effect interviewers and it become clear that interviews for senior positions had an important relationship as well as knowledge agenda. In the third session, using the whiteboard, I helped Louise to dispute her rule that she must give the perfect answer and then developed with her a statement of a more realistic rule.

Subsequent sessions incorporated the following interventions: more practice in the verbal, voice and body message skills of answering questions; making up a visualized rehearsal cassette starting with some brief mental relaxation skills, followed by appropriate calming, coaching and affirming self-talk for waiting outside interview rooms and then going in and answering the first few questions competently; and identifying and listing Louise's competencies and then cassette recording them twice – first with my voice and then with Louise's voice.

Stage 5, 'emphasize take-away and end', took place both during as well as at the end of counselling. During counselling, Louise was given a series of take-away assignments both to prepare for sessions and also to consolidate skills targeted in sessions. In addition, Louise was encouraged to practise her skills in her daily professional life, which she did with increasing success. This daily practice was especially important because Louise was not going for interviews. For both personal and professional reasons, she did not want to leave her present job unless it was for a substantial improvement. Indeed, a second agenda emerged as Louise realized that the skills she was learning for job interviews were similar to skills she required for holding and advancing in jobs. Louise saw me for about 25 sessions over two years. Over the last 18 months sessions were monthly and then bimonthly. As time went by, Louise was getting increasingly good feedback about how well she related in her company, first being promoted to company secretary and then being made a director, with an accompanying salary increase and the provision of a company car. Louise acknowledged that the lifeskills counselling approach had helped her to break down and address obtaining, holding and advancing in a job skills deficits that had, for a considerable period of time, held her back professionally.

REFERENCES

1 Nelson-Jones, R. (1984) *Personal Responsibility Counselling and Therapy: An Integrative Approach*. London: Harper & Row.
2 Nelson-Jones, R. (1988) *Practical Counselling and Helping Skills: Helping Clients to Help Themselves* (2nd edn). London: Cassell.
3 Nelson-Jones, R. (1993) *Practical Counselling and Helping Skills: How to Use the Lifeskills Helping Model* (3rd edn). London: Cassell.
4 Nelson-Jones, R. (1997) *Practical Counselling and Helping Skills: How to Use the Lifeskills Counselling Model* (4th edn). London: Cassell.
5 Nelson-Jones, R. (1996) *Relating Skills: A Practical Guide to Effective Personal Relationships*. London: Cassell.
6 Nelson-Jones, R. (1997) *Using Your Mind: Creative Thinking Skills for Work and Business Success*. London: Cassell.
7 Nelson-Jones, R. (1995) 'Lifeskills counselling', in R. Nelson-Jones, *The Theory and Practice of Counselling* (2nd edn). London: Cassell.
8 Nelson-Jones, R. (1997) op. cit.

SUGGESTED READING

Nelson-Jones, R. (1995) 'Lifeskills counselling', in R. Nelson-Jones, *The Theory and Practice of Counselling* (2nd edn). London: Cassell. This is a more advanced and thorough textbook presentation, about three times the length of the present chapter, of lifeskills counselling's theory and practice.

Nelson-Jones, R. (1996) *Relating Skills: A Practical Guide to Effective Personal Relationships*. London: Cassell. This book starts with four introductory chapters and then devotes a chapter each to the skills of: disclosing, listening, showing understanding, managing shyness, choosing a partner, trust, caring, intimacy, companionship, sexual relating, assertion, managing anger and solving relationship problems. The book concludes with a chapter on developing your relating skills.

Nelson-Jones, R. (1997) *Practical Counselling and Helping Skills: How to Use the Lifeskills Counselling Model* (4th edn). London: Cassell. This book is divided into seven parts: part 1 contains four introductory chapters; parts 2–6 contain fifteen chapters that systematically present the counsellor skills required for each of the lifeskills counselling model's five stages; and part 7 concludes the book with a chapter on developing your counselling skills.

Nelson-Jones, R. (1997) *Using Your Mind: Creative Thinking Skills for Work and Business Success*. London: Cassell. This book focuses on self-management in work and business settings. The first three chapters are on creating your thinking, creative thinking as skilful thinking, and learning how not to think skilfully. Then follows a series of chapters on application to work of the thinking skills overviewed in this chapter. The concluding chapter reviews how to keep using your mind.

DISCUSSION ISSUES

1 Critically discuss the notion of skills language as presented in this chapter.
2 Critically discuss the proposition that people create their thinking.
3 Critically discuss the usefulness of the DASIE five-stage model of counselling practice.
4 What relevance, if any, has the theory and practice of lifeskills counselling for how you counsel and live?

11

MULTIMODAL COUNSELLING AND THERAPY

Stephen Palmer

Multimodal counselling and therapy is a technically eclectic and systematic approach. The approach is technically eclectic as it uses techniques taken from many different psychological theories and systems, without necessarily being concerned with the validity of the theoretical principles that underpin the different approaches from which it takes its techniques and methods. The techniques and interventions are applied systematically, based on data from client qualities, the counsellor's clinical skills and specific techniques.

The approach uses a unique assessment procedure which focuses on seven different aspects or dimensions (known as modalities) of human personality. Not only is a serious attempt made to tailor the therapy to each client's unique requirements, but the counsellor also endeavours to match his or her interpersonal style and interaction to the individual needs of each client, thereby maximizing the therapeutic outcome.

DEVELOPMENT OF THE THERAPY

During the 1950s Arnold Lazarus, a psychologist, undertook his formal clinical training in South Africa. The main focus of his training was underpinned by psychodynamic and person-centred theory and methods. In addition, he attended seminars provided by Joseph Wolpe, a psychologist, thereby learning about conditioning therapies based on Behaviour Therapy (see Chapter 3). During 1957 he spent several months as an intern at the Marlborough Day Hospital in London, where the orientation was Adlerian (see Chapter 2). He believed that no one system of therapy could provide a complete understanding of either human development or condition. In 1958 he became the first psychologist to use the terms 'behavior therapist' and 'behavior therapy' in an academic article.[1]

Lazarus conducted follow-up enquiries into clients who had received behaviour therapy and found that many had relapsed. However, when clients had used both behaviour and cognitive techniques, more durable results were obtained. In the early 1970s he started advocating a broad but systematic range of cognitive-behavioural techniques and his follow-up enquiries indicated the importance of breadth if therapeutic gains were to be maintained. This led to the development of Multimodal Therapy which places emphasis on seven discrete but interactive dimensions or modalities which encompass all aspects of human personality.

More recently, in Britain, as a psychologist, counsellor and psychotherapist, I have developed multimodal therapy and applied it to the field of stress counselling and management.[2]

THEORY AND BASIC CONCEPTS

Modalities

People are essentially biological organisms (neurophysiological/biochemical entities) who behave (act and react), emote (experience emotional responses), sense (respond to olfactory, tactile, gustatory, visual and auditory stimuli), imagine (conjure up sights, sounds and other events in the mind's eye), think (hold beliefs, opinions, attitudes and values), and interact with one another (tolerate, enjoy or endure various interpersonal relationships). These seven aspects or dimensions of human personality are known as modalities. By referring to these seven modalities as Behaviour, Affect, Sensations, Images, Cognitions, Interpersonal and Drugs/biology, the useful acronym and *aide memoire* BASIC I.D. arises from the first letter of each.[3] ('Affect' is a psychological word for emotion and 'cognitions' represent all thoughts, attitudes and beliefs.)

From the multimodal perspective these seven modalities may interact with each other – for example an unpleasant image or daydream and a negative thought may trigger a negative emotion such as anxiety or depression. The multimodal approach rests on the assumption that unless the seven modalities are assessed, counselling is likely to overlook significant concerns. Clients are usually troubled by a multitude of specific problems which should be dealt with by a similar multitude of specific interventions or techniques.[4] For example, a client may suffer from a simple fear of spiders, anxiety about giving presentations at work, sleep disturbances, a lack of exercise and a poor diet. Each problem will probably need a specific intervention to help the client improve his or her condition.

Multimodal therapists have found that individuals tend to prefer some of the BASIC I.D. modalities to others. They are referred to as 'imagery reactors' or 'cognitive reactors' or 'sensory reactors' depending upon which modality they favour.

Principle of parity

In multimodal therapy the counsellor and client are considered equal in their humanity (the principle of parity). However, the counsellor may be more skilled in certain areas in which the client has particular deficits. Therefore it is not automatically assumed that clients know how to deal with their problems and have the requisite skills. The counsellor may need to model or teach the client various skills and strategies to help overcome his or her problem(s). It should be understood that having superior skills in certain areas does not make counsellors superior human beings!

Thresholds

One key assumption made in multimodal therapy is that people have different thresholds for pain, frustration, stress, external and internal stimuli in the form of sound, light, touch, smell and taste. Psychological interventions can be applied by individuals to help modify these thresholds but often the genetic endowment or predisposition has an overriding influence in the final analysis. For example, a client with a low tolerance to pain may be able to use psychological distraction techniques such as relaxing imagery, but is still likely to need an anaesthetic when receiving minor fillings at the dentist.

Theories underpinning multimodal therapy

Multimodal therapy is underpinned by a number of general theories. Multimodal therapists, however, do not inflexibly adhere to any one theory in a rigid manner.[5] These theories will be briefly discussed below.

People's personalities stem from the interplay between their social learning and conditioning, their physical environment and their genetic endowment. Social learning relates to what is learnt within social contexts such as how to behave in certain situations (see classical and operant conditioning, Chapter 3). Conditioning occurs consciously and sometimes non-consciously when people are rewarded or punished for particular behaviours. For example, a child who exhibits bad table manners may trigger a parent's wrath, and thus becomes conditioned to improve his or her table manners. However, other children may have observed how their parents eat at the table and without consciously thinking (that is, non-consciously) imitate their parents' good table manners. In this case the parents would have acted as good role models. This process is known as modelling. (Learning theory and social learning theory were developed by two well-known psychologists, Burrhus Skinner and Albert Bandura.) People respond to their perceived environment and not the real environment, and many factors can influence their perceptions: attitudes, values, beliefs, selective attention, problem-solving skills and goals. An individual's genetic endowment can greatly affect his or her ability to cope with different thresholds and favoured modalities. Therefore each client is unique and may need a personalized counselling programme to help him or her overcome his or her problem(s).

According to systems theory, people need other people to give purpose and meaning to their existence. This emphasis on relationships may be the focus of interpersonal difficulties and problems that clients may bring to counselling. For effective therapy to occur, sometimes all the people involved will need to receive group, couples or family therapy to deal with the problem concerned. For example, in sex therapy, if the male partner is impotent, often his partner will need to attend counselling too for therapeutic progress to be made.

Communications theory states that all actions or behaviour imply some kind of message. Communication goes beyond just talking and includes non-verbal messages such as eye-contact or posture. These messages make a statement about the two or more people communicating. For example, a manager could, in a relaxed manner, make a simple request of a member of staff: 'Can you please help Jane to finish that item of work'. This sentence is unlikely to lead to the employee becoming resentful. The body language, however, can send different messages. In this example the manager might hit the desk with his or her fist. The employee has a number of choices. He or she could immediately respond and start on the project, go through the motions of completing the task or could feign sickness and totally avoid starting on it. Although both parties are communicating with each other it is not necessarily in a productive manner.

The development of problems and how they are maintained

Problems develop and are maintained for a variety of reasons. Social learning, systems, and communication theories discussed in the previous section highlight some of these ways problems can arise and how they are maintained. Of course, underlying all problems is the biological and genetic dimension which goes to help make up a human being. In this section we will review the additional key factors.

Misinformation

Over a period of time people may learn incorrect assumptions and beliefs about life. For example, the beliefs 'I must perform well otherwise I'm a failure', or 'I'm worthless if my partner leaves me', or 'Life should be easy', may be learnt or imbibed by listening to significant others such as peers, parents or teachers. These beliefs may lead to considerable stress when external life events conflict with them. Couples may also hold on to unhelpful beliefs or myths such as 'If you feel guilty, confess.'

Due to misinterpreting their doctor's advice many people have misunderstood medical and health-related issues such as treatment of cancer or heart disease. Unless the health professionals correct these errors then patient compliance to medical procedures may be hindered or even non-existent.

Unlike the case with misinformation, with missing information people have not learnt the necessary skills, knowledge or methods to either understand or undertake particular activities or recognize specific problems. For example, people may not have in their repertoire of behaviour job interview skills, friendship skills, communication skills, or assertiveness skills etc. They may not realize that a pain in their left arm could signify heart disease and that it might be strongly advisable to have a medical check-up.

Defensive reactions

People avoid or defend against discomfort, frustration, pain, or negative emotions such as shame, guilt, depression and anxiety. Although it sounds quite natural to avoid fears or the unbearable pain of loss, people do not learn how to conquer them unless they confront them. For example, if a person has a fear of travelling by airplane he or she could easily avoid this mode of transport. However, there might be certain job expectations that require the person to fly across the Atlantic. If the person wanted to keep the job he or she would need to deal with this problem sooner rather than later. According to learning theory the main method of overcoming flying phobia is to experience exposure to flying. Although this can be partially undertaken using the person's imagination, the most effective technique is to fly on the airplane. Initially this might trigger very high levels of anxiety which only gradually subsides or to which the person habituates after an hour or two of exposure to flying. This is no different from the advice given to horse-riders who fall off their horse: 'Get straight back on the horse immediately.'

Lack of self-acceptance

People tend to link their behaviour skills deficits directly to their totality as a human being. Depending upon the particular belief the person holds, this tends to lead to anxiety, shame, anger or depression. For example, a person may believe, 'If I fail my exam, I'm a total failure as a human being.' A more realistic and logical way of looking at the situation could be, 'If I fail my exam all it proves is that I've got exam skills deficits. I can still accept myself as a fallible human being.' The unhelpful beliefs may have been imbided from parents and other significant people in the child's life but they may be reinforced and perpetuated by the person constantly re-indoctrinating him or herself on a regular basis throughout adulthood. In multimodal therapy the content of self-defeating or unrealistic beliefs is examined and is replaced by more self-helping and realistic beliefs.

From psychological disturbance to psychological health

The key issues discussed in the previous sections and the path to psychological health can be expressed in the form of the BASIC I.D. modalities below:

Behaviour: ceasing unhelpful behaviours; performing wanted behaviours; stopping unnecessary or irrational avoidances; taking effective behaviours to achieve realistic goals.

Affect: admitting, clarifying and accepting feelings; coping or managing unpleasant feelings and enhancing positive feelings; abreaction (that is, living and recounting painful experiences and emotions).

Sensation: tension release; sensory pleasuring; awareness of positive and negative sensations; improving threshold tolerance to pain and other stimuli.

Imagery: developing helpful coping images; improving self-image; getting in touch with one's imagination.

Cognition: greater awareness of cognitions; improving problem-solving skills; modifying self-defeating, rigid beliefs; enhancing flexible and realistic thinking; increasing self-acceptance; modifying beliefs that exacerbate low thresholds to frustration or pain (for example, 'I can't stand it' to 'I don't like it but I'm living proof that I can stand it'); correcting misinformation and providing accurate missing information.

Interpersonal: non-judgemental acceptance of others; model useful interpersonal skills; dispersing unhealthy collusions; improve assertiveness, communication, social and friendship skills.

Drugs/biology: better nutrition and exercise; substance abuse cessation; alcohol consumption in moderation; medication when indicated for physical or mental disorders.

PRACTICE

Goals of multimodal therapy

The goals of multimodal therapy are to help clients to have a happier life and achieve their own realistic goals. Therefore the goals are tailored to each client. A philosophy of long-term hedonism as opposed to short-term hedonism is advocated whereby the client may need to decide how much pleasure they may want in the present compared to the sacrifices they may have to make to attain their desires and wishes. For example, to go to college and obtain a good degree may necessitate working reasonably hard for a period of three years and not attending as many parties as previously.

The relationship between the therapist and client

The relationship is underpinned by core therapeutic conditions suggested by Carl Rogers, a psychologist who developed person-centred counselling. These core conditions are empathy, congruence and unconditional positive regard (see Chapter 13 for explanation). Although a good therapeutic relationship and adequate rapport are usually necessary, multimodal therapists consider that they are often insufficient for effective therapy. The counsellor–client relationship is considered as the soil that enables the strategies and techniques to take root. The experienced multimodal counsellor hopes to offer a lot more by assessing and treating the client's BASIC I.D., endeavouring to 'leave no stone (or modality) unturned'.

Multimodal counsellors often see themselves in a coach/trainer–trainee or teacher–student relationship as opposed to a doctor–patient relationship, thereby encouraging self-change rather than dependency. Therefore the usual approach taken is active-directive where the counsellor provides information, and suggests possible strategies and interventions to help the client manage or overcome specific problems. However, this would depend upon the issues being discussed and the personality characteristics of the client. Flexible interpersonal styles of the counsellor which match client needs can reduce attrition (i.e. premature termination of therapy) and help the therapeutic relationship and alliance. This approach of the therapist is known in multimodal therapy as being an 'authentic chameleon'. For example, if a client states that she wants, 'A listening ear to help me get over the loss of my partner', then she may consider an active-directive approach as intrusive and possibly offensive. On the other hand, a client who states, 'I would value your comments and opinions on my problems', may become very irritated by a counsellor who only reflects back the client's sentiments and ideas. Others may want a 'tough, no-nonsense' approach and would find a 'warm, gentle' approach not helpful or conducive to client disclosure.[6] This flexibility in the counsellor's interpersonal therapeutic style underpins effective multimodal therapy. Counsellors are expected to exhibit different aspects of their own personality to help the therapeutic relationship and clients to reach their goals. The term 'bespoke therapy' has been used to describe the custom-made emphasis of the approach.[7]

The process of change

The process of change may commence even before the first therapy session as clients are usually sent details about the approach with some explanation of the key techniques such as relaxation or thinking skills. Occasionally, therefore, the client has already started using simple self-help techniques before the therapy formally commences. In Britain, included with the details is a client checklist of issues the client may want to discuss with the counsellor at the first meeting[8] (see

Appendix 2). This checklist encourages the client to ask the counsellor relevant questions about the approach, the counsellor's qualifications and training and contractual issues, thereby giving the client more control of the session and therapy.

During the course of therapy, the client's problems are expressed in terms of the seven BASIC I.D. modalities and client change occurs as the major different problems are managed or resolved across the entire BASIC I.D. Initially, sessions are often held weekly. As client gains are made, then the sessions are held with longer intervals in between, such as a fortnight or a month. Termination of counselling usually occurs when clients have dealt with the major problems on their modality profile or feel that they can cope with the remaining problems.

Initial assessment

Assessment helps both the client and counsellor to understand the client's presenting problems and their degree of severity. The assessment procedure then leads on to the development of a counselling programme focusing on dealing with each problem. In multimodal therapy, the first or second counselling sessions are used to place the client's problems within the BASIC. I.D. framework (see later). The counsellor uses the initial interview to derive relevant information.[9]

1 Are there any signs of psychiatric disorder?
2 Is there any evidence of depression, suicidal or homicidal tendencies?
3 What are the persisting complaints and their main precipitating events?
4 What appear to be some important antecedent (i.e. preceding) events?
5 Who or what appears to be maintaining the client's problems?
6 What does the client wish to derive from counselling?
7 Are there clear indicators for adopting a particular therapeutic style?
8 Are there any indicators as to whether it would be in the client's interests to be seen as part of dyad (i.e. two), triad, family unit and/or group?
9 Can a mutually satisfying relationship ensue, or should the client be referred elsewhere?
10 Has the client previous experience of counselling, therapy or relevant training? If yes, what was the outcome? Were any difficulties encountered?
11 Why is the client seeking therapy at this time and not last week, last month or last year?
12 What are some of the client's positive attributes and strengths?

In the beginning phase of therapy the multimodal therapist is collecting information and looking for underlying themes and problems. During the first session the client is usually asked to give details about his or her problem(s) near the start of the session and often within only 20 minutes the client has provided information about a large majority of the 12 determinations. Further questioning will

TABLE 11.1   John's modality profile (or BASIC I.D. chart)

Modality	Problem
Behaviour	Eats/walks fast, always in a rush, hostile, competitive: indicative of type A behaviour Avoidance of giving presentations Accident proneness
Affect	Anxious when giving presentations Guilt when work targets not achieved Frequent angry outbursts at work
Sensation	Tension in shoulders Palpitations Frequent headaches Sleeping difficulties
Imagery	Negative images of not performing well Images of losing control Poor self-image
Cognition	I must perform well otherwise it will be awful and I couldn't stand it I must be in control Significant others should recognize my work If I fail then I am a total failure
Interpersonal	Passive/aggressive in relationships Manipulative tendencies at work Always puts self first Few supportive friends
Drugs/biology	Feeling inexplicably tired Takes aspirins for headaches Consumes 10 cups of coffee a day Poor nutrition and little exercise

normally fill in any gaps without appearing too intrusive. Then the counsellor will usually explain that it is useful to investigate the client's problems in terms of the BASIC I.D. modalities. This can be undertaken fairly easily in the session by using a whiteboard or paper that the client can see. With the counsellor's assistance, the client decides which Behaviours he or she would like to stop, introduce or modify. This is written on the whiteboard and then the next BASIC I.D. modality – Affect – is assessed. This process is continued until all of the seven modalities have been assessed. Table 11.1[10] is a BASIC I.D. chart, more commonly known as a 'modality profile', which in this example illustrates John's problems (see case study below). If appropriate, during the first session the counsellor will make a therapeutic intervention such as using a relaxation technique, to help the client cope with his or her immediate problem(s) and inject some hope into the situation.

Depending upon the time left in the session, the counsellor and client can either negotiate a counselling programme or postpone this to the following session. If the client reads an article or book about techniques and interventions that are used in multimodal therapy between sessions 1 and 2, then he or she is more likely to be constructively involved in negotiating a comprehensive counselling programme in the next session. The use of books, articles, handouts, and

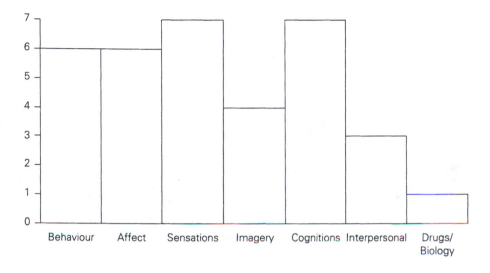

FIGURE 11.1   John's structural profile

audio-visual material is known as bibliotherapy. In addition, the client may be asked to complete a Multimodal Life History Inventory (MLHI)[11] at home. This is a 15-page questionnaire which can aid assessment and the development of a counselling programme. It has sections on each modality and includes routine history-taking and expectations regarding therapy. It prevents the counsellor asking too many questions during the first session.

In a later session an additional assessment tool is used. To obtain more clinical information and also general goals for counselling, a Structural Profile is drawn.[12] This can be derived from the MLHI or by asking clients to rate subjectively, on a scale of 1 to 7, how they perceive themselves in relation to the seven modalities. The counsellor can ask a number of different questions that focus on the seven modalities:

Behaviour: How much of a 'doer' are you?
Affect: How emotional are you?
Sensation: How 'tuned in' are you to your bodily sensations?
Imagery: How imaginative are you?
Cognition: How much of a 'thinker' are you?
Interpersonal: How much of a 'social being' are you?
Drugs/biology: To what extent are you health-conscious?

Then in the session the counsellor can illustrate these scores graphically by representing them in the form of a bar chart on paper. Figure 11.1[13] illustrates John's structural profile (discussed below in the Case Study). Then clients are

FIGURE 11.2 John's desired structural profile

asked in what way they would like to change their profiles during the course of counselling. Once again the client is asked to rate subjectively each modality on a score from 1 to 7. Figure 11.2[14] illustrates John's desired structural profile.

From assessment to an individual counselling programme

Multimodal counsellors take researcher Gordon Paul's[15] mandate very seriously: '*What* treatment, by *whom*, is most effective for *this* individual with *that* specific problem and under *which* set of circumstances?' (p. 111). In addition the *relationships of choice* are also considered. After the initial counselling or assessment session, assuming that the counsellor believes that he or she can offer the right type of help and approach to the client, they then negotiate a counselling programme.

As multimodal therapy is technically eclectic, it will use techniques and interventions from a variety of different therapies. Table 11.2[16] highlights the main techniques used. Although these are largely based on behaviour therapy, cognitive therapy and rational emotive behaviour therapy, techniques are also taken from other approaches, such as psychodynamic and Gestalt therapy. To avoid repetition, readers are guided to the other relevant chapters in this book to learn about the majority of these techniques. In this section we will focus on techniques and strategies which are used more exclusively in multimodal therapy.

TABLE 11.2 Frequently used techniques in multimodal therapy and training

Modality	Techniques/interventions	Modality	Techniques/interventions
Behaviour	Behaviour rehearsal	Cognition	Bibliotherapy
	Empty chair		Challenging faulty inferences
	Exposure programme		Cognitive rehearsal
	Fixed role therapy		Coping statements
	Modelling		Correcting misinformation
	Paradoxical intention		Disputing irrational beliefs
	Psychodrama		Focusing
	Reinforcement programmes		Positive self-statements
	Response prevention/cost		Problem-solving training
	Risk-taking exercises		Providing missing information
	Self-monitoring and		Rational proselytizing
	recording		Self-acceptance training
	Stimulus control		Thought stopping
	Shame attacking		
		Interpersonal	Assertiveness training
Affect	Anger expression		Communication training
	Anxiety/anger management		Contracting
	Feeling identification		Fixed role therapy
			Friendship/intimacy training
Sensation	Biofeedback		Graded sexual approaches
	Hypnosis		Paradoxical intentions
	Meditation		Role play
	Relaxation training		Social skills training
	Sensate focus training		
	Threshold training	Drugs/biology	Alcohol reduction programme
			Lifestyle changes, e.g. exercise,
Imagery	Anti-future-shock imagery		nutrition, etc.
	Associated imagery		Referral to physicians or other
	Aversive imagery		specialists
	Coping imagery		Stop smoking programme
	Implosion and imaginal		Weight reduction and maintenance
	exposure		programme
	Positive imagery		
	Rational emotive imagery		
	Time projection imagery		

A full modality profile

Once the modality profile consisting of the problem list divided into each modality has been noted down, then the counsellor and client negotiate techniques and interventions that can be used to help deal with each problem. Table 11.3[17] is John's full modality profile which will be discussed later in the Case Study. The modality profile guides the course of counselling, keeping the counsellor and client focused on the particular problems and the specific interventions. During the course of therapy, the profile is modified as new relevant information is obtained. It is important for clients to be involved with developing the counselling programme to ensure that they understand the rationale for each intervention

TABLE 11.3   John's full modality profile (or BASIC I.D. chart)

Modality	Problem	Proposed therapy programme
Behaviour	Eats/walks fast, always in a rush, hostile, competitive: indicative of type A behaviour	Discuss advantages of slowing down; disadvantages of rushing and being hostile; teach relaxation exercise; dispute self-defeating beliefs
	Avoidance of giving presentations	Exposure programme; teach necessary skills; dispute self-defeating beliefs
	Accident proneness	Discuss advantages of slowing down
Affect	Anxious when giving presentations	Anxiety management
	Guilt when work targets not achieved	Dispute self-defeating thinking
	Frequent angry outbursts at work	Anger management; dispute anger-inducing beliefs
Sensation	Tension in shoulders	Self-massage; muscle relaxation exercise
	Palpitations	Anxiety management, e.g. breathing relaxation technique, dispute catastrophic thinking
	Frequent headaches	Relaxation exercise and biofeedback
	Sleeping difficulties	Relaxation or self-hypnosis tape for bedtime use; behavioural retraining; possibly reduce caffeine intake
Imagery	Negative images of not performing well	Coping imagery focusing on giving adequate presentations
	Images of losing control	Coping imagery of dealing with difficult work situations and with presentations; 'step-up' imagery[18]
	Poor self-image	Positive imagery[19]
Cognition	I must perform well otherwise it will be awful and I couldn't stand it	Dispute self-defeating and stress-inducing beliefs; coping statements; cognitive restructuring; ABCDE paradigm;[20] bibliotherapy; coping imagery[21]
	I must be in control	
	Significant others should recognize my work	
	If I fail then I am a total failure	
Interpersonal	Passive/aggressive in relationships	Assertiveness training
	Manipulative tendencies at work	Discuss pros and cons of behaviour
	Always puts self first	Discuss pros and cons of behaviour
	Few supportive friends	Friendship training[22]
Drugs/biology	Feeling inexplicably tired	Improve sleeping and reassess; refer to GP
	Taking aspirins for headaches	Refer to GP; relaxation exercises
	Consumes 10 cups of coffee a day	Discuss benefits of reducing caffeine intake
	Poor nutrition and little exercise	Nutrition and exercise programme

recommended and take ownership of their own programme. Often clients will suggest interventions that will be helpful, such as joining an assertiveness, self-hypnosis, exercise, diet or meditation class. The counsellor will always take these ideas seriously as they may well be beneficial.

Second-order BASIC I.D.

Second-order BASIC I.D. is undertaken when the interventions or techniques applied to help a specific problem do not appear to have resolved it. This is a modality profile which solely focuses on the different aspects of a resistant problem, as opposed to the initial assessment which looks more at the overview or 'big picture'.

Tracking and bridging

Tracking is another procedure regularly used in multimodal counselling in which the 'firing order' of the different modalities is noted for a specific problem. Counselling interventions are linked to the sequence of the firing order of the modalities.

Clients often have a favoured modality which they may use to communicate with the counsellor, for example, talking about the sensations, cognitions or images they may experience. They would be known as 'sensory reactors', 'cognitive reactors' or 'imagery reactors' respectively. The highest scores on their structural profiles often reflect the modality reactor. Multimodal counsellors deliberately use a 'bridging' procedure to initially 'key into' a client's preferred modality, before gently exploring a modality that the client may be intentionally or unintentionally avoiding, such as the affect/emotion modality.

Format of a typical session

The format of sessions is adapted to what would enable the client to reach his or her therapeutic goals. However, it is often useful to employ a recognizable structure. This could include setting an agenda of therapeutic items the client and counsellor wish to discuss in the session. The agenda would usually include reviewing the client's homework assignments from the previous session; agreeing topics to be covered in the present session; negotiating further relevant homework assignments; eliciting client feedback about the session and tackling any problems that may have arisen during the session.

WHICH CLIENTS BENEFIT MOST?

Multimodal therapy has been shown to benefit children, adults and older client groups experiencing a wide range of problems. For example, those suffering from anxiety-related disorders such as agoraphobia, panic attacks, phobias, obsessive-compulsive disorders; depression, post-traumatic stress disorder; sexual problems; anorexia nervosa; obesity; enuresis; substance and alcohol abuse; airsickness; schizophrenia. As counsellors are expected to adjust their interpersonal style to each client, they may encounter fewer relationship difficulties when compared to other less flexible approaches. This flexible approach should lead to a reduced rate of attrition.

However, as with other therapies, multimodal therapy has its failures. Some clients are not prepared to face their fears, challenge their unhelpful thinking, use coping imagery, practise relaxation techniques, become assertive with significant others, etc. Others may have psychiatric disorders or other difficulties that prevent them from engaging in therapy. Some clients are in the pre-contemplative stage where they have not made up their minds to change and take on the responsibility of counselling. They may need to return to counselling at a later stage in their lives.

Case study

THE CLIENT

John was a 43-year-old married man with no children. He worked as manager of a branch of a large national food chain. He was referred by his doctor for counselling as suffering from occupational stress. He had been under pressure at work to reach new targets which he believed were unrealistic and unattainable. This led to angry outbursts at work which were causing interpersonal difficulties. For the past couple of months he had experienced sleeping difficulties, palpitations, tension and headaches. He was concerned that 'my performance at work is suffering and I just seem to be losing control'. His employers were concerned about the profitability of his branch and had become aware of his angry outbursts. They were willing to fund an initial six sessions of counselling.

THE THERAPY

John was sent an administration letter giving a time for the counselling session, details about the location, a client checklist (see Appendix 2) and a self-help book, *Stress Management: A Quick Guide.*[23]

At the beginning of the first session John was asked if he had any questions about the therapy or about the counsellor. He had read the pre-counselling material about the approach and enquired about the counsellor's qualifications and training. He understood the benefits of the counselling sessions being audio-recorded: he could listen to the tapes at home and go over any sections he had not fully grasped; the counsellor could listen to the sessions with his supervisor in confidence, to ensure that he had not overlooked any important issues and to receive useful guidance. (John liked the idea that three heads were better than two.)

John spent the next 15 minutes explaining his problems while the counsellor took a few notes of the key problems. The counsellor interjected occasionally to clarify any points he did not understand. The counsellor then described the BASIC I.D. assessment procedure:

Counsellor: In this approach to ensure that we have correctly understood the client's problems we usually focus on seven key areas or modalities. I'll use this whiteboard so we can both go through the different issues together. The first area to look at is Behaviour. [*Counsellor writes 'Behaviour' at the top left-hand corner of the whiteboard.*] You mentioned that you are 'always in a rush'. [*Counsellor writes this in central part of the whiteboard.*] Can you give me some specific examples?

John: I eat and walk fast. My wife always tells me to 'slow down'!

Counsellor: You mentioned that you are 'hostile' and 'competitive'.

John: Yes. Mainly at work although I can be outside of work too.

Counsellor: [*Counsellor writes 'hostile' and 'competitive' on the whiteboard.*] It sounds to me as if you have what is often known as 'Type A' behaviour.

John: You're right. I read an article about it once in a magazine.

Counsellor: [*Counsellor writes 'Type A behaviour' on the whiteboard.*] You mentioned that you avoid giving presentations at work and you've become accident prone. [*Counsellor writes these on the whiteboard.*] Are there any other behavioural problems that you would like to add to this list?

John: No. They are the main ones.

Counsellor: Okay. The next area we can examine is what is known as Affect or your Emotions. [*Counsellor writes 'Affect/emotions' on left-hand side of the whiteboard.*] You mentioned that you are 'anxious when giving presentations' and 'guilty when work targets not achieved'. [*Counsellor writes these on the whiteboard.*] Are there any other emotional problems that you would like to add to this list?

John: No. They are the main ones. Ah! I suppose that we should also mention my angry outbursts at work.

Counsellor: Okay. [*Counsellor writes this on the whiteboard.*]

This process was continued until each modality had been assessed. Table 11.1 is John's modality profile (see p. 148). As John had read the self-help book prior to the counselling session he was in a position to negotiate with his counsellor his own counselling programme. Table 11.3 (p. 152) is John's completed modality profile. The techniques and interventions were written on the right-hand side of the whiteboard corresponding to each particular problem. It was explained that the modality profile serves as 'working hypotheses' which can be modified or revised as new information arises. Before the end of the session John was introduced to the MLHI:

> *Counsellor*: I have found it very useful if my clients complete this questionnaire at home. [*Counsellor showed John the MLHI*.] It saves me taking up a lot of your time asking questions about different aspects of your life. It will not only focus on your anxiety and job performance, but may provide us with information that would help us deal with your other problems too.
>
> *John*: Sounds like a good idea.
>
> *Counsellor*: You can either bring it to the next session or send it to me beforehand to give me time to read it.
>
> *John*: I'll pop it in the post.
>
> *Counsellor*: In that case do make sure you mark it private and confidential.

Careful analysis of John's full modality profile indicated that teaching him a suitable relaxation technique would help him deal or cope with a number of different problems. This was brought to his attention and he agreed to listen to a commercially manufactured relaxation tape once a day before his evening dinner.

The next session was seven days later. An agenda for the session was set which included looking at how he had got on with the relaxation tape; queries regarding the MLHI; drawing his structural profiles; modifying his self-defeating beliefs; and a new homework assignment. Figures 11.1 and 11.2 were John's structural profiles. It is worth noting that his structural profile (Figure 11.1) had scores of 7 in sensation and cognitive modalities. When high structural profile scores occur in a particular modality, the person is often responsive to techniques used from that modality. John found the sensation and cognitive techniques were very helpful. John was both a 'sensory and cognitive reactor'. It was agreed that session 3 would be a fortnight later.

Over the remaining sessions John found that attempting to slow down, modifying his beliefs, using the relaxation exercises and coping imagery very beneficial. He reduced his caffeine intake and found that his sleeping improved. The intervals between the last two sessions were increased to four weeks to give him the opportunity to apply the range of techniques he had learnt in counselling.

By the last session John had learnt to slow down, had reduced his feelings of guilt and anxiety, and although he was still prone under extremes of pressure to become angry at least it was more controlled. Physically he was feeling much better and more relaxed with fewer headaches and better sleeping patterns. In addition he had modified his self-defeating beliefs.

The one area that required more hard work was the interpersonal modality. As he was feeling less stressed his interpersonal behaviour was less hostile and aggressive but he still wanted to improve it. John and the counsellor agreed that he would attend a follow-up session three months later to review progress and monitor how he was getting on using assertiveness skills.

REFERENCES

1 Lazarus, A.A. (1958) 'New methods in psychotherapy: a case study', *South African Medical Journal*, 32: 660–4.
2 Palmer, S. and Dryden, W. (1995) *Counselling for Stress Problems*. London: Sage.
3 Lazarus, A.A. (1989) *The Practice of Multimodal Therapy: Systematic, Comprehensive, and Effective Psychotherapy*. Baltimore: Johns Hopkins University Press.
4 Lazarus, A.A. (1991) 'The multimodal approach with adult outpatients' in W. Dryden (ed.), *The Essential Arnold Lazarus*. London: Whurr.
5 Lazarus, A.A. (1989) op. cit.
6 Palmer, S. and Dryden, W. (1995) op. cit.
7 Zilbergeld, B. (1982) 'Bespoke therapy', *Psychology Today*, 16: 85–6.
8 Palmer, S. and Szymanska, K. (1994) 'A checklist for clients interested in receiving counselling, psychotherapy or hypnosis', *The Rational Emotive Behaviour Therapist*, 2 (1): 25–7.
9 Palmer, S. and Dryden, W. (1995) op. cit. and Lazarus, A.A. (1989) op. cit.
10 Palmer, S. (1997) 'Modality assessment', in S. Palmer and G. McMahon (eds), *Client Assessment*. London: Sage.
11 Lazarus, A.A. and Lazarus, C.N. (1991) *Multimodal Life History Inventory*. Champaign, IL: Research Press.
12 Lazarus, A.A. (1989) op. cit.
13 Palmer, S. (1997) op. cit.
14 Palmer, S. (1997) op. cit.
15 Paul, G.L. (1967) 'Strategy of outcome research in psychotherapy', *Journal of Consulting Psychology*, 331: 109–18.
16 Palmer, S. (1997) op. cit.
17 Palmer, S. (1997) op. cit.
18 Lazarus, A.A. (1958) op. cit.
19 Lazarus, A.A. (1958) op. cit. and Palmer, S. and Strickland, L. (1996) *Stress Management: A Quick Guide*. Dunstable: Folens Publishers.
20 Lazarus, A.A. (1958) op. cit.
21 Lazarus, A.A. (1958) op. cit.
22 Lazarus, A.A. (1958) op. cit.
23 Palmer, S. and Strickland, L. (1996) op. cit.

SUGGESTED READING

Lazarus, A.A. (1989) *The Practice of Multimodal Therapy: Systematic, Comprehensive, and Effective Psychotherapy*. Baltimore: Johns Hopkins University Press. The key revised text on multimodal therapy written by the originator, Arnold Lazarus. It offers a practical, step-by-step guide to every phase of assessment and therapy and includes transcripts of actual sessions. A glossary of 37 therapeutic techniques is included.

Lazarus, A.A. (1997) *Brief but Comprehensive Psychotherapy: The Multimodal Way*. New York: Springer Publishing Company. This book illustrates how multimodal therapy can be brief yet still efficient. Lazarus writes in a lucid style and includes many case examples. The Appendices contain a number of useful questionnaires.

Palmer, S. and Dryden, W. (1995) *Counselling for Stress Problems*. London: Sage. This work provides a comprehensive view of stress counselling and stress management from a multimodal perspective. Techniques and strategies are discussed in depth and are illustrated by numerous case examples with session transcripts.

Palmer, S. and Strickland, L. (1996) *Stress Management: A Quick Guide*. Dunstable: Folens Publishers. Suitable for the layperson, this provides a working model of stress and key stress management techniques. This excellent self-help book covers the main methods used in multimodal therapy and helps the client to negotiate his or her own counselling programme.

DISCUSSION ISSUES

1 In what ways does multimodal therapy differ from other forms of therapy?
2 Critically discuss the usefulness of the BASIC I.D. assessment procedures.
3 Flexible interpersonal styles of the counsellor which match client needs can reduce premature termination of therapy. Discuss.
4 The practice of multimodal therapy places high demands on the therapist. Discuss.

12

NEURO-LINGUISTIC PROGRAMMING

Juliet Grayson and Brigid Proctor

NLP is a systemic way of working. This means we see people as a system of interactions (for example physical, mental, emotional and spiritual) and also see the system within a system within a system (for example, a child within a family, living in a village, living in England and so on).

NLP arose from studying the structure of an individual's everyday experience in detail, particularly focusing on people who were considered exceptional in their field. From this NLP developed:

- a set of presuppositions (guiding principles and attitudes)
- a methodology for modelling (what to observe and how to 'frame' that)
- a system of coding (the how to – a detailed description)
- a series of models (different ways of understanding)
- a trail of techniques (things to do)

An NLP therapist will encourage us to interact trustingly with our unconscious, and help us learn how to do that using movements, sensations, sounds, language and visualizations. The words we use will be taken seriously and literally. By paying close attention to language, and sharing an understanding of the deeper implications of using certain words, phrases and tenses, the therapist will help us to explore and experience different ways of thinking, and to consider alternative meanings behind our hopes, behaviours and experiences. When coming for help we will probably have explored most of the conscious solutions (those we are aware of). The NLP process is designed to help us become more aware and use *all* the possibilities which are within us, including the unconscious ones, which have been out of our awareness, lying dormant and unknown.

DEVELOPMENT OF THE THERAPY

Richard Bandler and John Grinder, two Americans at the University of Santa Cruz (Richard a student of mathematics, and John a professor of linguistics) became fascinated by the question 'What is the difference that makes the difference between everyday competence and excellence?' They decided to do an in-depth study of Fritz Perls (the founder of Gestalt therapy), Virginia Satir (a founder of family therapy and systemic therapy) and Milton Erickson (founder of the American Society of Clinical Hypnosis). They looked at their patterns of language and behaviour – what they *actually said and did* when doing their work, as opposed to what they said they were doing – what we would call their 'map of the world'. The modellers discovered that their maps were very impoverished versions of their actual practice, and discovered a rich variety of extra unconscious (out-of-awareness) attitudes and skills. Thus the field of NLP was born, in Santa Cruz, USA in the early 1970s. They were soon joined by a group of other people, and incorporated relevant skills, information and models from the fields of systems theory, anthropology, behavioural psychology and linguistics.

In Britain the Association of Neuro-Linguistic Programming (ANLP) is the accrediting body recognized by the United Kingdom Council for Psychotherapy (UKCP). ANLP has its own code of ethics, and has been a member organization of UKCP and its forerunners since 1987. It established a Psychotherapy and Counselling section in 1992.

THEORY AND BASIC CONCEPTS

NLP is curious about the rich complexity of people. The broad tools which each person uses to process the world (sight, sound, sensations, etc.) are the same, yet the way in which they use those tools is individual. It is an underpinning concept of NLP that the processes of generalization, deletion and distortion will be common to all.

Generalization, distortion and deletion

Humans need to selectively edit their experience of the world. Not to do so would be overwhelming. We all make generalizations. I have generalized that chairs are for sitting on, and that wood put together in a certain way is a chair.

We also delete large parts of our experience. Again, not to do so would bring too much information into the conscious mind. No doubt as you read this you are not aware of the pressure of your feet on the floor (or were not until I brought it to your awareness). By the way, which foot currently carries more weight? And how aware are you of the sounds outside your window? Much of what is happening around us is selectively deleted.

The third process that happens is that we distort – for instance we turn processes into completed events. Have you ever stereotyped a person on one short interaction or impression? Maybe later you realized that you had made an error of judgement – that judgement is itself an example of distorting by turning a process into an event and deciding 'how someone is'. You may then be closed to other information which does not fit with your original impression.

Because we are continuously generalizing, deleting and distorting, we each live in a model of the world which will be an impoverished and distorted version of what is actually there. Of course many people believe their versions to be the truth.

Modelling and coding

One of the skills NLP has crystallized is the ability to capture an individual's experience – a skill known as modelling. It involves discovering someone's 'map' or 'model' of the world, both that which they are conscious of *and* also that which is outside their awareness (for example their beliefs, or physiology). Such is the level of detail in the map that it can then be taught on to someone else. The chunks of information that will need to be discovered to pass the skill on are very small, and so a language or 'coding' has developed.

This modelling has various applications. We can model 'excellent' abilities, for instance how people who had a strong phobia about spiders overcame it (apparently) spontaneously. This skill can then be taught on to release other people who have a phobia and want to live free of that. We can also model 'stuck states' (for example, how a client sustains jealousy), and thereby gain greater awareness, understanding and choice about maintaining this state.

From modelling Fritz Perls, Virginia Satir and Milton Erickson a set of supportive and empowering beliefs about people emerged. These are known as presuppositions, and in NLP we act 'as if' these were true. As Robert Dilts, a co-developer of NLP said, 'An NLP technique used without a deep understanding and demonstration of the presuppositions is not actually NLP.'

The presuppositions

Basically there are two KEY presuppositions out of which others emerge, 'The map is not the territory' and 'Life and mind are systemic processes'.

'The map is not the territory'
This phrase coined by Alfred Korzybski – the father of semantics – means that each person is responding to his or her *perception* of how things are in the world, not to the world itself. It follows that if we are all responding to our own perceptions of reality then *each person will have his or her own individual map of the world*. We will all perceive the world slightly differently, and apprehend it through our own filters and perceptions, which means that *no individual has the 'right' or 'true' map* (although many believe their map is not a map but the truth). This underlying distortion is so deeply embedded in our culture that it is hard to see. Gregory Bateson was an anthropologist, psychologist and biologist interested in systems and their interaction, who had a profound influence in NLP. He once wrote:

The story is told of Picasso, that a stranger in a railway carriage accosted him with the challenge 'Why don't you paint things as they are?' Picasso demurred, saying that he did not quite understand what the other gentleman meant, and the stranger then produced from his wallet a photo of his wife. 'I mean', he said, 'like that. That's how she is.' Picasso coughed hesitantly and said 'she is rather small, isn't she? And somewhat flat.'[1]

A photo is a representation of reality, but we equate it with reality.

NLP further assumes that *people already have (or potentially have) all of the resources they need to act more effectively.* Acting as if this is true is very empowering. NLP also works from the 'belief' that *people make the best choices available to them* given the possibilities and the capabilities that they perceive available to them.

'Life and mind are systemic processes'

Each individual is a system, of the mind, body, spirit. Our relationships with others also form a system as do our societies, and our universe – joining together to create an ecology of systems and subsystems, all of which interact with and mutually influence each other.

Seeing things in this systemic way, like a series of wheels and cogs that turn each other and are inextricably linked, brings an awareness of and sensitivity to the larger system. Since *it is not possible to isolate completely any part of the system from the rest of the system*, and people cannot *not* influence each other, any change in clients in therapy may also cause a shift in clients' relationships with their partners and significant people in their lives.

People will also form feedback loops for each other, so that a person will be affected by the results that their own actions make on other people. As for interactions within a system – they are not all on the same level. For example, it is useful to separate behaviour from 'identity', and realize that what 'I do' is not all of 'who I am'.

Systems are 'self-organizing' and naturally seek states of balance and stability. This implies that *all behaviour has a positive intention* and there is a context in which every behaviour has value. So the positive purpose behind fear, for example, is often safety; and the positive purpose behind anger may be to maintain boundaries. So when exploring the expression of a problematic behaviour, we trust in and seek the positive intention.

Life itself is a process and not a completed event, and so we can say that all of the information that comes in life is merely information. This leads to the belief *there are no failures, only feedback.* We can only say we have failed when something is completed.

Human nature and health

In NLP we believe that living by these presuppositions will enhance people's lives. You may be curious to discover how NLP thinks of someone who does not seem to be living fully in the world in the way in which they might choose. This is what Bandler and Grinder have to say.

> In coming to understand how it is that some people continue to cause themselves pain and anguish, it has been important for us to realise that they are not bad, crazy or sick. They are, in fact, making the best choices from those of which they are aware, that is, the best choices available in their own particular models [maps of the world]. In other words, human beings' behaviour, no matter how bizarre it may first appear to be, makes sense when it is seen in the context of the choices generated by their model. The difficulty is not that they are making the wrong choice, but that they do not have enough choices – they don't have a richly focused image of the world. The most pervasive paradox of the human condition which we see is that the processes which allow us to survive, grow, change, and experience joy are the same processes which allow us to maintain an impoverished model of the world – *our ability to manipulate symbols, that is to create models* . . . we commit the error of mistaking the model for reality.[2] (our italics)

We have been systematically taught how to ignore some things, and include others. Most of us have been brought up with very poor maps of how feeling and behaviour works, both from within our family system, and also on a cultural level where, for example, not being successful the first time is construed as failure, and leads to feelings of shame.

So how does all this work in practice?

PRACTICE

The practice of NLP will vary according to the way individual practitioners choose to use their skills, tools and techniques, with each individual client. There is no set format for an NLP session. There will however be some broad goals that may generalize for all NLP practitioners, and some key points to which NLP practitioners will pay attention.

The goals of NLP

Building a relationship and working alliance between the therapist and the client, with the therapist holding the NLP presuppositions and attitudes (of respect, curiosity, open-mindedness and possibility), is the key to creating a space where the client can change.

Initially a conscious contract will be agreed, with clear goals for the work. The therapist will seek an explicit and detailed understanding of how the client (and therapist) will recognize that those goals have been achieved. What will the client be feeling, what will they see, what will they be saying to themselves?

The therapist will be particularly careful to ascertain the level at which the client is wanting and able to work. An NLP therapist will work differently with an identity level issue – 'I'm not that kind of person' – to an issue at the level of capability – 'I don't know *how* to . . .'

The therapist will encourage the client to ask questions of themselves, to find a wider map of the world, so that more choices become available. This might include deepening the client's experience of their own internal sensations, self-talk and visualizations that they have been disregarding.

The therapist will assist the client in appreciating the positive intention in behaviours that are (or have been) seen as 'problematic'. He/she will strengthen the clients' awareness of their conscious/unconscious feedback loop, thus helping the client to become aware of the signals that their own mind/body system is sending to them, so they can begin to be curious about what these signals may mean.

The therapist may wish to guide the client to explore and understand the deeper structure of the problem, for example the secondary gains, the benefits of maintaining the 'problem' state, and limiting beliefs that may have been formed – to uncover deletions, generalizations, and distortions of the problem so that a richer perception of the underlying issues and patterns can be obtained.

The relationship between the therapist and the client

One of the processes that Grinder and Bandler observed was the art of building deep rapport with the client, in order to enter into the client's world. Indeed the way Milton Erickson entered the system has been described as so complete that he was in the 'weave of the total complex'. Robert Dilts, a leading NLP trainer, author and co-developer, wrote that:

> The process of healing requires an intention [a goal], a relationship [rapport], and a ritual [technique] . . . While external techniques and tools may be used mechanically to . . . aid the healing process, the source of healing is within the system of the individual.[3]

Non-verbal clues from the client provide feedback to the therapist

The therapists whom the originators of NLP observed had an acute degree of sensitivity to tiny physiological changes, for example facial colour change, the size of the lips changing, tightness across the forehead, eye movements and breathing shifts. They used these non-verbal clues from the client as feedback, often without being consciously aware of what they were doing.

In NLP we place strong emphasis on reading tiny changes in body language. The therapist will use this as a guide in helping the client achieve their desired state. It becomes possible to explore and understand much of the unconscious internal communication, and how the client both manages and expresses what is happening for him/herself. Clients learn to know, trust and appreciate their own unique system.

NLP techniques

The therapist, having paid attention to how the experience of a particular client is coded, by noticing language patterns and physiological changes can offer a myriad of specific techniques that enable him or her to experience the effects of conscious and unconscious patterns of behaviour, memories and goals. Much NLP work uses such experiential play, which can be engaging, often amusing, whilst 'moving' clients profoundly. In outline, a few of these are:

Creating well-formed outcomes
Establishing goals which

- are achievable
- are stated in the positive ('I don't want to hold back in that meeting' may become 'I want to speak up')
- fit with the kind of person the client sees him or herself as being
- will have effects on the people around the client that the client is willing to tolerate
- have clear evidence that will let both the client and the therapist know when they have achieved the goal
- acknowledge the resources that are needed to achieve the goal

Anchoring techniques
These use the process of association to create a 'trigger' or an 'anchor' for a response. A naturally occurring experience of this is the smell of newly cut grass. When later we smell newly cut grass again, it acts as an anchor to elicit a state, and takes us back to an earlier time when we smelt that before.

In therapy we may help clients learn how to re-experience, for instance, a delightful, enjoyable, and creative occasion. By reliving this in the present, they explore and learn how they can 'trigger' this response for themselves, discovering how to re-access that 'creative' state appropriately and consciously whenever they wish to in the future.

First, second and third positions
This involves seeing a situation from three different perspectives.

First position is standing in your own shoes, living the experience. Second position is becoming the other person, seeing the world as if through their eyes, taking on their 'map of the world', beliefs and physiology. Third position is taking that of an objective observer – as if you are standing on a balcony. In third you are able to see from a dispassionate perspective the two people over there who are having a discussion or dispute – and you are not involved in the emotional reactions. By being able to get multiple perspectives on a situation, and also see yourself from someone else's point of view, this model can allow complex information to become available, often changing the way a situation is perceived and experienced.

Reframing

An event is given meaning according to the 'frame' within which it is set. When meaning changes, then a person's responses and behaviours also change. A client who complained of tiredness two weeks after a serious operation realized that this was in fact her body slowing her down in order to allow her to heal. This reframe allowed her to accept her condition and rest, thereby speeding her recovery. By changing the frame, we change the meaning.

Talking to parts

For many of us there is an internal dialogue which continues at a level that is barely conscious. This can be energy consuming. Talking between different parts of ourselves is one of the techniques used to enable clients to become more aware, and allow these conversations to happen more usefully. An NLP therapist may have the client communicate directly with different parts of the body, or different aspects of the self.

These are examples of some of the powerful therapeutic techniques NLP uses. We would like to stress that such techniques need to be underwritten by a developed self-awareness and integrity, respect for other people and appreciation of diversity.

The process of change

Bandler and Grinder say:

> People who come to us in therapy typically have pain in their lives and experience little or no choice in matters which they consider important. All therapies are confronted with the problem of responding adequately to such people. Responding adequately in this context means to us assisting in changing the client's experience in some way which *enriches it*. Rarely do therapies accomplish this by changing the world. Their approach, then, is typically to change the client's experience of the world.[4]

People get stuck in habitual ways of looking at things, making it difficult to think creatively and flexibly. By reframing their own experience, working 'as if' the presuppositions we have written about are true, we discover that people 'seem' to heal in a natural self-organizing manner. A behaviour that may have been seen as problematic, for example being depressed, may come to be seen as a useful, but ultimately ineffective form of self-protection.

In systemic terms, when fluctuations from the environment become too much for a system (for example a person), it cannot maintain its structure, and it becomes internally chaotic and unstable, to the point where the finest nudge brings things to a screeching halt. The system (person) here would be the current belief systems about him/herself and the universe, and the degree to which s/he can see and experience the infinite connections that make up their own personal universe. At this point the system has the possibility to break down, and cease to exist as an organized system; to revert to a previous condition by massive deletion and distortion; or to spontaneously reorder itself in a new way – out of the chaos comes a new order, a more evolved system. To 'choose' this option people usually need a minimum of social support and self-esteem. This is where counsellors are often called on, and where NLP practitioners will consciously engage with the client.

WHICH CLIENTS BENEFIT MOST?

As NLP has such wide interpretation, and there is no prescriptive format to follow then it can be of value to a wide variety of clients.

Traditionally NLP has been thought of as a short-term, effective therapy. However, many practitioners also use it for deep and long-term work. The basic orientation of NLP is solution-focused, looking forward to changes people want, and to how they might achieve those. It therefore has an orientation towards the future.

NLP has realized the benefits of being able to be fully 'in' an experience (associate fully into a particular state), and also to be able to step back and see a problem as separate from oneself (disassociate). The ability to associate and disassociate appropriately is particularly useful, and NLP has some particularly valuable techniques using this skill in relation to exams, phobias and traumas.

Case study

THE CLIENT

Jenny is in her mid-forties. Her mother died two years ago, and she has found this very difficult to accept. She came to therapy to resolve some of the issues around her mother. My intention here is to show one piece of work she did, and the subsequent impact.

THE THERAPY

I explained to Jenny that there is a process – a model – that is great for eliciting information. I mentioned that as we sort out where different pieces belong great changes can occur, that she would step back and see the problem clearly delineated, sorted into categories, and separate from herself. I pointed out that just these things in themselves can create a very different attitude to the whole issue. I asked if she would like to explore and experiment with this. She seemed enthusiastic.

We used a model called the SCORE.

S Symptom
C Cause
O Outcome
R Resource
E Effect

First we looked at the 'Symptom' space, and I framed this by saying, 'Let's look at the situation now, how is it for you now – what's the problem?' She said 'I'm not able to look at a photograph of Mum,' and as she said this I noticed she moved her head and body back, her face reddened, and her breathing quickened. She described how she physically could not bring herself to look at a photograph of her mother, had no photos of her mother in her house, and could not visit her father because he did have photos around.

I asked her gently what she wanted ('Outcome') – and she said: 'I want to be able to look at a photograph of my mother.' As she said this she breathed out a long sigh, and her hands became still and rested on her lap. I felt some resolution, that she had clarified her goal and I supposed that she did too. I suggested exploring the 'Cause'.

'So what led to this situation arising, a situation where the idea of looking at a photo of your mother has seemed hard?' Jenny talked of the close relationship she had had with her mother, and how hard her death had been, how Jenny still could not believe it was true. Jenny's voice became quieter, her breathing more shallow still, and the hands became clutched tightly across her chest.

It seemed time to move on to the 'Effect'. A number of things influenced this decision. She had been in a tense and distressed state for a while, and I was also aware of the time and the need to sustain the rhythm of the process. I began by pacing (carefully reflecting what she had said), then leading her on to look at the 'Effect'.

'So the situation has been about not wanting to look at a photograph of your mother, and you had a very close relationship with your mother, and she was always nearby. Let's leave those feelings behind for a moment, let's step out of all of that, and think instead of what you want. You want to be able to look at a photograph of your mother. Imagine now, that you *can* do this, and I know this may seem difficult right now, but just imagine being at a time in your life when you can enjoy looking at a photograph of your mother, and it feels absolutely OK, what does that do for you? What will the effect of that be in your life?'

Jenny began talking. At first I could see she was still in a state of distress – a necessary stage of the process in which it is almost physically impossible to tap fresh resources. As she talked I noticed her face began to light up and she gradually became more animated as she imagined herself . . .

'Well, I guess that being able to look at the photograph of Mum would mean that I have accepted her death, and then I could begin to remember her, and some of the happy times we had.' Jenny began to make larger gestures as she spoke of this.

'So as you are able to remember the happy times with your mother, because you can look at her photo and feel OK, what does that bring you, or allow you to do?' I asked, in a tone of gentle curiosity, reflecting back not only her words, the varied tone and faster speed, but also her gestures, thus matching the way she had expressed herself.

'Well', said Jenny, 'If I can bear to look at photos of my Mum then I'll be able to go to their house and visit Dad – at the moment he has to come round to me – I can't bear to go into his house and see pictures of her all over the place.'

At this point I felt it was time to move on. Jenny seemed to have a sense of the benefits, and I could see from her physiology, from the tone and speed of her voice, that she was in a very different state from earlier in the session. I asked what 'Resources' she might need. She told me that talking it through had helped, she had realized it was important not only to her but also to her father. She felt that remembering this would help in any difficult moments. She also remarked that breathing more deeply changed how she felt, and she could use that. She also said she just needed more time and said: 'When I look at the photo it will mean that I have accepted that I'm never going to see my mother in the flesh again, that she really has gone. A part of me knows that, but there's part of me that still doesn't want to accept that. Whilst I don't look then I can feel her to be alive and just away for a while.' This demonstrated an acceptance of the positive intention of what she had perceived as problematic.

I encouraged her to trust that her own wisdom would let her know when it was time to look at the photo, and that she would know when and how she wanted to do that.

When we considered what the original 'Symptom' had been, Jenny realized that her experience of it had completely shifted, that she no longer felt it to be such a problem. It wasn't that she would be able to look at a photo yet, but she no longer saw not looking as a problem. Now she saw it as a choice. She had already begun to organize her own healing in relation to this issue.

Jenny and I continued to work together for the next few months, working on issues mainly to do with Jenny's health which was not good at this time. We did not discuss the photograph again until about three months later, when Jenny walked in and said, 'I've brought the photo of my mum, it's in this carrier bag. I may not look at it today. I haven't looked at it yet.'

I said, 'You let me know if you feel you want to look. I'll leave it up to you to decide when or whether you want to look.'

Twenty minutes later Jenny said, 'OK, let's look now', and we spent the rest of the session with her looking, crying and talking to her mother in the picture. It was a very beautiful experience for me, and I was delighted to have been privileged to share it with her.

In the earlier session a number of things had been achieved. She had begun to make clearer distinctions and discovered extra information. Realizing that her physiology was linked to the state associated with each space, she had discovered the power of changing her breathing and how that changed her state. She also began to trust the wisdom of her own self, and her ability to understand her own healing process.

REFERENCES

1 Bateson, G. and Bateson, M.C. (1988) *Angels Fear: An Investigation into the Nature and Meaning of the Sacred.* London: Rider Books, p. 161.
2 Bandler, R. and Grinder, J. (1975) *The Structure of Magic: A Book about Language and Therapy.* Palo Alto, CA: Science and Behavior Books Inc. p. 14.
3 Dilts, R.B. (1995) *Strategies of Genius, Vol. III, Sigmund Freud, Leonardo da Vinci, Nikola Tesla.* Capitola, CA: Meta Publications, p. 293.
4 Bandler, R. and Grinder, J. (1975) op. cit., p. 156.

SUGGESTED READING

Andreas, C. and Andreas, S. (1989) *Heart of the Mind: Engaging your Inner Power to Change.* Utah: Real People Press. This book centres on case presentations and personal transformations using NLP. It includes areas dealing with abuse, shame and guilt, resolving grief, decision-making and motivation, weight loss, violence and more.

Bandler, R. and Grinder, J. (1993) *Frogs into Princes.* Utah: Real People Press. Written by the originators of NLP, this book teaches you about the basic NLP techniques in an immediate and humorous way.

Lankton, S. (1993) *Practical Magic: A Translation of Basic NLP into Clinical Psychotherapy.* Capitola, CA: Meta Publications. A book for established therapists who wish to use NLP in their work, this relates NLP techniques to other schools of psychotherapy.

O'Connor, J. and McDermott, I. (1995) *Principles of NLP.* London: Thorsons. This is a valuable introduction to NLP as well as a guide to applying the fundamental principles – the presuppositions – which are at the heart of NLP.

DISCUSSION ISSUES

1 (a) Close your eyes, and for a moment take on the belief that 'the world is a truly dangerous place'. Really allow yourself to step fully into believing that . . . take your time to build the internal feelings, and notice any sounds or pictures. After a few minutes open your eyes, look around, and notice what you see. Spend three minutes looking around you, maybe even walking around the room.

   (b) Shake that off – think of sitting on the top of a mountain looking at a breathtaking view – to let go of that other state.

   (c) Now close your eyes, and take on the belief that 'the world is a friendly and completely safe place'. Spend time allowing that sensation to build. After a few minutes open your eyes, looking around you notice what you notice, and maybe walk around the room.

(d) In small groups discuss the different experiences. Be aware that you just utilized two very different maps of the world. How fully were you able to engage in each one? What caught your attention when you opened your eyes? Which belief was easiest to take on?

2 (a) Imagine a particular issue which you consider a problem.

(b) Now think of the wisest person you know. Step inside their skin, take on their beliefs, and their physiology (posture, the way they hold their body, facial expression, gestures, etc.), *become the wise person*. Look at the problem from their perspective. What supportive insight would you, as a wise person, offer them about that problem, and what steps would you have them take in relation to moving the situation forward?

(c) Now become a very young child. Step inside his/her skin, and take on all of his/her beliefs. Allow yourself as this child to be really creative. What supportive insight would you, the child, offer them about that problem, and what steps would you suggest he/she takes in relation to moving the situation forward?

(d) Now become yourself towards the end of your life, as an old person. Look back at the person who had that problem in the past, see how they resolved it, what steps they took, what were the important things for them to understand. What would you pass on to the younger you, now you see the situation from this perspective?

(e) Discuss the experience, and the insight you have gained. What particularly surprised or delighted you in this exercise?

3 Think of something you have avoided doing (for example dancing in public, expressing anger, or writing a report). In small groups brainstorm what the positive intentions of this behaviour could be. Try each idea on, and see which of them fits the best. Understand that a part of yourself has had a positive intention in relation to this behaviour.

4 (a) Take the following two sentences and begin to notice the generalizations, deletions and distortions in them. 'The cat sat on the mat.' (Which cat, what colour was the cat, where was the mat, what kind of mat, was it a four-legged cat, was the mat a mat or a carpet . . . ?) 'Nobody loves me any more.'

(b) Discuss the impact of making these kinds of generalizations, deletions and distortions.

13

PERSON-CENTRED COUNSELLING AND PSYCHOTHERAPY

Sarah Hawtin

Person-centred therapy* is based on the fundamental belief that human beings are essentially trustworthy, social and creative. The practical expression of this belief is the willingness of the therapist to vacate the position of expert and instead to work to enable a client to realize their own resources and self-understanding. Person-centred counselling emphasizes our internal perceptual and emotional world as the source of understanding for our thoughts, feelings and actions. The approach is humanistic and also contains existential elements.

Although person-centred therapy stresses the importance of individual experience, in essence it is a theory of relationships; it acknowledges our interdependence in a way which provides a route to deep and acceptant communication with others. This is nowhere clearer than in person-centred group work. This has included vast encounter groups and cross-cultural gatherings, for instance in South Africa and Northern Ireland.

DEVELOPMENT OF THE THEORY

The founder of person-centred therapy was the psychologist Carl Ransom Rogers (1902–87). Rogers developed a passionate belief in the potential of all individuals to flourish in conditions which were supportive, respectful and genuinely trusting of them. This was in radical opposition to much established psychological theory of the time and owes a debt to the educational philosophers John Dewey and William H. Kilpatrick, both of whom were powerful influences in Rogers' early thinking. The mark of existential theologians Paul Tillich and Martin Buber is also clear in Rogers' understanding of human nature.

---

* In the person-centred approach there is no practical distinction between counselling and psychotherapy. Whether long- or short-term the fundamental nature of the therapeutic venture is the same. As a result, I have used 'counselling' and 'psychotherapy' interchangeably.

In 1942 Rogers published his ideas in his first book *Counselling and Psychotherapy* and followed this in 1951 with *Client-Centred Therapy*, thereby establishing his position as a major figure in the world of counselling and psychotherapy.

Debate and discussion has always ensured the growth of person-centred therapy, including the emergence of new 'variants'. Person-centred family therapy,[1] a separate school of Focusing[2] and the application of person-centred principles to working with clients diagnosed with major mental illness[3] are just three such developments. More recently the spiritual dimension of person-centred therapy has also been explored.[4,5] Despite his early religious aspirations, it was only in his later years that Rogers considered transcendental experiences within counselling.

The basic principles of the person-centred approach are now widely accepted as the basis for forming positive and enabling relationships and it has been profoundly influential in education and the provision of statutory and voluntary health and social services. As a therapeutic orientation it has a world-wide following, with practitioners on all continents.

THEORY AND BASIC CONCEPTS

At the heart of person-centred theory is a basic optimism about our capabilities and primary motivation. Given the right conditions, we will flourish and thrive and this will lead in turn to behaviour which is socially responsible and collectively enhancing.

Making the most of ourselves: the actualizing tendency

Rogers asserted that each person is a unified whole, or *organism*, with a single basic motivational tendency; the tendency to actualize. As Rogers put it: 'This is the inherent tendency of the organism to develop all its capacities in ways which serve to maintain or enhance the organism'.[6] This *actualizing tendency* is not an inner force which impels us, but rather a basic disposition we exhibit in ordering and approaching life. (This is similar to the fact that water always flows to the lowest point, not because something within a body of water drives it, but because the qualities and characteristics of water dispose it to behave this way.) It is an innate capacity to sort and order our internal and external experience in a way that is enhancing for us. Therefore, as we grow and develop, we naturally approach other people, the wider environment and our own experiences in a manner that takes us towards that which is positive and helps us avoid those things which are negative for our well-being.

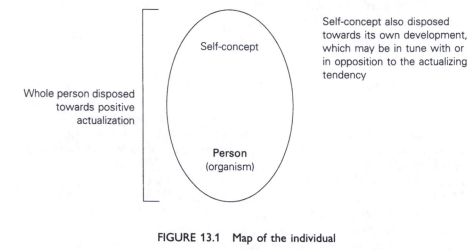

Self-concept also disposed towards its own development, which may be in tune with or in opposition to the actualizing tendency

Self-concept

Whole person disposed towards positive actualization

Person (organism)

FIGURE 13.1   Map of the individual

Learning who we are: the development of the self-concept

Although person-centred theory conceptualizes the individual as a unified whole, one aspect of our being plays a central role in our development and functioning. This is the *self-concept* and roughly corresponds with our conscious awareness of ourselves (see Figure 13.1). The self-concept begins to form at an early age, when we start to perceive that we are separate from those around us. We begin to think of ourselves in terms of 'I' and 'me'; as a unique person with various characteristics. This self-knowledge and awareness is not articulated at first, but as we grow, and particularly as we learn to speak, we gradually consolidate our ideas about ourselves. If the development of our self-knowledge occurs completely in tune with the actualizing tendency, that is if we come to know ourselves as the person we actually are, then we continue along the path of full and satisfying living. However, coming to know ourselves does not occur in isolation and it is the relational aspect of our being which causes problems.

Losing trust in ourselves and the source of distress

Our self-understanding develops at a time when we are heavily dependent upon others for our physical and emotional well-being. This sets up a potential conflict between our growth and the satisfaction of those around us. Giving and receiving affection, acceptance and love are positive in themselves, for such feelings are inherently satisfying; however, the need to gain approval and warmth from others may conflict with what we perceive as good for ourselves.

For example, imagine a small child drawing a picture of her house. She puts in a bright yellow sun and lots of pink and blue flowers. Her chosen surface is the flat cream walls of her parent's best front room which sets off her picture wonderfully. As she draws she feels happy and pleased that she can do something so nice for her parents. She loves them and feels this shows her love and will bring their affection in return. Needless to say, the response of her parents is unexpected and shocking. They become angry and their voices are hard and frighten her. She is sent to her room and is only allowed to come down sometime later to be told that drawing on the walls again will be severely punished.

How can the child come to terms with this? In creating the picture she is guided by the part of her that feels it is a creative and positive act. Now she has to absorb a completely different evaluation from her parents. She needs and wants their love, so, to maintain her trust in them, she begins to reinterpret her own behaviour and feelings. She comes to feel she was mistaken: for her parents to be so cold, she must have done something wrong. In doing so, she cuts off from her own feelings of hurt, creating a division within herself.

In one sense, responding this way is self-preservation, for it brings a greater certainty of being cared for by her parents. Yet such incidents put us at odds with the deeper and more intuitive valuing of our experience that we all possess. To a greater or lesser extent, we come to understand ourselves through the messages received from others and the emotional response they have to us. Unconditional positive regard is received where the messages allow and even fit our own experience: we feel both known and accepted and no inner tension is caused. However, when we are seen negatively or esteemed only if we conform to certain conditions, particularly if the people in question are powerful influences in our lives, the tendency is to take in their opinions, resulting in inner splits and conflicts. Rogers called this internalizing *conditions of worth* and these conditions become built into the conscious awareness we have of ourselves.[7]

The cost of preserving the self

Further problems arise, as what pleases one person may not please another. There can be a certain amount of flexibility in how we think about ourselves, for the self-concept is not a totally rigid monolith. It is more like a constellation of thoughts and feelings which cohere together in a reasonable fashion, for instance allowing us to show some aspects of ourselves more easily to one group of people than another. Yet despite this, we are still likely to run up against experience which challenges our self-understanding or brings different parts of ourselves into conflict and this will cause anxiety, for although we can suppress and even at times silence our true feelings and perceptions, they are not rubbed out altogether.

On these occasions our self-concept is threatened: a gap opens up between what we need to be true to maintain our understanding of the world and ourselves and what we sense is actually the case. Small discrepancies may be accommodated reasonably easily, but the greater the rift between experience and self-concept the greater the anxiety caused. Radical challenges can feel literally life-threatening, for some experiences drive such a deep wedge into the way we see ourselves, we no longer recognize who we are and such complete self-alienation is terrifying. As a result, we invest heavily in maintaining our self-concept.

To protect against internal discomfort and collapse, we filter internal and external experience by two processes known as *distortion* and *denial*.[8] In distorting an experience we selectively take bits of what is happening and leave out others, or we understand something in one way rather than another. For instance, a boy who is repeatedly told 'I won't love you if . . .' may absorb this to the extent of thinking he is unlovable. In later life, if he meets someone who is warm and friendly towards him, he may distrust them. Alternatively, he may feel he has misled the person and somehow duped them into thinking he is worthy of love, giving rise to guilt and an anxiety that the friend will leave once he is truly revealed. Both these outcomes protect the sense of himself as unlovable, one by projecting untrustworthiness outwards, the other by taking it upon himself. This in turn guards against knowing the pain of past rejections and the chaos of re-evaluating himself and his relationships.

By contrast, denying an experience means it is lost to conscious memory completely. We may simply never register certain feelings or we might avoid difficult knowledge, perhaps continuing to spend money as we always have when we are drastically overdrawn, or not making preparations for future events which we do not want to come. Also, denial is clearly evident in the amnesia which can occur in highly traumatic events.

Distorting and denying experience means that we continually shore up internal splits. Emotional and mental distress is the cost. For some the extent to which introjected conditions of worth are absorbed makes life a constant source of fear. In addition the flatness and emptiness which is so much part of depression shows the price paid for the suppression of feeling. Dissatisfaction, loneliness, confusion, anxiety, exhaustion, emotional deadness and even dissociation and so-called psychotic breakdown, can all come from our attempts to keep apart what we can consciously bear from our deeper knowledge. Self-protection becomes self-oppression and even self-destruction, and the externalization of this is prejudice, oppression and the destruction of others.

The transformation of distress

The aim of person-centred counselling is to offer the conditions which will allow the healing of inner splits and begin the process of reconnecting fully with experience and our innate valuing process. It rests on a single, but far-reaching premise, that offering respect, deep understanding and an honest and open presence to a client will create a climate of unconditional safety and trust. Gradually a client will have less and less need to defend against experiences which threaten to break through the protective layers they have built. Feelings, thoughts and perceptions which previously would have been transformed or banished can be held in awareness and reassessed, allowing a more satisfying absorption of experiences into the self.

PRACTICE

The goal of person-centred counselling carries an apparent paradox. There are no specific outcomes that the counsellor is working to achieve and yet there is a very clear sense of positive change (as outlined above). The resolution of the paradox lies in the person-centred understanding that the open, unthreatening and interested presence of another can in itself facilitate our growth and well-being. In addition, the impetus for growth already lies within us. With a client therefore, a counsellor needs to strive to *be* a certain way, rather than to *do* or achieve something. The counsellor is not the arbiter of the client's process, evaluating and directing events. Instead they create a facilitative relationship in which the client remains the expert on their own experience.

Arrangements for counselling

Care is taken over the practical arrangements for counselling. A warm, comfortable and quiet room is used, with the length of session agreed (often but not always 50 minutes to one hour). Regularity is common, but by no means necessary. Particular needs may require a particular response and, where possible and appropriate, more flexible arrangements may be made by mutual agreement.[9]

The relationship between client and counsellor

The relationship between counsellor and client is the axis on which person-centred therapy turns. Rogers stated that three *core conditions* should be present within the counsellor: *congruence, unconditional positive regard* and *empathy*. (Again, these are qualities of being, not indicators of preferable techniques or strategies.) Furthermore, if the therapeutic process is to unfold, the client, either consciously or unconsciously, needs to feel the presence of these qualities. For these factors alone to be sufficient for any successful therapy is a distinctive claim of person-centred counselling.[10]

The core conditions

Person-centred theorists have written extensively on the core conditions to explain their nature and to demonstrate their effectiveness. Traditionally the three core conditions are cited – however the therapist's *presence* is also discussed as an important quality and is sometimes known as the fourth condition.[11]

Congruence

Congruence involves the counsellor being self-aware and open and it has two dimensions. First, a counsellor must be wholly and genuinely themselves within the therapeutic relationship, being alert to the presence and movement of their thoughts, feelings and perceptions. Warmth, emptiness, boredom, fear, joy, excitement, concern, jealousy, anger, curiosity and so on may all come and go, but internally there should be no pretence or conscious concealment. Second, this genuine presence should extend out to the client. Engineering remoteness, presenting a professional façade or avoiding necessary or appropriate honesty with a client will inhibit the growth of the relationship.

In practice a major dilemma of congruence is how much the counsellor should actually disclose of their own thoughts and feelings: congruent disclosures on the part of the counsellor always risk diverting the focus from the client's experience. If I am irritated with a client, should I say? If a client asks questions about my own experience or life, should I answer? There is no absolute rule: what is right for one client may not be for another. For instance, in an initial session if a client says they have religious or spiritual feelings they want to talk about, and they ask if I believe in a spiritual dimension to life, I would probably answer straightforwardly and honestly. However, if I felt unclear about why my answer was important to them, I might first empathize with the seeming importance of my beliefs or disclose my uncertainty, before speaking of my own experience. This would not be to prevaricate or avoid the question, but to prevent an important issue for the client being lost.

Awareness and careful use of congruence also allows aspects of the relationship which persistently impinge on the counsellor to be raised. For example, if antagonism in the relationship is felt by the counsellor, but is not mentioned by the client, the counsellor may choose to speak of their own feeling of friction to create an opening for this mutual experience. In giving congruent expression to such feelings the counsellor would be careful to be clear they are saying something about themselves, rather than suggesting how it might be for the client. This leaves the client freer to check their own awareness and decide how they wish to respond. It invites mutual exploration, thereby building trust.

Clearly congruent disclosure by the counsellor is a complex issue. Mearns and Thorne offer useful guidelines by suggesting such disclosures should be a '*response* to the client's experience . . . *relevant* to the immediate concern of the client' and express feelings which are '*persistent* or particularly *striking*'.[12]

Empathy

The practical heart of empathy is deep listening to the internal world of another. It involves the whole person, including cognitive understanding, and bodily, emotional and intuitive responses. Crucial to empathy is becoming aware of a person's internal states 'as if' you are them, but without ever losing awareness of your own internal state.[13] In this way congruence and empathy become parallel processes.

Communicating empathy is important for the client to know they are understood and for the counsellor to check their understanding. In effect the counsellor is saying, 'This is how I sense it is for you. Have I got it right?' The expert on the client's experience should remain the client, reinforcing the mutuality of the process. Empathic responses often involve verbally conveying what is heard and felt, but facial expressions, tone of voice, gestures and even being a still and silent presence can all communicate the counsellor's understanding.

Experience can be approached at different levels and, as with congruence, what to say when is a key issue. Responding with surface aspects of a situation, when the client is experiencing feelings at great depth, or vice versa, is likely to jar the process of exploration because it is not close enough to the client's experience. Correctly pitching the level of empathic responses therefore also builds the sense of safety. Staying 'alongside' the client and sometimes picking up on things which are palpable, but not quite fully formed in the client's awareness is known as *staying with the edge of awareness*. This helps the client uncover new aspects of themselves, without taking them from areas or feelings they are engaged with.

Unconditional positive regard (acceptance)

For therapy to be successful, a counsellor must be able to hold some degree of liking or respect for a client. Unconditional positive regard is present when a counsellor accepts a client without needing the client to be a particular way to please or conform (the opposite to imposing conditions of worth). In practice this means trying not to judge the client's appearance, thoughts, actions and feelings and even forgoing a vision of a good or bad outcome to therapy. However, such acceptance is not a form of sterile inhibition or well-meaning latitude on the part of the counsellor. It is a deep interest which does not ask a person to distort themselves in order to be accepted.

A counsellor may well feel warmth towards a client. At times quite the opposite may be true. Strong negative or positive feelings on the part of the counsellor can hinder the therapeutic process. In particular they can inhibit empathy by clouding the ability to receive the client without distortion. When this happens the counsellor may need to use supervision to determine the root of these feelings and to find ways to unblock their empathic capacity. Positive or negative feelings that actually belong within the therapeutic relationship may call for sensitive congruent expression by the counsellor to prevent the relationship becoming stuck or dishonest.

Negative feelings usually bother counsellors more than positive feelings, though, interestingly, if we can allow ourselves to empathize with another person it soon becomes difficult not to feel positively towards them. In addition, the process of empathizing itself conveys enormous respect.

The unified nature of the core conditions

Each of the core conditions may be more obviously prominent at times, but their inter-relationship means the absence of one will cause the others to cease their therapeutic effectiveness. For instance, the positive effects of deep understanding and apparent respect will be void, if incongruence suggests dishonesty. Although the practical expression of person-centred counselling changes from client to client and with the same client through time, the core rationale is always about embodying the core conditions rather than directing the process or employing techniques.

Therapeutic process

The person-centred therapist does not work to achieve a particular outcome. However, if the therapeutic conditions prevail, then there is a common pattern of change amongst clients, known as the *therapeutic process*.[14]

Often a client will begin feeling cut off from themselves or frightened or overwhelmed by thoughts and feelings which feel uncomfortable or even alien. In theoretical terms this is conceived as a time of conflict between the self-concept and the actualizing tendency. This is captured in statements such as 'I don't know who I am any more' or 'I shouldn't feel this way. It isn't right.'

As counselling progresses the effect of the core conditions is safely to assist the loosening of the self-concept. Rigidity gives way to dispersal and new aspects of the self are encountered. This mid-point can involve rapid or slow fluctuation as a client explores new ways of looking at themselves and the world. Generally there will be greater absorption in the process of counselling and increased awareness of the flow and change of feelings that arise. Although this process can be pleasurable, disturbing feelings can also arise. These may relate to past experiences, present situations or apprehensions about the future. Another major feature is the move from talking about experiences outside the counselling room to exploring feelings that arise in the moment, including feelings about the counsellor and the relationship.

Gradually, cohesion into a more settled, but flexible self-concept occurs. This new self-awareness may have many different facets, but the potential conflict between different parts of the self is less troublesome: having mixed feelings becomes more acceptable and there is greater positive self-regard. The ability to respond to and experience the world without defences increases and life becomes more satisfying.

This process does not necessarily occur as smooth linear progression and is more likely to involve reversals, backtracking, circling round and periods of stuckness. Often one aspect of the self can begin to feel freer, but other parts have to 'catch up'. For example, a client may feel they have made progress in relation to relationships in the workplace, but faced with similar issues relating to parents or a partner may feel less certain.

WHICH CLIENTS BENEFIT MOST?

In theory there are no restrictions on who can benefit from person-centred therapy and counselling as long as the core conditions are present and the client can be aware of these at least to a minimal degree. Similarly, individuals bring an enormous range of issues to person-centred counselling. Although these are nearly always problematic to the client, this is not always the case.

This 'universality' is not without dispute. For instance, some argue that working in a person-centred way with those diagnosed as having major mental illness, such as schizophrenia or manic-depression is not possible. However, person-centred therapists do work in hospitals and mental health projects. One aspect of this work is known as 'pre-therapy', where the initial focus is on establishing contact with a client.

Doubtless some clients 'take' to counselling more readily than others. The extent to which a client feels actively involved in the issues raised and the ease with which they can engage the self in exploring the issues is likely to affect the outcome (though this is probably true for all therapeutic approaches).

The other important factor is the person of the counsellor. For each of us there are particular situations or issues which give rise to strong feelings or internal blocks. This partiality can be positive or negative. As therapists we bring our human limits to our work and although a major part of professional training and development for a person-centred therapist is building self-awareness, it may be the case that there will be clients with whom we should not work. This is not because of the client or the limits of the practice; it is because of who we are as therapists.

Case study

THE CLIENT

I first met with Grace in the autumn of 1995, when she came to see me at the GP surgery where I work part-time. My first impression was of the anxiety in her eyes as I met her in the waiting room. She looked down as we walked to the counselling room, but, as soon as she sat down, she began to talk about the 'terrible dilemma' she was facing. At 51 she was considering whether to leave her husband and had felt almost constant tension as she turned the problem over and over in her mind for several months. She now felt depressed and enormously tired.

THE COURSE OF THERAPY

For the first session I spent much of the time listening as intently as I could, working to empathize with Grace and tentatively conveying my understanding. Although the choice seemed clear – to stay or to go – Grace's internal stuckness and confusion came through strongly. She wanted to leave because she no longer felt there was any hope for resolving the differences in their marriage. What had started as a feeling of being slightly side-lined and occasionally belittled in the early years of the relationship had gradually developed into outright hostility from her husband. Grace's two daughters, Jane and Lindsay, had given her a purpose for staying while they grew up, but they had both left the previous year. Afterwards a sense of emptiness and bitterness towards her husband, David, had come creeping in. Yet alongside this there was a feeling that to go would be selfish. Even though Jane and Lindsay were now independent, it seemed to Grace that leaving would make her responsible for the destruction of the family. As a mother and a wife, she felt responsible for maintaining good family relationships. She also felt David would be bewildered and hurt.

For my part empathy and acceptance were in the forefront as we went through the next few sessions. It felt crucial to understand the whole of Grace's situation. To have responded only to the part of Grace that wanted to leave or conversely only to the wish to preserve her family and not to hurt David would have opened up a danger of my acceptance seeming conditional. It may have created the feeling that she was only partially understandable and that I would only be receptive to those things that fitted my thoughts about what Grace should do or be.

Over the weeks Grace's anxiety subsided as she felt less besieged by confusion and began to sense greater control over a complex potential decision. At the beginning of the seventh session she announced she had made up her mind. She was going to stay with David whatever and try to mend their relationship. She had tried talking with him about the gap between them and he said that, since Jane and Lindsay had left, the house had felt empty and life had been quiet. I felt a lurch of anxiety, having no real sense of how Grace might find happiness with David as things were. Remaining conscious of this I tried for the rest of the session simply to stay with Grace's exploration of the future possibilities.

Although my response had been swift and definite, it had also been accompanied by a sense of discomfort. I discussed this with my supervisor and despite my conscious commitment to Grace finding the best way forward in her own terms, I was brought up squarely against the fact that I did have a vision of a good outcome for Grace. Also, I could see parallels to Grace's experience in my own life, which I talked through with my supervisor and it was clear my own feelings were part of the intensity of that moment. Had there not been so much of myself influencing my response, giving congruent expression to the feeling of anxiety may have been helpful. In the event remaining aware, but not speaking of the anxiety, felt to have been a good choice.

The next time we met, Grace began by reiterating her decision. David had been 'unkind' during the week, but she thought he was making a great effort. They had even gone out for a walk together one evening – the first time for several years. I responded empathically by saying 'That is . . . I mean . . . David has been unkind, but . . . and also you have done something which feels like starting to make it better . . . something you remember enjoying before?' Grace nodded and then began to talk about the unkindness. The tension was palpable as she described David accusing her of not coping and of being the cause of their joint unhappiness. 'At first he seemed to listen, but then he accused me of blaming him for things not going right. If I loved him, I wouldn't go on all the time . . . I'd see that he is stressed, with work and everything . . . his children had left too. Maybe if we could talk . . . but he just shouted and finally slammed out of the house. All I could do was cry. He hasn't really said anything to me since. It was so nice when we went out for the walk . . . I just don't know how to keep that happening.'

Again, Grace talked about what she could do to make David feel better and this time I felt a flatness and she seemed slightly vague and distant. By contrast to the anxiety I felt previously, I was sure enough of the change that I was experiencing to risk giving voice to the feeling. 'Grace . . . I'm aware . . . um as you are talking . . . I have a sense of flatness . . .' (I held my hand against my chest as this was the area in my own body that I had the feeling and Grace looked at me more directly) '. . . heavy flatness . . . and somehow I feel you as further away.'

It was important to be clear that these were my feelings: it was not an empathic response. Instead I wanted to give congruent voice to a response within me to our relationship at that moment.

Grace looked down and paused. When she spoke again her voice was cracking with distress and a painful lump built in my throat. 'I really want it to work but sometimes it feels hopeless. And the worst part is being together for so long. Being alone . . . I don't know if I can survive. I've always had people round me. All those years . . . it wasn't all awful . . . [pause] . . . Maybe if I had gone when I was younger . . . but I kept thinking it would all be all right . . .' As she spoke tears began to roll down her cheeks and I felt Grace was touching a huge grief for the years she had kept her feelings locked away and the fear of facing a future without David.

Allowing the grief and fear to surface was accompanied by a change in the parameters of how Grace was thinking about herself and the dilemma of leaving/staying. She felt it opened up the question of whether she could conceive of herself as a single person and the extent to which her self-worth had always come through being with others. For instance, as the oldest child in a family of four, she had taken responsibility for her siblings at an early age, winning her mother's praise in the process.

Our work eventually came to a close several weeks later. Grace had begun to feel she wanted to try a period of separation from David and she took the opportunity to house-sit in the north of England for a friend who was going abroad. We were both conscious of the lack of support she might feel in moving away and investigated counsellors she could contact if need be.

A month or so later, Grace wrote to say that in living apart from David she was beginning to discover new interests and generally felt calmer. At the same time she was coping with considerable loneliness and sometimes deep fear when contemplating the future. For the time being, at least, she had chosen not to return to counselling.

REFERENCES

1 Gaylin, N.L. (1993) 'Person-centred family therapy', in D. Brazier (ed.), *Beyond Carl Rogers*. London: Constable.
2 Gendlin, E.T. (1981) *Focusing*. New York: Bantam.
3 Prouty, G. (1994) *Theoretical Evolutions in Person-centred/Experiential Therapy: Applications to Schizophrenic and Retarded Psychoses*. New York: Praeger.
4 Thorne, B. (1991) *Person-centred Counselling: Therapeutic and Spiritual Dimensions*. London: Whurr.
5 Purton, C. (1996) 'The deep structure of the core conditions: a Buddhist perspective', in R. Hutterer *et al.* (eds), *Client-centred and Experiential Psychotherapy: A Paradigm in Motion*. Frankfurt: Lang.

6 Rogers, C. (1959) 'A theory of therapy, personality, and interpersonal relationships, as developed in the client-centered framework', in H. Kirschenbaum and V. Henderson (eds), *The Carl Rogers Reader* (1989). London: Constable.

7 Rogers, C. (1959) ibid.

8 Rogers, C. (1959) ibid.

9 Mearns, D. (1994) *Developing Person-centred Counselling*. London: Sage.

10 Rogers, C.R. (1957) 'The necessary and sufficient conditions for therapeutic personality change', in H. Kirschenbaum and V. Henderson (eds), *The Carl Rogers Reader* (1989). London: Constable.

11 Rogers, C. (1986) 'A client-centered/person-centered approach to therapy', in H. Kirschenbaum and V. Henderson (eds), *The Carl Rogers Reader* (1989). London: Constable.

12 Mearns, D. and Thorne, B. (1998) *Person-centred Counselling in Action*. London: Sage.

13 Mearns, D. and Thorne, B. (1998) ibid.

14 Rogers, C. (1956) 'A process conception of psychotherapy', in *On Becoming A Person* (1967). London: Constable.

SUGGESTED READING

Axline, V.M. (1964) *Dibs, In Search of Self*. London: Penguin. This is an extraordinary account of the relationship between a play therapist and a gifted and withdrawn young boy. It conveys the enormous potential for healing and growth in a relationship which embodies genuine respect and understanding.

Brazier, D. (ed.) (1993) *Beyond Carl Rogers*. London: Constable. A compilation of interesting and challenging articles, published after Rogers' death, which develop new themes and implications for person-centred therapy.

Kirschenbaum, H. and Henderson, V. (eds) (1989) *The Carl Rogers Reader*. London: Constable. Incorporating early and later writings, this collection includes major pieces such as 'The necessary and sufficient conditions of therapeutic personality change'; 'A theory of therapy, personality and interpersonal relationships'; and 'Do we need a reality?'

Mearns, D. and Thorne, B. (1988) *Person-centred Counselling in Action*. London: Sage. By two well-known British practitioners, this accessible and comprehensive book discusses the practical implications of the core conditions and the nature of the working therapeutic relationship.

Rogers, C.R. (1961) *On Becoming a Person: A Therapist's View of Psychotherapy*. London: Constable. A popular and influential book bringing together lectures and writings. It is typical of Rogers' conversational style, and clearly lays out the central themes of person-centred therapy.

Thorne, B. and Lambers, E. (eds) (1998) *Person-centred Therapy – A European Perspective*. London: Sage. This volume brings together very recent developments in person-centred theory and practice from European practitioners.

DISCUSSION ISSUES

1 To what extent do you think the optimism of person-centred therapy about our basic nature is well founded?
2 Describe a relationship in your life where you feel genuineness, understanding and acceptance are present and one where they are absent. What difference does this make to you and the relationship?
3 Explore what you feel to be the limits and potential of the core conditions in practice?
4 Discuss the effectiveness of person-centred counselling at dealing with such differences as gender, culture, race or sexual orientation, between client and counsellor?

14

PERSONAL CONSTRUCT COUNSELLING AND PSYCHOTHERAPY

Fay Fransella

Personal construct psychotherapy and counselling do not fit easily into any one pre-existing category. The psychology of personal constructs that underpins them is *cognitive* in the sense that it deals with how people make sense of the world around them. It is *humanistic* in the sense that it deals with the total person and not just how we think or how we behave. But it is also *behavioural* in the sense that it gives a prominent and unusual place to our behaviour. In addition, it is more than any of these. As George Kelly says:

> Personal construct theory . . . is a theory about how the human process flows, how it strives in new directions as well as in old, and how it may dare for the first time to reach into the depths of newly perceived dimensions of human life.[1]

It is essentially an approach to helping those with psychological problems that focuses on how we experience the world as individual human beings. It does not see us as being the victims of our past history – although we can trap ourselves if we come to see past events in that way. We impose our own individual meanings on everything and the work of the counsellor or psychotherapist is to try to look at the world through the client's eyes. Only in this way can they get some idea of why the client is having the problems for which they are seeking help.

DEVELOPMENT OF THE PSYCHOTHERAPY AND COUNSELLING

To fully understand a theory it is important to know something about the theorist. The psychology of personal constructs was described by George Kelly in 1955.[2] He was born in 1900 and took his first degree in physics and mathematics. This was followed by another degree in education taken in Edinburgh, and then a higher degree in sociology and finally a doctorate in philosophy on neurological and physiological aspects of stuttering. With that background, it is not surprising that he suggested we might see how useful it would be to take 'the scientist' as our model of the person. This is coupled with his concern that we should be able to assess a person's construing – that is, get beyond the words (see Fransella[3] for more details of George Kelly).

When he started working on his theory in the 1930s, the approaches of Sigmund Freud and other 'psychodynamic' theorists and the behaviourists were dominant. Kelly saw his theory as being an alternative to both of these. He saw Freud as a genius who had come up with some very creative ideas but whose followers had done him a disservice. He had no time at all for the behaviourists. He thought they made the person into a puppet that reacted only when a 'stimulus' prompted them into action.

Personal construct counselling and psychotherapy are the application of the basic theory and methods of personal construct theory. While Kelly used psychotherapy as the focus of his theory, he saw that as only an example of what people might do with it. The theory is now used in very many settings including teaching, management, nursing and medicine.

The main development since 1955 has been the creation and elaboration of personal construct psychotherapeutic theories and practice for those with specific problems. These include the type of disorder of thinking found in some of those medically diagnosed as suffering from schizophrenia (summarized in *Inquiring Man*);[4] those who stutter;[5] those who are depressed.[6] Some have described how the personal construct approach can be used as an alternative to behavioural methods[7] and as a way of coming to understand the problems of children.[8]

THEORY AND BASIC CONCEPTS

Underpinning all of Kelly's thinking is his explicit philosophy, which he called *constructive alternativism* – not as complicated as it sounds. It says there are always alternative ways of looking at, construing, events. We are not stuck with what has happened to us in the past. Reconstruing is always possible but is not always easy.

The nature of construing

To understand what construing means, we can take Kelly's idea of looking at ourselves and others 'as if' we are all theory makers – 'as if' we are all scientists. Personal constructs indicate ways in which we have noted similarities between some events which thereby make them different from other events. We may construe some people as *intelligent*. By doing that we are, at the same time, saying that there are others who are *stupid*. An essential feature of personal construct theory is that all our personal constructs have two poles. You cannot know what *good* is without having some idea of what being *bad* means.

When making sense of someone, a person may go further and note that *intelligent* people are all *kindly* whereas *stupid* people are all *indifferent*. Now *intelligence, kindliness, stupidity* and *indifference* do not reside in the people we are construing but they reside in the eye of the construer. That person has a theory about others. Essentially what happens in practice is that every time she meets a person she construes as *intelligent* she behaves towards them 'as if' they were intelligent and makes a prediction that they will behave toward her in a *kindly* way. Construing is essentially about predicting. Whenever we make a prediction of any sort, we look to see whether this prediction is more or less right or wrong. Kelly was doing here something that had never been done before in a psychological theory; he made our behaviour *the experiment* we carry out to test the prediction we have made from our mini-theory. In this way, we are always launching ourselves into the future. Our behaviour is thus totally linked in with our construing.

As well as being a personal scientist, Kelly suggested we might usefully look at ourselves and others as a total entity. That may seem strange at first sight as one might ask how it is possible *not* to be a whole person. But behaviourists, for instance, certainly in Kelly's day, saw us in terms of our behaviour; cognitive theorists focus on how we think; and Freud or those who subscribe to psycho-dynamic theories focus on our unconscious processes. Kelly argued forcibly that it is not possible to separate our behaviour from our thinking or from our feelings.

Construing goes on in every aspect of our being. Our feelings are linked to an awareness of our construing in action. If we construe something that is happening as likely to challenge some core aspect of our notion of our 'self', we will have the unpleasant feeling of being threatened. Construing definitely does not just go on in the head alone, nor is it divorced from our behaviour or our feelings.

As well as being bi-polar, and predictive, construing goes on at all levels of awareness, from the level of the 'gut reaction' to the high levels of cognitive awareness as you try to understand the psychology of personal constructs. We are, each one of us, seen as a total construing process.

As has been touched on several times, construing is personal. No two people see the world which they inhabit in precisely the same way. But, to the extent that we have developed in similar cultures, so we may construe events in similar ways and so are able to communicate.

The nature of psychological disturbance

Kelly argued fiercely also against the use of concepts from medicine being applied to psychological problems. The psychology of personal constructs does not see clients who come for psychotherapy as being 'ill'. He suggests that we might use the concept of 'functioning' instead. A person who is fully functioning is someone who gets their predictions about other people and events more or less right most of the time. When things do not turn out quite as predicted, the fully functioning person may respond by saying, 'OK, I got it wrong that time, I'll hope to do better next time.' If that person concludes that the invalidation is more serious than that, they may deal with it by looking at the event from another viewpoint – they reconstrue.

A person who is not functioning so well may be incapable of dealing with much invalidation. He may resort to being *hostile*. Kelly gave personal construct definitions to some everyday words. Hostility is one of them. He wanted to be sure that all we experience could be accounted for within the same psychological theory. Not for him was there to be a theory of behaviour and another for emotion and another for learning and so forth. We are a totality. *Hostility* is used when we are aware, at some level, that our prediction is a failure but we cannot give up that way of construing because that would mean giving up some core aspect of how we see ourselves. So, 'intelligent people just must be kindly because my mother was intelligent and extremely kindly and this person is like my mother so she just *must* be kindly'. So he behaves in a way that forces the person to pay attention to him. There is nothing essentially 'bad' about such hostility. It is a way we protect ourselves against hard psychological times. Clients in psychotherapy will use hostility as a way of guarding themselves against the very success of the therapy if they see it as encouraging them to move psychologically too fast. But it can become a problem if an individual uses such a method too often, whether in therapy or in everyday life.

There are a number of ways in which an individual can be seen as acquiring a problem or 'symptom'. Remembering that all behaviour is seen as an experiment, a major way of acquiring a problem is to find yourself repeating the same experiment again and again in spite of persistent invalidating results. There is no reconstruing, no hostility. The person has ceased to be in charge of their own behaviour. The person has got psychologically stuck. They are, for some reason, unable to reconstrue. Such a person will only find it possible to reconstrue when they are able to understand why it is they have to keep conducting such experiments.

Another person may not have a problem with constant invalidation of their personal experiments, but rather find difficulty in making predictions at all. They are finding that the world is becoming an increasingly confusing place. In Kelly's sense, they are immersed in a sea of anxiety. Their way out is to anchor themselves to a 'symptom'. Perhaps they are feeling really bad and someone says 'you are depressed'; or they say 'I'm feeling bad because I am overweight.' They have found a reason for their otherwise chaotic experiences. Although not desired by the client, these symptoms are preferable to the anxiety. Many will find out that it is not the symptom that is the problem.

Other problems may be due to the use of personal construing that has been developed in early childhood, before the development of language. In one sense, this was Kelly's theory of 'unconscious' construing. Many people associate any discussion of 'the unconscious' with the ideas of Freud. And they would be right to do so. Freud gave the idea of human beings having an inner life public credibility and it has proved enormously useful. But George Kelly could not accept the idea that there were forces within us influencing our daily experiencing of the world. Kelly suggested the radical idea that there are no psychological forces within each one of us at all. He pointed out that in physics some concept of a physical force was necessary in order to explain why inanimate objects moved. A rock only moves if something hits it or gravity takes over – it does not move of its own accord. Freud brought the notion of physical energy into psychology and talks of 'psychic energy'. But Kelly asked the fundamental question, 'why do I have to start with the construct of force or energy?' Inanimate objects are different from human beings in that human beings are alive. One of the defining characteristics of living matter is that it moves.

Therefore, for Kelly, you do not need to invoke the idea of a force to explain why living matter moves – it does it of its own accord. What has to be explained is why we do what we do in the way that we do it. Kelly calls the construing developed before the onset of language as 'pre-verbal construing'. No force or energy is involved. Pre-verbal construing comes into play when a situation arises in adult life that makes the construing relevant. For instance, a child falls into a pond in the garden, cannot swim, feels panic but is rescued before any damage is done. For a time that child fears all water until he learns to distinguish the sink, the bath and the toilet as different from the pond, a lake and the sea. With a thoughtful and caring teacher the child learns to swim. That does not mean the fear of water disappears but only that swimming with a caring adult is all right. The child grows into adulthood and stays away from large stretches of water. He meets a girl who loves sailing. Problem. He starts quarrelling with the girl. The student counsellor manages to help him discover where his fear of water comes from. He can now talk about it and relate it to the fact that he can now swim. The situation is totally different from the one which caused his fear. In Kelly's terms, he has 'updated' his construing. By putting verbal labels on his pre-verbal construing he can reconstrue. Much of the psychotherapeutic process is to do with understanding the client's pre-verbal construing.

Kelly relates pre-verbal construing to two other aspects of human experiencing. One is what some call 'acting out'. What can one do with pre-verbal construing except behave it? The other connection Kelly makes is with psychosomatic complaints. This is obviously a complex connection. He argues that we are a total construing system, and that one way of expressing our construing is through our bodily processes.

PRACTICE

The goals of personal construct counselling and psychotherapy

Taken at its simplest, a person has a problem because they have become psychologically 'stuck'. They are not happy with the way things are and yet cannot find any alternative ways of dealing with life. Personal construct therapy, as well as theory, says that we *do* have choice, but can only operate that choice if we feel we can explore alternatives. In ordinary circumstances, the choice we make in elaborating our notions of our selves and what we make of others is always towards that which we imagine will enable us to make increasing sense of our world. When we get psychologically stuck we are unable to make that choice. So, a major goal of psychotherapy and counselling is to enable the person to 'get on the psychological move again'. Central to this is the idea that we are a form of motion. When we say we have a problem we say we are doing things we do not like.

Establishing the framework of the relationship

At the very start, the client needs to understand in a very general way, what they may expect from a personal construct psychotherapist or counsellor. For instance, they will have to work hard, for the personal construct counsellor has no specific answers to the problems the client has brought. The counsellor only knows some ways in which the client may be helped to reconstrue themselves, the people and the events in their life. The relationship is spelled out as something like a partnership – both work hard to understand how the client construes his or her world. To help their struggle to understand their own construing of the world and particularly the areas related to the problem, the client needs to understand that they will be asked to carry out tasks between sessions. These tasks will be agreed between psychotherapist and client and will often consist of trying out new or alternative behavioural experiments and so come to see that their own behaviour affects how others see them.

At the start of this understanding process, the therapist/counsellor listens to, and believes, everything the client says. That *credulous listening* is an essential starting point because everything the client says is deemed to have meaning for the client, even if the therapist knows it to be untrue. For it may not be untrue to the client or it may be of value to know why the client feels the need to tell an untruth to the counsellor. To be able to adopt the *credulous approach* the counsellor must be able to suspend their own personal values. That is, he or she has to be able to hear what the client is saying and not have it filtered through the therapist's personal ideas of what is right or wrong, good or bad. In personal construct counselling and psychotherapy it is no good the client looking to the therapist/counsellor for solutions. The client will be helped to find his or her own solutions.

A typical session

In the sessions themselves, there is no particular format, only some guiding principles. For instance, the therapist and counsellor will keep in mind that their own behaviour is a tool in providing validation for the client's own behavioural experiments. For instance, a client may inexplicably start behaving in a way the therapist/counsellor interprets as 'rude'. Their response will be very important since it will be seen by the client as supporting or negating the client's own experiment. It cannot be said too often that, when talking about construing, we are not saying that the client 'thinks' about their own behavioural experiments in a conscious way.

Sessions will usually include a discussion of the previous week's homework and the designing of work to be carried out the following week. Unlike some therapies, the personal construct approach sees the major work being done between sessions rather than during the sessions.

Defining the problem

Before a personal construct psychotherapist can start to help the client recon-strue, he or she has to formulate a theory about the nature of the client's problem. That formulation would be called 'the diagnosis' in a medical context. Kelly's formulation is in terms of personal construct theory using what he calls 'professional constructs'. It can be to do with the *process* of the client's con-struing or its *content*. Their construing may be too 'loose' for the client to pull their thoughts or feelings together sufficiently for them to have any meaningful perception of the world around them and so conduct behavioural experiments that have any clear-cut predictions. Alternatively, it may be seen as so 'tight' that any change at one level could cause a collapse of the entire system – just like taking away a card in the middle of a house of cards, the whole lot crumples. Change for clients with either of these process problems would be most likely to be seen by a personal construct psychotherapist rather than a counsellor. The personal construct practitioner makes a distinction here. A person who is having to change aspects of their whole construing system and not just the personal constructs themselves will require psychotherapy.

Problems with the *content* of construing can, of course, be almost anything. But some are as deep-rooted as the process problems and require psychotherapy rather than counselling. 'Pre-verbal' construing can cause us much trouble in adult life. For instance, if part of the diagnosis is that the client is continually behaving so that all attempts at forming close, long-term relationships fail because of some construing that evolved during early childhood, then the psychotherapist can expect to be with the client for many sessions. Only when these construings are given words to anchor them in present reality can the client construe them from their present perspective.

Part of the problem-formulation process involves making a best guess about why the client persists in being someone they are not happy with.

The change process

As we are seen as forms of motion, change is with us all the time. So what we are looking for here is a theory about how psychological change comes about. We are truly in the land of speculation because there is little hard evidence to show

how we actually do change our views, 'our minds' or 'our selves'. Kelly's theoretical speculations focus on 'diagnosis'. For that, a personal construct counsellor uses the 'professional constructs' mentioned in the last section. If a client's construing is seen as being too loose for comfort, leading to much anxiety, then part of the change process will include helping that person to tighten it and so make better sense of their world. If a man is construing his future wife as a waxwork image of his mother, then he will need to be helped to reconstrue. That might be a lengthy job if part of the 'diagnosis' included the professional construct that the man's construing of his mother was largely at a pre-verbal level. Basically, personal construct counselling and psychotherapy are based on the application of the whole of personal construct theory.

Major therapeutic strategies and techniques

Personal construct counselling and psychotherapy are heavy on theory and light on techniques. In fact, there no techniques that are a *must*. The counsellor or psychotherapist chooses that technique which they believe will bring about changes in construing toward which both client and therapist are working. Kelly puts it this way:

> Personal construct psychotherapy is a way of getting on with the human enterprise and it may embody and mobilize all of the techniques for doing this that man has yet devised. Certainly there is no one psychotherapeutic technique and certainly no one kind of inter-personal compatibility between psychotherapist and client. The techniques employed are the techniques for living and the task of the skilful psychotherapist is the proper orchestration of all these varieties of techniques. Hence one may find a personal construct psychotherapist employing a huge variety of procedures – not helter-skelter, but always as part of a plan for helping himself and his client get on with the job of human exploration and checking out the appropriateness of the constructions they have devised for placing upon the world around them.[9]

He created two techniques that might be used to come to a deeper understanding of how our client sees the world – the self-characterization and the repertory grid – and one for helping the client reconstrue – fixed role therapy.

The self-characterization

Kelly is reported as having said that, if he were to be remembered for only one thing, it would be his first principle: 'If you do not know what is wrong with a person, ask him, he may tell you'.[10] This is how he saw the self-characterization. The person is asked to write a character sketch of him or herself, in the third person, as if describing a character in a play. But this is written by someone who is very sympathetic to them and knows them better than anyone can ever know them. The person starts off with their own name, for example, in my case I would start: 'Fay Fransella is . . .'. There is no very detailed method of analysis, but it can reveal a great deal about someone if you become skilled at reading between the lines.

The repertory grid

This has become a technology in its own right and can be found in many forms. The original version was described by Kelly to 'get beyond the words'. A grid is basically a matrix made up of personal constructs and the 'elements' to be construed. Thus, if it is designed to look at interpersonal construing, the elements would most likely be people and relatives close to the client and the constructs would have been elicited from the client. The matrix can be analysed by several different statistical procedures. The pattern of relationships shows how an individual views important people and relationships.

Fixed role therapy

George Kelly was much influenced by the development of psychodrama by the psychiatrist, Jacob Moreno.[11] Kelly places considerable emphasis on role play and enactment as part of his psychotherapeutic and counselling approach. He elaborated this specifically into *fixed role therapy*. He did that to show how his theory might be put into practice rather than to spell out a specific technique. You take the client's self-characterization and write another that is similar to the original but different in certain respects. The client has to agree that the new sketch is someone he or she *could* be. Once agreed, the client adopts that role for a certain period of time. The aim is to show the client that one is not trapped forever in the same mode. We can all change; all re-create ourselves if we have the will. Writing the new sketch is not as easy as it sounds and Kelly spells out the procedure in some detail.[12]

WHICH CLIENTS BENEFIT MOST?

It is not possible to say which sort of people with which sort of problems may benefit most from the personal construct approach. It has been used with a wide range of problems. At one extreme there is the work of the psychologist, Don Bannister,[13] with those who have the disorder of thinking described as having 'schizophrenia' or those with long-standing problems such as stuttering,[14] to those with problems of depression or anxiety or phobias.

It should be said that, in most cases, where there is perceived to be a limitation, it is usually the limitation of the counsellor or psychotherapist rather than the client. One area that has not been extensively developed is the use of personal construct psychotherapy with groups of people. Some work has been done, however – for instance, by Landfield[15] who created the interpersonal transaction group method and Neimeyer[16] who described some clinical guidelines for carrying out such group therapy.

Case study

THE CLIENT

I have chosen to call her Flora for she was indeed flower-like. She glided into my room carrying with her a most pleasant scent. It is difficult not to become poetic about the impression she gave. Her hair was, indeed, the colour of pale gold, her eyes were indeed very blue and her skin that of the proverbial English peach. Her skirt came just the right distance above her knees proportional to her height, which was about five foot six inches, and showed off her very shapely legs.

As to Flora herself, she gave me the impression of being reasonably poised and self-confident. There was also a friendliness and warmth about her that suggested she was used to dealing with people. Her hand was cool and dry as we shook hands, suggesting she was probably not too stressed by the situation.

Flora had made the appointment by telephone. She explained she was having trouble with her personal life and would just like to talk to someone about it. She had read the book personal construct psychotherapist, Peggy Dalton, and I had written on personal construct counselling[17] and liked what she had read. She said she thought the personal construct approach was good because it would not impose some outside ideas upon her and the issues she wanted to talk about. It would not explain her problems in terms of her complexes or unconscious urges. It seemed to her that the approach would look at how she saw her life and herself and that was it.

The methods and procedures used in personal construct counselling make no distinction between gathering information about the client and their problem and the counselling or psychotherapy process itself. In some sense, the process has already started for many clients from the time they start to contemplate talking to a professional about their problem.

As we started talking, the question I had in mind was the extent to which this dazzling picture before me was indeed a picture, a front, or an accurate expression of the person herself. In addition, I was wondering whether the fact that Peggy and I were women influenced her choice of counselling as well as the personal construct approach itself.

Flora began to show signs of nervousness as she began to talk. She explained that her problem was that whenever she thought she had found a man who attracted her and who seemed to be attracted by her, the relationship never ended in marriage. They would start to have rows and eventually split up in acrimony.

She described herself as moderately intelligent but under-achieving at school because she did not think she would ever make the top class. By being in a lower class she could usually guarantee coming near the top in examinations – thus pleasing her parents. She had taken two A-level examinations, one in history and the other in economics. She now had what she described as a good job with a large travel agency and expected to rise to senior management level in a couple of years. She surprised me by saying that she was 39 years old.

She knew what to expect from personal construct counselling so we did not need to cover that. She agreed to my suggestion about a contract to meet for six sessions and then have a review to see where we had got to.

Before coming up with any formulation of the problem, it was necessary to get more information or data. It is by no means a requirement of personal construct counselling or psychotherapy to explore childhood experiences and parental attitudes, but it was clearly necessary here to explore earlier relationships, including ones with her parents. Flora had given the main theme of her problem – relationships with men always ending in failure. Was that recent or long-term?

She described her father first. A nice man, kindly, not spontaneous in his demonstrations of love but Flora clearly felt loved by him. However, she always felt that her father gave more of his attention to her brother, six years older than her and mentioned here for the first time. Her father was still alive and well and a successful accountant. Flora always felt welcomed by him when she visited home. I noted that she described the parental house as 'home' and not her own self-contained flat. Flora then went on to describe her brother, with whom she had a reasonably good, if somewhat distant, relationship. Her brother took up law and her father was demonstrably proud of this.

After a very long pause, she started to talk about her mother and slowly became more and more agitated. She loved her mother but never seemed able to please her. No, her mother did not reject her or say unkind things to her, she just never made her feel loved and wanted as a child – nor now as an adult. She always felt that her mother would really have liked another boy instead of a girl. Flora was vehement that her mother was a good mother and a good person, it was just that she never held Flora in her arms and gave her uninhibited love.

To explore Flora's construing of the world in greater depth, or as Kelly says 'to get beyond the words', I asked her to write a self-characterization. At this stage, the second session, I decided that a repertory grid would not add to our insights greatly. Flora was very articulate and able to introspect with some ease and to talk about her non-verbal or emotional experiences as well. Her self-characterization was quite short:

> Flora is a reasonably intelligent and lively person. She takes a pride in her appearance and thinks it important to make the best of oneself both in her work and in her private life. She is quite ambitious and wants to do well in her job. She has quite a lot of friends, both men and women, but increasingly wants to have a relationship with a man that lasts – she does not mind whether this includes marriage or not. She does not understand why, when she has most of the characteristics men seem to go for, no one seems to want her. I think she is really a little afraid that, nearly 40, she may spend the rest of her life alone.

If we take the first and second sentences as a description of how she sees herself now, we have a picture of a perfectionist, as least as far as her appearance is concerned. Then taking the last sentence as a description of where she sees herself as going, we have the picture of a bleak and lonely future.

With these data, and at the end of the third session, it was possible to formulate the first idea of what the problem might be in personal construct terms. Why is it that Flora kept failing in her relationships with men? Whenever there is a behavioural theme, one looks to see whether the client is 'extorting validational evidence for a social construction that has, at some level of awareness, already shown itself to be a failure'. Perhaps she was being *hostile* in Kelly's sense and 'making' it happen. She might be acting so as to ensure her relationships always fail. Where there is *hostility*, look for the *guilt*. What core role would she be dislodged from, in her terms, if she were to have a successful relationship? My idea was that, in her view, she was 'a person no one can love' or 'a person who can never please someone however hard I try'.

If this formulation were at all accurate, then this would involve helping her work on some pre-verbal construing. If she construed her mother as someone who really wanted her to be someone other than she was at a relatively early age, then it would be quite a struggle for her to accept this as true but that she now, as an adult, need not be a prisoner of that past. She would have to be helped to free herself. It was hypothesized that her father had not been able to compensate Flora for her lack of her mother's love.

This is an example of one difference between the personal construct view of counselling and psychotherapy. Psychotherapy involves helping someone change some aspect of their core construing of themselves; counselling does not.

The plan was to use the remaining sessions of the contract to explore just how open to the idea of change Flora was. To what extent did she see herself as having 'good' characteristics? To what extent was she able to see these as 'good' even though her mother did not/would not agree?

It transpired that 'Flora at work' was successful. She gave many examples of how her work was clearly valued, how she used her initiative, how she had good working relationships with senior and junior managers and so forth. The very gentle exploration of how her personal relationships with men failed revealed a theme here also. Her belief that no one could really love her for herself led her to start accusing them of being unfaithful to her/or not loving her enough with the result that they did, indeed, leave her.

This confrontation with her own construing had a profound effect on her. She accepted it as 'true'. She also came to glimpse that she, herself, might be afraid of loving someone and risking not having it returned – just like her relationship with her mother. Of course, knowing something is true does not mean that we can immediately change our behaviour. She had to disentangle it all from her construing of her mother. We agreed to extend the contract for another ten sessions.

These sessions focused on 'time-binding' her relationship with her mother as well as invalidating her view that no man could ever love her in her adult life. Much use was made of role play and enactment. She and I would enact mother and daughter, past man-friend and she herself, and other types of relationships. She came to see how she had made herself a prisoner of her past and gradually came to construe herself as someone who had the capacity to love as well as be loved. In this sense, we moved from counselling to psychotherapy. In a very real sense, she became a different person.

REFERENCES

1 Kelly, G.A. (1973) 'Fixed role therapy', in R.M. Jurjevich (ed.), *Direct Psychotherapy: 28 American Originals*. Coral Gables: University of Miami Press. p. 5

2 Kelly, G.A. (1991) *The Psychology of Personal Constructs*, vols I and 2. London: Routledge. (Previously published 1955, New York: Norton.)

3 Fransella, F. (1995) *George Kelly*. London: Sage.

4 Bannister, D. and Fransella, F. (1986) *Inquiring Man* (3rd edn). London: Routledge.

5 Fransella, F. (1977) *Personal Change and Reconstruction*. London: Academic Press.

6 Rowe, D. (1978) *The Experience of Depression*. Chichester: John Wiley.

7 Winter, D. (1988) 'Constructions in social skills training', in F. Fransella and L. Thomas (eds), *Experimenting with Personal Construct Psychology*. London: Routledge.

8 Ravenette, A.T. (1997) *Tom Ravenette: Selected Papers: Personal Construct Psychology and the Practice of an Educational Psychologist*. Farnborough: EPCA Publications.

9 Kelly, G.A. (1969) 'The psychotherapeutic relationship', in B. Maher (ed.), *Clinical Psychology and Personality: The Selected Papers of George Kelly*. New York: John Wiley. pp. 221-2.

10 Kelly, G.A. (1991) op. cit. p. 241.

11 Hare, A.P. and Hare, J.R. (1996) *J.L. Moreno*. London: Sage.

12 Kelly, G.A. (1991) op. cit. pp. 239-68.

13 Bannister, D. and Fransella, F. (1986) op. cit.

14 Fransella, F. (1977) op. cit.

15 Landfield, A.W. (1979) 'Exploring socialization through the interpersonal transaction group', in P. Stringer and D. Bannister (eds), *Constructs of Sociality and Individuality*. London: Academic Press.

16 Neimeyer, R.A. (1988) 'Clinical guidelines for conducting interpersonal transaction groups', *International Journal of Personal Construct Psychology*, 1: 181-90.

17 Fransella, F. and Dalton, P. (1990) *Personal Construct Counselling in Action*. London: Sage.

SUGGESTED READING

Button, E. (1993) *Eating Disorders: Personal Construct Therapy and Change*. Chichester: Wiley. This book describes how research and psychotherapy can be combined in a specific problem.

Dunnett, G. (1988) *Working with People*. London: Routledge. This gives an idea of the range of areas in which personal construct psychology has been shown to be of value.

Fransella, F. (1995) *George Kelly*. London: Sage. It explores Kelly the man, as well as his theory and its application to counselling and psychotherapy. It is part of the series 'Key Figures in Counselling and Psychotherapy'.

Fransella, F. and Dalton, P. (1990) *Personal Construct Counselling in Action*. London: Sage. As its title indicates, this is a practical account of working with personal construct theory in the counselling context.

DISCUSSION ISSUES

1 What are the implications of seeing behaviour as being 'the experiment' for understanding a client's problem?

2 If the philosophy states that no one person has direct access to 'the truth', who knows more about the problem – the client or the counsellor?

3 Discuss whether personal construct counselling is eclectic.

4 Discuss the differences between the psychoanalytic notion of 'the unconscious' and the personal construct notion of 'levels of awareness'.

15

PRIMAL INTEGRATION COUNSELLING AND PSYCHOTHERAPY

John Rowan

The word 'primal' means 'of the beginning' or 'of the origins'. The word 'integration' means 'making into one' or 'completing the whole'.

Primal integration is an approach which takes seriously the possibility of dealing with personal problems in a fundamental way by going back to their origins. In this, of course, it is not unique – many different therapies say the same thing. But primal integration has an open-ended notion of how far back those origins might be. Some forms of therapy will only consider childhood. Others will also consider infancy. Primal integration also takes into account the process of birth, and the foetal life which preceded that.

There is a knowing inside each of us about what we need to do to become more whole and actualize our potential. This knowing is part of the power within us all, the spark of self that we need to acknowledge and nurture. There are various ways of getting in touch with this source of inner strength – some are spontaneous and some are guided. In primal integration, we learn to trust the process and eventually to trust our own inner wisdom to guide us on our journey. Those of us who have been through this process have very often experienced very special moments of revelation and transformation. This is a form of therapy which is about liberation rather than adjustment to the established norms of society.

Primal integration is based on a natural phenomenon that has been recognized and used for a long time. It is a creative letting go of conscious control of the body and emotions which opens up the unconscious to awareness. This allows both insights and healing to emerge. The body wants to heal, to release the tensions and pains it is holding inside. Hence it is a form of therapy which is particularly good for people who have done some therapy before, and recognize the importance of this process of letting go of control. People who have done no therapy before tend to be too scared of the truth-telling effects of this process. But people who have done some therapy are more likely to recognize the necessity of facing and dealing with the truth, no matter how unpleasant it may be.

DEVELOPMENT OF THE THERAPY

It goes back to the early 1970s, when a number of people got together in the USA to form the International Primal Association. The founders included experienced therapists such as Bill Swartley, Tom Verny, Michael Broder and others. At the same time Frank Lake, a pioneering psychiatrist in Britain, was making the same sort of discoveries, and in 1966 published a book called *Clinical Theology*, which included a number of very striking case histories.

In the late 1970s, Bill Swartley led training groups in England, and since then a number of people have been practising in this country. My own work has been written up in a chapter in the book edited by me and Windy Dryden mentioned in 'Suggested reading' (p. 207). One of the main developments has been the group work which takes place at the Open Centre in London, under the very able guidance of Richard Mowbray and Juliana Brown (members of the Independent Practitioners Network), with assistance from Betty Hughes and others. All these were trained by Bill Swartley. They have written about their work in a book edited by David Jones.[1] At the same time some very interesting work has been going on at the Amethyst Centre near Dublin, under the direction of practitioners Alison Hunter and Shirley Ward. They have made some very interesting contributions to the theory and practice of the work. Shirley Ward's collected papers were published by the Centre in 1992. In 1993 there appeared, again from the Amethyst Centre, *The Fractal Dimension of Healing Conception*, a paper and video presentation prepared for the 6th International Congress of the Pre- and Perinatal Psychology Association of North America in Washington. In America there is active development of the practice in the International Primal Association (IPA), who hold yearly conferences and put on a number of other activities.

Another pioneer in Britain was William Emerson, also a member of the IPA, who spent a good deal of time in Europe. He had been trained as a clinician, and worked for some time in hospitals, but got more and more involved with regression and integration therapy. He also started calling his work primal integration, and was a quite separate source of influence in Europe. He pioneered the idea of actually working in a primal way with children, and produced a pamphlet on infant and child birth re-facilitation, and a video film of his work with them.

THEORY AND BASIC CONCEPTS

The theory says that most personal problems which need the attention of a therapist have their origins in early trauma, before the age of five years old, and will not be fundamentally resolved unless and until that origin is reached and dealt with. Some people still do not believe that babies can remember their own birth, but this is because they have not read the research by people such as David Chamberlain,[2] a highly respected psychologist, who has written very helpfully about these matters. The importance of early trauma is a very well-established theory in psychotherapy, and is held by many people other than primal integration practitioners. Sigmund Freud, the originator of psychoanalysis, and Carl Jung, the great psychiatrist who followed him, certainly held it, and so do such varied people as the body therapists and the hypnotherapists.

What tends to happen is that some very early event causes panic. This panic gives rise to a form of defence. This defence works sufficiently well at the time, and the person gets by for the moment. When the next emergency arises, panic is again dealt with by the same defence which worked before. But this defence then becomes part of the character structure of the person, and they are stuck with it. It gets to be too good. It protects all too effectively, cutting the person off from their real experience.

Because primal integration emphasizes early trauma, people sometimes think it is going to put all one's problems down to one trauma, happening just once in one's life. But of course traumas are seldom as dramatic as this. The commonest causes of mental distress are simply the common experiences of childhood – all the ways in which our child needs are unmet or frustrated. This is not necessarily a single trauma, in the sense of a one-off event – that is much too simplistic a view. Rather we would say, with the psychoanalyst Michael Balint,[3] that the trauma may come from a situation of some duration, where the same painful lack of 'fit' between needs and supplies is continued.

The goal of primal integration is to contact and release the real self. This is the part which was defended, and which therefore is now surrounded by all the defences which were erected over the years. But it has remained intact behind all the layers of defence, and can be contacted in therapy, with rich results. It is interesting to see, in book after book and paper after paper, how people do not really change in any substantial way unless they go through some kind of therapeutic work at this deep level.

Historically, this approach is close to early Freud, the early work of psycho-analyst Wilhelm Reich (who placed great importance on the body being directly involved in therapy) and Arthur Janov (author of *The Primal Scream*). But all of these adopted a medical model of mental illness, which primal integration rejects. As Thomas Szasz, the great critic of formal psychotherapy, pointed out long ago, neurosis is only a metaphorical sickness, not a disease in the true sense of the word. Rather does primal integration stand with those who are less concerned with cure than with growth.

As soon as one gets down into the early roots of mental distress, deep and strong feelings come up, because the emotions of early life are less inhibited, less qualified and less differentiated than they later become. In other words, they are cruder and clearer. And so the whole question of the importance of catharsis in psychotherapy arises here. Catharsis means the expression of strong emotions. It was Reich and Fritz Perls (originator of Gestalt therapy), not Janov, who discovered the techniques for deep emotional release that are used to produce primals. As many people now know, a primal is a deep emotional experience in which one gets in touch with the pain and terror of one's earliest bad experiences.

The Reichian-oriented therapist Charles Kelley used the term 'an intensive' years before Janov to describe experiences identical to primals.

It makes sense to say that catharsis has two related but separate components: one is cognitive (the thinking function) and relatively intellectual – the recall of forgotten material; the second is emotional and physical – the discharge of feelings in deep sobbing, strong laughter or angry yelling. But in the kind of work we are interested in here, it seems better to be more specific, and to say that catharsis is the vigorous expression of feelings about experiences which had been previously unavailable to consciousness. This lays more emphasis upon the necessity for the emergence of unconscious material.

What Bill Swartley, Frank Lake, Stanislav Grof (the great writer on the birth experience) and others did was to bring together the idea of catharsis and the emphasis on getting down to the origins of disturbance with another very important question – the transpersonal and the whole area of spirituality. This means that primal integration can deal with the major part of the whole psycho-spiritual spectrum mapped out by author Ken Wilber in his book *The Atman Project*.[4] What Ken Wilber is saying is that we are all on a psycho-spiritual journey, whether we like it or not, and whether we know it or not. We are moving from the pre-personal (infancy and childhood) through the personal (adult life, language and logic) towards the transpersonal (which goes beyond conventional thinking and everyday taken-for-granted beliefs). I have written about this at greater length in my book *The Transpersonal in Psychotherapy and Counselling*.[5] I believe primal integration is the only therapy which can handle this whole spectrum, except possibly for the holonomic (law of the whole) approach described by Grof,[6] which is so close as to be almost the same thing.

Much of the thinking behind Object Relations (the very popular branch of psychoanalysis associated with the names of Donald Winnicott, Michael Balint, Harry Guntrip and others in Britain) is compatible with what we find in primal integration. This is because these theoreticians also hold the idea of a real self behind all the defences.

In my belief primal integration is the fullest form of psychotherapy, because it covers all the four functions which Jung spoke of. It deals with the sensing function through body work and breathing. It approaches the feeling function through emotional contact and release. It handles the thinking function by means of analysis and insight. And it deals with the intuiting function through guided fantasy, art work, dream work and so forth. In terms of the theory of Ken Wilber, it covers the pre-personal (early experience and child development), the personal (adult life in the here and now) and the transpersonal (spiritual experience and visions of the future). So it runs the whole gamut of human experience.

PRACTICE

The practice is based on the theory of Stanislav Grof,[7] which says that our experience is organized into COEX systems. A COEX is a system of condensed experience whereby a certain pattern of physical sensations, emotional feelings, thoughtful ideas and spiritual impressions are held firmly together in the mind. This pattern comes from an experience we have had in the past. This experience, memorable and perhaps traumatic, sticks with us as a whole, not as a series of parts. When we come into a similar situation, it brings back the whole of that feeling in an exaggerated form, turning a whisper into a shout. This means that we are always meeting the same situation with the same reactions, the same defences.

So in therapy we may start with a recent experience of distress, such as being upset and angry with an authority figure. As the client is encouraged to express feelings of anger, etc., they may find the feelings really taking over. There is usually the sense of giving oneself permission to go with it. During that process, there may be a flash or vision from the past. In this case, it could be a parent figure and perhaps a memory scene. Then, if the client feels safe, he/she may re-experience a traumatic event and release the feelings from the past. A connection is made between that scene and the present. This generally releases the energy of the current situation and the client is able to function better. The more we can release our pent-up emotions, the more we can open to love and our own power within.

Now it is obvious that a procedure like this takes time, and it is really best to go all the way with a particular COEX in one session, rather than trying to take up the tail of one session at the head of the next, which usually doesn't work. This means that the primal integration therapist tends to prefer long sessions, which also enable the client to take a break or breather if need be during the session. I personally conduct some 1-hour sessions, but I also have some 1½ hour and 2-hour sessions; some people working in this area have used up to 10-hour sessions. The process is basically self-directed, so that each person will open up and progress at their own pace. This maintains safety and also provides support for those who are not ready or willing to go into the deeper parts of their psyche.

It is important to say, however, that all of this is primal integration, not primal trauma integration. It is not the intention to hive off traumas (bad and unforgettable experiences), and deal only with those. Whatever we do by way of therapy is part of an attempt to do justice to the whole of life, not just part of it. As Juliana Brown and Richard Mowbray[8] have well said, it is about 'continually bringing a deeper way of living into being, and a deeper way of being into living!'

One important piece of research that was done in primal integration by Ninoska Marina[9] found that it was particularly effective in dealing with such problems as relating to people, relating to oneself, having more energy and enjoying sex. The researcher found that people tended to discover 'a sense of self different to what it had been in the pre-therapy period.' This is a radical change, and not everyone is ready for this. So primal integration is a form of depth psychology, and needs to be taken in that light as something to tackle when we feel ready. In this process people open themselves up to deeper feelings, and thus become more vulnerable. So a high degree of trust has to be built up between client and therapist. But in reality, trust isn't a feeling, it's a decision. Nobody can ever prove, in any final or decisive way, that they are worthy of this trust, so the client just has to take the decision at some time, and it may as well be sooner as later.

If we believe, as Michael Broder (one of the earliest theorists of primal integration) suggests, that the primal process consists of five phases – Commitment; Abreaction (catharsis); Insight (involving the restructuring of thoughts and feelings); Counter-action (fresh behaviour in the world); and Pro-action (making real changes) – then it must be the case that the later phases are just as important as the earlier ones. In other words, working through is just as significant as breaking through. The glamorous part, and the controversial part, of our work is the 'primal', the cathartic breakthrough; but in reality the process of integration is necessary and equally exciting in its quieter way. For example, it is a great thing for a man to get to the cathartic point of forgiving his mother; it is another thing for him to start treating women decently in daily life, as a result of this.

One of the things that happens in primal work is that the deeper people go in recession and regression, the more likely they are to have spiritual experiences too. Shirley Ward of the Amethyst Centre in Ireland believes this is because the psychic centres open up. In other words, people get in touch with the higher unconscious – what the great Italian theorist Roberto Assagioli called the superconscious. However, in this area there is one very common error we have to guard against. Grof points out that blissful womb states, which primal clients sometimes get into, are very similar to peak experiences and to the cosmic unity which mystics speak of as contact with the Divine. This has led some people – David Wasdell (of the Unit for Research into Changing Institutions) for example – into saying that all mystical experiences are nothing but reminiscences of the ideal or idealized womb. This is an example of reductionism – that is, of always trying to reduce what is complex to what is simpler. The whole point is that we repress not only dark or painful material in the lower unconscious, but also embarrassingly good material in the higher unconscious. John Firman and Ann Gila[10] of the psychosynthesis school founded by Assagioli have recently written an important theoretical work on this subject.

WHICH CLIENTS BENEFIT MOST?

The ideal client is someone who has been in other forms of therapy which have introduced them to the basic ideas of working on themselves and exploring things at an unconscious level.

But really primal integration is very effective with such basic problems as depression and anxiety. These are the most common presenting issues for therapists of all persuasions today. It is also suitable for more immediate matters such as panic disorders, grief, rage, sexual abuse, rape, incest and the like. It can deal much better than most other approaches with pre-verbal traumas, issues around birth and pre-birth experiences, abandonment, rejection and other problems that are much more serious and troubling. These are some of the hardest issues for clients to work with, express, feel and release.

Because of its concern with the whole person in the social context, it is also able to pay attention to such things as sexism and racism. Sometimes people's problems come from outside, not from inside. Any adequate therapy must be able to handle this fact. We have to be able to listen with the fourth ear of political awareness as well as with the third ear of emotional awareness.

In reality, every problem has two components: the one has to do with the real situation as it exists in the everyday world, the consensus reality in which we all live. The other has to do with our own private reactions and responses to the world, which may be based on old tapes from the past, still playing in the present. In therapy we can handle the second of these two, and deal with whatever may be unrealistic or detrimental about that. Then when we have done that, the real situation will still remain, but we shall have greater strength and ability to deal with it in the best way possible, because we shall not be fighting against ourselves.

Case study

THE CLIENT

The client was a middle-aged man who had difficulty relating to women. They did not seem to like him, and he did not seem to understand them. In his younger days he had never been very successful with women, and had experienced a good deal of sexual frustration as a consequence. He was now married, with several children, but did not get on well with his wife. He had no idea why this was a problem, since at a conscious level he was not only appreciative of women, but also he was interested in feminism, and had even joined a men's consciousness-raising group.

THE THERAPY

He got into therapy, and had a number of experiences where he got in touch with his feelings, and started to open up the inner world of his mind. This was not an easy process, because being out of touch with his feelings had given him a sense of strength and invulnerability. It took some time before he could see the possibility of being strong and vulnerable at the same time.

Then he had an experience, which came quite spontaneously and unexpectedly, of reliving his own birth. He seemed to go through the experience from start to finish, and to have the sense of also seeing it from above. He seemed to see himself covered in green slime, and the words came to him – 'How could anybody love that?' He felt a terrible rejection, as if his mother had thrown him out of her womb, and taken her love away from him, and taken her milk away from him, and excluded him from her world. He had instantly decided upon revenge. She could do these things to him now, but just you wait! When he was big enough he would show her!

Some people doubt that babies so young can make decisions in this way. But as we saw earlier in the discussion of the COEX principle, similar experiences reflect forward and backward in the mind. The concepts and the language we acquire later can be reflected back into the earlier experiences to inform them and make them more complete. There is a lot of research now to show that very young babies are acutely aware of what is going on, and are well able to respond to them appropriately. David Chamberlain[11] in particular has made a special study of this. Each time the client felt rejected by his mother, the same decision was repeated, and repeated and repeated. By the time he grew up, at a deep level, below the level of conscious awareness, he hated his mother, and wanted to get revenge on her. And because this was an unacceptable feeling, all his feelings became unacceptable. And because she was a woman, this generalized to all women. As he came into adolescence and sexual feelings, he could not understand why he did not get on better with women. He was completely unaware that he hated them.

So when he had this breakthrough in his therapy, he was able to re-evaluate this decision, and to see that what he had done was understandable, but was not necessary. He could forgive himself, and forgive his mother, and dump the whole of that misunderstanding and decision-making. This is how therapy works – it enables a person to move on from an impossible situation by removing the misunderstandings from it. Immediately he found that he was getting on better with women. So that was phase one.

The next thing that happened was that he had an experience in primal integration group work where he had a vision of himself in the womb. He was the larger of a pair of twins, the other one a girl. And he had killed her: that was his belief. Ever since then, unconsciously, he had felt guilty about his treatment of women, and had reacted very strongly to any accusations they had made against him. This was one reason he had been affected so much by feminism. The group leader suggested that he go back into the womb, with a woman selected from the group, and this time preserve her instead of killing her. He did this, and once again felt relationships with women to be much easier. In fact, he met a militant feminist at a conference after that, and found her not to be threatening at all. She said to him, 'The hostility was yours, not mine.' And he now felt this to be true. So that was phase two.

Not long after that, he had an experience in the primal integration group where he seemed to be going back and back, and down and down, into the very depths of his early experience. Very early on, he had been faced with a fork in the road, so to speak, where he had to choose between relying on himself and relying on other people. He had chosen the path of relying on himself. And he had in fact been very independent, aided by the fact that his family had moved house many times in his youth. But now he went back to that fork in the road, it seemed, and decided to take the other path. The phrase came to him, 'I don't want to be alone.' And he seemed to come up from there with relays clicking and different connections being made all the way along the line until he came up to the present. And after the experience he seemed to be able to be intimate with a woman. He found a new partner, and became very different in the way he related to her. For the first time, he could genuinely be with another person.

It seems to me that other forms of therapy do not go as deep as this.

REFERENCES

1 Jones, D. (ed.) (1994) *Innovative Therapy: A Handbook*. Buckingham: Open University Press.
2 Chamberlain, D. (1998) *The Mind of Your Newborn Baby*. Berkeley: North Atlantic Books.
3 Balint, M. (1968) *The Basic Fault*. London: Tavistock.
4 Wilber, K. (1996) *The Atman Project* (2nd edn). Wheaton: Quest.
5 Rowan, J. (1993) *The Transpersonal in Psychotherapy and Counselling*. London: Routledge.
6 Grof, S. (1992) *The Holotropic Mind*. San Francisco: Harper.
7 Grof, S., ibid.
8 Brown, J. and Mowbray, R. (1994) 'Primal integration', in D. Jones (ed.), *Innovative Therapy: A Handbook*. Buckingham: Open University Press.
9 Marina, N. (1982) 'Restructuring of cognitive-affective structure: a central point of change after psychotherapy', unpublished doctoral thesis, Brunel University.
10 Firman, J. and Gila, A. (1997) *The Primal Wound*. Albany, NY: State University of New York Press.
11 Chamberlain, D. (1998) op.cit.

SUGGESTED READING

Blum, T. (ed.) (1993) *Prenatal Perception, Learning and Bonding*. Berlin: Leonardo Publishers. Fifteen articles by different writers, including an excellent chapter by David Chamberlain on 'Prenatal intelligence'. Quite academic and professional.

Noble, E. (1993) *Primal Connections*. New York: Simon & Schuster. A personal book using much material from her work with the late Graham Farrant, a pioneer of working with primal material. Makes many fascinating points.

Rowan, J. (1988) 'Primal integration,' in J. Rowan and W. Dryden (eds), *Innovative Therapy in Britain*. Milton Keynes: Open University Press. A fairly full account of primal work in action, paying attention both to the theory and to the practice.

Verny, T. (1972) *The Secret Life of the Unborn Child*. London: Sphere. A very well-written book giving much research evidence and many fascinating stories about prenatal experience.

DISCUSSION ISSUES

1 Is there conscious experience in the womb?
2 Is there such a thing as the trauma of birth?
3 Can anyone remember their own birth?
4 Can therapy in the present undo the experiences of childhood?

16

PROBLEM-FOCUSED COUNSELLING AND PSYCHOTHERAPY

Michael Neenan and Stephen Palmer

P roblem-focused counselling is a method of teaching or training individuals to identify current problems in their lives and then to learn a series of steps in order to overcome them. These problems can be of a practical nature (e.g. making a career decision) without any overlapping emotional difficulties (e.g. anxiety about making the wrong decision), but frequently these two elements, the practical and the emotional, are found together in clients' presenting problems. Therefore, the form of problem-solving presented in this chapter will be double-headed: first, tackling the emotional aspects of a problem; second, once this has been achieved, dealing with its practical aspects. For example, a client who is depressed (emotional problem) about being in debt (practical problem) struggles unsuccessfully to put his finances in order. This is because his negative view of himself as a hopeless failure prevents any clear thinking about climbing out of debt. By being helped to challenge and change his self-image and thereby lift his depression, he is then able to focus his restored energies on taking the necessary practical measures (e.g. cutting down on his drinking and gambling) to reduce or eventually eliminate his debts.

The double-headed or dual systems approach to problem-focused counselling that we describe in this chapter is essentially a cognitive-behavioural one because it emphasizes the significant impact our thinking has on our emotions and behaviour. As this problem-solving model draws on diverse psychological influences it can also be said to belong to the developing phenomenon of integrative counselling (see Chapter 9).

DEVELOPMENT OF THE THERAPY

Problem-focused counselling or training has been mainly developed over the last few decades by psychologists as a way of increasing clients' coping skills.[1] What each approach has in common is a sequence of problem-solving steps for clients to follow, starting with problem-identification and ending with a review of the solutions used to tackle the problem (the full steps will be described later). Skills acquisition is an important part of problem-solving training as some clients will not know how to put into practice some of their proposed solutions for change (e.g. learning time-management techniques or social communication skills). Problem-focused counselling is increasingly used in such situations as crisis intervention or stress management. This approach deals primarily with practical problem-solving and may be all that is required for some clients as they are not emotionally upset about their practical problems. If an emotional block did occur, then the therapeutic focus would be switched to tackling this block by using the ABCDE model (see below).

The counselling approach we use in this chapter to deal with emotional problem-solving is rational emotive behaviour therapy (REBT). REBT was founded in 1955 by Albert Ellis, an American clinical psychologist.[2] Ellis believed, like some ancient philosophers, that people are not so much disturbed by events themselves but by the views they hold about these events. In other words, emotional distress such as guilt, shame, depression or anxiety is a product of how individuals perceive and evaluate events in their lives (e.g. 'Because I lost my job, this makes me worthless').

Ellis was more interested in how individuals maintain their problems through their belief systems rather than how these problems were acquired (he rejected the view that present problems are rooted in early childhood experiences). For example, a 50-year-old man still sees himself as a failure because his parents predicted he would be one. REBT would encourage him to examine why he still agrees with his parents' opinion of him and the accuracy of his self-image. In over 40 years of REBT's development in treating a wide range of emotional disorders, Ellis has continually emphasized that individuals have to think, feel and act forcefully against their upsetting thinking if they want to achieve enduring change (for a fuller account of REBT, see Chapter 21).

THEORY AND BASIC CONCEPTS

ABCDE model of emotional disturbance and change

REBT offers a relatively simple model for understanding how aspects of our thinking can create our disturbed feelings and for tackling such disturbance-producing thinking:

A = activating event (e.g. losing one's job).
B = beliefs which sum up the individual's view of this event (e.g. 'As I've lost my job, which absolutely shouldn't have happened to me, this means I'm no good').
C = emotional and behavioural consequences largely determined by the individual's beliefs about this event (e.g. depression and withdrawal from the world prevent him from seeking another job).

D = disputing disturbance-producing beliefs (e.g. 'I would, of course, greatly prefer not to have lost my job *but* there is no reason in the final analysis why it must not happen to me. Without it, I can still be relatively happy and accept myself. I am too complex to damn myself as no good on the basis of losing my job').

E = new and effective rational outlook accompanied by emotional and behavioural changes (e.g. he feels sad about being made redundant but re-enters the world in order to find a new job. Self-acceptance now underpins his job-seeking efforts).

REBT asserts that rigid and absolute beliefs in the form of musts, shoulds, have to's, got to's, oughts, are usually to be found at the core of human emotional disturbance. These beliefs act as commands and demands that individuals make upon themselves, others, and the world (e.g. 'I shouldn't have to experience any stress at work'). Flowing from these musts, shoulds, etc., are three major conclusions:

1   Awfulizing – defining negative events as so terrible that they seem to slip off the scale of human understanding (e.g. 'Why are all these unpleasant things happening to me? It shouldn't be like this. It's awful').
2   Low frustration tolerance – an individual's perceived inability to endure discomfort or frustration in her life (e.g. 'Why does everyone hassle me as they shouldn't do. I can't stand it any longer!').
3   Damnation of self and/or others – giving oneself a negative label based on a particular action, life event or characteristic (see B in ABCDE).

These rigid beliefs are called irrational or self-defeating because they are seen as illogical and unrealistic. They block or interfere with clients' attempts to achieve their goals for change, and generate a good deal of emotional disturbance. Such disturbance then prevents or hinders clients from developing or implementing practical problem-solving skills. REBT asserts that all humans have a strong biological or innate tendency to think irrationally. This view is based upon the seemingly limitless ability of humans to disturb themselves over adverse environmental conditions or life events (e.g. lack of romantic relationships, difficult work colleagues, traffic jams). While the effects of these conditions upon human functioning are not minimized, nevertheless they are deemed to be an insufficient explanation for any resulting emotional disturbance.

In order to tackle our largely self-induced emotional problems and thereby attain emotional health, REBT suggests developing a belief system based on flexible and non-absolute preferences, wishes, wants, desires (e.g. 'I very much want your love but there is no reason why I must have what I want'). These beliefs are called rational or self-helping because they are seen as logical and realistic. They aid goal-attainment and usually reduce our level of emotional distress, thereby facilitating practical problem-solving. Flowing from these preferences and wishes are three major conclusions and constructive alternatives to the ones listed above:

1 Anti-awfulizing – negative or unpleasant events are judged on a scale of badness that lies within human understanding (e.g. 'As much as I don't like them, these unpleasant things are happening to me. They are bad but not awful').

2 High frustration tolerance – the ability to withstand or tolerate a great deal of difficulty or discomfort in one's life (e.g. 'A lot of people are hassling me at the present time but I can stand it without having to like it').

3 Acceptance of self and others – human beings are seen as fallible (imperfect) and in a state of continuous change, therefore it is futile to label them in any way (see **D** in ABCDE model).

REBT suggests that we have a second, biologically based tendency to think about our thinking, that is, to reflect rationally upon our irrational ideas and thereby counteract or minimize the potentially harmful effects of our distorted and crooked thinking. By developing a rational philosophy of living, individuals can learn to moderate their disturbed feelings as well as increase their striving for self-actualization (realizing one's potential).

Sequential model of practical problem-solving

Once the individual's level of emotional distress has been reduced and she is therefore free from her excessive self-absorption, she can now focus more of her time, energy and attention on practical problem-solving steps to achieve her goals for change. Wasik has proposed a seven-step problem-solving sequence and the corresponding questions that an individual can ask herself at each step.[3]

	Steps	*Questions/Actions*
1	Problem-identification	What is the concern?
2	Goal-selection	What do I want?
3	Generation of alternatives	What can I do?
4	Consideration of consequences	What might happen?
5	Decision-making	What is my decision?
6	Implementation	Now do it!
7	Evaluation	Did it work?

Step 1 This involves eliciting from the client clear and specific problems to work on; a problem list in order of priority can be drawn up if the client has a multitude of difficulties she wishes to address. This first step also includes identifying the client's own existing skills at problem-solving as these will be put to therapeutic use.

Step 2 The client's goals should be precise and realistic. This may involve negotiation between the client and counsellor. These goals should be stated in behavioural terms, that is, when, where and how often a particular activity is to be carried out.

Step 3 The client is encouraged to come up with as many possible solutions to her problems no matter how ludicrous some of them initially appear; in other words, to brainstorm. If the client has trouble suggesting few or any ideas the counsellor can suggest some himself as a means of prompting the client.

Step 4 This involves the client considering the advantages and disadvantages of each solution produced from the brainstorming session. The client may wish to rate the plausibility of each possible solution on a 0–10 scale (0 = least plausible to 10 = most plausible).

Step 5 The client now chooses which solution to pursue, based upon the calculation of probable success decided in the previous step.

Step 6 This involves the client rehearsing in the counselling session the behaviour she is going to carry out in real life. The counsellor can also help the client to suggest ways of handling the situation if setbacks occur (they usually do).

Step 7 At the next session, which is after the client has carried out the agreed solution, counsellor and client evaluate its outcome. Did it work and why? If not, why not? The client is taught that problem-solving is a process of trial and error and therefore there will be a head-scratching, back-to-the-drawing-board approach in the counselling sessions. If the proposed solution has been success-ful, then the client can pick another problem from her list and follow steps 1–6 again.

It is important to note that at any stage of the practical problem-solving process, clients can become emotionally disturbed (e.g. depressed, ashamed, angry) about their lack of progress, the frustrations they are experiencing or the length of time and amount of effort required to realize their goals for change. If this does happen, it is usually necessary for the counsellor to take the client back to the ABCDE model of emotional disturbance and change. This will help the client to undisturb herself emotionally by identifying, challenging and changing her disturbance-producing ideas (e.g. 'I can't stand all these bloody setbacks! I'm completely useless because I can't make much progress'). Once this emotional problem-solving has been achieved, the client can return her attention to the practical tasks at hand. Two important qualities that greatly assist clients in their problem-solving endeavours are self-acceptance and high frustration tolerance.

PRACTICE

The goals of problem-focused counselling are to help individuals tackle their emotional and practical problems in order for them to lead happier, healthier and more fulfilling lives. This is achieved by individuals thinking more rationally, feeling less disturbed and acting in more goal-directed ways. Through new ways of thinking, feeling and behaving, individuals' coping skills, both existing and learnt, will be improved. Problem-focused counsellors aim to make themselves redundant by teaching clients how to become their own counsellors for present and future problem-solving.

Socializing clients into problem focused counselling

This means teaching clients what is expected of them so that they can participate effectively in this therapeutic approach (this procedure may have to be postponed if the client is, initially, too upset to absorb this information). Clients are shown two forms of responsibility: (1) emotional – that their emotional disturbance is largely (but not totally) self-induced; (2) therapeutic – that in order to moderate or overcome this disturbance, they need to carry out a number of tasks, often on a lifelong basis, if they wish to maintain their counselling gains. These tasks are often described in counselling as 'homework'.

To help clients absorb these responsibilities, problem focused counsellors teach their clients to separate their presenting problems into their A (events or situations), B (beliefs) and C (emotions and behaviours) components. This therapist-as-teacher approach includes moving clients away from A–C thinking ('Traffic jams make me angry') to B–C thinking ('How do I make myself angry about traffic jams?'). Using B–C language helps to reinforce emotional responsibility.

Therapeutic relationship

Problem-focused counsellors agree that the conditions of empathy, warmth, respect, genuineness, and unconditional positive regard are necessary for the development of a therapeutic alliance. However, they have some reservations about displaying too much warmth as this may strengthen some clients' powerful needs for love and approval as well as convince them that lots of support from the counsellor rather than their own sustained effort is the key to tackling their problems. The development of a therapeutic alliance goes hand in hand with an early problem-solving focus. The message of counselling is: 'Let's get to work!'

Assessment

Problem-focused counsellors seek clear and specific information (where possible) from clients in order to place their emotional problems – tackling the practical ones comes later – within the ABC framework. This framework teaches clients a concrete way of understanding and tackling their emotional difficulties. For example, a client says he feels 'jittery' about confronting his best friend over an unpaid loan (A). What disturbed or unhealthy emotion does 'jittery' refer to? By encouraging the client to describe in some detail his uncomfortable feelings, the counsellor helps him to discover that the disturbed feeling is anxiety (C).

However, at this stage, neither the counsellor nor the client is aware of what the latter is most anxious about with regard to challenging his best friend over the unpaid loan (what a client is most upset about in relation to his/her presenting problem is known as the critical A). This is uncovered through a process known as inference chaining whereby the client's personally significant assumptions about this situation are linked through a series of 'Let's assume . . . then what?' questions. The aim of inference chaining is to identify the client's critical A which triggers his self-defeating belief about trying to get back the money:

> *Client:* I'm anxious that he might get angry if I ask him for the money back.
> *Counsellor:* Let's assume that he does get angry. Then what?
> *Client:* He might reject me and say he no longer wants my friendship.
> *Counsellor:* Let's assume that he does say that. Then what?
> *Client:* Well, that would mean I'm an unlikeable person.
> *Counsellor:* In whose eyes – his or yours?
> *Client:* His.
> *Counsellor:* Would you agree with his opinion of you that you are unlikeable?
> *Client:* Yes, I would. I would agree wholeheartedly. I have the same worries whether my other friends really like me.
> *Counsellor:* So with regard to this current problem, are you most anxious about asking him for the money back because you might be rejected and end up seeing yourself as unlikeable?
> *Client:* That's what I fear the most [*the client's critical A has been located*].

The next step is to help the client find his major demand about the critical A, for example, 'I must keep his friendship at all costs because without it I am unlikeable' (B). This irrational and self-defeating belief is composed of a must statement and a self-downing conclusion. A wide range of techniques is now employed throughout the course of therapy to dispute (D) this belief (the client probably has other self-defeating beliefs that also need to be addressed). From this disputing process, clients learn how to develop a new and effective rational outlook (E).

Cognitive techniques

These techniques help clients to think about their thinking in more self-helping ways. They are taught to examine the evidence for and against their self-defeating beliefs by using three major criteria:

1 **Logic.** Just because you would greatly prefer not to be unlikeable, how does it logically follow that you must not be unlikeable?
2 **Realism.** Where is the evidence that the world obeys your demands? If it did, then you would be guaranteed that you would never be unlikeable no matter what you did. Is this actually the case?
3 **Pragmatism.** How helpful is it holding on to this belief? Where is it going to get you if you keep on demanding that you must never be unlikeable?

Behavioural techniques

These are negotiated with the client on the basis of being challenging, but not overwhelming, that is, tasks that are sufficiently stimulating to promote thera-peutic change but not so daunting as to prevent clients from carrying them out (e.g. the client begins to say 'no' sometimes to his friends who expect him to drive them everywhere – he normally would always have agreed). While 'trying on' this new behaviour, he mentally challenges the demand that 'I must never be unlikeable.'

Emotive techniques

These involve fully engaging clients' emotions while they forcefully dispute their self-defeating ideas. Among these techniques are shame-attacking exercises whereby clients act in a 'shameful' way in real-life in order to attract public ridicule or disapproval, e.g. asking for roast beef in a vegetarian restaurant, at the same time vigorously striving for self-acceptance with such rational state-ments as 'Just because I'm acting in a stupid way doesn't make me stupid. If people want to see me as unlikeable because of my behaviour, then too bad!' Clients can learn from these exercises not to damn or label themselves on the basis of their behaviour or the reactions of others.

Imagery techniques

An important imagery technique is for the client to imagine remaining anxious for the rest of his life because he fears being disliked and is not prepared to do anything about challenging these fears (inaction imagery). The therapist encourages him to fill in specific details (e.g. letting himself be continuously used by others) in order to make his future as graphic as possible.

Conversely, the client imagines his future without the anxiety because he has learnt self-acceptance and assertion through hard work and struggle (action imagery). Again the client is encouraged to view his future in as much detail as possible (e.g. friendships based on mutual respect) and then contrast it with the inaction imagery. Clients usually need to go through this double imagery procedure frequently if it is going to be a spur to action, a commitment to change.

Practical problem-solving section of counselling

Once the client's emotional distress has diminished, he can then focus on what measures are required to address the practical aspects of his problems by using the seven-step model.

1 Problem-identification – the client's best friend has not returned the money he lent him.
2 Goal-selection – the return of the money, if possible.
3 Generation of alternatives:
   (a) 'Strangle him!'
   (b) 'Forget the money and put its loss down to experience.'
   (c) 'Become assertive.'
   (d) 'Report him to the police.'
   (e) 'Steal it from him.'
   (f) 'Ask him for it on every occasion I meet or phone him.'
4 Consideration of consequences:
   (a) 'If he was dead, it would be highly unlikely I would get my money back and I would end up in prison. Not a serious solution.'
   (b) 'That would reinforce my passivity.'
   (c) 'This sounds very promising as I am sorely lacking in assertiveness. I could learn to stand up for myself.'
   (d) 'I do not want the situation to become more complicated than it already is.'
   (e) 'Like (a), not a serious solution. He might claim that my money was actually his money because I stole it from him'.
   (f) 'The constant pressure might force him to return the money.'
5 Decision-making – the client chose steps (c) and (f).
6 Implementation – by learning and practising assertiveness skills in counselling, the client forcefully but unangrily asked for the money back on every occasion he communicated with his friend.
7 Evaluation – much to the client's surprise, his friend promised to repay the debt in two stages, the first of which was repaid before counselling ended. Even if the money had not been returned, the point of being assertive is to speak up unangrily for oneself without any guarantee that others will listen favourably or redress the grievance.

The real gains from counselling, the client concluded, were his new outlook based on self-acceptance and assertiveness. Getting the money back was a bonus.

The process of therapeutic change

This involves a number of steps for clients to learn and these include:

1 That individuals largely (but not totally) create their own emotional disturbances about life events or practical problems through their irrational and self-defeating thinking.
2 That individuals have the ability to minimize or remove these disturbances by identifying, challenging and changing their rigid patterns of thinking. Once this has been achieved, individuals can focus their energies on practical problem-solving.

3 In order to acquire a rational or flexible pattern of thinking, individuals need to think, feel and act against their irrational beliefs, usually on a lifelong basis, if they wish to remain emotionally healthy and problem-orientated.

The ABCDE and seven-step models provide the frameworks in which this process of therapeutic change can occur.

Format of a typical session

This would involve setting an agenda of things to discuss in the session in order to keep the counsellor and client focused on the latter's emotional and practical problems. The agenda would include reviewing the client's homework tasks from the previous week; agreeing the topics to be discussed in the present session; negotiating further homework tasks that directly arise from the work done in the session; and eliciting client feedback about the session. Problem-focused counsellors view agenda-setting as the most efficient way of structuring the time spent with the client.

WHICH CLIENTS BENEFIT MOST?

Problem-focused counselling has been shown to be effective in the following areas: crisis intervention; stress management; emotional problems such as depression, anxiety, guilt, shame, anger; work problems or career changes; interpersonal conflicts; procrastination; lack of assertiveness; performance or presentation anxiety (e.g. public speaking).

Failures with clients in problem-focused counselling usually occur because they do not accept (a) emotional responsibility – they blame other factors (e.g. a partner or job) for causing their problems and therefore demand that these factors change before they can; and/or (b) therapeutic responsibility – they avoid or resist the hard work required of them to tackle their emotional and practical problems.

Case study

THE CLIENT

Client's presenting problems

Jane was a 30-year-old married woman with a teenage son. She worked part-time as a cashier in a local supermarket. She sought therapy for her social anxiety, namely, fear of negative evaluation by others in social situations. She said it greatly restricted her social life because she usually avoided going out in the evenings (much to her husband's annoyance) and it also made her work relationships fraught with worry as she was often preoccupied with what her colleagues thought about her. A course of 10 sessions was agreed upon (this number could be re-negotiated depending on the course of therapy).

THERAPY

Beginning therapy

After gathering more background information on Jane and her problems, the process of socializing her into counselling began, including establishing her goals for change. Jane's chosen goal was to feel less anxious, have an active social life and feel more relaxed at work. In order to understand her problems within the ABC model, the counsellor asked for a specific situation in which she felt anxious so he could discover what she was most anxious about in that particular situation (locating the critical A):

> *Counsellor:* What was anxiety-provoking in your mind about that recent dinner party you very reluctantly attended?
> *Client:* I thought people were not interested in talking to me.
> *Counsellor:* Let's assume that's true. Then what?
> *Client:* They avoid me because I'm not as good as they are.
> *Counsellor:* In what way are you 'not as good as they are'?
> *Client:* I'm not good at making conversation; I'm awkward and clumsy.
> *Counsellor:* Let's assume that's true. Then what?
> *Client:* Then others will judge me as stupid and that's why I want to avoid these situations.
> *Counsellor:* Is this what you're most anxious about?
> *Client:* Yes [*the client's critical A has been located*].

The client's major demand (irrational or self-defeating belief) about her critical A was identified: 'I must avoid social situations otherwise I will reveal myself as stupid.' The client was shown that her self-image as 'stupid' made her anxious in social situations rather than the situations themselves. The client accepted this point but wondered how to change her anxiety. The first homework task was for the client to read a self-help book on understanding and managing social anxiety.

The course of therapy

In the following sessions, other homework tasks included: challenging her irrational belief with a newly emerging rational belief: 'I would prefer not to be seen as stupid but there is no reason why I can't be seen that way. If some people think I'm stupid I can still accept myself with my flaws.' This was reinforced by Jane carrying out shame-attacking exercises in which she deliberately invited ridicule or criticism from others (but nothing that would put her or others in danger or break the law) in order to strengthen her self-acceptance. She accepted more social invitations (much to her husband's delight) in order to tolerate uncomfortable situations. This was helped by learning relaxation exercises. The double imagery technique was used so Jane could imagine how the foreseeable future would be if she did not tackle her social anxiety (inaction imagery) and how different it could be if she overcame her problem (action imagery). Action imagery had the advantages Jane greatly desired and inaction imagery all the disadvantages Jane wanted to discard.

Once Jane's anxiety was under control, counselling focused on the practical aspects of her problem. The seven-stage model was introduced to Jane.

1 Problem-identification – lack of social skills.
2 Goal-selection – learn to be more socially competent.
3 Generation of alternatives:
   (a) 'Just be myself. Others can take it or leave it.'
   (b) 'Try to ingratiate myself with others. Always be interested in what they're talking about.'
   (c) 'Be a good listener. Let others do the talking.'
   (d) 'Learn the rules of the game so I can mix more comfortably with others.'
   (e) 'Learn from others and see how they do it.'
   (f) 'Pick things up as I go along. I'm sure it's not as difficult as I've always made it.'
4 Consideration of consequences:
   (a) 'That sounds too arrogant. I want to mix with others, not put them off.'
   (b) 'That would seem like I'm desperate to be liked. That's the opposite of self-acceptance.'
   (c) 'That's too unbalanced. I want to talk as well as listen.'
   (d) 'I'm sure there are some rules to learn but I don't want to see socializing simply as a game.'
   (e) 'Observation of others is a good way to increase my social skills.'
   (f) 'I've learnt many other things in this way. I'm sure this will be no different.'
5 Decision-making – the client selected elements from (d), (e) and (f).
6 Implementation – through rehearsal in the counselling sessions, e.g. maintaining eye contact, confident body posture, drawing out the other person on their hobbies, job, etc., and offering information about herself, Jane gained the confidence to enter a variety of social settings.
7 Evaluation – Jane found increasing success in social situations and improved relationships with her work colleagues. People remarked on how different she had become.

However, she did experience setbacks. When she struggled to make conversation in some social encounters her anxiety returned. At the next counselling session, she went back to the ABCDE model to pinpoint her anxiety-producing belief, namely, 'Things are going wrong, so this must mean I'm really stupid.' She was able to challenge such beliefs by focusing on what went wrong rather than damning herself because of these setbacks. Once she had reduced her anxiety, the emotional problem, she refocused on following the practical problem-solving steps.

By the end of therapy Jane's anxiety had greatly reduced and she said she was very pleased with the progress she had made. She said that her social life was full but if she turned down invitations it was no longer because she feared being negatively viewed by others. The problem-solving models she had learnt in counselling could be used to tackle any future eruptions of her social anxiety or new difficulties that might appear. Follow-up appointments were arranged for 3, 6 and 12 months' time to monitor Jane's progress.

REFERENCES

1 D'Zurilla, T.J. (1986) *Problem-Solving Therapy: A Social Competence Approach to Clinical Intervention.* New York: Springer.
2 Ellis, A. (1994) *Reason and Emotion in Psychotherapy* (2nd edn). New York: Birch Lane Press.
3 Wasik, B. (1984) 'Teaching Parents Effective Problem-Solving: A Handbook for Professionals'. Unpublished manuscript. Chapel Hill: University of North Carolina.

SUGGESTED READING

D'Zurilla, T.J. (1986) *Problem-Solving Therapy: A Social Competence Approach to Clinical Intervention.* New York: Springer. This excellent book provides in-depth information about problem-solving therapy and training accompanied by plenty of case studies. It also includes a chapter on outcome studies for readers interested in the effectiveness of this approach.

Milner, P. and Palmer, S. (1998) *Integrative Stress Counselling: A Humanistic Problem-Focused Approach.* London: Cassell. This book shows how the problem-solving approach is integrated with rational emotive behaviour therapy. The book includes case studies and a wide range of useful techniques for tackling stress.

Palmer, S. and Burton, T. (1996) *Dealing with People Problems at Work.* London: McGraw-Hill. An easy-to-read, no-nonsense book looking at how to deal with workplace problems created by one's colleagues as well as those that are largely self-induced. The book is packed with effective techniques that help individuals to improve both their workplace efficiency and interpersonal relationships.

Palmer, S. and Dryden, W. (1995) *Counselling for Stress Problems.* London: Sage. A comprehensive account of stress counselling and stress management which uses both the problem-solving models described in this chapter. The book details a great variety of interventions that can be used to tackle stress and supplies case studies to show these techniques in action.

DISCUSSION ISSUES

1   Do people's problems always need to be viewed as containing both emotional and practical aspects?
2   Problem focused counsellors usually argue that tackling emotional disturbance first is necessary before clients can focus on practical problem-solving. Why do they believe this and would you agree with the proposed order of therapeutic intervention?
3   What problem areas might this dual systems approach to problem-solving be unsuitable for? Give your reasons.
4   Is it realistic for individuals to learn and use both problem-solving models described in this chapter? Is this problem-solving approach too cumbersome to teach and too difficult for clients to learn?

17

PSYCHOSYNTHESIS

Jean Hardy and Diana Whitmore

Psychosynthesis is a psychology that addresses not only human problems but also our potential. While few ever reach their potential, in the searching we can learn to live our lives more fully. Psychosynthesis therefore has an optimistic view of the human race, but it is not a new way. It is based on thousands of years of consideration of what people are truly like, both in the West and in the East.

Psychosynthesis is a spiritual, or transpersonal psychotherapy. It has been called 'a psychology with a soul'. A core principle is that we share an inner wisdom, and a transcendent nature which is common to all peoples, but which is often unrecognized in the modern world, particularly in our rushed and materialistic societies. It is the function of the psychosynthesis therapist to respect the spirit within and to know that any person can find the answers to his or her own problems from within, with non-invasive guidance. Therapy is therefore gentle and creative, using art, guided imagery and visualization, autobiography and reflection.

DEVELOPMENT OF THE THERAPY

Psychosynthesis was developed by Dr Roberto Assagioli during the early part of the twentieth century. He studied with Freud and was a colleague of Jung, participating in the early international conferences on psychotherapy before the First World War. However, he split from Freud's work at the same time as Jung and for much the same reason – that psychoanalysis had no space for the spirit or soul. He developed much of his theory in Italy under the difficult conditions of Mussolini's government, which lasted from 1922 to almost the end of the Second World War. This meant he was cut off from easy access to European psychotherapy although he did publish articles in the *Hibbert Journal* in England in the 1930s, on his model of the person and his way of working with clients.[1]

It was not until the 1950s and 1960s that psychosynthesis became internationally known when Dr Assagioli began to travel abroad, attend international conferences and meet others working in his field. By that time what has come to be known as the 'fourth force', or spiritual, or transpersonal psychotherapy, had begun to attract several other well-known writers and clinicians. Victor Frankl had begun to write about the human need for meaning based on his experiences in concentration camps. Abraham Maslow had begun to study not only people with problems but people who seemed to live their life with exceptional openness and success, and also those who seemed in touch with a wider spirit and awareness of their purposefulness and place on this planet. This broader and deeper perspective had always been a part of Assagioli's vision.

Since the 1960s, psychosynthesis centres have sprung up all over the world and now exist in about 40 countries. Roberto Assagioli died in 1974. According to his wish and non-prescriptive way of working, these centres have developed each in its own way, as a network rather than a centralized system. International conferences are still held about every four years, and publications are regularly passed between different countries and centres. Psychosynthesis in Britain is now accepted as a BAC accredited course, and offers university validated training with Postgraduate and Masters Degrees.

THEORY AND BASIC CONCEPTS

Psychosynthesis has a well worked out theory about human nature, about who we are. This is represented by what is called the 'egg-shaped diagram', thus:

1 The lower unconscious
2 The middle unconscious
3 The higher unconscious
4 The field of consciousness
5 The 'I'
6 The higher self or soul
7 The collective unconscious

In this representation (Figure 17.1), 4 is the field of our consciousness – in other words, the way we experience our daily lives. It is all the things we are immediately aware of. For many people this field of consciousness seems to be the whole of life. But, as most depth psychologists in this century believe, human beings live in a depth of unconsciousness too – that which influences our lives but of which we are most often unaware. The rest of the diagram is about unconscious forces: 2 is the middle, 1 the lower, 3 the higher and 7 the collective unconscious.

We can reach the middle unconscious in ourselves relatively easily. It comprises dreams, memories of past times, and the deeper processes within us that are more accessible and of which we may be partially aware. It is where the line between the everyday world and the inner world is least well defined. The lower unconscious is the area first investigated by Freud – deep past material, childhood

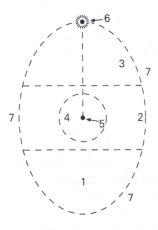

FIGURE 17.1 Assagioli's model of the human psyche

experience, trauma that has been covered up. It is here that we meet our many defensive strategies – perhaps ways of being cut off, or perhaps depressions, that we have used most of our lives to keep painful or disturbing material in some kind of control.

However, we are often as unaware of our great potential as we are of our deep problems. Psychosynthesis has a picture of the higher unconscious of which we can catch glimpses from time to time – of joy, of unity with the whole of life, of love, of beauty – that overwhelm us and place our lives in a much wider perspective. These glimpses, like those of all unconscious material can either be ignored and suppressed, or accepted and embraced. Through psychosynthesis therapy we can begin to recognize and then relate to all that we truly are, often uncovered from within those forces that affect our behaviour and actions of which we are largely unaware.

Both Jung and Assagioli also postulated a collective unconscious – that which we share in as members of our culture and race, of our gender, of nationality and as members of the whole human race. The view is that we carry these memories as much collectively as we do individually. In the twentieth century, for instance, most people in the West will carry with them at an unconscious level much knowing about the two world wars beyond what actual information they have about these wars. Now, late in this century, we might also feel that our unconscious influences are also ecological – a sense that we are collectively part of the amazing story of the whole universe and all the plants and animals within it. With the growing recognition of the interdependence of all life, few of us remain shut off from the experiences of the world we are a part of. The permeable lines in the diagram indicate there is movement within and between all the parts of who we are.

The diagram however is about more than this. The 'I' (5 in the diagram), is that part of ourselves which is the observer, which has always been present. When we feel 'together', centred, we are aware of the 'I' – but we can easily lose that awareness when swayed, disturbed and disorientated – which may be much of the time. In learning to become more centred we can more easily access the last part of the picture, 6, the higher self, or soul, which is all we may be not only as an individual, but also as a full part of the living web of life. Together, 5 and 6 are the process of living an aware, fully alive life, seeing life as a journey that makes sense. The higher self represents our fully alive being, that we can often glimpse through the higher unconscious, but which is fully aware. It is when we live out life most fully in the way we feel we are all meant to. As Marianne Williamson writes, 'we were all meant to shine as children do'.[2]

One part of Dr Assagioli's picture of the person is not on the diagram. It is the concept that we all consist of many 'subpersonalities'. The clown, the frightened child, the critic, the witch, the king, the mystic and the hermit are all possible components of one person. We each have our own array of them. These subpersonalities or characteristics are formulated by our life experiences and the strategies we employ to cope in times of trouble.

Though the diagram is necessarily static, the process in which we are involved is not so. Problems may erupt from any part of ourselves – subpersonalities get out of hand and take over, depressions and isolations emerge from the past, life crises potentially bring new awareness, or a feeling may arise of dissatisfaction because life seems less than it could be. Our lives, if they are to be satisfactory, cannot stay still. The psychosynthesis journey is a movement towards ever greater awareness – learning to recognize the whole orchestra which we are – even the quiet triangles stuck away at the back, and the out-of-rhythm drums. Learning also to recognize the conductor, who is the 'I', by which we manage that orchestra and therefore play more in tune, is an important part of that journey. We may even change the music through a realization of the higher self.

The task of the psychosynthesis therapist is to help his or her client get in touch with their own wisdom, in whatever stage of this journey they are. This is a lifetime process. The work does not impose any particular belief system on a client. A therapist will work with the beliefs that any person already holds or is reaching towards. Always the movement is towards the inclusion of the elements in the person that have been ignored and that are now causing problems. Always the work is towards more wholeness.

PRACTICE

Goals of psychosynthesis

Assagioli recognized two levels of psychosynthesis therapy which are necessary and indeed core to an individual's psychological health and spiritual well-being – *personal* psychosynthesis which aims to foster the development of a well-integrated personality, capable of actualizing itself through the individual's life; and *transpersonal* psychosynthesis which offers the possibility of realizing one's deepest, most essential self and its purpose in life.

The goals of psychosynthesis work could be summed up as the redemption of suffering and the evocation of potential in the client. It seeks to evoke our strengths and latent potential, to foster integration between our inner and outer worlds, to enable us to increasingly create our life as one which is rich with meaning and purpose, to enhance the quality of life and finally to enable us to find our own inner authority and wisdom.

Psychosynthesis does not hold a 'normative' view of psychospiritual health nor of what the client's process of therapy *should be like*. Instead, supreme importance is placed upon the individual's experience of inner freedom and upon gaining mastery over his or her own universe. A goal is to help clients enlarge their possibilities and choices in life.

The therapeutic relationship

Psychosynthesis holds that the human relationship is both core and essential to psychospiritual health and well-being. This principle forms the context and centrepiece of psychosynthesis therapy, with the relationship between client and therapist being foremost as well as sacred. Current research has shown that the quality of the human relationship has an important influence in determining the outcome of therapeutic work. Without a *bifocal vision* – one which sees both the light and the shadow in clients – and without a context which perceives the client as essentially much more than his or her problems, challenges and weaknesses – the therapeutic relationship would be limited and incomplete.

The heart of psychosynthesis work is based on an 'I–Thou relationship', in which the therapist fosters the strengths and potentialities of the client. The psychosynthesis therapist seeks to perceive the client as ultimately a self, a being, who has a purpose in life and has challenges and obstacles to meet in order to fulfil that purpose. The psychosynthesis therapist will relate to the client in a less mysterious and detached manner than classical analysis, and will seek to build a relational context which is holistic and healing.

Transference

The concepts of transference and counter-transference, the centrepiece of conventional analytic forms of therapy, are also an essential part of the psychosynthesis therapeutic relationship, but not the whole picture. Traditionally, transference is seen to be a 'playing out', with the therapist, of one's early relationships with parents or significant others. The client projects on to the therapist characteristics that he or she has in the past attributed to parents, and relates to the therapist with similar attitudes, behaviour patterns and emotional responses. Although Assagioli agreed with this Freudian definition and included it in psychosynthesis therapy, he stressed some essential differences in the importance placed on it and the strategy for working with it.

Assagioli *reframed* the concept of transference as a *healthy thrust* in the individual to complete a gestalt, finish unfinished business regarding our intimate relationships (of which parents are our first models) and to heal childhood trauma. This thrust is a part of the individual's continuing search for unity, to belong and be included in the universe. It is a response to the separation, alienation and isolation that many have experienced in childhood and represents an unconscious desire to heal the past. The therapeutic relationship offers a laboratory of sorts for us to work through these issues and learn to be intimate with another human being. If we learn to do this in the safe arena of therapy, we are learning skills for also doing so in life. The therapist helps the client evolve towards a more meaningful resolution of the transference by finding healthier, less dysfunctional ways of relating.

How does the therapist do this? In psychosynthesis therapy the goal is to dissolve the transference 'as it emerges' in the relationship. In the safety and contained environment of the therapeutic relationship, we will naturally and spontaneously experience ourselves regressing to more childlike states. We temporarily become dependent upon this person who accepts us unconditionally, mirrors to us that we are valuable and worthwhile, and supports us in dealing with childhood conflict and trauma. There is nothing pathological in this. The therapist will be watchful of the client regressing and relating to him or her in a more childlike manner, which signals the existence of transference.

With many clients, as the personal relationship becomes stronger, the transference will gradually lose its power and will resolve itself developmentally as we endure a process of maturation from child to adolescent to adult. It is often a matter of just letting it take its course. This is in accordance with the view of Perls who believed that the client will relate to the therapist as he or she related to parents, and depending on how well the therapist is able to hold and respond to this challenge, the client may go through a process of development.[3]

At any point along this journey, the psychosynthesis therapist may address and work with the transference with the client. This may occur through *intra-psychic* techniques, that is through consciously addressing the client's childhood and parental relationships, or *interpersonally* with attention being paid to the patterns of relating that are currently revealing themselves between client and therapist. Intra-psychic work with transference involves the client getting to know his or her own inner child. After all, it is this inner child who is transferring and who is seeking to become whole. The therapist's goal is for the client to know this wounded inner child intimately and eventually to provide, from her own inner resources, the wise parenting that every child deserves but seldom has. This builds the client's capacity for self-nurturing as well as independence and has a great impact on the transference.

Working interpersonally with the transference involves bringing the quality, the reality, the behaviour patterns that are being re-enacted in the therapeutic relationship into the foreground – at least the therapist must be aware of it, respond to it, but ideally the client too needs to become conscious of the perhaps childish, obsolete and dysfunctional way he or she is responding. With awareness comes the opportunity for change. It is the therapist's task to create the environment in which the client can learn more mature and healthy ways of relating.

Therapists are not immune from the relationship with the client evoking their past childhood patterns of relating and responding. Therapists must look within themselves for their own affective responses to clients. Transference cannot be addressed without looking at the counter-transference. Two people are involved in this relationship and both must learn to come to healthy intimacy. In addition, therapists will be unable to serve the client truly if their vision and perception of the client is obscured by their own psychological material.

The therapist must use discrimination and self-knowledge to monitor his or her responses and ways of relating to the client. For instance, if the client feels judged, the therapist must examine whether this might actually be happening through the counter-transference. How will the therapist respond to the moment in every therapeutic relationship when the client needs to assert his or her own identity and not conform or cooperate with the therapist's interventions? Will the therapist merely respond in the *same old ways* that the client experienced in the past and collude with the transference?

Some, but not necessarily all, of the counter-transference may stem from an earlier part of the therapist's life. However, it may also be an authentic human response to the client and not be judged as inappropriate. The therapist may also be sensing and feeling some of the affect that the client is unable to access in his or herself (projective identification). The therapist needs to become aware of 'blind spots' and historically repetitive behaviour patterns in his or her way of relating to the client.

The transpersonal context of psychosynthesis therapy trains the therapist to develop the ability to perceive the client as an inviolable being with immense potential. If this perception is lost, it is imperative for the therapist to ascertain and confront that in him or herself which is inhibiting the process.

The process of change

As previously mentioned, in psychosynthesis we do not follow normative definitions of what healthy human functioning *should* be like. There are no ultimate truths, no recipes to follow, but rather, the client is held as a unique unfolding self aspiring for meaning and purpose. Furthermore, the client's challenges, problems and presenting issues are seen as intimately connected with this journey and not merely the result of inadequacy, childhood conditioning or wounding.

Psychosynthesis acknowledges that all human states and experiences are valid in their own right, valuable moments that have something to offer and which contain the opportunity for growth or learning. Life is a journey and not a destination. Consequently, whatever the existential moment contains for the client is worth accepting, embracing and hopefully learning from. The process of change for an individual is not predictable.

What is guaranteed is that the process of change will include moments of darkness and despair to be faced; moments of joy and beauty to be embraced; there is an unknown to be allowed with no guarantees of security; disintegration may be necessary before integration. There will be times when we cooperate with this life process and our therapy will be creative and fruitful. On the other hand there will be times when we resist, rebel and try to suppress this very human condition. The process of change requires the full acknowledgement of the human condition and acceptance of the journey.

Basic strategies

The psychosynthesis therapist's first highly valued strategy for working with a client is to both encourage and allow the client to 'lead the way'. Consequently there is no set format which a psychosynthesis session would typically follow. Initially the therapist wants to learn what the client's history is, what difficult issues and challenges are being faced – and equally importantly, the way the client envisions the therapy going, what their goals are and what outcome they aspire to. This strategy (if it can be called one) evokes the client's own motivation for change and empowers him or her to commit to a forward direction. Then when the going gets rough, as it inevitably does as we face our own humanity, this motivation can be drawn upon.

Another strategy of the therapist for working through tenacious and difficult life issues is to address them on three complementary levels – the past, the present and the future. Our psychological history often contains the apparent roots of a problem or life issue. Therapeutic work may require us to delve into the experiences from our childhood which contributed to or sometimes created the problem in the first place. However, the client is experiencing these concerns in the present existential moment which is often the starting place. How the client experiences the problem, when, where and with whom, needs to be consciously addressed. Both levels of work are common to most forms of therapeutic work.

Psychosynthesis therapy adds a third level of inquiry, that of the future. By future we mean the creative potential contained within the problem, the possibility for the resolution of this issue to help the client evolve further on their life journey. In fact, we hypothesize that something 'new' is trying to be born for this client through the problem – there is a creative possibility immanent within the difficulty.

For example, the client's presenting issue may be that she is afraid to take risks in her life. The therapist's strategy will be to offer the client the opportunity to address the three levels mentioned above. First there might be an exploration of how the client experiences being unable to take risks presently, in what areas of her life she has the opportunity to do so and how she experiences emotionally and mentally her fear and resistance to doing so. This process may evoke memories from childhood where the client was unsuccessful with risk-taking and probably got hurt while trying to do so. Certain past relationships, such as with an authoritarian punishing figure, may have contributed to her inhibition. But equally importantly, the therapist may seek what qualities and strengths the client will cultivate through learning to take risks. How will it serve her to deal with this? What steps forward in her life will it enable her to take? What is the progressive context here in which the client can experience herself and make choices?

Basic techniques

The psychosynthesis approach is primarily pragmatic and existential. Although the overall goals and perspective may be similar among psychosynthesis practitioners, the methods they use may vary considerably. These will include relaxation, concentration, catharsis, critical analysis, psychological journal, subpersonality work, Gestalt dialogue, body movement, ideal models, symbolic art work and free drawing, mental imagery and the use of symbols, meditation, creative expression, inner dialogue and self-identification.

As the therapeutic relationship is central to psychosynthesis therapy it consequently uses the human interaction and traditional active dialogue as a ground for the work. Assagioli recommended first starting with a technique he called critical analysis. Critical analysis is a dialogue method which can be used to expand the client's self-knowledge, assess blocks and obstacles as well as creative potentials, and initiate an exploration of the unconscious in order to discover the 'history' of the client's issues. Psychological journal-keeping is another technique to achieve the same purpose and encourages the client to reflect subjectively. Early on, many psychosynthesis practitioners will invite the client to write an autobiography. This stimulates the unconscious and evokes awareness and understanding.

Active dialogue, psychological journal-keeping and autobiographical work can go a long way towards understanding psychological problems. Self-knowledge and awareness in itself can be healing and transformative. However, for many psychological issues the cognitive aspect needs to be complemented with *experiential* techniques designed to evoke and explore deeper levels of the unconscious.

Experiential work has the value of engaging the client on different levels when addressing an issue – the physical, the emotional, the imaginative and the mental. A psychosynthesis therapist might use a variety of practical experiential techniques. Among those most commonly used are the following:

Mental imagery work Images and symbols are the language of the unconscious. The imagination follows no rules of reality. Mental imagery work provides the client with a means of getting in touch with deeper levels of his or her unconscious in order to expand awareness and move towards change. The client's deep inner reality may be revealed in symbolic form through the use of imagery and visualization. For example, the client can evoke an imaginative image for her fear as well as recall a past experience where she felt that fear. The process can even be taken further with the use of the imagination to allow the symbols to change and transform – or by evoking an image of what needs to happen in order to heal the fear. The therapist may also invite the client to empower her images with speech and movement. We can get to know a part of ourselves, say the 'frightened child', by getting an image for it and imaginatively dialoguing with that image. This type of experiential work facilitates the process of change.

Mental imagery and visualization can also be used to 'reprogramme' the unconscious – that is, to recondition the psyche with images that are developmental and positive. The client can be offered selective images which set in motion chosen psychological processes – such as a flower blossoming or a tree with its roots firmly in the ground – which evoke the corresponding affective state.

Disidentification and self-identification   This is an experiential technique which is central to psychosynthesis therapy. It is based on the principle that firstly it is essential that we allow ourselves to experience 'what is' for us – be that feelings of fear, anger, resentment. We all live much of our lives unconsciously identified with emotional states. These states then give us a sense of identity. If we are feeling insecure, we imagine that we *are* an insecure person, or when an unacceptable emotion like anger surfaces, we cling to our preferred identification as a good 'nice' person, rejecting the anger. A basic tenet of psychosynthesis is that we are dominated by everything with which our self is identified – in a sense we are enslaved by a limited consciousness and we lose accessibility to the rest of our personality. This means that we lose the richness and resources of the rest of our being.

The disidentification technique allows us to recognize, own and accept these identifications and then to experience that we are *more* than them. It allows us to detach ourselves consciously from various aspects of our personality. This leads to a deeper sense of personal identity – the 'I' – and equips us with both self-awareness and choice. It enhances our inner freedom and capacity to regulate our lives and their expression.

As stated by Diana Whitmore,[4] this technique can be used in two ways. The therapist can encourage the client to learn the skill of being able to *disidentify* from limiting identities, beliefs, attitudes, behaviours, emotions or roles. For example, a client with a distorted self-image can become aware of the limiting impact this has on her life and *choose* to identify with her gifts and talents. Having the psychological skill to disidentify, the client can expand her perspective and create a more stable sense of identity. After disidentifying comes the possibility of choosing to identify with one's more stable sense of identity, which is the first step towards experience of our deeper self.

WHICH CLIENTS BENEFIT MOST?

Psychosynthesis can be practised as a form of brief therapy or as a long-term depth psychotherapy. It adapts itself to the needs and goals of the client which are often determined in the initial interview and the process of assessment and diagnosis. The potential client's own self-assessment and vision of what they would like from the work is an essential component in determining whether psychosynthesis therapy is appropriate for that individual.

Counselling and psychotherapy is today increasingly losing its 'stigma' of being primarily indicated for those individuals who are unwell and unable to function in their life and in society. With the stress of our modern life, with the breakdown of the nuclear family, with the social problems we face, more and more people are recognizing the need to turn inward, understand and deeply know themselves better. It is undeniable that many today experience life as lacking in meaning and purpose and are consequently depressed or feel isolated and alienated. Psychosynthesis work has proven itself to be highly effective with these issues and this type of existential reality. Many who seek psychosynthesis are inspired to address and enhance the *quality of their lives*.

As a transpersonal psychology or a psychospiritual psychology, psychosynthesis is especially useful for those who wish to reconnect with their own spirituality – their sense of fulfilment – and to explore their purpose in life. They seek a fuller experience of who they essentially are and where they are going with life. They long for their life to embody more richly their potential and capacity for goodness, for joy, for beauty and for creativity. They also most likely recognize that there are obstacles to this, that they have been unsuccessful in changing on their own and know that they would benefit from some support and mirroring. Basically, in Maslow's terms, they are seeking self-realization.[5,6]

Potential clients for psychosynthesis need to possess a reasonable motivation to understand themselves, their problems and life challenges. They must be interested in reflecting on life experience for the purpose of making use of the insights gained. A willingness to turn inward and explore one's inner world is important. A reasonable level of openness to engage in the intra-personal and interpersonal demands of therapy is essential. Although perhaps not yet conscious, a wish or desire to take some degree of responsibility for one's life circumstances is recommended. Although all of the above can be *grown into* through the course of therapy, the *potential* for these characteristics will greatly contribute to a successful outcome.

That is not to say that there may not be quite rigid defence systems to be overcome in the process, or dysfunctional behaviours to be addressed. Psychosynthesis therapy has long worked with individuals who experience strong life issues and problems that affect and inhibit their capacity to function in their daily life and in their community. Long-term psychosynthesis psychotherapy is most likely necessary when there has been severe trauma or abuse, or with addiction issues. This is also true with potential clients with a family history of mental illness. A general guideline is that the degree of disturbance impacts on the length of therapy required.

Case study

THE CLIENT

Susan was a 45-year-old woman who had been married for 20 years, had two children and a successful career. Although Susan's adult life had been incredibly busy, incessantly active with juggling a husband, home, career and family – she had been primarily well and happy until her fortieth birthday. Around that time life had started to feel flat, rather empty and meaningless. Susan found that the things that used to give her such a great sense of achievement – creating a nice home for her family, her activities as a helper (in her free time) at her children's school, her social life with her husband and colleagues – no longer did anything for her.

Before this Susan had never known boredom. She had never felt that her busyness was futile and in vain. She had never before questioned what she was doing and why she was doing it. Gradually she experienced a growing sense of greyness, emptiness and despair. She watched herself in her normal realm of activities and found them sorely lacking – but lacking in what she did not know. She constantly said to herself: 'What's it all for?' 'I have everything I need to be happy, but I'm not.' 'There must be more to life than this!'

For a couple of years Susan thought she needed a change. The family moved into a house needing major renovations which kept her busy for a while. But gradually the despair began to creep back. She went to her GP who also thought she needed a change and told her to take a holiday. This too proved fruitless. She decided to change her job and go to work for a firm that was more challenging and demanding of her skills and creativity. But it was to no avail. The feelings of meaninglessness and greyness did not leave her.

At a certain point Susan became suicidal and sunk into a deep depression. Her GP prescribed tranquillizers which only made her feel worse. Susan felt that she was dying – indeed she was experiencing a kind of psychological death, which she was interpreting as an impulse to take her own life physically. During Susan's period of despair, a friend told her about a psychosynthesis therapist. Although resistant, and feeling she must be really sick and bad to have to see a psycho-therapist, Susan rang the therapist and arranged her first session.

She arrived at the initial interview trembling with fear and trepidation but was immediately relieved to find the therapist to be quite a normal person. She began by saying that she feared she was having a breakdown, that too many people needed her, that she had lost her love for her husband and children, and that she often wanted to die but would not allow herself to entertain the thought except in her darkest moments.

The therapist was struck by what an attractive person Susan was. To look at her you would never guess that this woman was seething with despair and despondency. She presented herself as articulate, bright and in control. Her outer appearance and demeanour did not match the words with which she was describing her inner world of dark, dull, grey emptiness. One way that we can define psychospiritual health is that when our outer world is congruent with our inner world we experience well-being. This was anything but the case with Susan.

Susan began to speak a little about her childhood. The therapist needed to gather information and know Susan better before she could make an initial assessment of her needs and what the course of therapy could offer her. Susan had come from a working-class family with an alcoholic father. Her mother had more or less raised the children single-handedly and Susan, being the eldest, had carried much responsibility for the psychological care of both her mother and her two brothers.

When she was little, Susan's natural tendency had been to be a bit dreamy with a rich imaginative life. However, this could not be allowed because of the chaos and the demands her mother, albeit unconsciously, put on Susan to be the strong and capable one. She learned how to make others in her family smile, to distract them from their dysfunction, and she took charge – helping with the housework, baby-sitting her brothers, keeping everyone away from her father when he was drinking, and, most of all, protecting her mother.

As a child Susan vowed that *her* life would be different. As she matured, quite unconsciously she set about creating the perfect life for herself. She worked hard, achieved much and created a world for herself that was ordered and safe. She married at 25 and set about establishing first her career and then her family. Those viewing her life from the outside would never guess the inner turmoil that was motivating her actions and controlling her behaviour and direction in life.

So she had done it! She had created the seemingly perfect and normal existence for herself, which is how she imagined most people lived. To have that safe reality come crashing into nothingness was unbearably painful for Susan. Her therapist immediately warmed to Susan and felt compassion for her plight. Her story echoed a universal one – that all human beings have a need for a life that makes sense, is rich with meaning and contains moments of connectedness and unity. Susan in her present desperate state was devoid of all of that.

THE THERAPY

There were two major strands in Susan's experience that needed unravelling. The first was her childhood experiences of taking care of others and having to be the *together, strong one*, and the second her extreme depression and despair. The initial step was to make sense of Susan's childhood. The therapist helped her to define the many voices inside her that she recognized as coming from childhood. There was the 'pleaser' who knew how to make people happy and always give them exactly what they needed. There was also the 'critic' who constantly judged her and told her if she was doing things *right or well enough*. Upon discovering this critic (subpersonality in psychosynthesis terms) Susan burst into tears and with the therapist's encouragement cried throughout most of the session. She seemed to believe that this critic spoke the truth about her – she was never quite good enough. There were others, but the discovery of the critic was enough for the moment.

The therapist explained to Susan the principle of subpersonalities – that each of us may have many different parts inside, which are sometimes in conflict. Long lost was Susan's 'dreamer', the one in her who loved to be creative and poetic. With this knowledge Susan was immediately relieved and felt that some of her depression made sense to her now.

For several sessions the therapist worked mainly with Susan's presenting issues, establishing trust between them and using Gestalt dialogue to help her separate and identify the inner voices that were contained within her despair and depression. She found this new sense of clarity and self-awareness immensely relieving and already her depression was beginning to alter.

There was a period in the therapy when Susan began to feel aggressive towards the therapist. She had never before allowed herself to be dependent upon anyone – she liked to be in control and here was this individual who seemed to know more about her than she herself did. She found herself resisting the therapist's inter- ventions – something of a rebellion which Susan had never even contemplated in her childhood. She half expected to be punished for not being her usual compliant self and was not unaware of the unconditional positive regard her therapist seemed to give her. Although she knew she was being rather stroppy, she continued to feel respected and valued by the therapist. She had the sense that her therapist perceived her as *more than* her stroppy rebellion. This inclusion of a wider, more expansive view of Susan allowed her to feel safe enough to really explore these long-lost feelings of aggression and assertion. She found that she quite enjoyed being uncooperative and strong in herself. This enabled her to regain some qualities that she had forgotten.

The next phase of the therapy saw Susan diving head-on into her sense of despair and meaningless. The work she had done before this had enabled her to loosen the hold her depression had on her – but there was still the emptiness, the grey lack of anything that made her heart sing. In one session the therapist invited Susan to go back in her imagination to times in her past when she had felt *meaning* and a sense of life being *worthwhile*. To her surprise she was flooded with memories of moments in her life that had been stunningly meaningful – the birth of her first child, a sense of unity with her husband while on a walk in the woods, an experi- ence with gardening when she had sensed the *fundamental all-rightness* of the universe and her life. These memories had long been forgotten (or suppressed). She recalled her mother's hard-working life and how poignant it was that she cared so much for her family.

Susan began to ask herself the big questions about life: What am I here for? What is my place in the world? Without undue emphasis on finding the right answers to Susan's questioning, the therapist took her questions seriously and helped her to explore them – both with mental imagery looking at what the purpose of her life might be and with active dialogue focusing on her search for different and higher values. Underneath her despair, Susan actually had a longing for something she could only define as *spiritual*. She began to awaken to new potentialities within herself, such as her creativity and her impulse to be with others on a deeper level.

She found that her social contacts and life changed quite dramatically. When with friends she no longer made small talk but was keen to know the other on a deeper level. She had a series of experiences where she knew that life was fundamentally good and that human beings had a depth that was accessible in intimate moments.

This journey was not without its setbacks, moments of doubt – wondering whether she was conveniently making it all up in order to feel better. She began to 'reality test' her growing new awareness through her contacts with others. She found that some people could respond to her desire to relate on a deeper level and others were threatened by it. Her husband at first doubted that the therapy was actually helping Susan to come to terms with reality. But he gradually saw that in spite of the ups and downs, there was a renewed sense of vitality in Susan. Little by little she was coming 'home' to herself.

Susan's life did not necessarily 'look' much different externally from before. She did change her career to one that she felt offered more opportunity for connection to others and fulfilled her desire to contribute. However, Susan mainly learned that she needed time *just to be*, that much of her incessant *doing* in her life had led her away from something deep and essential in herself. She was more able to allow chaos and embrace the unknown. Her tight control of herself and others (to ensure that they were all right) loosened and with it came real meaning in her life.

Although psychosynthesis may be employed with a wide variety of presenting problems, we chose this client's therapy as an example of psychosynthesis in action because these kinds of existential issues are becoming increasingly common in today's world. Though we live in the information and communication age, it seems that more and more people are feeling alienated, isolated and hollow, as deeper human needs and feelings are subsumed to material and technological wizardry and quick fixes. We believe that the re-owning of our spiritual nature that is fostered by psychosynthesis offers real hope and help for humanity. If so, psychosynthesis, along with the other transpersonal therapies, will have an expanding healing role in the coming millennium.

REFERENCES

1 *Hibbert Journal*, vol. 32, October 1933–July 1934, and vol. 36, October 1937–July 1938.
2 Williamson, M. (1996) *A Return To Love*. London: Thorsons.
3 Perls, F. (1970) 'Four lectures', in J. Fagen and I. Shepherd (eds), *Gestalt Therapy Now*. New York: Harper & Row.
4 Whitmore, D. (1991) *Psychosynthesis Counselling in Action*. London: Sage.
5 Maslow, A.H. (1968) *Towards a Psychology of Being*. New York: Van Nostrand.
6 Maslow, A.H. (1978) *The Farther Reaches of Human Nature*. Harmondsworth: Penguin.

SUGGESTED READING

Assagioli, R. (1965) *Psychosynthesis*. London: Aquarian Press. The original textbook on psychosynthesis.

Ferrucci, P. (1990) *What We May Be*. London: Aquarian Press. An easily understandable introduction to psychosynthesis with exercises.

Hardy, J. (1996) *A Psychology with a Soul*. London: Woodgrange Press. A book which covers the historical roots of psychosynthesis and the major influences on Assagioli's thinking – from Plato to the *Divine Comedy* to western mysticism.

Whitmore, D. (1991) *Psychosynthesis Counselling In Action*. London: Sage. A practical book for those interested in the basics of psychosynthesis counselling and what could be expected from the therapy.

DISCUSSION ISSUES

1   How far do you believe that people are more than their personalities –
    in other words, do you believe that each of us also has a deeper and
    more essential self?
2   Do you think that inside we are actually many people? Do we have
    different parts of ourselves, that can sometimes clash? What are three
    of your own subpersonalities?
3   In what sense are our lives a journey? Can you trace any themes,
    consistent patterns or learnings in your own life, or in the life of
    someone you know very well?
4   Have you experienced moments of 'peak experience', glimpses of a
    deeper purpose or meaning to life that have been especially important
    to you and have informed your life? What does this tell you about
    human nature?

18

PSYCHODYNAMIC (FREUDIAN) COUNSELLING AND PSYCHOTHERAPY

Michael Burton and Lawrence Suss

P sychodynamic counselling is concerned with how we deceive ourselves as to our intentions, desires and beliefs and how these deceptions create conflicts between our expressed goals and our actions. The term psychodynamic means 'of/or pertaining to the laws of mental action', and its use presupposes that there are some principles that determine the relationship between mind and action and that these can be formulated as a basis for therapeutic intervention. Traditionally, the principles underlying psychodynamic counselling are presented as derivations of the ideas of the psychoanalytic school founded by Sigmund Freud, a doctor, neurologist and psychoanalyst. Current psychodynamic counselling draws from a much wider range of theoretical influences. One of the most fundamental tenets is that we are unaware of many of our motives and that if these are known to us we are able to make better, less conflicted choices. However, we are often resistant to or defended against recognizing these hidden motives, termed unconscious by most psychodynamic theorists, and hence are unable to change – indeed we seem to have a compulsion to repeat past behaviour. These repetitions are thought to arise because of earlier experiences where our behaviour successfully enabled us to cope by ignoring or repressing difficult feelings. Psychodynamic counselling thus has a theory of why we are unable to change, how this inability arises, and how it affects our lives.

DEVELOPMENT OF THE THERAPY

Psychodynamic counselling can trace its modern roots back to the early hypnotists of the eighteenth century, called mesmerists,[1] with their interests in ideas of unconscious subpersonalities and the psychological causes of illness. This led in the nineteenth century to the rise of psychotherapies aimed in one way or another at restoring some imputed imbalance of mind in the name of cure mostly by methods we would now think of as hypnotic.[2] In the late nineteenth century two theorists, Freud and Pierre Janet, a psychologist, began independently to formulate theories of mind which were to dominate much of the twentieth century. Freud's treatment system of psychoanalysis came to dominate the field of psychotherapy and, in the hands of psychoanalysts, to be seen as a therapy of five times per week stretching over a period of several years. It was left to several of Freud's students, notably Alfred Adler, Sandor Ferenczi, Wilhelm Stekel and Otto Rank, all doctors, to argue the case for a more pragmatic, briefer therapy which laid the seeds of psychodynamic counselling. They started a controversy in the early part of this century, which continues to this day, as to the efficacy of brief versus longer-term therapy.[3]

Exponents of brief therapy based upon psychoanalytic principles enjoyed a resurgence during and after the Second World War. The work of Franz Alexander, a psychoanalyst,[4] was particularly influential and emphasized the importance of the therapeutic relationship and the need for some flexibility in the therapist in the pursuance of a corrective emotional experience to repair some earlier loss or trauma. This drew upon the work of theorists such as Melanie Klein, a psychoanalyst, who had emphasized the importance of how we internalize images of important others as a derivative of our early relationships, especially with the mother. These ideas were later developed in Britain by the so-called 'object relations' therapists, particularly Donald Winnicott, a paedia-trician and psychoanalyst,[5] and attachment theorists such as John Bowlby, a psychiatrist and psychoanalyst,[6] who emphasized issues of attachment to and loss of the mother. This led to a vision of brief psychodynamic therapy in terms of corrective emotional experiences repairing the failures of early parenting. This is particularly exemplified by the work of David Malan, a psychiatrist and psychoanalyst, from which much British psychodynamic counselling derives.[7]

While these ideas of maternal bonding were strong in Britain, they show a cultural bias based on idealized visions (myths) of parenting behaviour. In America, where notions of individual identity expressed in terms of the development of the self were seen as important, a form of psychoanalytic counselling based on the work of so called self-psychologists developed[8] which saw therapy in terms of the strengthening of the self.

Alternative European ideas[9] based upon influences as diverse as existentialism, phenomenology, psychoanalysis, surrealism and Marxism theorize that ideas of the self derive from particular notions of what is private and what public. Such views would argue that the emphasis on singular and coherent selfhood (that could be held politically and legally responsible) leads to much of what is regarded as neurosis. The kind of psychodynamic counselling that is based upon these ideas is interested in how we develop and sustain a sense of identity and also borrows extensively from feminism, gay literature and post-modernism. The task of counselling is seen to be a challenge to the client's desire for an excessive sense of control and coherence. This demand is expressed in terms of the client's insistence that they know the counsellor and can predict what will happen in the counselling relationship because they admit to only those elements of the relationship which reinforce their fantasized vision of the world. The counsellor, by insisting on their mutual difference, challenges this fantasy and seeks to model the idea that a sense of meaning as a human being can only be obtained by negotiation and as a result of shared action, of which language is an example.

Perhaps most fundamental to psychodynamic counselling is the notion of 'relationship' in which we discover and develop our sense of identity in relation to the other. Freudian theory places great emphasis on the child's (typically boy's) developing relationship with the father in which the boy had to accept his subjugation to the father's greater potency and 'ownership' of the boy's mother, the so-called Oedipus complex. Modern theories tend to emphasize the role of both parents in the child's development, especially the mother, as formative in the production of adult personality. In counselling what is seen as most important is the way in which the client's own vision of their past influences their current relationships as demonstrated with the counsellor, so called transference. Indeed an important aspect of Freud's contribution was the realization that our memory operates selectively in the interest of producing coherent stories about ourselves and what we believe of our parenting may have little relation to other's recollections. The key ideas are that our inner world reflects the need to make some narrative sense of our external and internal perceptions. In early childhood, given our poor knowledge base, lack of control and limited cognition, events are often so traumatic to our sense of selfhood as to be unbearable and hence our perceptions have to be distorted to cope. A further important aspect of Freudian theory has been the idea that these traumatic experiences are actively repressed. This is seen to create the unconscious, a subdivision of mind with its own logic and rules, where the emotional components of experience are displaced on to previously neutral or less emotional stimuli, thus sufficiently mitigating their traumatic potential as to allow the displaced 'emotive material' to re-enter consciousness, typically as symptoms. Thus repression is seen as a way of leaving signposts to material which has remained unprocessed in the past. There has been a vociferous debate ever since Freud formulated this view as to whether traumatic events are thus repressed and subsequently recovered, particularly in relationship to sexual abuse. More commonly people appear to be aware, at least in terms of bodily distress, that they have areas of difficulty but actively avoid these topics when they arise in conversation by changing the subject in some way or another. This process is more like Janet's idea of dissociation or disavowal in which unacceptable thoughts or feelings are actively avoided.

The interests of early hypnotists in these dissociative phenomena were prompted by the observation that under conditions of relaxation and suggestion people would often report previously denied experiences and emerge apparently cured of other areas of symptomatic disturbance when awakened. Early hypnotists noticed that hypnotic cures often occurred when there was a close relationship between the therapist and client and used the term 'rapport' to describe this and the further effect that this relationship often became one of dependency of client on therapist. This led Freud to propose that during therapy patients would perceive him in ways which he believed related to earlier experience with significant others, the so-called transference. These transference effects appear to be closely related to imbalances of power, and psychodynamic counselling has developed an understanding of how symptomatic distress may mask or serve to express a desire to be cared for by a powerful other, originally presumably the mother. An important element of psychodynamic counselling is the struggle to bring these desires into the conscious awareness of the client so that they can recognize what is fantasized and what needs can be met in their relationships with others and what of these needs they should meet for themselves – for example, it is hard to perceive yourself as loved if you cannot conceive that you are lovable!

The positioning of the psychodynamic counsellor has many parallels with shamans, witch doctors and medicine men in other cultures.[10] All represent the possibility of speaking something that would under normal circumstances remain unspoken. In invoking the notion of the unconscious Freud reinvented a secular version of such worlds where the unspeakable could be spoken. Such speaking is usually only to be entertained under special conditions of arousal in the form of drug or exercise-induced trance (consider the importance of dreams and alcohol in our own culture). Equally these events are often conducted in special ritual or religious spaces (thus allowing a kind of deniability if the events still seem impossible to process in everyday life). Psychodynamic counselling places similar emphasis upon the special continuity of place and time, although the expressed reason is that people are actually extremely sensitive to such issues, especially when regressed. Perhaps this is a more acceptable explanation in a secular culture that sees therapy as having as its aim the reparation of early childhood traumas or losses.

This issue of degrees of regression, often expressed in terms of depth, has been central to a debate concerning the relative degrees of change that can be induced by low-intensity, brief therapies such as counselling versus high-intensity, longer therapies such as psychoanalysis. What research evidence there is has largely failed to show any significantly better results with longer, high-intensity therapies.[11] There is an increasing awareness that the client's decision to be different, signalled by coming to counselling, may express an openness both to change and to other people that has been previously lacking. This view, while emphasizing the importance of ritual space in the process of change, is far less didactic about the precise circumstances under which change can occur. In doing so it places much greater demands upon the therapist's flexibility in accompanying the client in a journey through anything from the ecstatic, to bereavement and madness. It also stresses that the counsellor's activities within the developing relationship should be constrained by an ethical concern for the client's safety and good, but not necessarily by the moral edicts of cultural probity.[12] Necessarily such a flexibility of positioning will mean that the counsellor too will experience him or herself in novel and disturbing ways. An awareness that being a counsellor can be a demanding and occasionally damaging experience has found expression in the requirement on most training courses that the trainee should have a long personal therapy and thus explore, and in some theories deal with, their own unconscious fantasies and conflicts. The extent of this demand from five times per week over maybe six or more years to 40 sessions over two years, is another factor that distinguishes the training of psychoanalytic therapists from psychodynamic counsellors.

Although personal therapy is important in psychodynamic counselling and, interestingly, also to many shamanistic inductions, the counsellor's task is better seen as an ongoing need to monitor and interrogate one's own defences and terrors than a closure created by a one-off period of therapy, no matter how intense or protracted. Thus psychodynamic counselling, while recognizing that the client's investment in the process of change is very different from the counsellor's, sees in the reciprocity of relatedness a potency for both counsellor and client to experience themselves differently. This notion of counsellor response was termed counter-transference by Freud, probably defensively, to imply that the counsellor's responses are largely prompted by the actions of the client. An area of psychodynamic counselling development has been the recognition of the complexity and fluidity of relational dynamics which defies easy definition and the way in which we are created as having gender, class and ethnicity by the way we speak and are spoken to. Since most therapy is conducted as a 'talking cure', an important aspect of psychodynamic counselling is the way in which clients seek to position themselves and their therapist in the forms and manner of their speech and in their expectation of the counsellor's listening to them.

Psychodynamic counselling places great emphasis on the idea that we speak as a subject with a physical body but that what matters is how we construct an image of our body, what we imagine it can do for instance. Freud tried to catch an idea something like this with his notion of the bodily ego, and what he sought to emphasize was that although human relations occur between two or more physical bodies it is how we imagine ourselves as embodied that critically determines the outcomes of such encounters. This idea that we are always dealing with our constructions of the world, not as it is, but as how it can be made meaningful in our lives, is critical in, for example, understanding the way individuals suffering from anorexia nervosa can cling to a body image of being too large despite overwhelming apparent evidence of starving to death. The task of understanding how we deceive ourselves is thus not simply to identify errors of thought, an activity common to both psychodynamic counselling and cognitive behavioural therapy, but also to understand how our particular perceptions of the world and the concomitant fantasies which support them serve to sustain such erroneous thinking. Freud thought that the bodily ego's development paralleled that of the relational importance of the body surfaces passing from initial issues of nutrition characterized by orality, through issues of retention and control characterized by the anus, through to issues of excitement and arousal characterized by the genitals. This developmental sequence has been largely superseded, although in emphasizing the constructive nature of body image Freud heralded almost a century of endeavour to understand how we develop ideas such as body, inside and outside, mind, and self and other. The movement of the last century has been away from physical, biological models towards ideas of how we symbolize and construct and are constructed by the social world, and psychodynamic counselling has been in the forefront of these movements.

PRACTICE

There is no one agreed set of practices in psychodynamic counselling, nor indeed an agreed set of theories, and courses bearing similar titles will offer profoundly different areas of study. Indeed, we are cautious of prescribing a specific methodology of practice as psychodynamic counsellors, preferring to argue that it is more the resultant of a reflexive and reflective attitude of mind. Each client presents in a different way and calls upon different responses in the counsellor. The critical issue is to attempt to maintain an ethical relationship in which the client's needs are kept in mind and the temptations of knowing, in the sense of producing or colluding with an overly prescriptive narrative, are resisted. This suspension of knowing seems in practice extremely difficult; the seductions of expertise are therapeutically attractive to clients and may be the only basis of most initial working alliances in therapy (see the earlier comments on hypnosis). Further, the kinds of expert discourse of therapy are personally and professionally very powerful, as evidenced on a weekly basis in the Sunday newspapers and by the burgeoning of new syndromes with their associated specialists.

In the presence of this wealth of competing claims and therapeutic nostrums some have sought the solution that promises validity for all by organizing taxonomies of disturbance, often based upon notions of developmental stages or biological dysfunction, and then arguing that different modes of treatment suit different clients. Indeed there is a considerable industry in attempting to map treatment on to symptomatology in terms of the most successful outcome. The problem has been to agree on what constitutes success. Most often this consists of a removal of symptomatic complaint and a diminished use of the caring services. The worry of such measures is that they can all too easily collapse into the positioning of the counsellor as the applicator of anaesthetic patches on the body politic or the broker of new lies for old. Perhaps the best we can urge is a vigilance as to where we find our power and at what costs to our clients.

At the more prosaic level of the session there is a general agreement that the purpose of counselling is for clients to be able to talk about aspects of their lives that they customarily avoid talking about, whether through social taboo or through processes keeping them from conscious awareness. What happens when this 'something' is spoken, and perhaps more importantly perceived to have been heard, is that both counsellor and client need to negotiate how they now perceive themselves to be positioned *vis à vis* the other. For example, an object relations oriented counsellor might look at how the client's habitual ways of relating, either to others in their story or in their relationship with the counsellor, seemed to deny any personal role or responsibility for negative happenings and to see these as the responsibility of others (often called projection). Through drawing these occurrences to the attention of the client in a non-judgemental way the counsellor might hope that these denied (split-off) parts might become more integrated into the client's personality, thus leaving the client freer to relate. A more classical Freudian might focus more on evidence in what is said of repressed sexuality as retold in the client's story (orality, anality, genitality and most important the Oedipus complex as mentioned earlier) and interpret the repression in the hope of gaining relief of symptoms through insight. An alternative approach based upon modern European ideas would be to try to keep open as many ways of understanding the client's experience as possible so that one interpretation by the client of their past or understanding of events is not given precedence over other as yet unspoken possibilities.

Given that the purpose is to help a client to speak freely it is also therefore to find and analyse the anxiety that motivates the blocks and resistances, to spot and challenge the absences in what is spoken, and to draw attention to the repetitions in behaviour. In part this can be achieved through a commentary on the therapeutic relationship and how the client expresses their spoken (conscious) and unspoken (unconscious) demands of the therapist, and in part from an analysis of the themes present in the stories that the client chooses to recall. There is considerable variation between schools as to whether the client's feelings and attitudes toward the therapist are taken up or allowed any validity beyond reflecting historical attitudes, and whether the client's narrative is treated as the subject of mutual exploration and negotiation or commented upon from a position of therapist expertise.

There are some practice issues that seem to occur in most psychodynamic approaches:

Assessment

This is an important aspect of psychodynamic counselling. It will include an assessment of: other support mechanisms (as counselling can make people feel worse in the short term); psychological mindedness (e.g. when a gap or repetition is drawn to the client's attention can the client reflect creatively on it); the ability to reflect on one's feelings rather than necessarily act on them (counsellors might check how the client has behaved in the past when at their worst e.g. are they a suicide risk); and their ability to make a relationship with the counsellor on which the work can be based (usually as demonstrated through at least one successful relationship outside counselling). The assessment will also include a history of the client so that the counsellor may build a fuller picture of the client's way of seeing his or herself and world. The history could include, for example, an early memory, details of siblings and their relationships, the relationship between mother and father, and other items important to the client.

Boundaries and limits

Establishing clear rules and boundaries for the start and end of sessions, the regularity of meeting, and holiday breaks and absences (of both counsellor and client) provides a setting in which any manipulation or attempts to control by the client might be seen and then explored with the client. This is sometimes thought by trainees to be quite a punitive approach but it does give a clear sense of control and also perhaps safety.

Expression of emotions

For some models of counselling, but not psychodynamic, the expression of strong emotions, often called catharsis, in counselling is sometimes seen as a goal in itself. Most psychodynamic counsellors believe that catharsis without accompanying insight is not very valuable, and perhaps a more important aspect of catharsis is the expression of trust and relational possibility with the counsellor.

Interpretation of the transference

Most psychodynamic approaches agree that clients will repeat behaviour, thoughts and feelings with their counsellor that might be seen as belonging to past relationships (normally thought to be with mother or father or other important carer, implying some power relationship is being brought into play). There is no general agreement about what to do with the transference (see above and Glossary), but it does give very important clues about how a client constructs and construes relationships in the world outside the consulting room. Karl Menninger, a doctor and psychoanalyst,[13] proposes a triangle of insight with the corners representing: parent or distant past; other or usually current or recent past; and transference or here-and-now with the counsellor. By careful listening it is sometimes possible to detect the client talking of similar patterns of relating in all corners of the triangle and a transference interpretation by the counsellor might bring all three experiences together, thus offering insight into the client's pattern of feelings or behaviour.

Use of the counter-transference

Broadly these are the thoughts and feelings (often including a pressure to act in some way) within the counsellor and are thought of as a measure of the relational process induced by the client. That is, as the transference is an unconscious positioning by the client of the counsellor, then the counter-transference can be seen as the counsellor's affective response to that transference. As such, the counter-transference is an important aspect of the counselling, as being able to monitor thoughts and feelings allows the counsellor insights into the client's unconscious processes. Counsellors should proceed with care before making interventions (interpretations) on the basis of their counter-transference and may have to hold on to these feelings for several sessions before their meaning becomes clear. At early stages in training it is not uncommon to 'act out in the counter-transference' (that is, act on the feelings induced rather than think about their possible meaning) but in general there is a 'rule of abstinence' – that counsellors do not act upon their counter-transference as this forecloses understanding what the client is trying to communicate. Discussion of these feelings in supervision can be very productive, giving a clue to the transference.

Acting out

Psychodynamic counselling, above all else, is a talking cure. Acting out, which is broadly defined as a client being unable to bear just to speak about something but instead feeling the need to act upon a feeling, can be seen as an avoidance of the act of speaking. Acting out can occur both within and outside the counselling room. For example, arriving late for counselling may be an acting out of frustration or anger with the counsellor (rather like a temper tantrum) but the client is not fully aware of the feeling unless and until the counsellor tries to get the lateness explored. It can be difficult for trainees to challenge a client over something that might appear trivial, like, for example, being late or choosing to go to the hairdresser rather than attend a counselling appointment or accidentally forgetting to bring the payment for the session. Rational (conscious) explanations by the client often cover (unconscious) feelings that have been acted on. The clear boundaries in psychodynamic counselling (as mentioned above) give the counsellor a better chance to see any acting out by the client.

Focus of the counselling work

In time-limited work there are two main schools of thought about whether there should be an overall focus for the work (for example, on a recent bereavement or difficulties in a current relationship or problems studying for examinations) or whether each session should be taken as it comes. The latter group suggest that to have a focus is in some way a denial of the pain of the fact that the work is time-limited, something which is important to be spoken about in the sessions.

Negative transference

When a client has strong negative feelings (for example anger, fear or hatred) towards the counsellor there is often an even stronger desire on the part of the client to act, perhaps by leaving the counselling or turning up late, rather than talking about this scary set of feelings. The counsellor's task is to try not to react defensively to any attack but try to help the client understand the underlying feelings.

WHICH CLIENTS BENEFIT MOST?

Psychodynamic counselling is most helpful to people who can discern the relationship between their thought and their actions, often expressed as thinking psychologically. It emphasizes the counselling relationship as a vehicle of change and is probably unhelpful to those who have severe difficulty relating (impoverished models of the other) or who insist on a fixed view of the world and themselves (the primacy of their own fantasy) or who would rather act in some way rather than reflect and think (that is, flee into action as a defence against thought). Another way of expressing this would be to say that it benefits those clients who already have some capacity to reflect on their actions as it assists in the development of reflexive thinking rather than uncritical action.

It may well be that the primary utility of psychodynamic counselling is to offer a supportive framework to the therapist to permit them a greater flexibility of action and interpretation of their own behaviour.[14]

Case study

The case study described is a faction composed of elements from one of the author's life.

THE CLIENT

The therapist explained that it was her custom to spend a couple of sessions to see if both therapist and client could work together and then to agree a contract in terms of a mutually agreed number of sessions. In the first instance the sessions would be for 50 minutes and occur once a week at the same time. The client was then invited to say a little more about what brought him. (*Setting clear boundaries.*)

The client was in his early thirties, working as a neuroscientist at a local university. Married for 11 years with a child of one year he described a history of marital difficulties which he located around his wife's manic depressive episodes. He seemed a personable and witty man who had dropped out of medical school in his late teens with a depressive episode which he explained as a result of taking amphetamines. He said that what had brought him was a repeated dream throughout his life which had become worse recently. He invariably awoke terrified and was then insomniac and anxious. (*Evidence suggests that a shared set of values and a personality match are indicators of positive outcome in therapy. A number of therapists from other cultures have been concerned by the way this may consciously or unconsciously promote a version of white, educated, liberal imperialism and part of the emphasis on language and identity is an attempt to become more aware of these political implications.*)

THE THERAPY

The disturbed sleep was partly due to his child of one year, the birth of whom had been traumatic and required a Caesarean section, and he said that the child slept very poorly and that his wife couldn't cope. The term 'cope' had occurred at least three times and the therapist commented upon how important coping was which elicited an agreement accompanied by huge sigh. (*Psychodynamic therapists look for inconsistencies and repetitions as evidence of areas of dissociation or paradox.*) The therapist had noticed that whenever the notion of research arose the patient would avoid eye-contact, and wondered in a speculative way whether there was something about the research that troubled him. There was a long pause and eventually he replied, 'the vivisection you see, I always get these terrible stomach pains and I have an irritated bowel much of the time, particularly when I operate'. Time was up and the therapist felt overwhelmed and exhausted, but was struck by the client's reluctance to leave and had to shoo him gently out of the door. (*The effects of dissociations are often marked by non-verbal signs and there is a view that prolonged denial of emotion may result in disturbances of the body or somatization, the cause of this being unclear.*)

After the session the therapist was struck by the absence of any early case history which she normally elicited, and was concerned at the range and severity of the presentation. (*Psychodynamic therapists often use their own feelings and alterations of expected behaviour as a measure of the relational process induced by the other, often called counter-transference.*)

Marriage, work, colleagues, all seemed fairly fraught and there was also the somatization that sounded serious and long-term. On the positive side was his relationship with his son and the fact that he seemed able to think psychologically about his own role in his life and to make connections; there was a clear sense that he wanted to do something about his life. The therapist felt she needed to check who his doctor was and how severe his previous breakdown had been since this would give some sense of how disturbed he might become in therapy. The therapist determined to offer a brief contract of 10 weeks focused around the dream and his need to carry so many burdens. (*Counselling often makes people worse in the short term.*)

The next session began with a description of breaking down at medical school when he was 18 and spending 'three months in the bin' (i.e. on a psychiatric ward) followed by a long period of recuperation. He commented that his father had been upset because he had wanted the status of having a son as a doctor, the sort of person he would have called 'sir'. The therapist commented that he hadn't mentioned his mother. There was another long silence and then a rather unemotional response about being close to his mother but her being ill. 'Then or now?' asked the therapist. 'Both', he said. 'She had a stroke recently but she was always ill when I was a child, my father always said she was all right until I was born. He had a cardiac arrest when I was in my first year at medical school . . . I was working it out, I've been looking after them for as long as they looked after me.' 'You sound as if you've always had to look after them.' 'Well in a way yes, I'm much bigger than them and neither of them had much formal education and I guess I was like a cuckoo in the nest.' (*Since the client set the scene it is assumed that there is some important communication. It seems to suggest that issues with the parents remain unresolved.*)

The therapist wondered what it had been like being bigger and cleverer and having the sense of being an object of admiration, and, she wondered, envy to his father. She said as much. 'Well my father always said he rather preferred my sister. When I got my 'A' levels he didn't speak to me for lays and yet I'd hear him boasting about me behind my back to his customers but he never said it to me.' He sighed again. 'What I want,' he said, 'is the peace that passeth all understanding.' 'I wonder if you've always felt so alone?' said the therapist. The patient began to cry – great seismic sobs shook him. The therapist's sense was that there were many issues, but perhaps the most pressing was how he seemed to accept such demands upon him and yet seemed so isolated; perhaps this could be looked at in the sessions together. (*The expression of emotion here was probably an indicator of growing trust and relational possibility by this rather academic and reserved man.*)

The client was late for the next session and apologized; the therapist wondered if he had disliked the suggestion he had some role in his struggle and isolation. (*Small changes in the nature of the meeting are often thought to be ways people use to express upset without consciously admitting it. The therapist verbalized one possible version.*) 'You sound like my wife.' There was a strong sense that the comparison was not complimentary. 'Silly cow', hazarded the therapist. 'Sort of', he said with a surprised twinkle. 'I think you get very angry because you take so much responsibility that it feels unfair that I suggest you take more but perhaps you do so much to advertise what you would like from others.' (*The therapist verbalizes what she surmises may be going on for the client and in so doing shifts the domain from fantasy to relational.*) 'I had the dream again', he said with she thought a sense of satisfaction at controlling the change of subject and an implicit complaint at the failure of the therapy. 'The dream was of an unnaturally still plastic blue ocean; it's weird I see the blue and feel paralysed and wake up screaming.' (*The way people use speech to increase or diminish the sense of relationship is an important aspect of training.*)

His associations were to a toy shop where he had seen a model plastic sea with battleships but nothing more. In a subsequent session he remembered that his grandmother had taken him and wondered why since it had usually been his mother. 'She was often ill when I was very small and then nothing.' It was only after several attacks upon the therapist had been survived that the memory of visiting his mother in hospital returned. He recalled 'the Eye hospital, they had a wooden horse'. (*The therapist clarifies and makes explicit what has been implicit.*) 'Your mother had an eye operation', the therapist prompted, 'Yes something to do with squint causing migraines, she had both eyes bandaged. I tried to hug her but they stopped me and said I'd hurt her. We went to the toy shop afterwards that's when I saw the sea.' There was a long silence. 'What colour were your mother's eyes?' the therapist asked as his tears began to fall unstoppably. 'I wonder if you felt you'd damaged your mother just as your father suggested?' 'But why has all this come back now?' (*The therapist makes the final connection when the client is on the edge of doing so.*)

In another session the issue arose again. 'When you first described the dream it was in association with your son', prompted the therapist. (*This kind of comment is often called reflection and is used to facilitate connections which the patient may avoid. It also prompts a sense that the therapist has been listening carefully.*) 'When he won't sleep it makes me so angry, I shook him the other night and he went all silent and I spent the rest of the night worrying I'd damaged him.' 'I guess you damage animals in your work and then there's your wife's ill health – damage seems quite a theme. I wonder if you take on so much to prove that you aren't damaging but in doing so it makes you even more angry so that you end up not having time to do anything properly, like often being late for therapy?' 'I wouldn't take that from anyone else but maybe you're right.' (*This is a summarizing interpretation which tests the therapeutic relationship, sometimes called the alliance. Evidence suggests that such comments damage the sense of trust and this has to be rebuilt before initiating any further comments. In the light of the planned ending in three sessions it is probably excessive given that the issues of ending had not been adequately explored.*)

He missed the planned ending, rang a few days later but missed the re-booking and then rang to say goodbye. On follow-up at one year the dream had not recurred but the pattern of overwork remained.

REFERENCES

1 Crabtree, A. (1993) *From Mesmer to Freud*. New Haven: Yale University Press.
2 Ellenberger, H.F. (1970) *The Discovery of the Unconscious*. London: Fontana Press.
3 Bauer, G.P. and Kobos, J.C. (1995) *Brief Therapy*. Northvale: Aronson.
4 Bateman, A. and Holmes, J. (1995) *Introduction to Psychoanalysis*. London: Routledge.
5 Phillips, A. (1988) *Winnicott*. London: Fontana Modern Masters.
6 Greenberg, J.R. and Mitchell, S.A. (1983) *Object Relations in Psychoanalytic Theory*. Cambridge, Mass.: Harvard University Press.
7 Malan, D. (1976) *The Frontier of Brief Psychotherapy*. New York: Plenum.
8 Paton, M.J. and O'Meara, N.M. (1994) *Psychoanalytic Counselling*. Chichester: Wiley.
9 Frosch, S. (1986) *Psychoanalysis and Psychology*. Basingstoke: Macmillan.
10 Stoller, P. (1997) *Sensuous Scholarship*. Pennsylvania: University of Pennsylvania Press.
11 Bergin, A.E. and Garfield, S.L. (1994) *Handbook of Psychotherapy and Behaviour Change* (4th edn). New York: Wiley.
12 Lomas, P. (1987) *The Limits of Interpretation*. Harmondsworth: Penguin.
13 Menninger, K. (1958) *The Theory of Psychoanalytic Technique*. New York: Basic Books.
14 Davey, T. and Burton, M. (1996) The Psychodynamic Paradigm, in W. Dryden and R. Woolf (eds), *Handbook of Counselling Psychology*. London: Sage.

SUGGESTED READING

Bauer, G.P. and Kobos, J.C. (1995) *Brief Therapy*. Northvale: Aronson. Provides an historic overview, key elements of three main contributors (D. Malan, P.E. Sifneos and H. Davenloo), assessment and selection of patients, technique, use of transference and termination. Provides a good comparison of the three important contributors to brief psychodynamic psychotherapy.

Davenloo, H. (ed.) (1994) *Basic Principles and Techniques in Short Term Dynamic Psychotherapy*. Northvale: Aronson. A wide range of contributors including H. Davenloo, P.E. Sifneos, D.H. Malan, and H.H. Strupp provides comprehensive coverage of the main approaches to short-term work including interesting and helpful detailed clinical material and discussion of technique.

Frosch, S. (1989) *Psychoanalysis and Psychology*. Basingstoke: Macmillan. Good critical look at models of the mind, development theory, language and meaning, gender and sexual differences, and racism. A scholarly work.

Jacobs, M. (1988) *Psychodynamic Counselling in Action*. London: Sage. This provides a logical and structured approach to psychodynamic counselling, giving good coverage of the basic ideas, themes and issues (including first sessions, assessment, boundaries and endings) but perhaps giving a false sense of cohesion to the work.

McLoughlin, B. (1995) *Developing Psychodynamic Counselling*. London: Sage. A more hands-on approach to working psychodynamically with a focus on the client–counsellor relationship. Lots of interesting clinical examples to illustrate the points.

Paton, M. and O'Meara, N. (1994) *Psychoanalytic Counselling*. Chichester: Wiley. This is a research-based text detailing developmental and ego-based models of counselling, American-style. It is a valuable and unusual resource as it integrates research, theory and practice.

DISCUSSION ISSUES

1 To what extent do you think we fool ourselves in the cause of producing plausible stories of ourselves?

2 If the child is the father of the man is this because we endlessly repeat familiar patterns, thus reinventing ourselves, or because we store an image of ourself which has to be changed?

3 Why would the myth of mother–infant innocence be so important for our culture?

4 How might processes of power be played out in a therapeutic relationship? What factors would make the patient especially vulnerable?

19

PSYCHODYNAMIC (JUNGIAN) COUNSELLING AND PSYCHOTHERAPY

Jean Stokes

J ungian therapy is a psychodynamic therapy. It places value on the lifelong struggle towards awareness of how our inner and outer worlds relate and on personal growth and development throughout life. The focus is on fostering relatedness both to self and others. The aim is for the client to become both psychologically stronger and more aware of what is creative and destructive in themselves and their lives. This represents an inner journey of self-discovery and personal meaning, sometimes arduous but profoundly rewarding, and unique to each person. The client is then in a position to pursue psychological growth independently and in their own individual way.

DEVELOPMENT OF THE THERAPY

Carl Gustav Jung (1875–1961) was a Swiss psychiatrist who worked in Zurich with psychotic patients. He also brought to his work a keen interest in myth, philosophy and religion. He became interested in the ideas of the neurologist and psychoanalyst, Sigmund Freud, whose ideas about the unconscious he found initially sympathetic to his own. In fact from 1907 until 1913 he was the key member of Freud's psychoanalytic circle. However, by 1912 he was finding Freud's view of psychological energy as rooted in the sexual instincts too limited and concrete. For Jung it was something more neutral, closer to a life energy, and so capable of taking many forms: biological, psychological, spiritual and moral. Jung's differing views were unacceptable to Freud and the famous rift between them occurred.

Where Freud had worked with neurotics needing to recover the ability to 'love and work' Jung worked out his theory firstly from his experience with psychotics. His own experience of near breakdown also had a creative outcome for his theories and work which he then saw also applied to other kinds of troubled people. Jung saw many people in mid-life desperately seeking personal meaning despite outwardly successful lives, and in this way widened the group of people who could benefit from psychotherapy, previously limited to the younger adult. To distinguish his ideas from Freud's, Jung used the term *analytical psychology* for his work.

In his clinical work he stressed that both therapist and patient are affected by the work they do together. He regarded the therapist's emotional response to the patient as invaluable information. Recognizing, however, the emotional demands and responsibility this inevitably placed on the therapist, Jung pioneered the necessity for all would-be therapists to themselves have an analysis as part of their training. His ideas were attractive to people from all walks of life, resulting in the formation of Analytical Psychology Clubs from which grew today's Jungian professional societies. This included in the 1940s the British Jungian movement with Michael Fordham at its centre. As a child psychiatrist Fordham related Jung's ideas to working with children. He further developed Jung's ideas by connecting them with those of the object relations school of psychoanalysis, especially Klein's work.

THEORY AND CONCEPTS

Jung used the word *psyche* (from the Greek, meaning 'mind, spirit, soul') to describe people's inner world, their subjective experiences and attitudes. Some of these we are fully aware of and able to articulate. These are our *conscious attitudes*. However, we also have attitudes of which we remain unaware, or are unwilling or unable to acknowledge to ourselves, let alone to others. These are *unconscious attitudes*. They tend to reveal themselves in our behaviour – for example, we 'forget' the birthday of someone we can't admit we dislike. Jung called these unconscious attitudes, which were rooted in our personal history of family and society, *the personal unconscious*.

The personal unconscious contains those attitudes which were not seen as acceptable by those around us in early life and so were pushed out of consciousness. For example, a child with parents who frowned when he got angry will learn to deny these feelings, first to his parents and, if there is no other outlet, eventually to himself. The personal unconscious also contains those aspects of ourselves we have simply not yet developed, such as our adventurous side. These less acceptable or unknown aspects of ourselves Jung described as the *shadow* of the personality.

What we have pushed out of consciousness or not yet become conscious of we tend to attribute to others. This is called *projection*, and it means that we rely on the other person to carry the projection for us, that is, to be what we think they are. We criticize or unduly admire others for what we are not getting to grips with, for example our sexuality, success, ability to make money, etc. Scapegoating in families and groups is the result of *projection of the shadow* at work. The problem in attributing (projecting) either negative or positive qualities on to others is that we are depleting our own personality by remaining unconscious of these aspects of ourselves. This will limit our potential to develop psychologically. Seen in this light, if through relationships with others we can 'own' what is in our shadow and so *withdraw the projections*, then we have a chance to enrich the personality by becoming more conscious and less at risk of the shadow contents taking us over – for example, the sudden judgemental attack on someone who has done something we ourselves secretly do or want to do.

Jung saw consciousness and unconsciousness as the two primary opposites of our inner or psychological life. Psychological development and health mean bringing conscious and unconscious attitudes as far into balance as possible. He called this *holding the tension between the opposites*, suggesting that this is a balance we are constantly having to redress as new experiences in both our inner and outer worlds challenge the status quo. This is the basis of human development. At each stage of life from infancy through to old age, we are faced with new tasks in all areas: physically, mentally, psychologically, morally and spiritually. How we negotiate the tasks of one stage will affect for good or ill how we face and negotiate the next stage. The mid-life crisis is a case in point: the person who behaves like an adolescent is making a statement both about fear of the second half of life and about something unfulfilled in the adolescent task of leaving the child behind. The drive to redress this imbalance comes from what Jung calls the *Self*. *The Self is the central core of the personality, which perpetuates psychological development throughout life*. It is the Self which strives to balance our need to live in society with the need to feel personally alive in a unique way. This process, which is ongoing, Jung called the *individuation process*.

Jung viewed the psyche as *self-regulating*, like the body. The unconscious attitudes will make their presence felt through symptoms, such as depression, when the clash with conscious attitudes becomes too great and holding the tension between the opposites therefore becomes too stressful. This is often the point of crisis at which someone will seek help. Therefore the unconscious has a *compensatory function* in relation to the conscious mind. It is exactly this self-healing capacity which can be harnessed in therapy where the client learns to see symptoms as indicators of psychic stress as well as problems in themselves.

As part of the individuation process we all struggle to hold the same opposites. We all try to separate from and to merge with others, to address good and bad in ourselves and others, to love and to hate, to face the unknown in our lives and in ourselves. We struggle to commit and to be alone, to relate to parents, friends, lovers, siblings, partners and children. We struggle with the need to find a balance between being outward-looking (extroverted) and inward-looking (introverted), to be a member of a group and yet unique. Jung saw the same themes and figures expressed symbolically in myth and religion, fairy-tales and the arts, and across different cultures. He saw that they resonated psychologically for people down the ages, and posited the existence of a *collective unconscious* containing the residue of human psychological evolution.

To these universal figures and experiences, images of which he observed often appeared in people's dreams, Jung gave the name *archetypes*. Examples of *archetypal images* are: the forces of good and evil, the union of masculine and feminine, the witch mother/tyrannical father, the nourishing earth mother, the

Wise Old Man and Woman, the Puer or Peter Pan figure. Other archetypal images are the heroic fight with a monster, the journey into the unknown (present even in *Winnie the Pooh*, and a powerful metaphor for the experience of counselling and therapy), and 'the dark night of the soul'. We come across modern versions today in films, on the television, in politics, children's stories, novels, and even cartoons.

An archetype is a human predisposition. It is an innate psychological readiness to relate to people: to a mother, to a father, to parents as a couple, to siblings and friends, to partners, to one's children. It is also a readiness for key human experiences such as birth, separating from the parents, the emergence of sexuality, marriage or partnering, becoming a parent, the loss of innocence, awareness of mortality and death. Each involves initiation, sacrifice and gain. It is a sort of DNA for psychological development, the basis for individual human experience. Every child is born but each child's experience of this rite of passage into the world will be individual and unique, depending on the child themselves and the actual physical and technical circumstances of birth, the mother's state of health and mind, and family and social attitudes. Even at this early stage the balance of inner and outer, of positive and negative will colour the child's conscious and unconscious attitudes.

The conscious part of our personality Jung called the Ego. The Ego develops as a result of relating, through human interactions first with the parents and then with others. Through these crucial interactions the child's innate, *archetypal expectations* or *projections* of 'Father' and of 'Mother' meet with experience of an actual relationship with a mummy and a daddy and are modified. (Children's books with their witches and fairy godmothers, giants and princes, reveal just how archetypal and unmediated by experience a young child's inner world tends to be.) A network of experiences and fantasies forms around these early significant relationships and these *associations* become the basis for expectations/projections about future interactions and relationships.

Growth occurs as at each stage of life from infancy onwards we struggle with challenges to these archetypal expectations. For adult life to have a secure basis and change to be tolerated and even welcomed there need to be good enough conditions for the inevitable losses and gains of each stage to be tolerated. This means that if the child is neither inappropriately hastened on, nor held back by circumstances or unconscious family influences then all will go well. The child will become an adult with realistic expectations of self and others. Where things go wrong the adult is likely to have an inflated sense of self to compensate for feelings of unworthiness and insecurity, or tend to be anxious and controlling of others to avoid what they feel to be the inevitable disappointment of relationships.

When the network of associations to these early important relationships is largely negative, for example a mother's depression clouds joy in her child, or a father is overly critical, then a *complex* is formed with the problem relationship at its core. This is a kind of 'psychological magnet,' a heightened sensitivity to any subsequent situation perceived as similar. The protective strategies (*defences*) the child developed at the time to cope with the original distress and anxiety come into action again in the adult. "Then" becomes "now" – the client with the depressed mother is unconsciously attracted to close relationships with depressed people in which he feels he must be bright and cheerful to survive. He has a negative mother complex. He remains unconscious of the fact that as an adult he could behave differently and constantly repeats the experience. The complex has him in its grip and he sees all important relationships through the lens of this complex.

The mature adult also needs to have a flexible *persona*, the role we take on in different social contexts, together with the accompanying behaviour, dress, language, manner, etc. Problems occur when either the range of roles is too limited or, more commonly, someone becomes *identified with their persona* (for example, the teacher who 'teaches' whoever s/he is with) and where loss or change of role results in feeling a profound loss of self.

Jung also noted that partnerships begin with projections. Falling in love involves projecting the image of the archetypally ideal partner on to an otherwise ordinary man or woman whose 'warts and all' humanity is temporarily obscured. When this goes on too long individuals become limited and the relationship stifled because partners collude in carrying each other's projections – for example, one person projects his nurturing side on to his partner who allows him to carry his/her assertion in the world. Tied by their mutual projections they each remain only half a person. Psychological maturity for both the individuals and their partnership depends on withdrawal of these projections from each other so as to learn from the partner and develop these qualities and capacities in themselves. In this way the Self can also use partnership as a route to individuation.

PRACTICE

The goals of the approach

Jungian therapy sets out to bring about inner change of a long-term nature. It aims to facilitate the client in making conscious those projections, complexes, unconscious attitudes and protective strategies (*defences*) which, as long as they have been unconscious, have held up development and therefore the process of individuation. By helping the client to put into words previously unconscious ideas (fantasies) about him or herself and others, the therapist aims to enable the client to develop his own capacities for understanding his feelings, thoughts and relationships. Through a process of experiencing and reflecting, the client is gradually helped to come to terms with what he is and is not, and realize what he still can be: to move from an inflated inadequacy to accept being ordinary and yet unique.

The counsellor aims to provide a setting both physical and psychological in which the client can begin to build sufficient trust to allow the often painful re-living of complexes and accompanying fantasies to take place. Continuity over time is therefore important. Consequently Jungians usually work within an open-ended or long-term contract, of at least a year and often longer. The ending is planned for at a point when the client feels able to take over the work on his own inner process.

The general format of sessions

These take place at regular intervals – weekly, or more frequently in the case of psychotherapy. They last for 50 minutes each. This boundary of time and of confidentiality is firmly maintained by the counsellor, who does not usually interact with the client in other capacities as this interferes with the counselling relationship and the potential for necessary projections to emerge. Client and counsellor sit in similar comfortable chairs positioned so that the client can both look and be looked at or not, as he wishes. A couch is also available for the psychotherapy client wishing to get more in touch with the inner world.

As this is one of the 'talking therapies', the client is encouraged to say whatever comes to mind. There is no set agenda or focus. In fact the client is actively encouraged to go with whatever spontaneous images, feelings and thoughts come up, and to relate dreams and fantasies as they occur. Silence can mean just as much as talking. For this reason the counsellor will probably not interrupt a silence unless she feels the client is struggling. The client is also encouraged to voice feelings about the way he experiences sessions and the relationship with the counsellor as well as exploring life and relationships outside the sessions. The counsellor offers her understanding of the meaning of what is being said and experienced both in and out of the session, and encourages the client to reflect and offer further associated memories, feelings, and fantasies. If the client chooses, he can also use poetry, painting, music, etc., to explore his inner world, his experiences and his relationships.

Often the first session with a client will contain in a condensed form the central complex(es), such as negative father complex, Oedipal or exclusion complex. Sometimes an early dream indicates the central issues that the client is unconsciously concerned with, by showing in dramatized form via the dream figures the state of the person's relationship to themselves and others. (In the dream the I is the conscious personality, the ego, while the dream itself is a spontaneous product of the Self.) For instance, a woman very enmeshed in the relationship with her mother, dreams that she walks past a mother and child playing on a beach. She knows in the dream that the child is her. She leaves them and walks on to join friends. This dream had a powerful effect on the dreamer and was something she often came back to in sessions, where the main work was around separating psychologically from the mother.

Throughout the sessions the Jungian counsellor will be listening for whether the client's expectations of themselves and of relationships are of actual people or archetypal figures. Does their description of their partner suggest a god or goddess or a real person? Have they come to see their parents as human beings or do they still seem more like a witch and a tyrant? Or perhaps mother is the archetypal ideal woman or father the perfect man? These standards that they strive to live by and constantly feel they fail, how realistic are they? And this same-sex friend of whose snobbery they are so critical – does this person represent their shadow?

Jungian counselling often starts with helping the client to come to terms with their shadow, that rejected undiscovered part of themselves. As she gets to know the client the counsellor will become aware of both negative and positive pro-jections, and those attitudes which the client has unconsciously absorbed, without question, from significant others. In addition, because the relationship between client and therapist is crucial, the Jungian counsellor will be noting how the client responds to her, and monitoring her own responses to the client himself and his story. The importance of this is that there will be triggers in the therapeutic relationship for the client to relate to her as he has related to significant others in his past and as he relates to others in the present. He will not only consciously tell the counsellor where his difficulties are, in so far as he can, but he will also *show* her by the way he experiences and treats her. He will enact the unconscious attitudes in the session. In the counselling setting this form of projection is called *transference*. Through the transference the Self brings the core complex straight into the counselling process.

To facilitate the emergence of transference projections the Jungian counsellor will not reveal a great deal about herself beyond what is professionally essential or obvious from where she works or who she is. This is in order not to deprive the client of the opportunity to experience feelings towards her which he may otherwise feel he needs to hide, as he has done in the past.

As the counselling situation is not equal in the sense that one person is seeking help from another, a common archetypal projection on to the counsellor is of one or other of the parents. If the client has an authority complex because he experienced his father as a harsh, critical, god-like figure or his mother as a cold and withholding 'stone mother', then at different times he will perceive the counsellor as critical or cold, and struggle for a while with a *negative trans-ference*.

The counsellor's task is to help the client put into words (*make conscious*) his perception of himself and others, and to assist him in taking back the projections which inhibit real relationship and individuation. She does this by pointing out how she observes and experiences him perceiving his relationships through the lens of the complexes that grip him, and endeavours to help him link these up with other experiences past and present – for example, 'From the closed-up look on your face and the way you go silent when I say something, I think you feel I've taken over just as you did when you talked with your older brother.' This work of understanding and connecting by the therapist is called *interpreting*. The therapist will also encourage the client to reflect on when, and with whom, such feelings and thoughts have been around before. Then the client will be able to make his own connection or interpretation of his experience. Gradually he will begin to develop his own capacity to think about and understand his feelings, fantasies, thoughts and bodily sensations, and so be less dominated by his complexes.

Earlier we mentioned the importance that Jung placed on the therapist's own emotional response to the client. This is known as the *counter-transference* and refers to the feelings aroused in the counsellor by the client, what he says and the way he is in the sessions. The counsellor feels what the client is feeling uncon-sciously or she may feel with him as others do in his presence. The counter-transference is a vital source of information about the client's unconscious inner world, about how he relates and about how others relate to him. It is a more primitive, unconscious form of communication between people on a par with that between mother and child, which Jung called 'participation mystique'. The Jungian counsellor needs to monitor this important emotional response during the session and make conscious what the client seems not yet to know or be able to put into words himself. The counter-transference may take the form of an image, an intuitive perception, a thought or a feeling. Or the counsellor may experience a bodily sensation when with the client – one counsellor described feeling very puffed up and then suddenly very small with a client who swung between feeling an inflated sense of self and feelings of great inadequacy.

As reflects the nature of the complex, the 'work' client and counsellor do together has a spiral nature. The 'psychological magnet' of the complex and the compensatory nature of the unconscious means that in an unconscious effort to understand what seems incomprehensible, the client repeatedly finds himself in situations and relationships where the same painful feelings and defences are triggered. As the counsellor helps to make him conscious of this *compulsion to repeat* and the fantasy behind it, the client is helped to explore its meaning. He unravels the network of associated experiences and feelings that has built up around a particular formative experience. The grip that the complex had on him gradually lessens as it cannot stand the light of consciousness.

However, this much-longed-for change, is also feared and *resisted*. Change means risk and giving up the familiar 'devil I know'. So to help establish and maintain a *working rapport* the counsellor also helps the client to think about the anxiety, which means he both wants to change, and to protect himself against change. The counsellor observes what protective strategies (defences) the client relies on, when he resorts to them and what may be the reason, for example changing the subject when a painful point is reached, or denying anger when anxious of the effect expressing it would have. Then by being encouraged to get in touch with the fantasy behind the need to protect himself (for instance, fear that the counsellor, like his father, would withdraw if he got angry), the client can begin to give up those protective strategies which get in the way of life, intimacy and further development. The Ego is stronger, there is less anxiety and change is really on the way.

WHICH CLIENTS BENEFIT MOST?

Many clients who find their way to a Jungian therapist complain of lack of meaning in their lives, of the feeling that 'there must be something more to life than this'. Others are seeking to renew or find a sense of inner purpose lost or greatly changed through life experiences such as a relationship crisis, death of a loved one, or a major change of circumstances such as redundancy. Some may come because they feel an inner purpose has never been established and they have no sense of their identity, or of self-worth. Because relationship is at the heart of Jungian therapy clients with difficulties in making relationships can be helped over time. Clients with difficulties in early life, such as repeated losses or parents themselves struggling to be emotionally mature, or where early circumstances have meant they have had grow up too soon (sick parents, abusive experiences, childhood illness or handicap), find the long-term nature of Jungian therapy valuable. It helps the Self to unfold and the Ego to strengthen through a gradual approach to increased consciousness. Creative people, who fear the analytic stance will by definition damage their creative capacities, often respond well to a Jungian approach as their art, music, writings, etc. can become part of the work and be viewed as an expression of the Self.

Jungian therapy is less suitable for the person who has a problem-solving attitude to difficulties, as they are likely to find it slow and frustrating. Nor is it for the person who seeks cure, rather than insight into themselves and growth. Some very extroverted people may struggle with the emphasis on the inner world but this can shift if they are able to persevere. Clients with seriously disabling behavioural problems such as addictions, incapacitating panic attacks, or eating disorders, which are severe enough to prevent the person from leading anything like a normal life, would only be able to benefit from any form of psychodynamic counselling once the symptom was sufficiently under control to enable the person to attend regularly and to tolerate some degree of psychic pain.

Case study

THE CLIENT

Paul was in his mid-twenties, a professional single man working in finance. Despite aptitude he hated the work, and rebelled against the 'business man' persona in his appearance and dress. His real interests lay with people, and with writing and composing songs and music for the group he played in.

Presenting problem

Paul sought help because 'There are parts of myself that I don't understand', and 'relationships with women go wrong'. He felt he didn't know how others saw him or how he saw himself. He could no longer sort this out on his own.

In fact both actually and symbolically there were unknown parts of himself, for Paul had been adopted as an infant. He had always known this and it had been a successful adoption. However, he knew nothing about his birth parents and when he looked at his adoptive parents and adopted sibling Paul did not see himself mirrored back. The 'dual mother' motif portrayed in many myths and fairy-tales, and children's fantasies about really being the child of much more exciting parents, was right there for Paul in his actual experience. He had a negative mother complex with anxieties about rejection, and a negative father complex to do with belonging.

Paul's problems had come to the fore during adolescence – the turbulent period of identity crisis. He was rejecting his own Celtic culture, imagining his birth father was English. He felt unrelated to his own masculinity and aggression, which he projected out on to his adoptive father and male relatives as 'all machismo'. He had good male friends, but was more aware of their deficiencies in the feeling and sensitivity area than their strengths, suggesting an over-developed relationship to the inner feminine. With women he formed archetypally intense short-lived relationships which echoed his unresolved relationship to his birth mother.

THE THERAPY

From the outset Paul's early experience of relationship reflected in the process. He was referred shortly before the therapist went on her summer break, so just as bonding began to take place, separation followed. His high anxiety and undifferentiated feeling meant he was likely to unconsciously perceive this separation through the lens of the complex as abandonment and rejection. Without bringing this to consciousness the chances were that the relationship would not survive the break. So the therapist interpreted the connection between this potential attachment and immediate separation and that with his birth mother. Paul was able to see the similarity, as well as the differences which his therapist pointed out (namely that their separation was temporary, they would meet again soon, etc.) and hold on to it, which augured well for his capacity to use the therapy. It also brought immediately into the open the negative mother complex in the form of a potential negative transference towards the therapist/mother. However, unlike with his birth mother, these feelings could be expressed prior to the separation. The working rapport thus established survived the break.

Very shortly afterwards, Paul's shadow, his undeveloped capacity to handle aggressive feelings in himself or others, came abruptly into the process, when one night he was hit in the face by a man and was concussed. His passivity in response symbolized his inability to assert himself appropriately, while his tendency to be 'hit in the face' by his own unconscious feelings remained a useful image in the work – once the traumatic event itself had been processed.

Paul's songs were very important in his psychic process. Through them he articulated raw feelings of rage and despair about separation and rejection in images archetypal in their power – of sirens who lured men on to the rocks, of black holes and neglectful women. At one level these referred to the painful on–off nature of his relationship with his girlfriend, but they were equally applicable to the raw pain of that first separation. Paul's therapist treated them as spontaneous unconscious material like dreams, and so a product of the Self which was guiding his work on himself.

The rejection and abandonment complex inevitably continued to surface in the transference. Paul would leave sessions feeling he had been thrown out and left to cope with his own feelings, and report back that he hadn't known what he was doing in his car when he left the session. Genuinely concerned about this potentially dangerous dissociated behaviour, the therapist patiently interpreted the negative transference feelings towards her as the mother who each session abandoned him to his fate. She engaged his ego in thinking with her about the risk of such behaviour.

Paul became more able to voice rather than act out negative feelings and so to manage his anxiety better himself. As he began to see that life lived more consciously was actually less painful, he developed more of a capacity to wait. The plan of searching for his birth mother went on hold, as he realized that seeking out his external identity was not enough on its own. Instead he paid more attention to how he experienced his existing relationships, with his adoptive parents and with the girlfriend who attracted so much of the archetypal good mother projection. For a long time the mother complex was split between therapist and girlfriend. The therapist was experienced as sometimes the abandoning mother and sometimes the adoptive mother who offered, as he came to realize, continuing care and availability. The adoptive triangle of birth mother and adoptive mother and Paul also appeared in the transference. In the counter-transference the therapist was aware, as she imagined his birth mother had been, of the neediness of her patient, of guilt at the ends of sessions. She felt the intolerable pain that, like his adoptive mother, she could only nurse him through but not assuage, and she had to withstand the angry attacks for not being there all the time, and his disappointment that she was only a poor substitute for the perfect mother he felt he had lost.

As the rejection complex emerged in his projections on to his therapist and others, and as these were explored in the work, Paul realized that to protect himself he either disengaged from relationships before rejection could happen or he failed to see it coming. He noticed that when anxieties about rejection began to surface again, it was a sign that he was under psychic stress.

After about 18 months Paul felt that to seek out his birth mother would no longer be a quest for the archetypal ideal mother but to know his origins, her story and discover who he looked like. His relationship with his adoptive parents had matured into one in which he could feel supported by both as his actual parents, having faced the fear that they too might reject him if he went ahead with the search for his birth mother. In the sessions Paul and his therapist worked hard on his anxieties about the momentous meeting with his birth mother and how best to be in control without being controlling. Further strengthening of his ego thus took place.

Gradually Paul showed in various ways that he did now know who he was. He made a good friendship with his birth mother and had more realistic expectations of relationships with women. More at ease with his masculinity and able to identify with his Celtic background, he also found his own style at work. He sought out and met his Irish birth father, and processed the feelings this evoked with the minimum of help from his therapist and a greater ability to find support in friends and family. He made conscious his wish to settle down and to become a father himself in time, and re-developed a relationship which had blossomed too early in his therapy and gone on hold.

After two years he had a dream which he and his therapist both felt presaged his readiness to end therapy: *We are in the hall that leads to your consulting room, near the front door. You are showing me a map and helping me plan a journey.* His associations to this were that the hall was between the inner and the outer world and that it represented a stage of transition. Both Paul and his therapist recognized how important it was that he should be the one to leave her, and also that the ending of the therapy should be one that allowed for gradual letting go. This experience of ending would in itself be a key part of Paul's therapy and one that only long-term work could have offered him. So, over several months, the therapy wound down by increasing the gaps between sessions, allowing Paul the opportunity to explore feelings about ending and new beginnings. He left with a New Year and potential long-term relationship on the threshold, knowing that his therapist's door remained open to him should he want to knock, but with both feeling he would not need to do so.

SUGGESTED READING

Hyde, M. and McGuinness, M. (1992) *Jung for Beginners*. Cambridge: Icon Books. An introduction to Jung's ideas through a combination of both text and cartoon-type pictures which is the style of this series of books on seminal thinkers. The approach is refreshing while dealing well with the ideas.

Jacoby, M. (1984) *The Analytic Encounter: Transference and Human Relationship*. Toronto: Inner City Books. A short, very clear and readable account of basic principles of the Jungian approach with good case examples to illustrate.

Kast, V. (1992) *The Dynamics of Symbols: Fundamentals of Jungian Psychotherapy*. New York: Fromm Psychology. A more extended account of how a Jungian therapist works and thinks about the psychological development of clients with particular emphasis on the relationship between conscious and unconscious complex and archetypes, and the way they appear in dreams, drawings and fairy-tales as part of the therapeutic process. Very accessible and brought alive with examples and case material.

Redfearn, J. (1992) *The Exploding Self: The Creative and Destructive Nucleus of the Personality*. Wilmette, IL: Chiron. Redfearn applies Jungian ideas to society as a whole as well as to the individual and explains the relevance of Jungian concepts to both. Clear and well-written, with the lay reader as well as the therapist in mind.

Storr, A. (1973) *Jung*. London: Fontana Modern Masters. A short account of Jung's life and work and the relationship between the two.

DISCUSSION ISSUES

1   The notion that unconscious thinking and action is compensatory to conscious action and thinking is an important one in Jungian therapy. Choose a life issue such as relationship, job, friendship, and discuss how a client might reveal conscious and unconscious attitudes which are in conflict with one another. How might the counsellor help the client towards a more integrated attitude?

2   Consider the idea that projection is both limiting and a means of growth. How can experiencing a transference on to a therapist help a client to grow? You might like to refer to the case study as a starting point.

3   The case study could be said to exemplify the Ishmael complex (Ishmael was Abraham's illegitimate son who, with his mother, was cast out of the tribe into the wilderness). Many myths, legends and fairy-tales, ancient and modern, portray complexes and the task of unravelling them. Choose a favourite story and discuss the meanings it holds for you and others.

4   Compare and contrast the information about the aims and practice of Jungian therapy with another psychodynamic approach or a humanistic or cognitive one. What differences and similarities do you observe?

20

PSYCHODYNAMIC (KLEINIAN) COUNSELLING AND PSYCHOTHERAPY

Julia Segal

The Kleinian approach to psychodynamic psychotherapy depends on the capacity of therapists to make contact with their clients' inner world, including the hidden anxieties which disrupt their clients' lives. Therapists' sympathetic but realistic understanding of frightening and frightened elements of clients' minds and personalities can enable clients to reassess, reclaim and modify previously rejected aspects of themselves. At the same time clients are able to reassess memories and experiences of other people in their lives, both past and present. With the help of the therapist, the client's inner world is rebuilt on firmer foundations. This has lasting and significant consequences for future relationships, both with the self and with others.

Some of these concepts may seem strange: Kleinians are sometimes noted for their difficult and odd ideas. However, many people find that once they get used to them, the ideas are both comprehensible and useful. Children seem to have less difficulty understanding them than some adults.

Many forms of counselling and psychotherapy have developed in opposition to the ideas of Freud. Kleinian therapists of all kinds, however, are more likely to emphasize the debt owed to the psychoanalytical inheritance. Melanie Klein[1] herself was a psychoanalyst: although she disagreed with Freud over some important issues, fundamentally she saw his method and understanding as the foundation on which she based all her work. Similarly, Kleinian counsellors and psychotherapists see Klein's method and understanding as providing the foundation on which they base their work. Their emphasis on the value of carrying over into the counselling relationship much which has been learnt in the more intensive setting of psychoanalysis gives their work a distinctive aspect.

Kleinian therapists, for example, are very strict about their own time-keeping; they are unlikely to discuss any aspect of their own lives with clients; they are likely to keep their rooms, setting and own appearance as unchanging as possible. All of these things, they believe, have significance to clients which clients may not immediately recognize, but which affect the work which can be done. They also pay attention to the unspoken anxieties of the client and do not rely simply on what the client says directly.

DEVELOPMENT OF THE THERAPY

Melanie Klein began work in Vienna with Sandor Ferenczi and moved to Berlin where she had the support of Karl Abraham. In 1926 she moved to Britain, where she remained until her death in 1962. In Vienna she already found that Freud's ideas about the interpretation of dreams[2] gave her insight into her own son's fantasies and play. Detecting some anxieties she talked to him about them and his response was immediate. One day, for example, he told her he was 'not afraid any more of the things that have been explained to him even when he thinks of them'.[3] Although Klein discouraged others from analysing their own children, this could stand for the essence of the Kleinian method. By enabling the person to understand frightening thoughts and feelings, the fear is reduced *without the need to avoid thinking.*

Klein paid meticulous attention to the words and actions of her patients, and was rewarded with remarkable insight into the ways the mind works. Her followers learned to understand some of the fears behind psychotic states of mind as well as more 'normal' ones, and developed important insight into the feelings and reactions of therapists themselves. They became convinced of the importance of careful observation as a means of understanding the client's reaction to the therapist; and thereby of getting in touch with anxieties forming the most significant basis for a client's relationships with others.

Klein herself believed that analysis five times a week was the only way to allow the deepest anxieties to emerge and to enable fundamental changes. However, many therapists and counsellors offering sessions once, twice or three times a week see the work of analysts as research which they can apply in their own practice. Even small reductions in anxiety obtainable in a one-off session can sometimes have significant effects on the lives of clients.

THEORY AND BASIC CONCEPTS

Klein's ideas about the way our minds work were revolutionary. Her observations led her to believe that children were very much aware of the world, dynamically interacting with it and actively making sense of it from a very early age. She developed a concept of Unconscious Phantasy[4] by which she meant something more than the fantasies which children and adults weave to entertain themselves. Unconscious phantasies are the mental representations of the child's first experiences. For example, Klein thought that a child might experience being angry as an unconscious phantasy in which the child was fighting someone. A baby feeling loving towards its mother experiences love in some concrete way, for example, as a phantasy of giving her something wonderful. She found that children experience their mothers in phantasy in age-appropriate ways; to begin with as something with the vastness, power and swell of the ocean; later closer to a living, warm, containing and loving room; a comfortable piece of furniture.

Only gradually do they become aware of their mother's relationship with other people and her ability to go and to return. To begin with her absence may be felt concretely, as darkness is felt as more than the absence of light.

Such phantasies, created very early on out of primitive experiences and attempts to make sense of them, leave their mark in the ways we later relate to our living spaces; or to the ocean, the moon and the sky – as poets have always described. Our earliest phantasies involved us doing things to, and things being done to us by, those closest to us; these most basic phantasies have two important consequences. Because they are dynamic, they depend on outside events as well as internal ones. For example, if a baby in phantasy fights with a monster-breast coming at it (when its stomach hurts and it doesn't want to feed, for example); the phantasy goes on; the breast monster (probably) goes away. What happens next is important. The pain may also go and the breast return and be experienced as a wanted, loving good object which can fill the beginnings of a hole. Alternatively, the pain may not go away. The baby may feel the loving breast is lost forever. From the baby's point of view the fight with the breast monster had an outcome. Phantasies develop in relation to events; and they may not always be entirely under the baby's control.

Secondly, such phantasies form the basis for the child's and then the adult's understanding of the world. A child whose phantasies regularly include a sense of control over a basically good world will understand events and people in a different way from a child whose phantasies always involved a sense of dissatisfaction, frustration and impotent helplessness. Expectations aroused by early experiences will be carried over into later ones. So, for example, a baby which has experienced the world as a good place is likely to develop into an adult who expects to give and to get good things from life. Equally, someone who lost a parent at the age of 10 may in some deep sense 'expect' to lose their partner after 10 years; or when their own first child is 10. They may behave in a way which is determined by this fear – and may actually bring it about.

It is important to note that the baby's experience of the world depends only partially on those around. Melanie Klein observed that the child's experience seemed to depend not only on what was actually provided, but also on the child's ability to make use of it. Some children are more tolerant and forgiving; others more demanding. Although some of this can be understood as a reaction to the parenting the child receives, Klein thought there were other factors at work as well. In particular she thought the child's tolerance of pain and its constitution were important elements of experience. Bad experiences may be made worse by cruel or neglectful parenting; and good parenting may mitigate them; but good experiences may also count for more for some children than for others.[5]

As babies grow into children and then adults, the ways they relate to the world continue to be influenced by early phantasies, modified to a greater or lesser degree by later ones. For example, when we are small we do not know how much effect our angry or loving phantasies have in the outside world. If we became very angry with our mother and she then went away or went into hospital, we may be afraid it was our phantasied attacks which caused it, and that our phantasies of making her better were useless. We may grow up afraid of attacking people in phantasy: afraid our anger can cause injury.

There are many ways we can behave if we fear our own anger too much. We may, for example, try always to be very nice to people in the hope that they will be nice to us. This may work for strangers, but it may be obvious to close family that this niceness at times covers up fury; and they may react angrily themselves. When they are angry we know *we* are not angry but *they* are; and this may in a way be satisfying.

A new lover, our own children, or a therapist may all have the capacity to challenge our fear of our own anger, and may gradually enable us to recognize and use it appropriately. However, in less happy circumstances, we may choose a lover who will act to confirm our belief that our anger is dangerous; or we may be unable to be overtly angry with our children. We are likely to be afraid of being angry with our therapist – but if we are lucky, he or she will recognize this, point it out and help us to examine and lose our fear.

Klein drew attention to the ways in which we try to get rid of our own uncomfortable states of mind, and how damaging this can be. Work done since has increased our understanding of such processes, and of the role of therapy in modifying them. In phantasy we can cut out bits of our minds; thrust them into others; or have bits of others thrust into us; we then claim that all of these are 'not me'. 'It is my child/spouse/mother who is angry/sad/dependent/frustrated, not me'. Therapy can help us to see where we have done this, and to reclaim disowned aspects of ourselves.[6]

Painful emotions of grief and mourning are involved when we bring together parts of our minds which previously we kept separate. In order not to admit we have lost someone, for example, we may maintain a phantasy that we are them; or that they inhabit our body. We may feel we act in ways which are 'them' not 'us' at times; and perhaps feel out of control of parts of our body or mind. Recognizing that a lost person 'lives' inside us metaphorically though not concretely can only happen after grief and mourning, in which feelings of loss are experienced.[7] In phantasy we have to recognize what of 'them' is really us; what is them which we can make ours; and what of them we have truly lost. Kleinians see mourning as a powerful process in which the person may make new discoveries about themselves and the world; a process of growth. However, they also recognize how painful it is. The presence of an understanding person makes the pain of mourning easier to bear and less likely to be cut off from perception in a damaging way.

Klein found that even small children can have powerful feelings of hatred towards both their parents, as well as very strong desires to keep them alive and well.[8] These conflicts are both a spur to development and, sometimes, a cause for difficulty. Some awareness of having attacked the person they love, for example, can make a child want to make things better; this can be a motive force for creative work of all kinds, in childhood and adulthood. However, too much guilt about damage done to the mother in infancy, for example, can be paralysing; or can motivate attacks on the self and on others.

Adults can find it reassuring as well as surprising to recognize in therapy some aspect of their emotional life which they have always considered bad and have tried to hide all through their life. Jealousy, hatred or envy are emotions which are commonly denied and may be uncovered in this way. Although these are emotions people dislike having, there is a sense of security in no longer having to maintain a lie about oneself. There is also some security in the discovery of the extent and limits of the badness; one woman was astonished that it was possible to consider just how much she hated her mother; for the thought had always seemed so bad she had to 'stuff it down a well' and obliterate it from her mind. She was shocked when the counsellor asked how bad it was; did she want her mother actually dead? Or perhaps a million miles away? Oh no, she said; she just wanted her to come round rather less often every week. Once it was spoken she realized it was not such a terrible thought after all.

PRACTICE

In the work of Kleinians, understanding the fears or anxieties connected with relating to others is seen as the main force for change. Such understanding is achieved through the relationship between client and therapist. By providing a safe setting in terms of the physical and emotional surroundings, the therapist enables the client to allow feelings and thoughts into consciousness which previously were unrecognized or rejected. By observing and reporting on links the client appears to be making without recognizing them, the therapist uncovers connections the client has been unaware of making – but which may have been highly significant in determining actions and beliefs.

The therapist also models a more tolerant and sympathetic way of understanding less desired aspects of the self, thus enabling clients to be less harsh on themselves. This helps to reduce clients' anxieties and tension. Clients have to work less hard to maintain illusions about themselves and others. With this relaxation comes a new tolerance of the self and others which improves clients' relations with themselves and with the rest of the world.

The goal of psychodynamic psychotherapy or counselling is to open up areas of the mind and emotional responses to conscious awareness. In this way it differs from those therapies (including many drugs) which work to close down aspects of the mind. The therapist works on the assumption that reality is safer than pretence; that knowing is ultimately more bearable than not knowing; that much can be tolerated within a good relationship with a therapist which could not be tolerated alone, and that the expansion of consciousness and strength which such therapy can offer will bring benefits to the client and to those around.

People are sometimes afraid that psychodynamic counselling and psychotherapy may open up 'cans of worms'; but the goal is to allow the 'worms' to melt away or transform into quite different objects under the clear light of day. Therapy may bring out things which were previously 'swept under the carpet'; and the client may want to push everything back under the carpet as they leave – but the bump will be smaller and less liable to trip people up.

How theory is applied

The therapist's beliefs about the importance of the client's relationship with the therapist govern much of the way in which therapy is offered. For example, the therapist is aware that very primitive phantasies can be stirred by feelings of dependence and consequent fears of change and of abandonment, and will pay considerable attention to making arrangements for sessions clear and predictable and avoiding as far as possible changes to the room, to the timing of sessions and even to the general appearance of the therapist. The therapist looks for ways in which the client reacts to breaks in therapy, such as at Christmas, Easter and the summer. These reactions can tell the therapist – and ultimately the client – how the client responds to being left to their own devices. Old conflicts connected with being left by parents, perhaps through illness or death, may emerge at such times; if these issues are not taken up and understood sufficiently, clients often miss sessions just before or just after a break.

The therapist also uses the theory to help understand what is going on for the client and to try to show the client his understanding. For example, a client who appears very self-confident but makes the counsellor feel quite useless might be using a mechanism Kleinians call projective identification[9] to 'get rid of' feelings she cannot bear into the counsellor. The counsellor will wonder first if he is really being useless; he will then use his recognition of this process to wonder (aloud or in his own head) whether the client too feels quite useless inside, but cannot bear the feeling. Suggesting this tentatively to the client may give some indication of whether the client is prepared to work in this way with the counsellor; where one client would experience a relief in being understood, another client may furiously reject the suggestion.

Change process and therapeutic relationship

In the here-and-now relationship with the therapist, the client's past and present difficulties will be reflected. Focusing on this relationship can bring into the room in a lively way issues which have been neglected for years. For example, a woman who does not stand up to her husband is likely not to stand up to the therapist: the therapist may be able to discover and understand some of the roots of the hesitancy in the relation with himself, and thus ultimately transform the relation with the husband. (If the therapist does not ensure the client understands why he is working in this way, some clients become annoyed at the apparent over-valuing of the relation with the therapist at the expense of consideration of 'real-life' relationships. Because of this, in short-term work some Kleinian counsellors restrict the use of overt transference interpretations. They may, for example, use their understanding of the client–counsellor relationship to illuminate the client's relationship with her husband, but talk to the client of it mainly in terms of the relationship with the husband, using material from the relationship with the therapist only to make it more convincing.)

Kleinian therapists focus on their clients' anxieties; the worries which seem to underlie the ways they think and behave. For example, a client was talking non-stop and not allowing the counsellor time to think or answer. Using the client's appearance – very thick make-up – and something of the content of what she was saying as clues, the counsellor took advantage of a moment's break to wonder gently if the client was afraid that she had to put up a real barrier of words between herself and the counsellor in order to prevent the counsellor getting in and seeing that underneath the bravado and the fun she was afraid she was 'really' a terrible person. The client took a deep breath and stopped talking. When she began again it was with a completely different tone and she began to tell the counsellor how her mother had often told her she had killed her twin brother who had died in infancy.

Questions will seldom receive direct answers from a Kleinian therapist or counsellor. How they react will depend on the context. Counsellors may explain that they find it more helpful to try to understand what a question is about, rather than to answer it. If a client asks if the counsellor has children, for example, an answer either way may block the client's willingness to reveal their own feelings about children and parenthood. Exploring the significance of the question for the client without answering it may be far more revealing. (For further discussion of this see Segal (1993).[10])

Partly because there is an expectation that their clients (unlike many counselling clients) will already have some idea that they need psychotherapeutic help, psychodynamic psychotherapists are less likely to explain; they may simply interpret the client's response in terms of their perception of the client's anxieties. Some clients find this irritating, particularly at first. It demonstrates that the therapist or counsellor is working in his or her own way and is not prepared to go along with everything the client wants. It also shows up the distinction between professional and friend. This itself may become a focus of discussion; along with irritation the client may also experience relief. A social relationship brings with it responsibilities as well as rewards; the relationship with the counsellor works under different rules and the counsellor holds responsibility for these. This can liberate a client, particularly if they have always felt responsible for looking after others, for example. The counsellor is saying very firmly that they can look after themselves, and it is not the client's responsibility to be considerate and caring if they do not feel like it.

Format of a typical session

A psychodynamic counselling or psychotherapy session is likely to start with the counsellor or psychotherapist greeting the patient in a serious but warm manner, saying very little, if anything. The counsellor will listen carefully to any 'small talk' and will respond courteously, but will be trying to understand what it betrays about the client's state of mind. The counsellor will probably not join in discussing, say, the weather or the journey. The first thing she says will probably be addressed as closely as possible to the client's anxieties as understood by the counsellor at that moment. What the client has said will be understood as conveying something to the counsellor about his state of mind, his hopes and anxieties at that moment about coming to counselling.

The session will continue with the client talking about whatever occurs to him. The counsellor will respond; listening and commenting on what seems to be important for the client.

The counsellor will be constantly on the look-out for what is going on in the relationship, and the ways the client is talking as well as what they are saying. For example, a client who claimed to be very keen on counselling greeted everything the counsellor said with 'no . . .'. Eventually the counsellor pointed this out, whereupon the client said 'no I don't' – and they both laughed. The client was then able to use this intervention in a way she had been quite unable to use anything the counsellor had said before; together they could begin to explore what it was that made her so scared to allow anyone else to have an idea and give it to her. In this case it led to exploration of a very painful childhood memory, when she had been unable to say 'no' effectively to an uncle who abused her regularly. The 'no' not only constantly asserted her ability to keep people out of her body and her mind; together with her seductive enthusiasm for counselling it also created in the counsellor something of the feeling of being misused and perversely ill-treated.

The counsellor or psychotherapist may say at least one thing about the relationship between the client and herself in the session. In particular, she will be alert for any negative reactions which betray any sense of unease or discomfort towards the counsellor or therapist. For example, she may pick up the way a client seems to be trying to please; or the way he has not mentioned anything about a coming holiday, though there is reason to believe he is afraid of being left to his own devices at this time. If a client is talking about troubles with his partner, the counsellor may pick up some way in which the relationship with the counsellor may be related to the particular issue which seems to be troubling the client on that day. Idealization of the therapist will probably be understood by the therapist as a defence against persecutory beliefs or phantasies; a client who is always pleased or happy with what the therapist says may have quite terrifying secret beliefs about how dangerous it is to question what is going on, or to admit to any dissatisfaction. In looking for ways the client feels about counselling the counsellor will not be simply listening for the client to say 'I was unhappy with what you said last week . . .', which very few clients are capable of admitting directly. More subtle hints may be have to taken, and there must be a careful and sensitive process of checking out whether the counsellor's understanding is correct.

It is comments about what is going on in the room, between client and therapist, if sensitively timed and directed, that Kleinians think are likely to bring about the most change.[11] If used insensitively, however, they can simply give the client the feeling that the therapist is feeling left out and wants to be noticed; or that issues which really matter to the client are being ignored. For this reason, the therapist is likely to acknowledge seriously the overt issue which is being discussed as well as any possible underlying transference issue. The client's immediate response, as well as material brought up later, will help the therapist to work out whether their intervention made sense to the client and was useful, or whether it needed modifying or rejecting outright.

The session will include careful attention to any imminent changes of date or time caused by therapist or client; there will be some attempt to elucidate any meaning such changes might have for the client. These are important, since unspoken reactions can be 'acted out' by sessions being cut short or missed, or the therapy being brought to an abrupt end.

WHICH CLIENTS BENEFIT MOST?

Psychodynamic counsellors and psychotherapists may cater for slightly different client groups. Counsellors tend to work in settings where the clients may consider there is nothing basically wrong with themselves. Counselling clients may see themselves as fairly normal people having to deal with a difficult situation – such as some aspect of student life; an illness; the death of someone close; a loss of some other kind; or a marital problem which is not necessarily of their own making.

Psychodynamic psychotherapists may have a greater expectation that their clients know there is something *in themselves* which needs attention. Their clients are perhaps more likely to have tried the new lover, the new job, the New Year's resolution – and still be finding that they are not happy; that their life is not as they wished or planned. They may have a greater recognition that there is something wrong in their own approach to the world which might be put right by a therapist. These clients may also have some sense that their problems may take some time to solve; they have tried the 'quick fixes' and they have not worked.

Unconsciously, clients have all kinds of beliefs about therapy and counselling, which may or may not emerge over time; but unless there is some sense of wanting understanding and insight, and of these being worth having, clients are unlikely to appreciate work with psychodynamic counsellors or psychotherapists.

Case study

THE CLIENT

Ann arrived in a state of despair. She wept as she told the counsellor how unfair she felt her family was towards her. In her twenties she had worked in films and earned a lot of money; she had always given her sister and her mother expensive presents and had kept regular contact with them. But when she had had a child by a married man, shortly after being diagnosed with arthritis, they had completely failed to support her. She felt absolutely at the end of her tether. Her mother hated her; her sister hated her; her neighbours were no support at all, and her friends all had their own problems. By the age of 46 she felt she really ought not to need support like this, but she just could not cope. Her arthritis made every action painful and she had very little money but nobody was prepared to help her. The only good thing in her life was her son, who was all a son could be to her.

She had tried various kinds of therapy earlier in her life; after a suicide attempt in her thirties, she said, one therapist had told her she disgusted him. This was all she remembered.

THE THERAPY

The counsellor herself felt somewhat overwhelmed by Ann's predicament and the way she presented herself; and she was afraid Ann would expect her to be disgusted, as her previous therapist had been. She acknowledged to Ann how unsupported Ann felt, and how she must be afraid that she, the counsellor, would turn against her too. Ann's response to this was to relax visibly and become more thoughtful.

In many of her sessions Ann talked almost non-stop. It was as if she was completely overloaded. The counsellor pointed out that Ann seemed to feel she had to do all of the work herself. This led to Ann talking about the way she had never felt supported. Her father had died when she was 10; her older sister had left home and she had felt she had to support her mother. The counsellor linked this with Ann's sense of being unsupported now; in particular because her son was now nearly 10 too. Though Ann was surprised that there could be a link, she talked for the first time of her father and how she had felt about him. She talked of his sudden death; how nobody had ever told her anything about it, and how she never thought about him as she was growing up. She did remember feeling very lonely as a teenager.

When she was a young woman, men had wanted to marry her, but she had left each of them; two after six years or so. The counsellor wondered with her if this was because she was afraid they would leave her, like her father had. Ann was not sure about this; they would all have made good husbands; she was still not sure what had been wrong about the relationships. She 'didn't know'.

The counsellor helped Ann to focus on the way she used 'I don't know' to stop trains of thought in the session. The thoughts often seemed to run 'So-and-so is not very nice to me, it must be my fault – oh I don't know.' The counsellor pointed out that she seemed unable to think about whether it was her fault or not; she wondered if Ann had had similar thoughts about her father's death, thoughts which she had stopped before discovering that it really was not her fault that her father had died. Ann did not respond by talking further about her father, but she did begin to allow her thoughts about other people to develop further. Gradually the counsellor helped Ann to talk in more detail about the many people in her life who were really *not* very nice to her. This seemed to be a new process for Ann, who felt somehow that nice people should not think such thoughts.

The counsellor helped Ann to see that she could actually make clear judgements about the behaviour of certain members of her family; about her employer and about her friends. She could discriminate between those who were 'nice to her' and those who were not. She remembered with tears how much she had supported her much older sister through a bad marriage, and how the sister had then turned against her, accusing her unjustifiably of being in love with her husband. She remembered with a shock how her sister's first husband had in fact made a pass at her, and how disgusted she had been. She also remembered her envy of her sister for being older and prettier, and the times she had not been nice to her, but she was able to evaluate this differently. She no longer felt that all her sister's ill-treatment of her was justified. She could now recognize that her sister and brother-in-law were not supportive people; they never helped her mother but constantly borrowed money from her which they did not repay.

This clearer view enabled Ann to stop asking them for help and affection which she had finally realized she was not going to get. Her relation with her mother improved too, partly because she stopped constantly trying to get her mother to condemn her sister; she accepted that her mother too did not want to see how mean and selfish her sister was.

During the counselling Ann remembered more about her previous therapy; she remembered that the therapist had actually been very supportive at times, though she was still hurt by his comment. She now wondered if he had been trying to say something different from what she had thought. Her new ability to think things through had enabled her to regain some memories of a good relationship; it was no longer lost in the memory of the bad ending.

When Ann decided she was able to stop counselling, she still did not have a partner but she was feeling much more self-confident. She could recognize that she was bringing her son up well and had a good relationship with him; she was also encouraging him to see his father regularly. She had completely changed her social circle, so that she was no longer seeing people who had been cruel to her, and had made a stronger friendship with some kinder friends. Her mother was no longer unkind to her; and she had found a new job where she was much happier. She was grateful to the counsellor for helping her to feel more secure and less in a state of constant panic; though she was also disappointed she had not managed to find a husband.

The counsellor was pleased that Ann's life had changed so much for the better, but she was also left feeling that there were important issues which had not been fully addressed. Counselling had to stop after two years: this was not long enough for some of Ann's most painful feelings about her father to emerge and be worked through. The counsellor was aware that some of Ann's relationships showed signs of reflecting an ambivalent attachment to and identification with her father, and would have liked to be able to address this further. However, although Ann could now allow herself to think a little more clearly about other people, there still seemed to be an embargo on further thoughts about her father, just as there had been when, as a teenager, she 'never thought about him'. The counsellor was afraid this had meant that she had not properly separated from him in her unconscious phantasy, and that this was preventing her from attaching herself to a new partner. However, Ann had talked through some of her feelings about separating from the counsellor and the counsellor was hopeful that Ann would be able to take some of the work further on her own.

I am grateful for permission to use this case. I have altered several details to disguise identities.

REFERENCES

1 Segal, J.C. (1992) *Melanie Klein*. London: Sage.
2 Freud, S. (1901) *On Dreams*, in vol. 5 of the *Standard Edition of the Complete Psychological Works of Sigmund Freud*, ed. J. Strachey. London: Hogarth Press and Institute of Psychoanalysis.
3 Klein, M. (1921) *The Development of a Child*, in vol. 1 of *The Writings of Melanie Klein* (1975). London: Hogarth Press and the Institute of Psychoanalysis. p. 42.
4 Segal, J.C. (1985) *Phantasy in Everyday Life*. London: Pelican Books. (Reprinted London: Karnac Books, 1995; and New Jersey: Aronson, 1996.)
5 Klein, M. (1957) *Envy and Gratitude* in vol. 3 of *The Writings of Melanie Klein* (1975). London: Hogarth Press and the Institute of Psychoanalysis.
6 Segal, J.C. (1992) op. cit.
7 Klein, M. (1940) *Mourning and its Relation to Manic-Depressive States*, in vol. 1 of *The Writings of Melanie Klein* (1975). London: Hogarth Press and the Institute of Psychoanalysis.
8 Klein, M. (1937) *Love, Guilt and Reparation*, in vol. 1 of *The Writings of Melanie Klein* (1975). London: Hogarth Press and the Institute of Psychoanalysis.
9 Segal, H. (1981) 'Countertransference', ch. 6 in *The Work of Hanna Segal: A Kleinian Approach to Clinical Practice*. New York and London: Jason Aronson. (Reprinted London: Free Association Books (1986) with a new title: *Delusion and Artistic Creativity and Other Psychoanalytic Essays*.)
10 Segal, J.C. (1993) 'Against self-disclosure', in W. Dryden (ed.), *Questions and Answers in Counselling in Action*. London: Sage.
11 Malan, D.H. (1963) *A Study of Brief Psychotherapy*. (Reprinted New York and London: Plenum, 1975.)

SUGGESTED READING

Orbach, S. (1978) *Fat is a Feminist Issue*. London: Hamlyn. I am not recommending this for the feminist theory but for the way it illustrates many unconscious phantasies people have about their bodies. Orbach is a psychodynamic psychotherapist.

Segal, J.C. (1985) *Phantasy in Everyday Life: A Psychoanalytical Approach to Understanding Ourselves*. London: Pelican Books. (Reprinted London: Karnac Books, 1995; and New Jersey: Aronson, 1996.) A readable introduction to psychoanalytical ideas, as applied to ordinary relationships.

Segal, J.C. (1992) *Melanie Klein: Key Figures in Counselling and Psychotherapy*. London: Sage Publications. An introduction to the life and work of Melanie Klein.

DISCUSSION ISSUES

1 Should a counsellor share their own experiences with a client? Why do psychodynamic counsellors oppose this?
2 What goes on in the process of mourning?

3 What is the role of the psychodynamic counsellor or psychotherapist for a client suffering from depression?

4 How would you define or describe what is meant by the *inner world*? How does it relate to the concepts of *conscious* and *unconscious*?

21

RATIONAL EMOTIVE BEHAVIOUR THERAPY

Michael Neenan

R ational Emotive Behaviour Therapy (REBT) is a system of psychotherapy which teaches individuals how their belief systems largely determine how they feel about and act towards events in their lives. For example, three people working for the same firm lose their jobs at the same time. The first person is angry because she believes she should have been promoted and not sacked; the second person is depressed because she believes that without a job she is worthless; and the third person is happy to have lost her job because she always found it boring. The important lesson to learn from this story is that though the loss of the job contributes to the various emotional reactions, it does not cause them: how each individual perceives being made redundant is the key factor in determining these emotional reactions.

REBT's emphasis on the way thought influences feeling places it within the cognitive-behavioural school of therapy of which it is a founding member.

DEVELOPMENT OF REBT

REBT was founded in 1955 by Albert Ellis, an American clinical psychologist.[1] He originally practised psychoanalysis but came to disagree profoundly with its viewpoint that present emotional problems have their roots in early childhood experiences. In seeking to develop a different therapeutic approach he found inspiration from, among other sources, Epictetus, a first-century AD Greek philosopher. It is a quote from Epictetus that forms the cornerstone of REBT: 'People are disturbed not by things, but by the views which they take of them.' In other words, emotional disturbance such as anger, anxiety or depression is mainly a product of how individuals perceive and evaluate events in their lives, for example, 'I see myself as unlovable when my wife won't speak to me.' Ellis was more interested in how individuals maintain their problems through their belief systems rather than how these problems were acquired. For example, a 40-year-old woman still sees herself as unlikeable because of parental neglect when she was a child. REBT would examine how she uses current events or circumstances to reinforce her negative self-image.

In order to highlight the use of reason in tackling disturbance-producing thinking, Ellis initially called REBT 'rational therapy'. However, this name created the false impression that exploring clients' emotions was of little or no importance to Ellis. To counter this view, he changed the name in 1961 to Rational-Emotive Therapy (RET). This twin focus on thoughts and feelings in the process of change still did not sufficiently reflect the actual practice of Ellis' approach – it seemed to overlook the role of behaviour in this process. Therefore in 1993 RET became Rational Emotive Behaviour Therapy. It took Ellis nearly 40 years to state clearly what he had been practising from the outset: namely, that clients have to think, feel and act against their upsetting thinking. REBT had come full circle.

THEORY AND BASIC CONCEPTS

ABCDE model of emotional disturbance and change

REBT offers a simple model to understand how aspects of our thinking can create our disturbed feelings and how to tackle such disturbance-creating thinking. In the model:

A = activating event (e.g. being rejected by a partner).
B = beliefs which sum up the individual's view of this event (e.g. 'As I no longer have your love, which I must have, then I'm worthless').
C = emotional and behavioural consequences largely determined by the individual's beliefs about this event (e.g. depression and withdrawal).
D = disputing disturbance-producing beliefs (e.g. 'I would greatly prefer to have her love *but* there is no reason why I must have it. Without it, I can still be happy and accept myself. I am too complex to damn myself as worthless because of this sad chapter in my life').
E = new and effective rational outlook accompanied by emotional and behavioural changes (e.g. sadness and a return to socializing based on self-acceptance).

REBT asserts that rigid and absolute beliefs in the form of musts, shoulds, have to's, got to's, oughts, are usually to be found at the core of our emotional disturbance. These beliefs act as demands we make upon ourselves, others and the world (e.g. 'My life *should* be easy and free from problems'). Flowing from these musts and shoulds, etc. are three major conclusions:

1 Awfulizing – defining negative events as so terrible that they seem to slip off the scale of human understanding (e.g. 'These horrible things shouldn't be happening to me. It's awful').

2 Low frustration tolerance – an individual's perceived inability to endure discomfort or frustration in her life (e.g. 'There's so much pressure at work, as there shouldn't be, and I can't stand it!').
3 Damnation of oneself or others – giving oneself a negative label based on a particular action, life event or characteristic (see **B** in ABCDE example).

These rigid beliefs are called 'irrational' or self-defeating because they are seen as illogical and unrealistic. They block or interfere with individuals achieving their goals for change and generate a good deal of emotional distress. Ellis believes that all humans have a strong biological or innate tendency to think irrationally. This assertion is based upon the seemingly limitless ability of humans to disturb themselves over harsh or unpleasant environmental or life conditions (e.g. inadequate housing, poor job opportunities, failed relationships). While the effects of these conditions upon human functioning are not minimized, nevertheless they are deemed to be generally insufficient as an explanation for any resulting emotional disturbance.

In order to tackle our largely self-induced emotional problems and thereby attain emotional health, REBT suggests developing a belief system based on flexible preferences, wishes, wants and desires (e.g. 'I want an easy and problem-free life but there is no reason why I *must* have what I want'). These beliefs are called 'rational' or self-helping because they are seen as logical and realistic. They aid goal-attainment and usually reduce our level of emotional disturbance. Flowing from these preferences and wishes are three major conclusions and constructive alternatives to the ones listed above:

1 Anti-awfulizing – negative events are judged on a scale of badness that lies within human understanding (e.g. 'These things are happening to me and they are very bad but not awful').
2 High frustration tolerance – the ability to tolerate or withstand a great deal of difficulty or discomfort in one's life (e.g. 'There is a lot of pressure at work but I can stand it without liking it').
3 Acceptance of self and others – human beings are seen as fallible (imperfect) and in a state of continuous change, therefore it is futile to label them in any way (see **D** in ABCDE model).

REBT suggests that we have a second, biologically based tendency to think about our thinking, that is, to reflect rationally upon our irrational ideas, and thereby counteract or minimize the potentially harmful effects of our distorted and crooked thinking. By developing a rational philosophy of living, individuals can greatly moderate their disturbed feelings as well as increase their striving for self-actualization (realizing one's potential).

Two types of disturbance

REBT argues that two types of emotional disturbance underlie most, if not all, neurotic problems, that is, these are problems, such as guilt, which do not involve loss of contact with reality or are not caused by physical disease. The first type is called ego disturbance and relates to demands a person makes upon him or herself, others or the world and when these demands are not met he or she engages in some form of self-depreciation, such as, 'As I'm not a good public speaker, which I must be, then I'm totally incompetent.' The second type is called discomfort disturbance and involves demands a person makes upon him or herself, others or the world that comfortable life conditions must exist and when they do not he or she usually displays low frustration tolerance, such as, 'I can't stand any longer this turmoil in my life. It shouldn't be this way!'

Ego and discomfort disturbance are separate categories but frequently overlap in emotional distress as when, for example, a woman condemns herself as weak (ego) for not being able to cope with a hectic home and work schedule (discomfort).

Understanding emotional states

REBT suggests that emotional reactions to unpleasant life events can be divided into unhealthy and healthy negative emotions as follows:

Unhealthy negative emotions	Healthy negative emotions
Anxiety	Concern
Depression	Sadness
Guilt	Remorse
Shame	Regret
Hurt	Disappointment
Damning anger (of person)	Non-damning anger (of behaviour)
Jealousy	Concern about one's relationship
Envy (malicious)	Non-malicious desire to possess another's advantages

Underlying unhealthy negative emotions are demands and their conclusions (e.g., the anxiety-producing belief 'I must do this task well otherwise I will see myself as useless'). Underlying healthy negative emotions are preferences and their conclusions (e.g. the concern-producing belief 'I would very much prefer to do this task well but I don't have to. If I make a mess of the task this just shows I'm presently unskilled in this area but I'm certainly not useless as a person').

The above list of negative emotions is not meant to dictate to clients how they should feel about events in their lives, but acts as a means of establishing which emotions may require therapeutic intervention in order to alleviate clients' suffering (e.g. focusing on a woman's prolonged damning anger and depression over being rejected by her partner rather than on her non-damning anger when the morning papers are delivered late). Transforming unhealthy negative emotions into healthy negative ones through belief change can help individuals to bear what they perceive to be unbearable and thereby help them to adapt constructively to harsh or grim reality. These lists of emotions are not set in stone and therefore are modified and added to from time to time.

Self-esteem versus self-acceptance

Many counselling approaches want to raise clients' self-esteem so that they can 'feel good about themselves'. From the REBT viewpoint, this approach has serious drawbacks. Self-esteem is seen as a form of measurement or judgement of the individual based upon her actions, traits, achievements, possessions, and so on (e.g. 'I have lots of self-esteem because I have a good job, a loving partner, a new big house, the respect of my colleagues, and I've been tipped for promotion. Everything is going well for me'). Although these things are pleasurable to have, the individual's self-respect is built upon them. If she loses some or all of these things it is highly likely that she will condemn herself (e.g. 'I'm a failure') as the foundations of her self-respect begin to crumble. Therefore self-esteem usually works temporarily and carries the potential for emotional disturbance when things go wrong in one's life.

To guard against such developments, REBT advocates unconditional self-acceptance whereby individuals refuse to measure or value themselves no matter what is happening in their lives. Individuals are neither raised up nor cast down, like shares on the stock market, depending on their fluctuating fortunes in life (e.g. 'I lost my job and the respect of my colleagues and we'll have to move to a smaller house. Too damn bad! What I haven't lost is my self-acceptance because it was never on the line in the first place'). Unconditional self-acceptance is not a recipe for complacency in life but is more likely to be an enduring basis for constructive change and striving for life goals.

The role of insight

As discussed earlier, REBT's view of the acquisition of emotional distress is largely biologically based with significant reinforcement from environmental conditions. The perpetuation of such distress is more complex but can be summarized in three major REBT insights:

1 Emotional disturbance is largely determined by irrational (self-defeating) beliefs. We feel the way we think.
2 We remain disturbed in the present because we continually brainwash ourselves with these beliefs, that is, we accept them uncritically.
3 The only enduring way to overcome our disturbance is through persistent, often lifelong, hard work and practice – to think, feel and act forcefully against our irrational beliefs.

Goals of REBT

REBT helps individuals to overcome their emotional and behavioural problems in order for them to lead happier, healthier and more fulfilling lives. This is achieved through individuals thinking more rationally, feeling less disturbed and acting in goal-directed ways. REBT therapists aim to make themselves redundant by teaching clients how to become their own self-therapists for present and future problem-solving.

Elegant and inelegant solutions

The preferred strategy of client change in REBT is for them to surrender all rigid musts, shoulds, etc., not only from their presenting problems but also from their lives, to minimize future emotional distress. This will achieve what Ellis calls a 'profound philosophical change' and therefore he views this as the elegant solution to emotional problem-solving. Not all, or even most, clients will wish to embark on such an ambitious course and therefore these clients favour the inelegant solution or non-philosophical change.

This kind of change does not focus on challenging and changing disturbance-producing musts and shoulds – the root of the problem – but is more:

1 Behaviourally based – for example, an individual uses distraction techniques (such as relaxation) to cope with her anxiety instead of directly confronting her fear that 'I must not faint in the supermarket.'
2 Inferentially based – an individual's assumptions about his life are examined rather than the rigid ideas from which they derive, for example his claims to be friendless are proved false instead of the therapist encouraging him to assume the worst and thereby learn to accept himself even if no one else does.
3 Changing activating events – that is, avoiding or modifying unpleasant situations rather than facing them; for example, an individual changes from a difficult college course to an easier one rather than staying with the harder course to challenge her idea 'that life must be easy'.

While these inelegant goals may make sense to the client, REBT argues that the underlying irrational ideas are still intact and therefore likely to be reactivated under similar circumstances at a later date.

Socializing clients into REBT

This means teaching clients what is expected of them so that they can participate effectively in this therapeutic approach. Clients are shown two forms of responsibility: (1) emotional – that their emotional disturbance is largely self-induced even though they may blame others for it; (2) therapeutic – that in order to overcome this disturbance they need to carry out a number of tasks often on a lifelong basis if they wish to maintain their gains from counselling.

To help clients absorb these responsibilities, REBT therapists teach their clients to separate their presenting problems into their A (events or situations), B (beliefs) and C (emotions and behaviours) components. This therapist-as-teacher approach includes moving clients away from A-C thinking ('Public speaking makes me feel anxious') to B-C thinking ('How do I make myself anxious about public speaking?'). Using B-C language helps to reinforce emotional responsibility.

The relationship between the therapist and client

This relationship is usually based upon certain core therapeutic conditions advanced by Carl Rogers.[2] These core conditions are empathy (understanding the client's viewpoint accurately), warmth, respect, genuineness (the therapist acting in a natural and open way), and unconditional positive regard (the client is accepted without any reservations; REBT calls this unconditional acceptance). REBT agrees that these conditions are necessary for the development of a relationship that will help the client to achieve his/her goals for change. With regard to warmth, REBT therapists are usually wary of displaying too much of it as this may reinforce some clients powerful needs for love and approval as well as convincing them that lots of support rather than sustained hard work is the answer to tackling their problems.

Assessment

This is a process which seeks to understand the client's presenting problems and their degree of severity. REBT therapists seek clear and specific information (where possible) from clients in the first session in order to place their problems within the ABC framework. This teaches clients a concrete way of understanding and tackling their difficulties. For example, a client says she feels 'uptight' about public speaking (A). What unhealthy negative emotion does 'uptight' refer to (see p. 281)? By encouraging the client to describe in some detail her uncomfortable sensations, the therapist helps her to reveal that the disturbed emotion is anxiety (C).

However, at this early stage in therapy, neither the therapist nor the client is aware of what the latter is most anxious or disturbed about with regard to public speaking (what a client is most upset about in relation to his presenting problem is called the critical A). This is uncovered through a process known as inference chaining whereby the client's personally significant assumptions are linked together through a series of 'Let's assume . . . then what?' questions. The aim of inference chaining is to identify the client's critical A which triggers her irrational belief about public speaking which then, in turn, directly leads to her anxiety:

> *Client*: I'm anxious that I might give a poor presentation.
> *Therapist*: Let's assume that you do. Then what?
> *Client*: My colleagues might look down on me, see me as incompetent.
> *Therapist*: Let's assume they do see you as incompetent. Then what?
> *Client*: They would be right: I would be incompetent.
> *Therapist*: So are you most anxious about seeing yourself as incompetent if you give a poor presentation?
> *Client*: Correct [*the client confirms that the critical A has been located*].

The next step is to help the client find her major demand (that is, a must, should, have to or got to statement) about the critical A, for example 'I must give a good presentation otherwise I'll be incompetent' (B). This irrational belief is composed of a must statement and a self-downing conclusion. A wide range of techniques (see below) is now employed throughout the course of therapy to dispute (D) this irrational belief (the client probably has other self-defeating beliefs that also need to be addressed). From this disputing process, clients learn how to develop a new and effective rational outlook (E).

Cognitive techniques

These techniques help clients to think about their thinking in more constructive ways. They are taught to examine the evidence for and against their irrational beliefs by using three major criteria:

1 **Logic**. Just because you very much want to give a good presentation, how does it logically follow that therefore you must give one?
2 **Realism**. Where is the evidence that the world obeys your demands? If it did, then you would be guaranteed to give a good presentation all of the time without experiencing any anxiety. Is this actually the case?
3 **Usefulness**. How helpful is it holding on to this belief? Where is it going to get you if you keep on demanding that you must give a good presentation?

Behavioural techniques

These are negotiated with the client on the basis of being challenging, but not overwhelming, that is, tasks that are sufficiently stimulating to promote thera-peutic change but not so daunting as to possibly prevent clients from carrying them out (e.g. the client agrees to give two presentations a month to her col-leagues rather than one a week – normally she would have avoided doing them if possible). While carrying out the presentations she mentally challenges the demand that 'I must give a good presentation', while endorsing her strong preference for giving one.

Emotive techniques

These involve fully engaging clients' emotions while they forcefully dispute their irrational beliefs. Among these techniques are shame-attacking exercises whereby clients act in a 'shameful' way in real life in order to attract public ridicule or disapproval, e.g. taking an imaginary dog for a walk, and at the same vigorously striving for self-acceptance with rational statements such as 'Just because I'm acting foolishly doesn't make me a fool.' Clients can learn from these exercises not to damn or rate themselves on the basis of their behaviour or the reactions of others.

Imagery techniques

The principal technique is rational-emotive imagery whereby the client is encouraged to feel anxious by imagining giving an incompetent presentation to her colleagues and then, without altering any details of this mental picture, to change her emotion to one of concern. This emotional shift is brought about by the client replacing her underlying irrational belief with a rational belief.

The process of therapeutic change

This involves a number of steps for clients to learn and these include:

1 That individuals largely (but not totally) create their own emotional disturbances about life events through their irrational thinking about these events.
2 That individuals have the capacity to minimize or remove these disturbances by identifying, challenging and changing their rigid patterns of thinking.
3 In order to acquire a rational or flexible pattern of thinking, individuals need to think, feel and act against their irrational beliefs, usually on a lifelong basis.

The ABCDE model provides the framework in which this process of therapeutic change can occur.

Format of a typical session

This would involve setting an agenda of things to discuss in the session in order to keep the therapist and client focused on the latter's problems. The agenda would include reviewing the client's homework tasks from the previous week; agreeing the topics to be discussed in the present session; negotiating further homework tasks that directly arise from the work done in the session; and eliciting client feedback about the session. REBT views agenda-setting as the most efficient way of structuring the time spent with the client.

WHICH CLIENTS BENEFIT MOST?

REBT has been shown to help, among others, the following groups: adults with relatively straightforward emotional problems such as moderate anxiety and/or depression; severely disturbed adults who seem to be stubbornly resistant to change (e.g. clients who display long-term anti-social behaviour); those who are suicidally depressed; individuals who are chronic substance abusers; adolescents who may be withdrawn and exhibiting behavioural problems such as excessive temper tantrums; and children as young as 7 or 8 years with, for example, difficulties making friends at school.

Failures with clients in REBT usually occur because they do not accept (a) emotional responsibility – they blame other factors (e.g. a partner or job) for causing their problems and therefore demand that these factors change before they can; and/or (b) therapeutic responsibility – they avoid the hard work required of them to make progress.

Case study

CLIENT'S PRESENTING PROBLEMS

John was a 46-year-old married man with two teenage children. He worked as a sales executive. He sought therapy at the request of his wife because of anger problems related to increased pressures at work. He described himself as 'always pushing forward' and as someone 'with great energy and drive' but his increasingly 'explosive outbursts' were getting out of hand. His family were finding it difficult to deal with his angry behaviour and were on tenterhooks a lot of the time. A course of eight sessions of REBT was agreed upon (this number could have been renegotiated depending on the flow of therapy).

BEGINNING THERAPY

After gathering more background information on John and his problems, the process of socializing him into therapy began, including establishing his goals for change. John's chosen goal was to retain his energy and drive but give up the accompanying performance-diminishing anger. In order to understand his problems within the ABC framework, the therapist asked for a specific example of an occasion when he lost his temper in order to find out what he was most angry about in that situation (locating the critical A):

> *Therapist*: What was anger-provoking in your mind about that slow queue in the supermarket?
> *John*: Other people were holding me up, wasting my time, preventing me getting back to the office.
> *Therapist*: Let's assume they were doing that. Then what?
> *John*: I can't get on with what I want to do. I've got a lot of work these days.
> *Therapist*: And if you're blocked or delayed from doing this work . . .?
> *John*: I'll fall behind with my work schedule.
> *Therapist*: And if you fall behind . . .?
> *John*: I have even more work to do to catch up. I can't stand it!
> *Therapist*: So would you say that what you're most angry about is the extra work you have to do, through the catching up, when people hold you back in some way?
> *John*: That's it exactly [*the client confirms that the critical A has been found*].

The therapist taught the client the differences between beliefs based on demands (rigid musts and shoulds) and beliefs based on preferences (wishes and wants) and how they lead to unhealthy and healthy negative emotions respectively. The therapist asked the client which belief system was present in his thinking:

> *John*: I'm demanding that my life must not be made any more difficult than it is already otherwise I won't be able to cope any longer.
> *Therapist*: And if you want to give up your anger about these additional difficulties in your life, what needs to change?
> *John*: My rigid beliefs.

Other situations were identified (e.g. getting stuck in traffic jams, temporarily losing the keys to his home or car, long meetings, people not getting to the point) where this rigid belief was present. The client appeared to have a philosophy of low frustration tolerance to setbacks, frustrations, blocks in his life (discomfort disturbance). Having established the ABC components of the client's presenting problem, John was next shown how to dispute (D) this belief using the criteria of logic, realism and pragmatism. John found the usefulness disputes the most convincing and therefore the ones most likely to help him change:

> *Therapist*: You say that people or things waste your time and block you from doing your work, but how much additional time do you waste with your angry outbursts?

John: I'm only stuck in a supermarket queue for several minutes but I waste about an hour before I eventually calm down, then I feel ashamed and guilty about my behaviour which wastes even more time. I'm such a damn fool for behaving like this.

Therapist: I wonder how many hours per week your anger wastes at work?

John: Too much.

Therapist: Would you like to keep a diary in order to find out?

John: Yes, that's a good idea.

Therapist: Who or what actually wastes most of your time?

Client: I do, and I want it to stop.

The client was shown that he was largely responsible for his own emotional disturbance, not events or other people, and his first homework task was agreed.

THE COURSE OF THERAPY

In the following sessions other homework tasks included: reading an REBT self-help book on anger; noting on a card, which he carried at all times, the benefits of surrendering his anger; carrying out daily imagery exercises whereby he changed his anger in frustrating situations to non-damning anger, that is, expressing his irritation at individuals' behaviour but not damning them for it. The client's rational belief which challenged the irrational one was: 'I would greatly prefer not to have to suffer inconveniences, frustrations, more pressures, but there is absolutely no reason why I must not suffer them. If I do, I can learn to stand them without liking them.'

At first, John found that his new rational belief lacked conviction because he was still losing his temper frequently, but by applying sustained force and energy to his homework tasks and vigorous disputing of his irrational belief he eventually achieved a 'breakthrough':

John: I was at a meeting that was going on for too long and I could feel my anger rising but I quickly stepped in with my rational belief and squelched the anger. I was able to continue to focus on the meeting and went back to my office afterwards and got straight on with my work. Previously I would have been in a foul mood and wouldn't have been able to concentrate on anything else. I think this is the breakthrough. I certainly have been thinking and feeling differently since that day.

Therapist: Good news, then, but you need to go over your rational belief a thousand times and ask: why it is more helpful than the irrational one? This will help to consolidate the breakthrough. Dispute, dispute, dispute!

John: Okay, I get the message.

As therapy passed the midway point and John was making substantial reductions in the frequency, intensity and duration of his angry behaviour, the focus switched to his other emotional problems of guilt and shame which he had mentioned in the first session (the ego disturbance aspects of his presenting problems). He called himself a 'damn fool' for his angry outbursts and another goal of therapy was to teach him self-acceptance as a fallible human being, that is, that he could accept himself for his behaviour while at the same time attempting to change it.

However, John resisted this message and believed he could not accept himself 'while I behave in such a deplorable way'. His solution was based on self-esteem – that is, he felt better about himself when his anger was reduced. He could see that he was making himself vulnerable to future bouts of self-condemnation if his anger became unmanageable again, but he believed that in order to avoid such an occurrence he would have to work even harder on himself.

As therapy neared the agreed termination date, John had clearly demonstrated competence and confidence in using the ABCDE model to understand and tackle his problems as well as devising his own homework tasks. In other words, he had become his own therapist. The last session was devoted to reviewing his progress in therapy which he said 'has brought my anger firmly under control and my family can now breathe a huge sigh of relief'. He now accepted the grim reality of an increased workload at his office but was no longer putting himself under pressure because of it. Future outbursts of anger could be dealt with by again looking at the ABCs of the problem (the therapist was attempting to be realistic about the probable setbacks John would encounter). John's feelings about termination were discussed: 'Sad but necessary if I'm to go it alone.' Follow-up appointments were arranged for 3, 6 and 12 months' time to monitor John's progress.

REFERENCES

1 Ellis, A. (1994) *Reason and Emotion in Psychotherapy* (2nd edn). New York: Birch Lane Press.
2 Rogers, C.R. (1957) 'The necessary and sufficient conditions of therapeutic personality change', *Journal of Consulting Psychology*, 21: 95–103.

SUGGESTED READING

Dryden, W., Gordon, J. and Neenan, M. (1997) *What is Rational Emotive Behaviour Therapy? A Personal and Practical Guide* (2nd edn). Loughton, Essex: Gale Centre Publications. Explains the theory and practice of REBT in straightforward terms. Also includes a chapter on teaching REBT and how the authors used REBT to tackle their own problems.

Ellis, A. (1988) *How to Stubbornly Refuse to Make Yourself Miserable About Anything – Yes, Anything!* Secaucus, NJ: Lyle Stuart. A lively and entertaining book on how people make themselves needlessly miserable and, more importantly, how to achieve lasting mental health and happiness.

Hauck, P. (1988) *How to Be Your Own Best Friend*. London: Sheldon Press. An enlightening self-help book which shows individuals how to get the best out of life by avoiding self-neglect, that is, not letting people walk all over them or always putting others first.

Walen, S.R., DiGiuseppe, R. and Dryden, W. (1992) *A Practitioner's Guide to Rational Emotive Behaviour Therapy*. New York: Oxford University Press. A clear and easy-to-read account of how to do REBT. The book is aimed at practitioners new to REBT. Contains a glossary of REBT terms and questions on various chapters to test the reader's understanding of REBT.

DISCUSSION ISSUES

1 REBT views our beliefs about events rather than the events themselves as the main cause of our emotional reactions. Does REBT go too far in suggesting that no event can totally determine our emotional response to it?

2 Why does REBT view striving for self-acceptance rather than raising self-esteem as likely to be the more enduring form of change?

3 REBT's focus is on identifying, challenging and changing people's irrational or self-defeating ideas. Does this mean that people's feelings are of little or no importance in therapy?

4 REBT's emphasis on how people's problems are being maintained rather than how they were acquired can appear to minimize the importance of past events. Is it always essential to look back in order to understand the present?

22

REALITY THERAPY

John Brickell and Robert Wubbolding

R eality therapy is a cognitive-behavioural method of counselling and psychotherapy that is highly focused and interactive, and one that has been successfully applied in a wide variety of settings. Due to its focus on the current life issues perceived by the client (their 'current reality') and the use of skilful questioning techniques on the part of the reality therapist, reality therapy has proved itself to be very effective in shorter-term therapy, although it is, most certainly, not limited to such.

Reality therapy is based on psychiatrist Dr William Glasser's 'Choice Theory' that rests on the principle that all of our motivation and behaviour is an attempt to satisfy one or more of our (five) universal human 'needs', and that we are responsible for the behaviours we generate or choose. A core idea is that regardless of what may have happened to us, what we may have done, or how our needs may have been violated in the past, we can re-evaluate our current reality and choose behaviours that will help us to satisfy our needs more effectively now and in the future.

What has been found time and again, is that when a person learns to meet his or her needs more effectively in the present, any impact or influence of past events begins to dissolve and the person can move from strength to strength. To be happy and effective we must live and plan in the present.

DEVELOPMENT OF THE THEORY

Reality therapy was developed in the mid-1960s in two settings: a mental hospital and a correctional institution, both in Los Angeles, California. Its founder, William Glasser MD, received his psychiatric training in the traditional psychodynamic, insight-centred theories which aimed at helping clients get in touch with their early childhood and understand, maybe after many years of therapy, how their neurotic symptoms and behaviour were derived from their unconscious conflicts. However, during his training he became increasingly concerned that even when these processes achieved their initial goals, there was far too often little change in the client's behaviour, particularly in the longer term.[1]

From his own extensive observation and practice, what he found was that by enabling clients to take responsibility for their own behaviour, rather than accepting that they were victims of their own impulses, their past history, or of other people, events or circumstances around them, that they were able to make dramatic changes.

Since its introduction, Glasser and others have gradually refined both the theory and practical application of reality therapy and has continually demonstrated the comprehensiveness of the theory and its wide applicability as a method. Indeed, to date, reality therapy has been applied to virtually every counselling/psychotherapy setting, but perhaps most extensively in the areas of addictions (where it has been successfully used in conjunction with the 'Minnesota Model' and the 'Twelve Steps' of Alcoholics Anonymous), relationships, stress and 'burn-out', social work, probation, and schools and education.

THEORY AND BASIC CONCEPTS

The theory that underlies reality therapy, called 'choice theory',[2] is one which explains not only how we function as individuals, both psychologically and physiologically, but also how we function as groups and even societies.

Glasser adapted and expanded choice theory from an already existing model called 'control theory' (devised by theoretician William Powers in 1973). Indeed, numerous books have been written by Glasser on control theory and its applications to many areas, including psychotherapy, schools and education, and management. However, in the spring of 1996, Glasser decided that because the numerous adaptations and expansions he had made to the original control theory were so significant he would call what he now teaches 'choice theory'.

This renaming was indeed very apt because the name 'control theory' implies 'external control' whereas Glasser had always emphasized and taught that the 'control' referred to was the person's sense of 'inner control' and, further, that most if not all of our behaviour is internally motivated and 'chosen'. Indeed, Glasser emphasizes that human behaviour is generated or chosen not because of external stimuli (despite how influential such stimuli might seem to be), nor because of past unresolved conflicts. Rather, that human motivation and behaviour is generated or chosen in an attempt to fulfil one or more of the five basic needs that are universal (that is, everybody has them) and genetic.

The five major principles of choice theory

1 **Our basic needs** All human motivation and behaviour is designed to fulfil one or more of the five basic '**needs**' that are built into our genetic structure, which are:

(a) *Survival, health and reproduction*: this includes all of the physiological functions performed by the body in an attempt to establish and maintain our health and homeostasis (our 'healthy balance'). It also includes our sexual drive which in turn, of course, enables our species to survive.

(b) *Love and belonging*: the important need that we have for love and friendship, to share and cooperate.

(c) *Self-worth/power*: other words that could be included here are competence, self-esteem, empowerment, or 'to be able'.

(d) *Freedom*: meaning the ability to make choices; to move around; to be independent; to feel unrestrained and unconfined (including having enough physical space).

(e) *Fun and enjoyment*: a need that can express itself in almost every human activity. It includes 'interest' and play which, according to Glasser, is essential to learning.

It is important to point out that these needs are not in a hierarchy, although, of course, for most of the time we will choose to fulfil our survival need first. However, history is littered with examples of people who have laid down their life in the name of freedom or, indeed, for the love of other people. Additionally, research shows that a high percentage of people who commit or attempt suicide do so for reasons of intense loneliness – which demonstrates how much stronger the need for love and belonging was for such people at that point in time. Indeed, Glasser states that our need for love and belonging, for caring and relationships and 'connectedness' to other people is by far the most prominent of the needs and, further, contends that all long-term human problems are in essence relationship problems. For this reason, in the practice of reality therapy the counsellor helps the client to extensively explore the significant relationships (or perhaps lack of significant relationships) in their lives and encourages them to evaluate all they are doing by the choice theory axiom: *Is what I am doing getting me closer to the people I need?* If the choice of behaviours is not getting people closer, then the counsellor works to help them find new behaviours that lead to better relationships.

2   Our **'quality world'** Although we all possess these needs, each of us tries to fulfil them in very specific ways. We develop an 'inner picture album' or what Glasser refers to as our 'quality world' of specific and unique wants or desires of how we would best like to fulfil our needs. Our quality world contains images or representations of people, places, things, beliefs, values and ideas which are important or special and have quality for us.

3   **Frustration** The difference (frustration) between what people want (and therefore 'need') and what they perceive they are getting from their environment causes them to generate specific behaviours. 'Behaviour' is seen as 'total' or holistic, comprising actions, thinking, feelings and physiology, which are inseparable. Thus behaviour is purposeful; that is, it is intended to close the gap between what the person wants and what they perceive they are getting. Sometimes this behaviour is successful, and at other times it is unsuccessful. Either way it is the person's best attempt at the time to try to fulfil their wants and, therefore, needs.

4 **Total behaviour** As referred to above, actions, thinking, feelings and, even, physiology, are regarded as inseparable components of ('total') behaviour and are generated or chosen from within; they derive from unmet or violated wants/needs, and not from external stimuli. Thus, most of them are choices.

Glasser uses an analogy of the 'behavioural car' to explain further the practical value of total behaviour in counselling. The idea here is that each of the four components of total behaviour represent the four wheels of the car. The front two wheels represent actions and thinking, and the back two wheels represent feelings and physiology. As we steer our behavioural car down the road of life, we only have direct control over the front two wheels (actions and thinking), but as we steer the front wheels, the back two wheels (feelings and physiology) always follow. Likewise, in the real world, although it is extremely difficult – if not impossible – to change our feelings directly (and, even more, our physiology), purely by will alone, nevertheless we do have an almost complete ability to change our actions (what we do), and some ability to change what we think, regardless of how we may be feeling at the time. And when we change our actions and thinking, our feelings and physiology change also.

This has great practical value for the reality therapist who, rather than talking endlessly with the client about their upset feelings (be it depressing, angering, anxietizing, or whatever), over which they have no direct control, the reality therapist will *gradually and empathically* help the client to begin focusing on what they do have control over (the 'front two wheels' of actions and thinking) and, further, to help them to develop a plan of action; to *do* something different to what they've been doing – in order to feel better as well as meet their 'wants' and 'needs' more effectively.

5 **Perceptions and 'current reality'** How people perceive the world around them, as well as how they perceive themselves, does of course constitute their 'reality' of the world and themselves at that point. This is the person's 'current reality'. Understanding the client's perceived current reality and helping them to evaluate and re-evaluate such perceptions is understood by the reality therapist to be an extremely important aspect of the counselling process. Examples of the kind of perception questions a reality therapist might ask a client who was being counselled for, say, a relationship problem, could include: 'How do you see your relationship right now?' 'How do you think your partner sees it?' 'What would a close and loving relationship be like?' 'How much influence do you think you have in improving your relationship?' 'Whose behaviour can you control when trying to improve this relationship?' 'Can you control anybody's behaviour but your own?' And so on.

In summary, choice theory contends that the source of all behaviour is in the here and now (current reality). Whatever human beings do, think and feel has a purpose – to try to fulfil current wants and, therefore, needs. And so choice theory challenges deterministic theories of human nature which suggest that behaviour is caused by external stimuli, and it differs from other theories that stress the influence of the past or unconscious conflicts on current behaviour. However, this in no way suggests that in reality therapy counselling, a client's past experiences (in respect of their needs being violated or unfulfilled in the past) are regarded as irrelevant or that they should be ignored or dismissed.

Indeed, having such information about the client's history can enable the reality therapist to be aware of the length or extent of the presenting problem, as well as of the time when they may have been more successful, or happier, or more effective in the past; situations which the client may be able to learn from and build upon. The client may have an extensive history of past unfulfilled or abused needs, or their problem may be caused by some long-past violation of their needs, but the reality therapist understands that the client's real problem (or conflict) is that their needs are still being unfulfilled *now*. And so, the reality therapist will gradually and empathically bring the focus of the counselling to help the client to identify and choose more strength-building and need-satisfying behaviours *now* and in the future. What has been found time and again is that when a person learns how to meet their needs more effectively in the present, the possible impact or influence of any such past memories begins to dissolve and the person can move from strength to strength. Invariably, such change is only achieved through persistence and hard work by the client and with caring and empathic support by the counsellor.

PRACTICE

The practice or method of reality therapy is seen as two major (but interconnecting) strategies: (a) establishing a *trusting* counselling relationship or environment, and (b) the procedures that lead to change which have been summarized by Dr Robert Wubbolding as the 'WDEP System'.[3]

Establishing the counselling relationship/environment

As with most other theories, reality therapy regards the establishment of a warm, accepting and trusting relationship to be absolutely essential for effective counselling to occur. Clients must feel safe to discuss their inner worlds – their thoughts, feelings and actions – without fear, criticism or blame.

Reality therapy counsellors endeavour to communicate that their style will be very interactive; that they will intervene by asking questions and discussing issues; and that they will cling relentlessly to the belief that the client can make better or more effective choices *now* in order to live a happier, more satisfying and need-fulfilling life.

The specific skills for establishing this therapeutic environment are beyond the scope of this introductory chapter but are covered extensively elsewhere.[4]

Procedures: the 'WDEP system'

Reality therapy uses questioning to a much greater degree than many other approaches and, therefore, in their training, reality therapists learn to develop extensive questioning skills. The **WDEP System** provides a questioning frame-work that is applied very fluidly and *is* not *intended to be used as a simplistic series of steps*. Each of the letters represents a cluster of ideas. However, for the purposes of this chapter, they are summarized as follows:

W = **Wants** asking clients about their wants, needs, perceptions and level of commitment.

Most clients will readily talk about what they don't want; yet by helping them to clarify and articulate what they *do* want, clients invariably learn, in a very insightful way, many aspects of their inner worlds that they, perhaps, were previously only vaguely aware of.

Clients are given the opportunity to explore every facet of their lives, including what they want from specifically relevant areas such as their friends, partners, children, job, careers, spiritual lives, manager, subordinates, and, importantly, what they want from themselves and from counselling. Asking clients what they want from themselves, includes helping them to determine the level of commit-ment they are willing to apply in order to fulfil their wants.

D = Doing and Direction

'What are you doing?' and, 'In which direction is your behaviour taking you?' The 'doing' here extends to exploring all of the four components of total behaviour: actions, thinking, feelings and physiology. In doing so, the skilled reality therapist endeavours to move from the general to the specific; that is, from what the client generally does to what they have specifically been doing, thinking and feeling, and even how they have been physically (for example symptoms experienced such as headaches, tenseness, tiredness and so on).

As counselling progresses, the reality therapist will ask the client to describe 'exactly what happened', or even to describe in detail their behaviours and the events of a specific day. Such specific, precise and unique information provides both a deeper level of understanding for the therapist and, importantly, a much greater *awareness* by the client of their own (total) behaviour. Based on the establishment of such awareness, the next and most important component of the WDEP System can be even more effectively applied.

E = Evaluation – helping the client to self-evaluate

The self-evaluation by the client is without doubt the heart of reality therapy and is invariably where the greatest emphasis is applied in the counselling process. Clients are asked to make a searching evaluation of their own specific behav-iours, as in: 'Is what you're doing helping or hurting you get what it is that you say you want?' They are also asked to extensively evaluate the appropriateness and attainability of their wants; their perceptions; their level of commitment; their behavioural direction; their thinking or 'self-talk'; their perceived place of control (whether they perceive it as inside them or outside them); the efficacy of their plans; and many other areas. The reality therapist will therefore ask such questions as:

'Is what you are doing getting you closer to the people you need?'
'Is what you want realistic or attainable?'
'How committed are you to working things out?'
'Is your overall direction a satisfying one for you?'
'If nothing outside of you changes (e.g. at work, other people, etc.) what will you do?'
'Does it help or hurt to repeatedly tell yourself that you're "useless"?'
'Can you really have what you want when you want it, 100 per cent of the time?'
'What else could you do?'

These and literally hundreds of other self-evaluation questions are the cornerstone of the WDEP system and, as with all other aspects of the counselling process, need to be asked with empathy, care and a positive regard for the client.

P = Planning – helping the client to make a plan of action

The process of the WDEP System culminates in helping the client to make a plan of action. The focus is more on action because this is the component of total behaviour (actions, thinking, feelings and physiology) over which we have the most control. The Alcoholics Anonymous axiom, 'You can act your way to a new way of thinking easier than you can think your way to a new way of acting', most certainly fits with reality therapy.

Additionally, the reality therapist – in understanding choice theory – is aware that the four components of total behaviour are inseparable; so when people change their actions, their thinking, their feelings and their physiology change also. By contrast many people stay 'stuck' or 'put their lives on hold', by waiting until they feel better before they'll do anything. Some people wait forever!

The characteristics of an effective plan have been extensively described (by Wubbolding) elsewhere[5] but include certain criteria. An effective plan is: (a) formulated by the client; (b) attainable or realistic; (c) put into action as soon as possible; and (d) is within the complete control of the client and not dependent upon someone else.

In conclusion, it should be re-emphasized that the WDEP System is not a series of steps to be followed mechanically one after the other. Rather it is a flexible system, any part of which can be applied at any given time and one that needs to be used in counselling with empathy and care, as well as with skill.

WHICH CLIENTS BENEFIT MOST?

Reality therapy, based on choice theory, is a system for human interaction which embraces universal ideas. Choice theory offers an explanation for healthy as well as unhealthy behaviours. It is multicultural at its core in that it explains how all human beings function. All people, as seen in this theory, are motivated to satisfy the innate needs of survival or self-preservation; love and belonging; self-worth/power; freedom or independence; and fun or enjoyment.

Some people make healthy and effective choices while others make unhealthy or even destructive choices. Reality therapy can be used by parents in parenting their children, by therapists and counsellors to intervene with clients; by managers to coach employees and build work teams; by educators to motivate students; and by partners or spouses to grow in their relationships.

The WDEP formulation provides a usable methodology for the above relationships. It has been successfully applied in a wide variety of counselling settings: in addictions, mental health, education, social work, criminal justice, and in the workplace. It is a method that can readily be used in groups, as well as in one-to-one counselling. It is most effective when clients are willing to move to the level of motivation expressed by the internal statement, 'I want to change.' If clients have adamantly chosen not to be helped, not to make more effective choices, or are prevented from living more effectively because of brain damage or perhaps some of the personality disorders, neither reality therapy nor any intervention can help. But individuals beyond all help are very rare.

The more important limitation is the skill of the user of reality therapy. Creative counsellors find ways to become part of even the most resistant and disturbed client's quality world. When that occurs clients are more likely to self-disclose, evaluate their own behaviour and make effective change. In the last analysis, however, effective change is a choice made by clients on their own. It is often said that therapy happens in the office. Change takes place outside.

Case study

THE CLIENT

Paul, 17, was referred to a private counsellor by a teacher who said that he was clearly depressed and had written several papers for her class in which he alluded to suicide. The teacher was quite aware of the importance of taking all suicide ideation seriously. She consulted with the head teacher, discussed the issue with his parents and referred him for more intensive help.

The counsellor met with the parents in order to establish a relationship, gain their trust, and gather information from their perspective. He asked them to be sure to tell their son that they were meeting with him and to summarize the content of the session for him.

They stated that he'd always been something of a loner with few friends. There were one or two people he seemed to 'hang out with' occasionally, but for the most part he kept to himself. In fact, lately he had remained in his room over the weekends with the shades drawn. His grades were above average as he liked to read and had a good vocabulary, which the parents said impressed the teachers and probably gave them the idea that he was even more studious than he was. They hastened to add that he was a good student and had no intention of diminishing that fact. His long history of good work habits made his spiral downward even more puzzling. They found no evidence of drug use or anti-social friends. Coming for counselling seemed acceptable to Paul. He even admitted he needed some help and was not happy.

THE THERAPY

When the time came for the first appointment he changed his mind, but agreed to talk on the phone to the counsellor. The counsellor's plan was to assess the need for counselling and the lethality of the suicide ideation. Part of the conversation was as follows:

> *Counsellor*: Paul, I'm glad you called. I talked to your parents and they gave me their perspective on how things are going.
> *Paul*: Yeah. They're worried.
> *Counsellor*: They're definitely worried, but what do you think about how things are going for you?
> *Paul*: They told you I spend time in my room on the weekends.
> *Counsellor*: With the shades drawn.
> *Paul*: Yeah.
> *Counsellor*: What do you think about that?
> *Paul*: That's about right.
> *Counsellor*: What's the purpose of staying in your room?
> *Paul*: I just don't feel like doing anything.
> *Counsellor*: What do you feel like?
> *Paul*: I'd like to escape from all of this.
> *Counsellor*: I'm going to ask you a question which I ask my clients when they say they are feeling bad. Are you thinking about suicide?
> *Paul*: Yeah, sometimes I think about it.
> *Counsellor*: I can help you feel better if you would come and talk with me.
> *Paul*: What's the use?
> *Counsellor*: Why not try? What can you lose?
> *Paul*: Not much, I guess.
> *Counsellor*: How about today?
> *Paul*: So soon?
> *Counsellor*: I have time late this afternoon.
> *Paul*: I guess I could do that.

The purpose of the counsellor's comments was to encourage a face-to-face meeting and initiate a counselling relationship. The counsellor also wanted to assess further the seriousness of the suicide threat.

In the first real counselling session the counsellor asked the other important questions about suicide: Have you tried to kill yourself previously? Do you have a plan? Do you have the means available? Will you make an agreement not to kill yourself accidentally or on purpose?

In the counselling session he determined that Paul clearly did not present a serious suicidal threat and so they were able to set this issue aside and move on.

In the next few sessions the counsellor proceeded slowly without 'pressuring' Paul to change. In fact at the end of the second session he told Paul: 'Don't make any radical changes just yet. We need to explore things further.' This kind of vague paradoxical technique called 'restraining' fits with choice theory in that it implies but does not state explicitly that the client has more control and more choices than he, at first, imagined. This is an effort to help prepare the client for a more explicit discussion of choices.

In the second session the discussion focused on Paul's behaviour prior to the downward trend which he was currently experiencing. School and school work were always enjoyable and he always had acquaintances but never close friends. Girls seemed to like him as he was witty and clever. Sports appealed to him and he even played in teams but he stated that he 'was not a sports fanatic'. Following professional sports was a 'semi-hobby' in that he read the sports pages in the newspaper every day. These activities had diminished over the last few months and he became even more lonely and alone to the point where he stayed in his room on weekends. He talked freely about his behaviour, including how he was lonely and depressed. Part of the session included the following dialogue:

Counsellor: Paul, I want to understand that when you played sports, made the effort to meet other students, talked to the girls you liked, and exercised more, you felt better than you do now. Is that right?

Paul: That's right.

Counsellor: So it helped you when you were actively doing things?

Paul: Yes.

Counsellor: Paul, if you continue to be uninvolved where will you be in the future?

Paul: I guess uninvolved and miserable.

Counsellor: And you came here to feel better? Right?

Paul: Yes, and to make my parents happy.

Counsellor: Now, do you think you can just choose automatically to feel better?

Paul: No, but I don't feel like doing anything. I just want to get over these wretched feelings.

Counsellor: I believe you can.

Paul: But I can't seem to feel better.

Counsellor: Do you want to feel better?

Paul: Of course. You've asked me that before.

Counsellor: I do repeat questions occasionally. Now, here's a question I have not asked you and it is the most important one I brought up so far. Are you ready?

Paul: Yes.

Counsellor: Do you want to work hard enough to feel better to push yourself to do some things, even though you don't feel like it?

Paul: I sure don't want to be so miserable.

Counsellor: I think it is a good idea to stay in your room this weekend. But I think you need to open the drapes and let the light in.

Paul: I don't think that will do anything.

Counsellor: Will it hurt?

Paul: I guess not.

Counsellor: Let's put it this way. If you make no changes in anything you do, will anything change for you?

Paul: Well, no, I guess not.

Counsellor: I believe I can help you if you don't rush into change but if you are willing to try a few things.

Paul: OK. I can do that.

The counsellor's comments were designed to be enigmatic for Paul. He wants to help Paul gain control of his life and more effective need-satisfaction through an action-centred plan. He does not wish to 'out-muscle' Paul's resistance. This behaviour would not only stiffen Paul's resistance but might result in Paul's failure to return. On the other hand, he wants to communicate to Paul that change is possible and a better life is possible if he makes better choices. In this way the client can begin to move toward a more satisfying life.

Subsequent sessions

Each session included a discussion of movies and books and other seemingly irrelevant information. But conversing in this manner is intentional and very useful. By deepening the relationship Paul grew to trust the counsellor and put him deeper into his quality world.

Paul gradually made better choices in which he spent an increasing amount of time out of his room on the weekends. He began to speak to other students more, play football and relate in a friendly way to his parents. At one point a girl asked him for a date.

Included in the counselling were repeated questions centring on self-evaluation. 'Is staying in your room helping you?' 'When you talked to the girl at the football game, how did you feel – better or worse?' 'What do your parents think?' 'What difference do they see in you?' 'What are you doing when you feel happy? Does that specific action help you?'

People only change to live more happily and healthily when they decide they are not getting what they want, examine their behaviour in an evaluative way and make specific plans to be involved with other people (belonging), to perform activities which result in a sense of achievement (self-worth), to repeat these choices (freedom), and to have fun on a regular basis.

REFERENCES

1 Glasser, W. (1965) *Reality Therapy*. New York: Harper & Row.
2 Glasser, W. (1998) *Choice Theory*. New York: Harper Collins.
3 Wubbolding, R. (1988) *Using Reality Therapy*. New York: Harper & Row.
4 Wubbolding, R. (1988) ibid.
5 Wubbolding, R. (1988) ibid.

SUGGESTED READING

Glasser, W. (1965) *Reality Therapy*. New York: Harper & Row. The original book by the founder of reality therapy.

Glasser, W. (1998) *Choice Theory*. New York: Harper Collins. This new book explains the theory which underlies reality therapy and expands on Dr Glasser's original ideas contained in his preceding book *Control Theory* (1984), published by Harper & Row.

Wubbolding, R. (1988) *Using Reality Therapy*. New York: Harper & Row. A very practical, easy-to-read book on how to implement the principles of reality therapy.

Wubbolding, R. and Brickell, J. (1999) *Counselling with Reality Therapy*. Bicester: Winslow Press. A comprehensive book on choice theory and the practical application of reality therapy to a wide range of counselling settings.

DISCUSSION ISSUES

1 In what ways is reality therapy different from many other methods of counselling/psychotherapy?
2 Reality therapy focuses on helping people to fulfil their five basic needs and *not* necessarily just on trying to help them solve the 'presenting problem'. The presenting problem may only be an outcome or 'symptom' of their unmet needs. Explain these statements by giving some examples.
3 Dr William Glasser's Choice theory maintains that all we can do from birth to death is behave, and that all of our behaviour is 'total behaviour'.

   (a) What is total behaviour?
   (b) Which components of total behaviour are under our voluntary control?

4 Choice theory argues that our behaviour is *not* simply a response to some external stimulus, but rather that human motivation is internal (or intrinsic) and behaviour is generated or chosen in an attempt to fulfil our wants and needs. Give some examples to explain these statements.

23

SOLUTION FOCUSED THERAPY

Bill O'Connell

Solution Focused Therapy (SFT) is a form of brief therapy which builds upon clients' strengths by helping them to evoke and construct solutions to their problems. It emphasizes the future, more than the past or the present. In a solution focused approach the counsellor and client devote a greater proportion of time to solution construction than to problem exploration. They try to define as clearly as possible what the clients would like to see in their lives.

SFT fosters a sense of collaboration between the counsellor and the client, with the latter being viewed as competent and resourceful. It pays little attention to the 'roots or causes' of a client's problem. This stance could be compared with driving a car where it is useful to look in the rear mirror from time to time but it is advisable to spend most of your time looking through the front windscreen! Solution focused counsellors believe in minimal intervention in the client's life – their task being to initiate an impetus for change which the client will continue after the counselling. The counsellor negotiates with the client to identify a priority concern which has attainable goals.

The solution focused approach originated in family therapy. The key founding figures were the family therapists Steve de Shazer, Kim Insoo Berg and colleagues at the Brief Family Therapy Centre in Milwaukee, as well as Bill O'Hanlon, a therapist in Nebraska. The members of the Brief Therapy Practice in London pioneered the method in the United Kingdom. Many professionals in fields such as teaching, management, health and community care use the core skills and interventions advocated in SFT. It is now used in a wide range of settings including schools, psychiatric hospitals, counselling services, voluntary organizations, therapeutic groups and probation and social work teams. It is used with a wide variety of clients – problem drinkers, offenders, survivors of abuse, employees suffering from stress, couples and families.

DEVELOPMENT OF THE THERAPY

Solution focused therapy belongs to the constructionist school of therapies, so called because they subscribe to a constructionist theory of knowledge. Other approaches which share this theoretical basis are personal construct therapy, neuro-linguistic programming and the brief problem-solving model developed at the Mental Research Institute in Palo Alto, California.

The social constructionist theory of knowledge which underpins SFT states that the meaning of words is known only through social interaction and negotiation. We have no direct access to objective truth because our attempts to articulate meaning take place in a context which includes the person who makes the observation. The 'knower' actively participates in constructing what is observed. Constructionism claims that this inseparability of the known from the 'knower' destroys the myth of absolute truth. Instead it offers a much richer, more diverse way of looking at our world and thereby extends personal choice. It contends that no one person or school of thought possesses more of 'the truth' than another. The therapist does not have access to hidden truths denied to clients. In therapy, the two parties can explore an extensive repertoire of meanings in relation to the client's experiences, in order to reach an understanding which will help the client to deal with his or her 'problem'.

Therapy is a dialogue in which both partners construct the problem and the solution. The problem does not have an objective, fixed meaning which the clients bring with them. Instead they tell and retell their story using language which reshapes the social reality by which they live. As Paul Watzlawick, a therapist and philosopher, said, 'reality is invented, not discovered'.[1] Language does not reflect reality, but creates it. In our scientific culture we tend to assume that there is a necessary connection between a problem and its solution. The solution should fit the problem. If, for example, a client has had a problem for a long time it is expected that it will be a lengthy process before a solution emerges. If the problem is complex, then it is thought that the solution must also be complex. SFT challenges these assumptions and instead of trying to make the solution fit the problem, aims to find a solution which fits the client. This shift in thinking alters the content and direction of the counselling. The focus becomes the changes the client wants, rather than the causes of the problem. In the psychological realm, the search for causal connections is often tenuous and elusive. Is a person depressed because he has a genetic predisposition towards depression, and/or because his family life was disrupted by his parents' separation when he was 10, and/or he lacked the social skills and confidence to make close relationships, and/or he has low self-esteem, and/or he is long-term unemployed? What weight ought we to give to each explanation? How do we prove they are 'true'? How do we know when we have gone far or 'deep' enough? Where does the counsellor start to work on such a complicated agenda? Is such an approach dictating the need for long-term therapy? Most forms of therapy seek causal mechanisms for clients' problems. Understanding the origins of their problems helps many people. However, solution focused counsellors do not believe that it is always necessary to identify origins of problems for lasting solutions to emerge. They regard problems not as symptoms of pathology, but as an integral part of human experience. In SFT the emphasis is on how our future shapes what we do at the moment. Being clear about our preferred future motivates and clarifies our approach to the present. An analogy would be a journey in which the driver or pilot plans a drive or flight according to the time he or she wants the car or plane to arrive at its destination. With that end in view, decisions are made about the course, speed, amount of fuel required and stopping-off places along the way. The end point determines the means. When clients' lives are blighted by a major problem it tends to obscure the future or even destroy any hope for a better future. Problems represent ways in which people have lost their bearings or failed to use the skills or resources required to travel to their chosen destination.

Clients and counsellors often assume that there is a necessary sequence of events which needs to take place before the client will be 'better', that X has to happen before Y can happen. For example, that the client must learn to express emotions before she will be able to resume a normal life. The SF therapist questions such connections and is often able to demonstrate to the client that change can take place prior to the client's feelings changing. It challenges the ways in which clients view their problems, if these attitudes are making change more difficult or unlikely.

The SF approach takes the position that certain types of conversation are more likely than others to motivate and support a client towards change. These empowering narratives stress the competence, skills and qualities which the client can utilize. It may be helpful for the reader to compare a problem focused model with a solution focused one. Some of these questions will be verbalized, others will not.

How can I help you? versus **How will you know that counselling has been helpful?**

The introductory phrases used by the counsellor indicate how she sees the process of counselling. The former stresses the expert role, the 'privileged position' of the counsellor. The latter emphasizes what the client hopes to achieve and how he will know when he has achieved it. This question actively recruits the client as a partner in a joint enterprise. Similar questions include: 'How long do you think it will take before things will get better?' 'How will you know that it has been worth your while coming here today?' 'How do you think counselling might help you?' 'How will you know when things are getting better?'

Could you tell me about the problem? versus **What would you like to change?**

The former invites an account of the problem, the latter invites a description of the specific behaviours the client wants to alter. The latter sets a climate of expectancy of change and implies that the client has potential to change.

Is the problem a symptom of something deeper? versus **Have we clarified the central issue on which you want to concentrate?**

The former has been the dominant form of enquiry in therapy for much of its history (apart from behaviourism). It is not always verbalized by the counsellor,

TABLE 23.1 A comparison between a problem focused and a solution focused approach

Problem focused	Solution focused
• How can I help you?	How will you know that counselling has been helpful?
• Could you tell me about the problem?	What would you like to change?
• Is the problem a symptom of something deeper?	Have we clarified the central issue on which you want to concentrate?
• Can you tell me more about the problem?	Can we discover exceptions to the problem?
• How are we to understand the problem in the light of the past?	What will the future look like without the problem?
• How is the client protecting himself?	How can we use the qualities and skills of the client?
• In which ways is the relationship between the counsellor and the client a replay of past relationships? (psychodynamic models)	How can the counsellor collaborate with the client?
• How many sessions do we need?	Have we achieved enough to end?

but will guide and inform her thinking. The latter seeks a clear definition of the priority focal issue which will form the centre of the therapeutic agenda.

Can you tell me more about the problem? versus **Can we discover exceptions to the problem?**

A problem focused approach seeks to gather as much information as possible about the patterns of problem behaviour in order to design an intervention which will break the vicious circle. The latter question invites descriptions of those times when the problem is not happening. The implication is that the client is already engaging in solution behaviour, as much as, if not more than, in problem behaviour.

How are we to understand the problem in the light of the past? versus **What will the future look like without the problem?**

The former implies that the 'truth' about the problem lies in understanding the past. The latter focuses attention on the client's picture of the future in order to establish goals and to motivate the client.

How is the client protecting himself? versus **How can we use the qualities and skills of the client?**

The former directs the counsellor's thinking about the client's self-defence strategies. The latter emphasizes the need to identify the resources which the client could utilize to solve the problem.

In which ways is the relationship between counsellor and client a replay of past relationships? versus **How can the counsellor collaborate with the client?**

In the former, the therapist uses the current therapeutic relationship, which is believed to echo past relationships in both parties' lives, to work cooperatively with the client and to formulate the nature of the client's problem. In the latter, the collaboration revolves more around a sense of shared goals than in the nature of the relationship itself.

How many sessions do we need? versus **Have we achieved enough to end?**

The former question may constitute the basis of a contract with the client, for either a fixed (possibly reviewable) number of sessions, or an open-ended arrangement. The latter emphasizes the minimal intrusion principle and focuses attention on goal achievement, in the belief that the effect of therapy continues long after the sessions have ended.

PRACTICE

The goals of the therapy are the goals which clients bring with them, providing they are ethical and legal. The counsellor's role is to help clients to begin to move or continue to move in the direction they want. They do this by helping:

- to identify and utilize to the full the strengths and competencies which the client brings with him;
- to enable the client to recognize and build upon exceptions to the problem, that is, those times when the client is already doing (thinking, feeling) something which is reducing or eliminating the impact of the problem;
- to help the client to focus in clear and specific terms on what they would consider to be solutions to the problem.

The counsellor acknowledges and validates whatever concerns and feelings the client presents, and seeks to develop a rapport, a cooperative 'joining', in which the counsellor offers the client a warm, positive, accepting relationship and the client feels understood and respected. In SFT, the counsellor shares expertise with the client by adopting a learning position, 'a one-down position', in which the client is encouraged to teach the counsellor about her way of looking at the world. The counsellor matches the language of the client, offers encouragement and genuine compliments and adapts her stance according to what the client finds helpful. The client is respected as being an expert in her own life, while the counsellor has expertise in creating a therapeutic environment.

It is not the usual practice to offer clients a fixed number of sessions. It is more common to consult with the client at the end of a session to hear what she feels about meeting again, and if a further session is necessary, when that should take place.

Focal issue

SF therapists stress the importance of negotiating a focal or central issue for the work. The clearer and more defined the agenda, the greater the likelihood that the counselling will be efficient and effective. SFT attends to the problem as presented by the client. The closer the counsellor can keep to the client's agenda, the more likely the client will be motivated to change. It is not always possible to achieve this at the beginning as clients are often confused, anxious, overwhelmed and unsure how counselling can help them. The priority is to find a common language to describe what the client wants to change and to begin to explore how those changes would affect the client's life. The counsellor needs to find leverage – a solvable problem which the client both wants, and is able, to work upon.

Clients who present with broad, diffuse, and poorly understood problem patterns and who need considerable time to form a trusting alliance are more likely to need an extended period of exploratory work. It is a great advantage when clients can articulate their problem and their goals, but it does not mean that initial vagueness about the future disqualifies them from brief solution focused work. It simply means that the counsellor has to work harder and take longer.

The message

Near the end of each session, the SF counsellor will compliment the client on what he is doing, thinking or saying which is helpful. She may also give him a task to perform. At the end of the first session, clients are usually asked to 'notice between now and the next time we meet, those things you would like to see continue in your life and come back and tell me about them'.

Principles

There are a number of principles which guide SF work. They apply both to how the client should approach the problem and to how the counsellor should conduct the counselling.

- **If it isn't broken don't fix it.**
  SFT emphasizes that people *have* problems, rather than that they *are* problems. It avoids a view of clients as being sick or damaged and instead looks for what is healthy and functioning in their lives.

- **Small change can lead to bigger changes.**
  Change is regarded as constant and unavoidable. Initiating a force for change can have repercussions beyond the original starting point. Experiencing

change can restore the person's sense of choice and control in his or her life and encourage the making of further changes.

- **If it's working keep doing it.**
  The client is encouraged to keep doing what she has shown she can already do. This constructive behaviour may have started prior to the counselling. Clients may need to continue with a new pattern of behaviour for some time before they feel confident about maintaining it.

- **If it's not working stop doing it.**
  Clients in SFT are encouraged to do something different (almost anything) to break the failure cycle. This may run counter to family scripts such as, 'If at first you don't succeed, try, try again.'

- **Keep counselling as simple as possible.**
  There is a danger that the beliefs of the counsellor, particularly if they demand a search for hidden explanations and unconscious factors, will complicate and prolong the relationship.

Interventions

The following interventions are commonly found in solution focused practice. How and when they are used will depend upon the judgement of the therapist.

Pre-session change
When making an appointment, the client is asked to notice whether any changes take place between the time of making the appointment and the first session. Typically, the counsellor will enquire about these changes early on in the first session. By granting recognition to pre-session change, the counsellor can build upon what the client has already begun. The client may present the counsellor with clear clues about strategies, beliefs, values and skills which are transferable into solution construction. This 'flying start' helps to accelerate the process of change and increases the likelihood of the counselling being brief. Positive pre-session change is empowering for the client because the changes have taken place independently of the counsellor and, therefore, the credit belongs solely to the client.

Exception seeking
The counsellor engages the client in seeking exceptions to the problem, that is, those occasions when the problem is not present, or is being managed better. This includes searching for transferable solutions from other areas of the client's life, or past solutions adopted in similar situations.

Competence seeking
The counsellor identifies and affirms the resources, strengths and qualities of the client which can be utilized in solving the problem. Coping mechanisms which the client has previously used are acknowledged and reinforced.

The miracle question

This is a central intervention typically used in a first session, but which may also reappear in subsequent sessions. It aims to identify existing solutions and resources and to clarify the client's goals in realistic terms. It is a future-oriented question which seeks to help the client to describe, as clearly and specifically as possible, what her life will be like, once the problem is solved or is being managed better. The question as devised by Steve de Shazer follows a standard formula:

> Imagine when you go to sleep one night, a miracle happens and the problems we've been talking about disappear. As you were asleep, you did not know that a miracle had happened. When you wake up what will be the first signs for you that a miracle has happened?[2]

This imaginary format gives the client permission to rise above negative, limited thinking and to develop a unique picture of the solution. An open expression of what they believe they want can either motivate them further towards achieving their goals, or perhaps help them to realize that they really don't want these changes after all. It can also highlight conflicts between what they themselves want and what other people in their life want for them. The counsellor helps the client to develop answers to the miracle question by active listening, prompting, empathizing and therapeutic questioning.

Scaling

The counsellor uses a scale of 0–10 with clients – 10 representing the morning after the miracle and 0 representing the worst the problem has been, or perhaps how the client felt before contacting the counselling service. The purpose of scaling is to help clients to set small identifiable goals, to measure progress and to establish priorities for action. Scaling questions can also assess client motivation and confidence. Scaling is a practical tool which a client can use between sessions. The use of numbers is purely arbitrary – only the client knows what they really mean.

Reframing

Using the technique of reframing, the counsellor helps the client to find other ways of looking at the problem, ones which are at least as valid as any other, but which, in the opinion of the counsellor, increase the chances of the client being able to overcome the problem.

WHICH CLIENTS BENEFIT MOST?

SFT does not automatically exclude any clients. However, it does assess their 'position' in respect of counselling in order to ensure that time and effort is not wasted. Berg[3] uses the terms 'visitor', 'complainant' and 'customer' to distinguish between clients with different agendas. A visitor is someone who does not think he has a problem and/or does not want to participate in counselling. A complainant is someone who is willing to discuss the problem but sees the solution as lying elsewhere, in the actions of other people. A customer is someone who recognizes that he has a particular problem and wants to do something about it. It would be a mistake to treat these three 'types' of clients in the same way. On occasions, the counsellor can manage to encourage the visitor or complainant to become a customer, by negotiating a clear benefit which the client could gain from counselling.

Case Study

THE CLIENT

The client was a white female in her forties, married, with three children. She had a well-paid 'white-collar' job in which she had to work long hours while juggling child care and responsibilities for an elderly mother. Her husband often worked away from home. Approximately two years prior to coming for counselling, she had felt 'on the verge of a nervous breakdown' and had to take time off work. She had returned to work after three months and had re-negotiated a less stressful role in the organization. However, she had again begun to experience similar stress-related symptoms and immediately prior to presenting for counselling had taken sick leave. She described herself as being anxious, indecisive and short-tempered at home, particularly with the children. Her memory and concentration were poor and she was not sleeping well.

THE THERAPY

During the first session the client talked at length about her problems at home and at work, although she said she had felt unsure about doing so. The counsellor validated the client's feelings and experiences, while listening for examples of coping strategies. He asked the miracle question and received an answer which included:

- sleeping better;
- feeling mentally calmer;
- being more supported by her husband;
- playing with her children and not shouting at them;
- being back at work and coping with the pressures, without being snappy and making mistakes.

The counsellor asked, 'On a scale of 0 to 10, 10 representing the morning after the miracle and 0 the worst you've ever been, where would you put yourself today?' The client answered that she was at 3. At the end of the session the counsellor invited the client to notice times when she managed to control her worry habit even a little and to remember what she did to achieve that. She was also asked to write down a list of things which she thought she could do in order to reduce her stress levels. The client appeared motivated and keen to use the time off work to 'sort herself out'.

When she returned for the second session, the counsellor asked, 'What's better?' She described situations when she felt free from stress – gardening, going out with her friend to an evening class, reading, taking her children to the cinema. The feedback given by the counsellor congratulated her on what she had managed to do. In terms of utilizing her skills and experience, the counsellor noted that she had a lot of energy and was creative and caring in her approach to the problem. The counsellor reminded her that she had overcome this problem before and wondered whether she could remember anything which had worked the last time. She felt that her husband had been very supportive then and that she needed him to support her more at the moment.

During the third session the client reported that she was surprised (as was her husband) at how well she was doing.

> *Client*: I've been able to stop thinking about going back to work without it wakening me up in the middle of the night.
> *Counsellor*: How did you manage to do that?
> *Client*: I think I've come to see that there's more to life than just working all the time. I've begun to stand back from it.

The client had begun to change her 'viewing' of her problem. The counsellor invited the client to continue doing what was working and to think through the implications of her new way of looking at her job.

At the fourth session she reported that she found scaling helpful and used it each day to measure how she had dealt with particularly stressful situations. She felt calmer, more relaxed and had 'stopped flying at' her daughter. She was experimenting in taking small manageable steps towards controlling her anxiety.

She reported that she was at 6 on the scale. She was sleeping better and had come to realize that things would never be perfect. She would be happy to achieve a 7, not a 10. The counsellor affirmed the client's self-awareness and problem-solving strategies and reinforced her repertoire by expressing the view that, once acquired, these skills would not be lost, as long as they were consolidated by regular practice. The counsellor also suggested that skills used in the domestic arena were transferable to the work environment. This belief helped to increase the possibility that the counselling could be effective and brief.

> *Counsellor*: I've seen you make progress and there's every reason to think that you can maintain that. I think people can transfer these skills. I think it's important to realize it's basically the same stuff. It's just a different place or environment. You've got the tools there. You're doing the job already.

By the sixth session the client felt she was handling relationships at home much better, but felt anxious about the impending return to work. Despite her apprehension, she had developed a 'survival plan' for her first few weeks back. Her solutions included a determination to say no to extra work, a request for a meeting with her boss to get more resources and avoidance of any unnecessary travel. The feedback to the client complimented the client on her self-care skills and her courage in facing up to a stressful situation. The client wanted reassurance that the counselling could continue for a few more weeks until she felt more confident about work.

In the next session the client said that she felt that she had had a setback and that she was quite depressed about work again. She had visited her workplace but had felt quite overwhelmed and her colleagues had not been very friendly. The counsellor reassured her that 'practising new habits is often bumpy'. He also explored how she was managing to stop things getting worse. Her answer was the increased support at home. In the final two sessions the client revisited the miracle question and applied it to her work situation – for example, how colleagues would be treating her, the amount and kind of work she would be doing. She recognized that she had 'moved down a gear' and was more in control. She liked her 'new self'. After nine sessions she felt that she had learnt sound strategies for handling her stress. She decided to end counselling.

REFERENCES

1 Watzlawick, P. (1984) *The Invented Reality*. New York: W.W. Norton.
2 de Shazer, S. (1988) *Clues: Investigating Solutions in Brief Therapy*. New York: W.W. Norton.
3 Berg, I.K. (1994) *Family Based Services*. New York: W.W. Norton.

SUGGESTED READING

de Shazer, S. (1991) *Putting Difference to Work*. New York: W.W. Norton. The most influential figure in solution focused therapy explains the theory behind the practice. Advisable to read a 'how to do it' book first.

George, E., Iveson, C. and Ratner, R. (1990) *Problem to Solution – Brief Therapy with Individuals and Families*. London: Brief Therapy Press. A good introduction to practice from the pioneers of the method in Britain.

Letham, J. (1994) *Moved to Tears, Moved to Action*. London: Brief Therapy Press. Particular emphasis on working with women and children in a British context.

O'Connell, B. (1998) *Solution Focused Therapy*. London: Sage. This practical book clearly identifies and explains the main skills needed to practise solution focused brief therapy.

O'Hanlon, B. and Weiner-Davis, M. (1989) *In Search of Solutions*. New York: W.W. Norton. Packed with practical ideas.

DISCUSSION ISSUES

1 What do you think about the idea that it is preferable to spend more time exploring solutions than understanding problems?
2 We tend to think of clients as having defined problems. What part do you think the counsellor plays in negotiating the problem definition?
3 'Counselling should be as brief as possible so that people can get on with their lives.' Discuss.
4 Answer the miracle question in relation to a problem area in your own life and share your observations with a colleague.

24

TRANSACTIONAL ANALYSIS

Ian Stewart and Tony Tilney

Transactional analysis (TA) is a model for understanding human personality, communication and relationships. TA got its name because it was originally developed as a way of analysing the patterns of communication – *transactions* – that people use when they are relating in pairs and groups, and this is still an important emphasis within the approach.

A central supposition of TA is that – with practice and appropriate training – you can reliably judge someone's internal experience from their external behaviour. In particular, you can judge by the person's *observable behaviour* whether she is 'in the here and now', or replaying part of her childhood, or unawarely copying the behaviours, thoughts and feelings of one of her own parent-figures.

TA therapy* is most often classed among the *humanistic* approaches to personal change, because of its emphasis on personal responsibility, equal relationship between client and therapist, and the intrinsic worth of the person. However, TA also shares some characteristics with the *behavioural* approaches, notably in its use of clear contract-making; and TA's central theoretical ideas were drawn directly from the tradition of *psychodynamic* thought, in ways we shall explain below.

THE DEVELOPMENT OF TA

With a history dating back to the 1950s, TA is among the older-established of today's therapies. Like many other therapeutic approaches, it derives essentially from the work of one person – in TA's case, the psychiatrist Eric Berne (1910–70).

Berne was originally trained as a Freudian psychoanalyst, and the roots of TA lie in the psychodynamic tradition. Among Berne's early mentors were two analysts who had themselves developed their own theories from Sigmund Freud's ideas, namely Paul Federn and Erik Erikson. It was from Federn that

---

* Throughout this chapter we shall use the word 'therapy' to mean 'psychotherapy or counselling', and 'therapist' to mean 'psychotherapist or counsellor'.

Berne first learned the concept of *ego-states*, which he built into his own theory (see below). Erikson saw human development as comprising a sequence that occupied the person's entire lifetime, and this also Berne incorporated in his own theory, as the idea of *life-script*.

Berne was a talented and prolific writer. His book *Transactional Analysis in Psychotherapy*,[1] published in 1961, is still an indispensable professional source for the theoretical ideas of TA. In 1964 came the publication of Berne's *Games People Play*. Intended for a professional audience, the book unexpectedly became a best-seller, catapulting both Berne and TA to international media fame. From then until the mid-1970s, TA enjoyed the dubious status of a 'pop psychology'. Numerous books and articles appeared, featuring TA in often watered-down, over-simplified or downright distorted versions. It took TA many years to recover from the harm done by the media image that was widely peddled during that period of mass popularity.

Even during this episode, however, serious professional activity in TA continued unbroken. Since Eric Berne's death in 1970, transactional analysts have continued to refine and expand both the theory and practice of TA. The approach is widely used in psychotherapy and counselling, as well as in a range of other applications such as education, management and communications training. Today there are professional TA associations in more than 60 countries of the world. The European TA association has over 4,000 members, and the membership roll is still expanding, with interest growing especially strongly in the countries of Eastern Europe.

THE THEORY AND BASIC CONCEPTS OF TA

Philosophical assumptions

At the heart of TA lie certain philosophical assumptions – fundamental belief-statements about people, life and the nature of change. These assumptions are as follows:

People are OK.
Everyone has the capacity to think.
People decide their own destiny, and these decisions can be changed.

People are OK This means: everyone has intrinsic worth, value and dignity. This is a statement of essence rather than behaviour, and is held to be true irrespective of race, age, gender, religion or any other personal feature.

Everyone has the capacity to think Everyone except the severely brain-damaged has the capacity to think. Therefore it is the responsibility of each of us to decide what he or she wants from life. Each individual will ultimately live with the consequences of what he or she decides.

Decisional model TA holds that when a grown-up person engages in apparently self-defeating behaviours, or repeatedly feels painful feelings, she is in fact following strategies she *decided* upon as a young child. These strategies appeared to the child to be the best way of surviving and getting her needs met. The child was not *made* to feel or behave in particular ways by her parents, or by 'the environment'.

TA assumes that the same is true for the adult person. Other people, or life circumstances, may exert strong pressures on her, but it is always her own decision whether to conform to these pressures. The person is thus held to be personally *responsible* for all her feelings and behaviour.

Since the person himself is responsible for making these childhood *early decisions*, it follows that later in life he can change any of these decisions – that is, *redecide*. If some of his infant decisions are producing uncomfortable results for him in adult life, he can trace the outdated decisions and change them for new and more appropriate ones.

Thus, TA takes an assertive view of the possibility of personal change. The person will achieve change not merely by gaining 'insight' into old patterns of behaviour, but by deciding to change those patterns and taking action to achieve this change.

TA theory

There are certain key ideas that form the foundation of TA theory, and serve to distinguish TA from any other psychological system. They are as follows:

The ego-state model (PAC model)

Central to TA is the *ego-state model*. An *ego-state* is a set of related behaviours, thoughts and feelings. It is a way in which we manifest a part of our personality at a given time. The TA model portrays three distinct types of ego-state: *Adult*, *Parent* and *Child*.

If someone is behaving, thinking and feeling in response to what is going on around him here and now, using all the resources available to him as a grown-up person, he is said to be in an *Adult ego-state*.

At times, the person may behave, think and feel in ways which are a copy of one of her parents, or of others who were parent-figures for her. When she does so, she is said to be in a *Parent ego-state*.

Sometimes the person may return to ways of behaving, thinking and feeling which he used when he was a child. Then he is said to be in a *Child ego-state*.

In TA theory, the initial capital letters are always used when we want to indicate that we are referring to the ego-states (Parent, Adult, Child). A small letter beginning the word shows we mean a real-life parent, adult or child. The ego-state model is often known alternatively as the *PAC model*, after these three initial letters.

When we use the ego-state model to understand various aspects of personality, we are said to be employing *structural analysis*.

Transactions, strokes, time structuring

If I am communicating with you, I can choose to address you from either an Adult, Child or Parent ego-state. You can reply in turn from Adult, Child or Parent. This exchange of communications is known as a *transaction*.

The use of the ego-state model to analyse sequences of transactions is referred to as *transactional analysis proper*. The word 'proper' is added to show that we are talking about this branch of TA in particular, rather than TA as a whole.

When you and I transact, I signal recognition of you and you return that recognition. In TA language, any act of recognition is called a *stroke*. Everyone needs an adequate supply of strokes to maintain their physical and psychological well-being.

When people are transacting in groups or pairs, they use time in various specific ways which can be listed and analysed. This is the analysis of *time structuring*.

Life-script

TA assumes that each of us, in childhood, writes a life-story for himself or herself. This story has a beginning, a middle and an end. We write the basic plot in our infant years, before we are old enough to talk more than a few words. Later on in childhood, we add more detail to the story. Most of it has been written by the age of 7. We may revise it further during adolescence.

As grown-ups, we are usually no longer aware of the life-story we have written for ourselves. Yet we are likely to live it out faithfully. Without being aware of it, we are likely to set up our lives so that we move towards the final scene we decided upon as infants.

This unaware life-story is known in TA as the *life-script* (often shortened simply to *script*).[2] The concept of life-script ranks with the ego-state model as a central building-block of TA.

As we have already said, TA assumes that the young child *decides upon* her life-script. That is, she 'writes her own story'. She does this as the best means she can find – with an infant's powers of thinking and experience – for surviving and getting needs met in a world that can often seem threatening.

Though the parents cannot force a particular script upon the child, they are naturally likely to exert a strong influence upon that child's early decisions. In particular, parents give their children *script messages* – instructions about how to be or not be, what to do or not do. Especially significant in most people's scripts are negative messages called *injunctions*. These take the form 'Don't . . .', for example Don't Feel, Don't Be Important, Don't Exist, Don't Be You. Injunctions are communicated to the child from the Child ego-state of the parent, and usually have their origins in the parent's own unmet childhood needs.

In *script analysis*, we use the concept of life-script to understand how people may unawarely set up problems for themselves, and how they may set about solving those problems.

Discounting, redefining, symbiosis

The young child decides on a life-script because it represents the best strategy that the child can work out to survive and get by in what often seems a hostile world. When we are in a Child ego-state, we may still be believing that any threat to our infant picture of the world is a threat to the satisfaction of our needs, or even to our survival. Thus we may sometimes distort our perception of reality so that it fits our script. When we do so, we are said to be *redefining*.

One way of ensuring that the world seems to fit our script is to selectively ignore information available to us about a situation. Without conscious intention, we blank out the aspects of the situation that would contradict our script. This is called *discounting*.

As a part of maintaining our script, we may sometimes get into relationships as grown-ups which re-play the relationships we had with our parents when we were children. We do this without being aware of it. In this situation, one of the partners in the relationship plays the part of Parent and Adult, while the other acts Child. Between them, they function as though they had only three instead of six classes of ego-state available. A relationship like this is called a *symbiosis*.

Rackets, stamps and games

As young children, we may notice that in our family, certain feelings are encouraged while others are prohibited. To get our strokes, we may decide to feel only the permitted feelings. This decision is made without conscious awareness. When we play out our script in grown-up life, we continue to cover our authentic feelings with the feelings that were permitted to us as children. These substitute feelings are known as *racket feelings*.

If we experience a racket feeling and store it up instead of expressing it at the time, we are said to be saving a *stamp*.

A *game* is a repetitive sequence of transactions in which both parties end up experiencing racket feelings. It always includes a *switch*, a moment when the players experience that something unexpected and uncomfortable has happened. People play games without being aware they are doing so.

To summarize so far: the idea of life-script is central to TA's model of personal problems. When people are playing out their script, they are likely to feel racket feelings and to play games.

Thus, the process of personal change means moving *out of script*. But if you move out of script, what do you move *into*? We outline some answers in the next section.

PRACTICE

The goals of personal change in TA

Berne urged that the proper goal of TA treatment is not 'insight', nor 'progress', but *cure*. While most of today's transactional analysts agree with Berne that cure is their goal, they have differing views about what constitutes cure. Some simply equate cure with completion of the treatment contract between client and therapist.

Berne himself saw cure not as a one-off event, but as a progressive process that moved through four stages:

- social control
- symptomatic relief
- transference cure
- script cure

At the first stage, *social control*, the client may still feel the discomforts and troubles she has brought to therapy, but she has become able to control dysfunctional behaviours in her interactions with others. Moving to *symptomatic relief*, the client now also experiences relief of subjective discomforts such as anxiety, depression or confusion. In *transference cure*, the person has become able to stay out of script so long as he can 'keep the therapist around', either literally or in his head. Finally, at the stage of *script cure*, the person's own Adult takes over the role of the therapist, making it possible for the person to 'put a new show on the road'. This means that she moves substantially and permanently out of script patterns and into script-free thinking, feeling and behaviour.

Autonomy

As another way of framing 'cure', Eric Berne proposed the idea that the goal of personal change is *autonomy*. Being autonomous implies the ability to solve problems using the person's full adult resources to think, feel and behave in response to here-and-now reality. The components of autonomy are *awareness, spontaneity*, and the *capacity for intimacy*. By *awareness*, we mean the ability to experience things – to 'hear the birds and smell the flowers' – with here-and-now immediacy, rather than in the way we were taught to do by others. *Spontaneity* means the ability to move freely and by choice between Adult, Parent and Child ego-states. *Intimacy* with others, in its TA sense, means the open expression of wants, feelings and needs as they arise, without game-playing or manipulation.

Contractual method

The TA therapist assumes that he and his client will take *joint responsibility* for achieving whatever change the client wants to make.

This follows from TA's philosophical assumption that therapist and client relate on equal terms. It is not the therapist's task to do things *to* the client. Nor can the client expect that the therapist will do everything *for* her.

Since both parties take an equal share in the process of change, it is important that both know clearly how the task will be shared. Therefore they enter into a *contract*. Eric Berne[3] defined this as: 'an explicit bilateral commitment to a well-defined course of action'.

Berne's colleague Claude Steiner[4] has suggested four requirements for sound contract-making. These are widely accepted by transactional analysts. They are:

1 *Mutual consent*: therapist and client must explicitly agree the terms of the contract.
2 *Valid consideration*: the client must give the therapist some agreed recompense for the service that the therapist offers. This will usually be financial, but other forms of consideration are also possible.
3 *Competency*: the therapist must have skills to provide the service contracted for. The client must also be competent to undertake therapy; for example, she must have sufficient Adult ego-state available to understand and agree to what is going on in the session.
4 *Lawful object*: everything agreed on in the contract must be legal, and must meet appropriate professional and ethical norms.

The term *overall contract* is used to describe the client's main longer-term contract. This will often be for an important script change. Client and therapist are likely to address the overall contract over a number of sessions or for the full duration of therapy. A *session contract*, as its name implies, is a shorter-term contract taken for a single session, or even for part of the time within one session. A *(working) assignment* means a contract for some activity that the client will carry out between one session and the next.

Open communication

Eric Berne insisted that the client, as well as the therapist, should have full information about what was going on in their work together. This follows from the basic assumptions that people are OK and that everyone can think.

In TA practice, case notes are open to the client's inspection. The therapist may often encourage the client to learn the ideas of TA. These measures invite the client to take an equal role with the therapist in the process of change.

Treatment direction

TA is an actionistic approach to personal change. The TA therapist does not assume that the 'therapeutic relationship', of itself, will necessarily bring about desired changes. Instead, she develops an analysis of the client's problem, and agrees a contract for the changes he will make. She then intervenes actively in a planned and structured manner to help him achieve these changes. This process of planned intervention is summed up in the phrase *treatment direction*.

There is a continual three-way interplay between contract, diagnosis and treatment direction. For example, you may revise your diagnosis of the client because you have got to know him better or because he has already changed in the course of treatment. The changed diagnosis may call for a re-negotiation of the contract; and the new diagnosis and new contract will then require you to re-think your choice of interventions.

The 'three P's': permission, protection and potency

The TA writer Pat Crossman[5] suggested that a crucial function of the therapist is to give the client *permission* to go against the prejudicial commands of the Parent 'in her head'. To do this, said Crossman, the therapist has to convince the client that she has more *potency* – more power – than that internal Parent. At the same time, the therapist needs to provide the client with appropriate *protection* from the wrath of the internal Parent, at least until the client can develop his own protection. This trilogy – of permission, protection and potency – is now usually referred to in TA simply as the 'three P's'.

Practitioners in the redecision school of TA (see the section below on 'Three schools') play down the significance of 'permission-giving' in Crossman's sense. Instead, they see the client herself as *taking permission* to go against the script. They argue that it is the client, not the therapist, who possesses the potency to make this change.

Transactional analysts from all schools, however, would agree on the central importance of ensuring protection for the client. In practical terms, this includes setting up a physically safe environment, guaranteeing confidentiality, and using an effective system for medical and psychiatric referral. Another crucial element of protection is to guard against the three tragic script outcomes: suicide, homicide or going crazy. This is most often accomplished by inviting the client to 'close escape hatches' – a process that we describe in the next section.

Closing escape hatches

To 'close escape hatches', the client makes and states an unconditional decision that she will never, in any circumstances, kill or harm self, kill or harm anyone else, or go crazy. Crucially, this undertaking is not a *promise* to the therapist; it is a decision that the client takes *for herself*. The therapist's task is to offer the procedure, then act as witness while feeding back to the client any sign of incongruity.

The closing of escape hatches has two purposes. First, it serves as practical protection against the tragic outcomes of suicide, homicide or going crazy. Second, it facilitates movement out of script. Experience of script analysis indicates that many people's scripts are directed towards a final scene (*script payoff*) that entails one of the three tragic outcomes. The form of the child's early decision in such cases is: 'If things get bad enough, I can always . . . (kill myself, kill someone else, go crazy)'. By closing escape hatches, the person takes an unconditional Adult decision to turn away from these outcomes. The effect of this is to destabilize the entire structure of the script, making therapeutic movement easier. This therapeutic shift may sometimes be bought at the cost of some temporary discomfort to the client.

By the time of Eric Berne's death in 1970, three different 'schools' of TA had already begun to emerge, and they are still recognized today. They are the *classical, redecision* and *Cathexis* schools. Each school has its favoured theoretical ideas and techniques; the relationship between client and therapist also differs somewhat as between the practice of the three schools. It is worth adding that in TA (unlike some other therapeutic approaches) the different schools are not 'at war' with each other, but co-exist peacefully. Few TA therapists specialize in one school alone; indeed, TA's professional accreditation process requires candidates to show competence in all three schools.

The *classical* school is so called because its practitioners have stayed closest to Berne's original ideas and ways of working. A central aim in the classical approach is to help the client strengthen his Adult functioning – that is, to bring his thinking, feeling and behaving more into the here-and-now instead of responding to his script. Classical therapists seek primarily to make Adult-to-Adult contact with their client, using a whole array of analytical diagrams, questionnaires and problem-solving frameworks. At the same time, they follow Berne's example in using the power of their intuition and encouraging their client to do the same. In ego-state terms, this entails use of the intuitive power that resides in a Child ego-state, often dubbed the 'Little Professor'.

While *redecision* therapists also encourage Adult functioning, they start from the assumption that the client will achieve her most fundamental personal change by working in a Child ego-state.[6] The reasoning is that since people make their original script decisions during childhood, they can best change these decisions while directly re-experiencing their childhood. To achieve this, redecision therapists often use techniques derived originally from Gestalt therapy, such as 'two-chair work'. They ask their clients not to 'talk about' childhood problems, but to 'be there' in imagination and deal with these recalled scenes in new and more resourceful ways. Though redecision therapists invite their clients to move into Child ego-states, the therapist herself is careful *not* to assume the complementary role of Parent. Instead, she asks the client to converse with the imagined 'Parent' in the other chair or in a remembered past scene.

In the *Cathexis* approach also, emphasis is placed on the client's use of Child as well as Adult ego-states in change.[7] But in contrast to redecision work, the Cathexis therapist actively assumes the role of Parent – all the while working within contractual boundaries and the time boundaries of the therapy. Within these bounds, the therapist 'becomes' a new parent for the client, offering more positive parenting than the client got from her original care-giver.

WHICH CLIENTS BENEFIT MOST?

TA is notable for the breadth of its application. It has been used successfully to help clients deal with many different types and levels of problem and dysfunction. These range all the way from simple problem situations, through temporary stress reaction, to deeper-seated emotional and relationship difficulties and personality disorders. Used in specialized and protective settings, TA therapy has had good results in the treatment of some kinds of psychosis.

Case study

In this case study, we have used *italics* to highlight TA concepts and methods already described in the sections above. The therapist was Tony Tilney.

THE CLIENT

First impressions

Celia came into the therapy room and sat down stiffly in an upright position as if thinking about how to do it. She turned to me with a nervous childlike smile. My immediate impression was of a child trying to be grown up. She was a professional woman in her mid-forties with a senior and highly responsible job, in which she presented herself as confident if somewhat aloof. Within herself she was anxious and insecure and had low self-esteem. With her friends and her partner she alternated between anger and desperate attempts to please.

Script analysis

Celia was not yet clear what she wanted out of therapy. I explained the significance of the *life-script*, the set of decisions made in childhood which shapes both what we do and how we see the world. We made a contract to start with *script analysis* for four sessions and then to look again at the outcomes we were aiming for.

This contract-making process – of agreeing a way forward and then taking another look from the new vantage point – was often repeated as therapy proceeded. Contracting was therefore not a once-only process but was integrated into the whole of the therapy. Each review gave a clearer picture of the desired outcome and enabled us to adjust the *treatment direction* in order to achieve it as quickly as possible.

We began script analysis by working through a *script questionnaire*, a systematic way of questioning to establish the client's history, in particular around early influences, the relationships with the parents and the family situation. Here also we find clues as to how the client reacted and what *early decisions* she may have made.

Celia first described her mother as 'loving'. She had certainly often told Celia how much she loved her. In return for this love she imposed on Celia a duty to make her happy – an impossible task, as her mother alternated between extreme dependency, withdrawn depression and violent emotional outbursts. As the eldest child Celia had to hold the family together, do the housework, calm her mother's outbursts or draw her out of depression when she threatened suicide. Her father withdrew from the family, spending his time at work or drinking with friends.

Celia had struggled with the task of being little mother to the family and keeping her mother alive, and became very competent. When she reached her teens she started to rebel against this role and demanded some space for herself. Shortly afterwards her father abandoned the family and her mother killed herself.

I now understood the significance of the stiff way she had sat down in the first session and the placatory childlike smile. In her *Child ego-state* she held an *early decision* that she had to get things right for others or they would die. To do this she had to be very grown-up and efficient. She must not let her own needs and feelings get in the way of this, so she had no right to feel, to be herself, perhaps even to exist; she could only win the right to exist by working hard. She believed that if people say they love you, you become totally responsible for them. Also in her Child she struggled with her anger at not getting her needs met together with a deep sense of sadness, inadequacy and guilt that she had (as her Child saw it) allowed her mother to die. From her Parent ego-state she still received messages telling her she was not getting things right or giving enough of herself.

We were now able to draw a diagram known as a 'script matrix', showing *script messages* from her parents and decisions she had made as a child which now had pervasive influences on her thinking, feeling and behaving. We identified the most powerful *injunctions*: Don't Feel, Don't Be You, Don't Be Important and Don't Exist from her mother and Don't Be Important and Don't Exist from her father.

We were also able to understand her mother's behaviour in terms of what the *Cathexis school* of TA calls *symbiosis*. Her mother had attempted to get Celia to use her Parent and Adult ego-states to look after her while Celia's Child and her mother's Parent and Adult were discounted.

THE THERAPY

Starting therapy

My first aim, beginning even in these exploratory sessions, had been to invite Celia to feel at ease by relating to her in an open, contactful and respectful way. I wanted to establish an *OK-OK relationship* between her and myself. At first this took precedence over the content of the therapy process proper.

Our next task, also accomplished in the opening sessions, had been to establish how we were to work together. This process of making a *contract* was essential if we were to maintain an equal, respectful, OK-OK relationship throughout the therapy. Business details of times, fees, etc. had been easily settled in the opening session, and we had agreed the rules regarding confidentiality.

Social control

With script analysis completed, we now went on to work mainly in the *classical school* of TA. The initial aim was to develop the strength of the Adult. Celia could now take an adult view of what her mother had told her and the events of her childhood. She understood where the problem was coming from and was able consciously to take steps to control it, such as thinking clearly about criticism from others and noting the way she discounted positive feedback. She had achieved the stage of cure known as *social control*. She was functioning better with her colleagues and her partner, though she still found it difficult to hold on to the gains.

She also now had a clear view of the way ahead and we made a new *contract* for the changes which would indicate the successful outcome of the therapy. These would include asking clearly for what she wanted and not inappropriately rescuing others (doing things for them which they were well able to do for themselves). We made this contract clearer by specifying behaviours which would indicate when it had been achieved.

Transference cure

Another change occurred which made Celia's life easier. In the course of therapy I had been able to give her many positive messages which were contrary to those she had received from her parents. She was beginning to take me into her Parent ego-state as a good parent resource, resulting in *transference cure*. However, this might be difficult to retain if she left therapy prematurely.

(*Note*: you will realize that in Celia's case, the second of Berne's stages of cure – *symptomatic relief* – was not clearly distinguishable from the stages before and after it. I noted this fact at the time, but was not concerned by it: Berne's 'four stages' are intended as a flexible *aide-mémoire*, not a rigid set of laws).

Closing escape hatches

Particularly in view of Celia's mother's suicide, and the presence of the script message 'Don't Exist', I had been clear since an early stage that *closing escape hatches* would be a crucial step for Celia in achieving lasting script change. I had mentioned the procedure to her at the stage of script analysis. Celia had been well aware at that point that she was not yet ready to give up these three 'last-resort' outcomes to her script. I made no attempt to persuade her to do so, since it is crucial that the closure of escape hatches must be the client's own autonomous choice; I knew the procedure would be of no effect if Celia were to carry it out merely to 'please me'.

It was only after several months of therapy, when Celia had already moved to a position of much more secure Adult understanding of her own and her parents' history and motives, that she told me she was ready to close all three of the escape hatches. She stated to me her own unconditional decision that she would never kill or harm self, kill or harm others, or let go of her sanity, no matter what might happen in her life. Observing her closely, I judged that she was making these statements congruently. I congratulated Celia for having taken a crucial step in change.

Script cure

I had foreseen that the final stage of cure would involve Celia in changing some of the *early decisions* that she had been holding in her Child ego-state, so that she could substantially release herself from her script. We achieved this through *redecision* work. Celia contracted to imagine her mother was sitting on a cushion. While keeping some energy in Adult, so that she could think clearly, she contacted her Child ego-state. She told her 'mother' from Child how she now understood what had happened in her childhood. She moved through anger into sadness for her lost childhood and the love she had not had.

Celia *redecided* in Child that she was lovable. She did not have to justify her existence and had a right be loved, to be important and be herself. As she made this new decision, her features softened and she adopted a more relaxed body posture.

Termination

Celia was disoriented for a time by this change. She had lost much of the script which she had used to structure her life. The new situation presented her with many new opportunities and challenges and she needed a period of adjustment to deal with it fully. She continues to be successful at work but is no longer over-stressed and has been promoted. After a period of readjustment her relationships with her partner and her friends have greatly improved. In our final session we checked our *contract* and agreed that it had been fully achieved.

REFERENCES

1 Berne, E. (1961) *Transactional Analysis in Psychotherapy*. New York: Grove Press. (*Other editions include*: London: Souvenir Press, 1991.)

2 Steiner, C. (1974) *Scripts People Live: Transactional Analysis of Life Scripts*. New York: Grove Press.

3 Berne, E. (1966) *Principles of Group Treatment*. New York: Oxford University Press. (*Other editions include*: New York: Grove Press, 1966.)

4 Steiner, C. (1974) op. cit., note 2.

5 Crossman, P. (1966) 'Permission and Protection', *Transactional Analysis Bulletin*, 5 (19): 152–4.

6 Goulding, M. and Goulding, R. (1979) *Changing Lives Through Redecision Therapy*. New York: Brunner-Mazel.

7 Schiff, J. *et al.* (1975) *The Cathexis Reader: Transactional Analysis Treatment of Psychosis*. New York: Harper & Row.

SUGGESTED READING

Berne, E. (1961) *Transactional Analysis in Psychotherapy*. New York: Grove Press. (*Reprint edition*: London: Souvenir Press, 1991.) This was Berne's first book-length statement of TA principles. It is still the essential source text for some of the central ideas of TA, in particular for Berne's original theory of ego-states.

Stewart, I. (1989) *Transactional Analysis Counselling in Action*. London: Sage (Counselling in Action series). Written for practising and trainee counsellors and therapists, this book gives detailed practical guidance on using TA to help people change. The techniques are illustrated in an extended case study, and the book includes suggestions for self-supervision.

Stewart, I. and Joines, V. (1987) *TA Today: A New Introduction to Transactional Analysis*. Nottingham: Lifespace. This book explains current TA ideas in straightforward language, starting from basic principles. It is structured around the syllabus of the 'TA 101', the standard international entry-level examination in TA. The teaching material is reinforced by numerous examples and exercises.

Tilney, T. (1997) *Dictionary of Transactional Analysis*. London: Whurr. This gives definitions and full descriptions of all the terms used in TA theory and practice. It is designed to be useful not only to the TA professional, but to the general reader who wants an accurate understanding of current TA.

DISCUSSION ISSUES

1 *Ego-state shifts* Think back over the past 24 hours. Do you recognize any situations in which you thought, felt and behaved as though you were back in your own childhood (i.e. in a Child ego-state)?

   Were there other situations in which you thought, felt and behaved in a way that now reminds you of one of your own parents or parent-figures (Parent ego-state)?

   And were there still other situations in which you thought, felt and behaved neither as a Child nor a Parent, but as your age-appropriate self (Adult ego-state)?

   For each type of ego-state: if you were to observe yourself on a video replay of that situation, how would you and others see and hear you behaving?

2 *Choosing transactions* Is there anyone with whom you seem often to get into a 'locked' pattern of relating, in ego-state terms? For example, you may find you typically get into Child with them, while they come from Parent. If you would like to find a new way of communicating (transacting) with this person, think of several creative and safe ways in which *you* can deliberately shift to a different ego-state while communicating with them. What difference does this make?

3 *Games* Do you recall any occasions, in relating to others, when you have said to yourself something like: 'Why does *this* always happen to me?', or 'This is so painfully familiar, but I don't know how I got into it again'? If so, think back through the sequence of behaviours (a game) by which you got yourself into that repetitive outcome. What clue do you now recognize that lets you know you are just *beginning* the game? How could you change your behaviour in future so that you get *any* outcome that is different from the repetitive painful one?

4 *Life-script as a story* Do you have a favourite story? It might be a fairy-tale recalled from your childhood, or a novel, or an ancient myth, or a film, or . . . What is this story? If you were to imagine that this story tells you something about the story of your own life, what would that something be? If you first learned the story in childhood, what do you think of it now? How do you feel about the story? Do you want to change it in any way?

25

RESEARCH ISSUES IN COUNSELLING AND PSYCHOTHERAPY

John McLeod

I t will be clear to any reader of this book that there exist many different approaches to counselling and psychotherapy, and that much remains to be understood about the extent to which each of these approaches is (or is not) effective in any particular case. From the very beginnings of the counselling and psychotherapy professions, therapists have attempted to find ways of recording and analysing their work. This is mostly an informal process, carried out through supervision and talking with colleagues. However, in recent years an increasing number of therapists have been engaging in more formal research projects. This type of research can be defined as: *a systematic process of critical inquiry leading to valid propositions and conclusions that are communicated to interested others.*[1] One of the implications of this definition is that it is possible to see that 'research' is a broad concept. There are many different kinds of inquiry that can yield useful knowledge. The aim of this chapter is to introduce some of the approaches to research that have been most widely employed in the field of counselling and psychotherapy, and to explain how and why they have been used. The chapter is also designed to help readers to find their way through the published research literature, which represents an invaluable source of ideas and learning for anyone interested in therapy.

THE DEVELOPMENT OF RESEARCH INTO COUNSELLING AND PSYCHOTHERAPY

To understand the research that is being carried out and published today, it is necessary to know a little about how this area of work has developed over the last 50 years. Most research is at least partially built on the methods and findings of previous studies. Also, the focus of therapy research has shifted over the years, as some research questions have come to be seen as more important than others.

It could be argued that the earliest attempts to carry out any form of systematic inquiry into therapy were the case studies published by Freud, Jung and their colleagues around the turn of the century. These psychoanalytic therapists took careful notes of what their patients said in sessions, and wrote elaborate case studies which showed how the process of therapy could be explained in psychoanalytic terms. To this day, the knowledge base of psychoanalytic psychotherapy and psychodynamic counselling is still heavily reliant on this kind of case study report. For many therapists outside the psychoanalytic community, however, there were significant weaknesses in this approach to creating valid knowledge about therapy. How reliable were Freud and his colleagues in recording what happened during sessions? To what extent might their interpretations have been influenced by personal biases and assumptions? Might not other observers have arrived at different interpretations? How valid is it to generalize from a small number of cases? These criticisms resulted in many therapists being sceptical about this approach to research, and motivated them to look for more objective methods of finding out about the therapy process. Nevertheless, it cannot be denied that psychoanalytic case studies have made, and continue to make, a major contribution to the overall knowledge base of psychology and psychotherapy.[2]

As counselling and psychotherapy became more firmly established in the health care systems of North American and European countries, during the 1950s and 1960s, there emerged a growing pressure to demonstrate their effectiveness. Those picking up the bill for therapy – governments and independent health insurance companies – demanded evidence that therapy was money well spent. During the period between 1950 and 1980, therefore, there was a great deal of research attention given to the question of how best to evaluate the *outcomes* of therapy, in terms of beneficial changes to client well-being, level of psychological adjustment or ability to cope. There are many issues involved in evaluating the outcome of therapy. For example: who decides on whether the client has benefited – the client, the therapist, an independent observer, a close family member, the client's employer, or all of these? Another issue concerns the comparison between the amount of improvement that clients experience following therapy, and the improvement that might have been expected had they never consulted a therapist. It is known that many psychological problems are episodic or cyclical, and will therefore reduce somewhat even in the absence of treatment. In designing a fair test of the effectiveness of therapy, it is therefore essential to include some kind of control or comparison group. But how can this comparison group be created? To use potential clients who had been denied therapy is ethically indefensible. To use people who were not seeking therapy is ethically acceptable, but introduces other difficulties. Outcome researchers have, over the years, had to work hard to develop satisfactory solutions to these problems.

By the early 1980s, there was an impressive amount of evidence which demonstrated that counselling and psychotherapy were effective for about 60 per cent of clients. The focus of research then began to shift towards the question of *process*: what are the elements or ingredients that contribute to success or failure in therapy? Alongside this movement toward process research, there has been a continuing strand of outcome research, but now targeted at more specific issues. In many countries, health care purchasers are looking for evidence not only that therapy is effective in general terms, but that *this* kind of therapy is effective for *that* kind of client in *this* setting, and that it will cost less than alternative forms of care (for example, drug treatment). The recent trend in outcome research, therefore, has been in the direction of more locally based studies, and of incorporating ways of measuring the financial costs and benefits of the treatment package offered to clients. Some of the impetus for this kind of research has also come from users of services, who are becoming more aware of issues around accountability and consumer choice.

Although research into the process of therapy has gained in prominence in recent years, it has nevertheless been around for a long time. Psychoanalytic case studies are one means of examining the process of what happens in therapy. In the 1940s, Carl Rogers and his colleagues were among the first to make recordings of counselling sessions, and to use transcripts of sessions to study the connection between the statements made by the therapist and the growth in self-acceptance of the client. The recent interest in process research has built upon Rogers' work by developing new ways of gaining access to the complex and often hidden 'interior' of the therapy session. For example, researchers have constructed brief and easy-to-use questionnaires that measure client and ther-apist perceptions of such process factors as empathy or therapeutic alliance. Other researchers have used video and audio recording techniques to assess levels of emotional experiencing and transference patterns, or as the basis for sophisticated multi-observer case studies.

WHO IS RESEARCH FOR? DIFFERENT AUDIENCES

Implicit in the preceding review of the historical development of research in counselling and psychotherapy is the notion that therapy research has been driven by a number of different agendas or groups of stakeholders. When reading therapy research, it can be useful to keep in mind that it may have been written for one or more of a variety of audiences. One very important audience for therapy research has been the purchasers of therapy, comprising a range of government, private sector and voluntary organizations. These stakeholders have been highly influential; not only are they in a position to pay for therapy services, but they are also in a position to pay for research. Typically, this audience is interested in research that looks at outcomes, which clearly specifies client groups (for example, in terms of standard diagnostic categories) and which includes a large enough sample size to maximize the reliability of the findings and their generalizability to other settings. Policy-makers and institutional pur-chasers of therapy have been particularly interested in the results of *randomized controlled trials* of therapy. These are studies in which clients or patients are randomly assigned to different treatment conditions, or to a treatment condition and control/comparison group. By contrast, psychotherapists and counsellors themselves represent a quite different audience for research. Practitioners tend to be much more interested in small-scale intensive studies which include plenty of detail on the characteristics of clients and the types of interventions used with these clients. On the whole, practitioners are looking for research findings that will make a difference to their practice, that will help them to be better therapists. A third audience for research comprises academic researchers and theorists. These are people who are usually based in universities or research centres, and are often driven by an interest in theoretical and methodological issues. Finally, the actual clients or consumers of therapy represent a potential audience for research. In principle, research findings should be able to help clients select which type of therapy they might enter, or decide whether they need therapy at all. Unfortunately, very little research has been directed toward the interests of consumers. A widely reported recent survey of therapy clients carried out by the Consumers' Association in the USA[3] illustrates some of the potential for consumer-oriented research.

Having some understanding of the intended audience of a research paper is helpful for anyone trying to find their way around the research literature. However, the relative power and influence of these different audiences means that the majority of published studies tend to reflect the interests of purchasers/policy-makers and academics, rather than practitioners and clients. This imbalance has led to another key issue, which is the existence of a research–practice 'gap'.

THE RESEARCH–PRACTICE 'GAP'

Surveys carried out in the USA[4] have found that, when therapy practitioners are asked about which sources of information or learning have informed their work with clients, then research findings comes low on their list. Practitioners report that their knowledge of therapy comes from training, learning from clients, talking with colleagues, engaging in supervision. When asked about research, they reply that they seldom read research articles, but that when they do they find the research papers irrelevant, over-statistical or containing insufficient clinical detail. It is important to note that these attitudes were reported by therapists in the USA whose training required them to learn about research methods and undertake a research dissertation. Clearly, in countries such as Britain, where training as a counsellor or psychotherapist does not necessarily include a research element, awareness and use of research will inevitably be even lower. The existence of a gap between research and practice in this field has sparked considerable debate: what use is research if it does not have the potential to influence practice? Out of this debate has come a willingness to develop new approaches to research which may be more practice-relevant.

THE SEARCH FOR THE MOST APPROPRIATE METHODS

Traditionally, research into counselling and psychotherapy has been carried out within university departments of psychology or psychiatry, or in clinics attached to such departments. These disciplines have been dominated by an approach to research which places great emphasis on accurate, objective measurement and experimentation. Until very recently, as a result, the bulk of therapy research has relied on methods of *quantitative* analysis of data. This style of research usually requires fairly large numbers of 'subjects' each of whom completes standardized questionnaire measures of variables such as anxiety, depression, stress, self-esteem, etc. Standardized questionnaires are carefully constructed so that their reliability (does the questionnaire measure the same variable under different circumstances?) and validity (does the questionnaire actually measure what it is supposed to measure?) can be ensured. Often, norms on these questionnaires are available, so that the scores of therapy clients can be compared against a national or occupational 'average' score. Client change is estimated by comparing questionnaire scores at different times, for example at the start of therapy, at the end, and then finally after a follow-up period.

Without denying the value of quantitative methods, it is possible to argue that there are aspects of the therapy process which these methods do not capture. There is an increasing appreciation of the relevance of *qualitative* methods. More and more, researchers are using open-ended interviews, or compiling case studies, rather than administering questionnaires. The combination of qualitative and quantitative techniques in a truly pluralist approach to inquiry is becoming more widely accepted.

The essential point here is that it is intrinsically difficult to study the processes and outcomes of therapy. Each case, and even each session, is complex and in many ways unique. At the same time, if knowledge is to be built up over many cases, some way must be found of simplifying the phenomena of therapy and making comparisons between one case and another. Qualitative methods are well-suited for intensive exploration of the experience or meaning of therapy for the client or therapist. Quantitative methods are perhaps better suited to comparisons between groups of clients or models of treatment.

GAINING ACCESS: RESEARCH TOOLS AND THE RESEARCH LITERATURE

One of the real issues for many therapists who are interested in research is concerned with the problem of gaining access to relevant information. Table 25.1 lists just some of the journals which publish research in counselling and psychotherapy. This is a very long list. While it may be possible for some therapists to take out personal subscriptions to one or even two of these journals, it is clear that to keep in touch with the field as a whole means having access to library facilities. Very few university libraries will actually stock more than a fraction of the journals in this field, so it is necessary to use on-line search facilities, which produce lists of articles under key-word headings. These computerized literature search packages will usually also provide an *abstract* (brief summary) of each article. Two of the most useful of these on-line systems are Psyc-Lit and BIDS. Any university or public library information desk should be

TABLE 25.1 Journals regularly publishing research in counselling and psychotherapy

American Journal of Orthopsychiatry	Counselor Education and Supervision
American Journal of Psychiatry	European Journal of Counselling, Psychotherapy and Health
American Journal of Psychotherapy	International Journal of Group Psychotherapy
American Psychologist	Journal for Specialists in Groupwork
Archives of General Psychiatry	Journal of Behavior Therapy and Experimental Psychiatry
Behavior Therapy	Journal of College Student Development
British Journal of Clinical Psychology	Journal of College Student Personnel
British Journal of Guidance and Counselling	Journal of Consulting and Clinical Psychology
British Journal of Medical Psychology	Journal of Counseling and Development
British Journal of Psychiatry	Journal of Counseling Psychology
British Journal of Psychotherapy	Journal of Eclectic and Integrative Psychotherapy
Canadian Counsellor	Journal of Humanistic Psychology
Changes	Journal of Mental Health Counseling
Clinical Psychology Review	Professional Psychology: Research and Practice
Counseling Psychologist	Psychiatry
Counselling	Psychotherapy
Counselling Psychology Quarterly	Psychotherapy Research
Counselling Psychology Review	Small Group Research

able to arrange access to these facilities, and will be able to order printed copies of any papers of special interest. At the time of writing, none of the British publishers or professional associations produces digests of new research in counselling and psychotherapy. Other professional groups (for example medicine, social work, probation) have generated such services, and it is to be hoped that this feature will become available to European counsellors and psychotherapists before very long, possibly on the Internet. However, current digests are of limited use to those seeking to review knowledge in particular areas, since the relevant studies may easily stretch back over 30 years.

Another difficulty faced by many people wishing to carry out research into counselling and psychotherapy is that a great deal of research has relied on standardized questionnaire measures of variables such as anxiety and depression. The research and development costs of producing these questionnaires is considerable, and as a result many of them are disseminated through commercial publishing companies, which charge for their use. Sometimes, questionnaires are only released to persons with appropriate qualifications and training (usually in psychology and psychometrics). In these circumstances, a counsellor or psychotherapist who does not possess the appropriate qualifications will need to find a co-worker with that type of expertise. An alternative approach would be to use a questionnaire which is in the public domain, or to get permission directly from the author of the scale (as long as he or she has not assigned copyright to a publisher). Usually, people who design questionnaires are very happy for anyone else to use them, as long as they can receive a copy of the results in a form that they can use in their ongoing validation of the instrument. The name and address of the person who designed a questionnaire would normally be displayed in the papers that he or she has written.

Access to a general range of research skills, including how to design studies, analyse quantitative or qualitative data, write for publication, can also present problems for some counsellors and psychotherapists. Most people who are involved in therapy research have acquired their initial research skills through taking a university MA or MSc course which includes at least one module on research methods, and a research dissertation. There are two research networks in Britain which enable therapy researchers to keep in touch with each other. These are operated by the British Association for Counselling and the Society for Psychotherapy Research, and are both linked in turn to wider European and North American networks. There is also a growing number of websites that display dialogue and information on therapy research.

ETHICAL DILEMMAS

Research into counselling and psychotherapy involves enquiry into areas of high personal sensitivity. The confidentiality of client disclosure to the therapist, and any other client information, must be respected in any research study. Steps must be taken to make sure that the collection of research data does not interfere with or distort the therapeutic process. Practitioners, and managers/administrators of counselling and psychotherapy organizations, tend to guard with vigour the well-being of clients and it can be difficult in many situations to gain permission to carry out research. Within Health Service and some Social Services settings there are formal Ethics Committees which approve research proposals. Although it can be time-consuming to deal with these Committees, they at least present the researcher with a set of procedures and guidelines to follow.

One of the most difficult areas of ethical decision making in therapy research concerns the principle of informed consent. Whenever a client is invited to take part in a research study, he or she should be fully informed of the nature of the study and what will be required from them, and then asked to sign a consent form. In most situations it would be ethically questionable to make treatment contingent on consent to participate in research. This would be coercive. Yet it can be quite difficult to convey to clients at the outset of therapy that they are free to participate or not in a research study. They may assume that completing the research questionnaire is the cost they must pay to be seen. They may be in a state of distress or confusion that makes it hard for them to assimilate the information on the consent form. One way to safeguard the interests of the client is through a system of *process consent*, in which informed consent is sought not only at the start but also at later stages in the process of the therapy.

Voluntary participation in research, and informed consent, are even more problematic when the researcher and the therapist are the same person. If a client has had good service from the therapist he or she may feel obliged to help them with their research. The act of carrying out research into ongoing clients places the therapist in a dual relationship, in which the primary ethical consideration of acting solely to meet the needs of the client may become compromised. For example, if the therapist is studying gender issues in therapy, he or she may unconsciously lead the client into talking about gender relationships.

The ethical issues arising from therapists researching their own practice can be resolved, but require careful planning and continual monitoring.

An emerging ethical issue in therapy research involves the fact that sometimes clients report that their participation in research has made a positive contribution to their therapy. Clients may say that filling in a questionnaire, or being interviewed by a researcher, has helped them to identify their core issues, or to realize why their therapy was not proceeding as well as it might be. An implication of this type of observation is that there is a sense in which it might be unethical to *deny* clients the benefits of participating in research. Conversely, if research techniques are powerful enough to help clients, they must also be impactful enough to damage at least some clients. The whole question of how research can be better integrated into therapy practice needs much more discussion.

Finally, it should be noted that the movement toward health services and insurance companies only being willing to support evidence-based care therapies has an ethical dimension. The argument here is that it is only ethical to offer forms of therapy for which there exists evidence of effectiveness. Therapists or agencies who do not monitor or evaluate their practice can, from this perspective, be criticized on moral grounds, on the basis that clients or service users may be exposed to inappropriate or damaging interventions. So, the decision *not* to do research also has ethical implications.

CONCLUSIONS

Many counsellors and psychotherapists have strong feelings about research, both positive and negative. Some practitioners believe very strongly that it is essential that their work is researched and evaluated so that they can be publicly accountable and be seen to be striving to improve their service. Other practitioners argue that the research that is carried out (or at least most of it) just is not relevant to their work, and that there may be a danger that research will influence therapy in the direction of becoming more technical and detached, with an ensuing loss of humanity and creativity. The politics of research is also an important issue for many therapists. Who does research, and who is it for? There is an absence of research into therapy with clients from gay, lesbian, multicultural or disabled groups. There is a lack of research into feminist or transpersonal therapies. The power of certain groups within the therapy establishment is reflected in the contents pages of research journals. There are, therefore, many challenges associated with therapy research, and many important methodological problems to be sorted out. However, there is also much to be gained from engaging in these issues. Reading and doing research is a means of reflecting on the complex practice of therapy, of gaining a handle on what we do. It can be argued that involvement in professional writing and research is a key aspect of counsellor or psychotherapist development.[5] On beginning to be a counsellor or psychotherapist, the main challenge is around gaining sufficient competence, being good enough. Later on, the challenge is one of constructing a professional identify and having one's own voice.

REFERENCES

1 McLeod, J. (1994) *Doing Counselling Research*. London: Sage.
2 Kvale, S. (1996) *InterViews*. London: Sage.
3 Seligman, M. (1995) 'The effectiveness of psychotherapy: the Consumer Reports study', *American Psychologist*, 50: 96–104.
4 Morrow-Bradley, C. and Elliott, R. (1986) 'Utilization of psychotherapy research by practising psychotherapists', *American Psychologist*, 41: 188–97.
5 McLeod, J. (1997) 'Reading, writing and research', in I. Horton and V. Varma (eds), *The Needs of Counsellors and Psychotherapists*. London: Sage.

SUGGESTED READING

Bergin, A. and Garfield, S. (eds) (1994) *Handbook of Psychotherapy and Behavior Change* (4th edn). New York: Wiley. This is a very long book, to be consulted in a library rather than bought (although a paperback edition is available). It contains authoritative reviews of research, and developments in research methods, written by the leading figures in the psychotherapy research community. If you are interested in a specific research topic or area, one of the best ways to start is to look up that topic in the index and follow where it leads. Updated roughly every eight years.

Hill, C.E. (1989) *Therapist Techniques and Client Outcomes: Eight Cases of Brief Psychotherapy*. London: Sage. An interesting read. Clara Hill combines quantitative and qualitative methods to explore the question of the relative importance of therapist technique as against general relationship factors. Mainly written up as a series of case reports.

McLeod, J. (1994) *Doing Counselling Research*. London: Sage. An introduction to all the main techniques and approaches used in therapy research, expanding on the issues raised in the present chapter. Relevant to psychotherapists as well as counsellors.

Roth, A. and Fonagy, P. (1996) *What Works for Whom? A Critical Review of Psychotherapy Research*. New York: Guilford Press. This book emerged from a review of psychotherapy services carried out on behalf of the English Department of Health by Tony Roth and Peter Fonagy, who are well-known therapy researchers. The book offers a comprehensive review of counselling and psychotherapy research on health-related areas of practice, and a very helpful discussion of the issues involved in translating research findings into recommendations for policy and practice.

Sexton, T.L. and Wilson, S.C. (eds) (1996) Special feature. Counseling outcome research: implications for practice. *Journal of Counseling and Development*, 74: 588–622. A set of papers which offer suggestions on how existing research findings can give some pointers toward good practice in counselling and psychotherapy.

Toukmanian, S.G. and Rennie, D.L. (eds) (1992) *Psychotherapy Process Research: Paradigmatic and Narrative Approaches*. London: Sage. Contains some very interesting examples of new qualitative techniques for exploring the experience of therapy.

DISCUSSION ISSUES

1   Reflect on what you have read in earlier chapters of this book. How important has research been in relation to establishing and developing the theoretical approaches to counselling and psychotherapy which most interest you? In relation to these approaches, what research do you feel should now be carried out?

2   Imagine that you are a client attending a counselling centre or therapy clinic for the first time. When you arrive an administrator tells you that they are carrying out an evaluation of the work of the unit, and invites you to spend 20 minutes in a side room filling out questionnaires. The first piece of paper that you read is an informed consent form. How do you imagine you might react to this scenario?

3   Imagine that you are a therapist participating in a research study. Each of your therapy sessions with clients is video-recorded and analysed. Clients complete a package of questionnaires before each session, and are interviewed by the researcher after each fifth session. What kinds of thoughts, feelings and fantasies might be evoked in you by this situation?

4   Find a published research study that has been carried out into an aspect of therapy in which you are interested. Read the study carefully. What are the strengths and weaknesses of the way this study has been carried out? Are there any alternative interpretations of the results that might be plausible? How might this study have implications for practice? What further research should/might be carried out on this topic?

GLOSSARY

The contributors provided a number of short explanations of terms taken from their chapters. The Glossary includes over 140 entries and can be used as a mini dictionary of counselling and psychotherapy which relates specifically to this book.

It is worth noting that several therapeutic approaches may use similar terms but give them different meanings. To overcome any possible confusion that this may cause, when necessary definitions have the affiliated approach included. For ease of reference, abbreviations have been avoided. In this Glossary the three psychodynamic approaches have been referred to by the particular progenitor, which reflects the various chapters, that is, Freudian, Kleinian, Jungian.

ABCDE model a way of representing the development, maintenance and eventual improvement in a client's emotional disturbance. *Rational emotive behaviour*

actualizing tendency the innate capacity of all human beings to develop and grow in positive and fulfilling ways. *Person-centred*

anchoring the process of connecting an internal response with an external trigger so that the internal response can be activated at will. *Neuro-linguistic programming*

archetype universal and innate motifs/ideas which structure human perception of life experience. Transcending the personal, they come from the *collective unconscious*. They cannot be experienced directly but through their manifestations in dreams, myths, fairy-tales and legends and such universal experiences as birth, marriage, death and separation. By their very nature archetypal images are infinitely varied and exert a fascination and power. *Jungian*

assertion standing up unaggressively for one's opinions, rights, interests, etc., but without any guarantee of redress of grievances or that others will listen favourably. *Problem focused*

attending skills the use of body language such as eye-contact and posture as a way of expressing a positive interest in what the client is saying. *Integrative*

authenticity this involves an openness to existence and an acceptance of what is given, something we only experience infrequently. *Existential*

automatic thoughts (also known as cognitions) and images reflect the client's 'internal dialogue', i.e. what they are saying to themselves. Negative automatic thoughts are unhelpful in their content and contribute to the individual's moods, such as anxiety or depression. Underlying the client's automatic thoughts are their core beliefs/**schema**. *Cognitive*

autonomy that quality which is manifested by the release or recovery of three capacities: awareness, spontaneity and intimacy; any behaviour, thinking or feeling which is a response to here-and-now reality, rather than a response to script beliefs. *Transactional analysis*

avoidance avoidance is a term which has a particular meaning in behaviour therapy, and refers to a person with anxiety evading the object or situation which they fear. It prevents *exposure* and needs to be challenged in therapy. It is a major difficulty in phobias and obsessive-compulsive disorders. *Behaviour*

awareness awareness is the process of identifying and owning our thoughts, feelings, bodily sensations and actions. *Gestalt*

BASIC I.D. an acronym and *aide-memoire* used to remember the seven key modalities: Behaviour, Affect, Sensation, Imagery, Cognition, Interpersonal, Drugs/biology. *Multimodal*

behavioural analysis a behavioural analysis is a detailed description of a person's problem behaviour including items which precede the unwanted behaviour and items which maintain it (through reinforcement). These 'items' may include thoughts, feelings, actions, body sensations and environmental circumstances. This analysis is used to finely tune the focus of therapy. *Behaviour*

being-in-the-world Existentialists use this phrase to describe our inseparable relation to the world – we are inevitably involved with all there is, including others. *Existential*

borderline personality disorder a personality disorder characterized by instability in interpersonal behaviours with intense fluctuations in mood and self-image. *Hypnosis*

brainstorming spontaneous offering of as many ideas as possible, no matter how ludicrous some of them appear to be initially, in order to find a solution or solutions to a problem. *Problem focused*

bridging a method that involves a therapist initially 'keying into' a client's preferred modality and then taking an indirect route via a second (and occasionally third) modality and then finally arriving at the avoided modality. *Multimodal*

catharsis The vigorous expression of feelings about experiences which had been previously unavailable to consciousness. This generally produces a purging or cleansing effect, which enables radical restructuring of consciousness to take place. *Primal integration*

choice theory the theory which underlies reality therapy. It is a theory which attempts to explain not only how we function as individuals, both psychologically and physiologically, but also how we function as groups and even societies. It explains that all we do lifelong is to behave and that our behaviour is 'total behaviour' consisting of our actions, thinking, feelings and our physiology. Further, our behaviour is internally motivated and chosen. Choice theory maintains that our behaviour is always our best attempt at a given time to satisfy one or more of the five basic needs built into our genetic structure. *Reality*

'closing escape hatches' protective procedure in which the client makes and states an unconditional decision that she will never, in any circumstances, kill or harm self, kill or harm anyone else, or go crazy. *Transactional analysis*

complex the network of emotionally charged associations which builds up around significant experiences and people and affects subsequent encounters with people or situations perceived to be similar. At the centre of the complex is an archetype. *Jungian*

conditions of worth the judgements and conditions placed upon us by others or ourselves, which effectively say 'I/you are only acceptable if . . .'. They are the opposite of unconditional acceptance. *Person-centred*

congruence the congruent person is self-aware and freely and acceptantly themselves. This internal openness is also extended into relationships and includes a transparency which allows a true person-to-person meeting. On occasions such transparency may include self-disclosure. *Person-centred*

conscious mental contents which are known and can be called upon at will (see **unconscious**). *Jungian*

constructionism a philosophy which asserts that we co-create meaning in our lives by negotiating with each other through language. *Solution focused*

constructive alternativism this philosophy underpins the whole of personal construct theory. It states that there are always alternative ways of construing events, even though they may be hard to find. That means no one need be the victim of their past, although we can make ourselves a victim if we come to construe it that way. *Personal construct*

contract an explicit bilateral commitment to a well-defined course of action; a commitment to oneself and/or someone else to make a change. *Transactional analysis*

core conditions known as empathy, congruence and unconditional positive regard, the core conditions are the qualities of being that a therapist must bring to the counselling relationship in order to facilitate therapeutic movement. *Person-centred*

counselling is a usually talking-based, disciplined approach to problems in living or aspirations towards greater self-fulfilment, with the aim of helping clients to discover their own inner resources. It is characterized by certain theories, training and ethical parameters.

counter-transference is the therapist's (originally unconscious) response to the client. Often used as an important guide to processes occurring between therapist and client outside of conscious awareness. It raises a difficult issue of when the therapist's own feelings and thoughts about the client derive from the therapist's desires and when they are a response to the client. The entire problem derives from Freud's need to position the therapist as an objective observer rather than a participant in the relationship and is often used as an argument for the importance of therapy during training in order to resolve the therapist's own transference issues. Often replaced in post-modern psychodynamic counselling by ideas of the therapist's positioning(s) in terms of the ebb and flow of power in the relationship. *Freudian*

counter-transference the feelings and phantasies activated in the therapist/counsellor as a result of the client's transference phantasies. *Kleinian*

creative adjustment children deal with the normal socializing process by doing the best they can in the circumstances in which they find themselves. Adaptation in a hostile environment is a means of survival in childhood but can lead to problems in later life. *Gestalt*

critical A the part or aspect of a client's problem that he/she is most upset about and which triggers his/her irrational belief which then, in turn, directly leads to his/her emotional reaction. *Rational emotive behaviour*

DASIE model DASIE stands for lifeskills counselling's five-stage model of counselling practice focused not just on managing current problems but on altering underlying problematic skills to prevent and manage future problems. *Lifeskills*

dilemmas a type of 'procedure' in cognitive-analytic therapy which describes choices about how we act or feel (in relation to ourselves or others) and which appears to be unnecessarily false or narrow. Usually we are unaware of this process and therapy is about promoting awareness and discovering new options. *Cognitive-analytic*

directive counselling and psychotherapy may very broadly be divided into two approaches: directive and non-directive. Directive approaches assume that the therapist brings knowledge and skills about particular types of problems to the therapeutic encounter and, with these, directs the course of therapy with the client's collaboration. Non-directive approaches assume that the client has within him or her the key to the resolution of his or her problems and the therapist therefore leaves the client to determine the direction of therapy. *Behaviour*

disputing the process of challenging a client's irrational belief and constructing a rational belief to replace it. *Rational emotive behaviour*

dissociation the process whereby some ideas, feelings, or activities lose relationship to other aspects of consciousness and personality and operate automatically or independently. *Hypnosis*

distortion and denial the process of suppression or filtering of experience which allows us to defend against those things that threaten our understanding of ourselves and the world. *Person-centred*

double imagery procedure a technique that encourages a client to visualize her/his future if she/he continues to avoid her/his problems (inaction imagery), and then contrast it with another view of her/his future based on tackling her/his problems (action imagery). This procedure is designed to motivate clients to change. *Problem focused*

dual systems approach procedure used in problem focused counselling which deals with the emotional aspects of a client's problem (e.g. anxiety about a career change) before focusing on the problem's practical aspects (e.g. upheavals involved in a career change). *Problem focused*

eclecticism in counselling, eclecticism refers to the combining of techniques and/or approaches from different schools of therapy. Multimodal therapy is an example of an eclectic approach.

ego one part of a tri-division of mind including id and superego. The ego was proposed by Freud and others to describe the development and interplay between components of mind. The term derived originally from Freud's attempt to develop a neurophysio-logical correlate of mind and was that part of the nervous system that was connected to the sense and hence in receipt of stimulation from the periphery. This was contrasted with stimulation arising from internal processes or drives such as thirst, hunger and later sexuality that Freud called 'id'. The task of therapy was, in Freud's famous phrase, to let ego be where id was, or, put differently, to release ourselves from the promptings of our drives to meet them through social means. The superego is thus seen as the internalization of the injunctions of rationality, expressed as socializing prohibitions to immediate gratification. Most terms in psychodynamics have been through an extended period of evolution, not least in Freud's own writing. *Freudian*

ego-state a consistent pattern of feeling and experience directly related to a corresponding consistent pattern of behaviour. *Transactional analysis*

empathy the process of becoming accurately aware of the internal experience of another and conveying this awareness to them. *Person-centred*

encouragement the emphasis on the positive in a person by the therapist. Clients are helped to appreciate the good things they have to offer. They learn to acknowledge that they have value as people. *Adlerian*

experimentation in personal construct theory our behaviour is the experiment we conduct to test out our construing – predictions – about each event that confronts us. Our subsequent behavioural experiment will be directly related to whether our last prediction proved right or wrong. Seeing behaviour as an experiment rather than as an end in itself is one of the unique features of personal construct theory. *Personal construct*

exposure or **exposure therapy** terms used in behaviour therapy. A person is encouraged to remain with the object, such as a spider, or situation, such as open spaces, which they fear. Initially, their anxiety increases, but will gradually lessen over time. This reduction in anxiety will become established if the *exposure* is regularly practised. The reduction of fear, in this way, is known as *extinction*. See also **avoidance**. *Behaviour*

family constellation the pattern of positions that the children take in their family when they are young. The children unconsciously choose through trial and error what sort of children they will be and take up their own unique positions like stars in a constel-lation. *Adlerian*

first, second and third positions different perspectives for looking at the same issue. First is seeing the issue through our own eyes, second involves stepping into someone else's shoes and seeing the issue from their point of view, and third involves stepping right outside the whole situation to be able to gain an objective view of the whole situation. *Neuro-linguistic programming*

flooding this is a form of **exposure** to the worst feared situation for a prolonged period of time, continuing until anxiety reduces. This may take place in reality or in imagination. Great care and professional guidance are recommended. *Behaviour*

freedom from the existential perspective we are free to respond to the limitations in which we find ourselves and are therefore responsible for the choices we make. *Existential*

game a repetitive process of behaviour with an ulterior motive that is (a) outside of conscious awareness, (b) does not become explicit until the participants switch the way they are behaving, and (c) leaves the people concerned feeling confused, misunderstood, and each wanting to blame the other person. *Transactional analysis*

givens those aspects of existence which are universal (e.g. death, freedom) and particular (e.g. our parents, the time and place of our birth). *Existential*

goal setting the acronym SMART helps clients focus on what they want to achieve. SMART refers to goals which are Specific, Measurable, Achievable, Relevant and Time bound. *Integrative*

homework assignments are considered integral to cognitive and cognitive behavioural therapy. They can take the form of bibliotherapy, that is reading self-help books, or the practice of cognitive or behavioural techniques outside the counselling sessions on a regular basis in order to help clients overcome their problems quickly and effectively. *Cognitive*

hypnoanalytical approaches these approaches assume that the presenting problem is being dynamically maintained by repressed historical experiences or current conflicts. In order to resolve the problem the client needs to access the repressed experiences in order to gain insight and to 'work through' the associated feelings in order to re-evaluate the conflictual material in the context of the present time. *Hypnosis*

hypnotherapeutic approach the utilization of the client's own unconscious resources for psychosomatic healing by providing suggestions which, by implication, activate the process of 'unconscious searching for solutions'. *Hypnosis*

id See **ego**.

identity the experience of being authentically oneself. *Psychosynthesis*

ideodynamic exploration a utilization approach that is particularly useful for uncovering repressed traumatic events, and their associated distressed feelings, related to current psychological and psychosomatic problems. Changes may be *ideomotor*, i.e. a movement of the finger (finger signalling) or *ideosensory*, i.e. changes in sensations experienced in the finger or hand. *Hypnosis*

implosion a form of prolonged flooding carried out in imagination usually with a great deal of anxiety. *Behaviour*

individuation the process which goes on throughout life, but is particularly important in the second half, of becoming more fully and consciously oneself, facing both strengths and limitations. Paradoxically it involves recognizing both one's uniqueness and ordinariness. *Jungian*

inner world our inner world is our own personal (three-dimensional and dynamic, changing) 'map' or construct which is made up of all the phantasies we have about ourselves and others, and which we use to understand the external world. The inner world is influenced by what happens in the external world, and vice versa. For example, we may relate to our partner as if he or she were the partner 'in our head', or in our internal world, rather than in the actual one. The partner in our internal world may be very similar to the one in the external world or may have important differences. *Kleinian*

integrative in counselling and psychotherapy 'integrative' refers to the integration or merging of two or more usually distinct therapeutic approaches. Cognitive analytic therapy is an example of an integrative approach. *Integrative*

Interpretation an attempt by the therapist to name the processes or material which the client is defending themselves from recognizing. It is typically seen as the moment of resolution in which what has been denied or repressed is brought into relational speech, thus freeing the client from having to keep it away. Often the denial or repression is so strong that a number of interpretations addressing the same issues have to be offered by the counsellor during the work together. *Freudian*

introjection the 'swallowing whole' of the attitudes, values, beliefs and opinions of significant people in our lives. This process shapes the development of our attitudes to self, others and the world (our intrapsychic process). *Gestalt*

irrational belief a rigid idea, often in the form of a must or should, which can create emotional distress and block goal-attainment. *Rational emotive behaviour*

levels of awareness personal construing can take place at different levels of awareness ranging from the clearly conscious level to the level of construing that we all evolve before we have acquired language. *Personal construct*

life-script a pre-conscious life-plan made in childhood, reinforced by the parents, 'justified' by subsequent events, and culminating in a chosen alternative. *Transactional analysis*

lifeskills sequences of choices affirming or negating psychological life that people make in specific skills areas. *Lifeskills*

lifestyle Adler's term for the unique and consistent pattern of behaviour in people consisting of their short- and long-term goals, their beliefs and feelings. People form their lifestyles in childhood. *Adlerian*

map of the world as humans we can never know reality, in the sense that we have to experience reality through our senses, and our senses are limited. A bee looking at this page would perceive it very differently because the way a bee perceives things is very different from the way a human perceives things. Our individual perception of how the world is, and what is important, forms our own unique 'map of the world'. *Neuro-linguistic programming*

miracle question a central intervention in solution focused therapy which invites the client to describe in detail their vision of life without the problem. *Solution focused*

modality profile This consists of an analysis of a client's identified problems divided into the seven **BASIC I.D.** modalities with the specific interventions written adjacent to the problems. *Multimodal*

modelling young children are often observed to imitate adults' behaviour, such as feeding themselves with a spoon. Not only children *model* others' behaviour. In behaviour therapy, specific behaviours are demonstrated to the client who then models them. For example, an unassertive client may observe a therapist acting assertively by saying no to a request and be encouraged to replicate this behaviour. *Behaviour*

Multimodal Life History Inventory 15-page questionnaire used in multimodal therapy to assist in assessing the **BASIC I.D.** modalities, history-taking and client expectations of therapy. *Multimodal*

non-directive counselling see directive

one-down position an attitude adopted by the counsellor of sharing expertise with the client. In this way the counsellor learns from the client how to cooperate effectively with him or her. *Solution focused*

organismic self-regulation the human organism is in constant interaction with the environment. In this process a person will be able to receive what is nourishing and reject what is toxic, thereby completing gestalts. In an ideal world there would be no unfinished business (incomplete gestalts). *Gestalt*

outcome study an investigation into the effectiveness of counselling or psychotherapy, designed to evaluate the degree of benefit or client change that can be attributed to the therapeutic intervention.

personal construct system this is the sum total of personal constructs we have created to make sense of (interpret, construe) events in our world as they take place and, in so doing, we are able to make predictions about their outcomes. *Personal construct*

phantasies mental constructions we use to make sense of our experiences. They involve people and things phantasised as inside us or outside us, doing things to each other and ourselves. They are dynamic and constantly changing. They influence our under-standing of the world around us as well as being influenced by it. *Kleinian*

phenomenology the method of existential therapy where an attempt is made to suspend prejudice and explanation so that what is observed can be more accurately described. *Existential*

presenting problem is the problem or issue identified by the client and/or counsellor on the client first presenting for counselling (e.g. depression, panic attacks, inability to cope following divorce, etc.). Over the course of counselling this focus may change, be resolved, or become irrelevant as wider or deeper issues emerge.

private logic refers to the unconscious beliefs and ideas that people have about themselves and the world and how they will move through life. *Adlerian*

procedure a term in cognitive-analytic therapy that decribes the sequence of beliefs, thoughts, feelings and actions behind any intended activity. Activity here is thought of in the broadest terms (e.g. thinking, feeling, relating, doing) and can include unconscious processes (see **PSORM**). *Cognitive-analytic*

process research a study which aims to investigate one or more of the elements or 'ingredients' of therapy. This kind of research may attempt to develop a detailed descriptive account of the process element (e.g. the therapist's or client's *experience* of empathy) or may examine the correlation between the presence of that element and successful outcome (e.g. are high levels of therapist-supplied empathy associated with good-outcome cases?).

projective identification a phantasy whereby someone gets rid of into another person an emotional state they cannot bear in themselves. In reality many subtle means are used to bring this phantasy to life. It is the most primitive means of communication between parent and infant or therapist and client. It may be used as a form of unconscious attack. *Kleinian*

PSORM the model that underpins cognitive-analytic therapy. It stands for 'Procedural Sequence Object Relations Model' and describes the way in which inner worlds (e.g. beliefs, perceptions and thoughts) relate to the outer world (e.g. acts) in a series of cyclical patterns ('**procedures**'). The model brings together cognitive and analytic theories and includes an explanation of how our sense of self develops. *Cognitive-analytic*

psychodynamic refers to the constantly changing aspect of the way we relate to others and ourselves; perceiving ourselves and others differently from moment to moment, according to our unconscious phantasies. *Kleinian*

psychopathology originally a psychiatric term referring to mental sickness or to an underlying personality problem, often classified into disorders such as depression, agoraphobia, post-traumatic stress disorder, borderline personality disorder, etc. Many counsellors dispute the reality behind or helpfuless of such labelling.

psychospiritual a psychological term used to denote that there are always two levels of experience, the first psychological and the second more essential or 'spiritual'. *Psychosynthesis*

psychotherapy is a usually talking-based approach to problems in living or aspirations towards greater self-fulfilment. It is a field characterized by multiple theories and generally lengthy training, usually including substantial therapy for trainees.

qualitative methods a style of doing research that relies on representing experience and action through written text. The key features of this approach are: use of interviewing as a means of data collection, concern for researcher reflexivity, use of hermeneutic and interpretive techniques to analyse data, research designs that employ case studies or intensive analyses of the experiences of particular groups.

quality world is a term used in **choice theory** (the theory which underlies reality therapy). Our 'quality world' is a small, simulated 'world' that we build into our memory which contains images or representations of all we want, or which has 'quality' for us. *Reality*

quantitative methods a style of doing research that relies on representing experience and action through numbers. The key features of this approach are: the use of measurement instruments such as questionnaires and rating scales, concern for the validity and reliability of instruments, application of statistical techniques in the analysis of data, and research designs that involve comparisons between groups.

randomized controlled trial (rct) a form of outcome study in which clients or patients are randomly assigned to different treatment conditions, or to a treatment condition and control/comparison group. The advantage of this method is that outcomes can be unambiguously attributed to treatment mode (other factors being held constant). Disadvantages of this method in therapy research: client preferences may make true randomization difficult to achieve; large numbers of clients are necessary to generate sufficient statistical power to detect differences; relevance of results for clinical practice is sometimes problematic.

rational belief a flexible idea, often in the form of a wish or want, that reduces or eliminates emotional distress and aids goal-attainment. *Rational emotive behaviour*

reciprocal role procedure a particular type of **procedure** in cognitive-analytic therapy, used to describe recurring patterns of relationships. Relationships are thought of as comprising a search for complementary roles. The term can describe forms of relationship with another person (externally) or with oneself (internally). *Cognitive-analytic*

reflective skills the use of paraphrasing and summarizing what the client has said to help the client explore his or her problem. Paraphrasing is the ability to sum up the content of what the client has said in one or two sentences. Summarizing is the ability to reflect back both the content and possible feelings the client may have expressed. *Integrative*

reflexivity personal construct theory is reflexive in that the theory applies as much to the construing of the counsellor as it does to that of the client. *Personal construct*

reframing offering an alternative meaning for similar constituent parts – like a jigsaw which can be made into two different pictures. Examples of reframing would be 'thinking about things differently', 'taking another point of view', or 'taking other factors into consideration'. *Neuro-linguistic programming*

regression going back in time to an earlier part of one's life. This means actually re-experiencing and reliving early life, not just remembering it. It is important to realize here that early experiences are registered in the cells and muscles of the body, not only in the brain. There is little benefit in regression in psychotherapy unless it is also accompanied by recession – that is, the move inward into the depths of one's own inner world. *Primal integration*

repertory grid a technique for creating mathematical relationships between the personal constructs of an individual. George Kelly described it as a way of 'getting beyond the words'. There are now many versions and many statistical and non-statistical ways of making sense of the data. *Personal construct*

response prevention clients often avoid further exposure to particular anxiety-provoking objects, situations or thoughts, collectively known as cues, by carrying out rituals which lessen the anxiety. In response prevention, the client is encouraged not to carry out the ritual which is usually triggered by the cue, so that continued exposure is allowed to take place. *Behaviour*

restatement in skills terms taking a client's problem and breaking it down into hypotheses about the component thinking skills and action skills deficits that maintain the problem and require addressing during and after counselling. *Lifeskills*

schema also known as 'core beliefs', these are usually developed in childhood. They are rules or themes which help the person make sense of the world and other people and serve to influence a person's automatic thoughts in certain situations. *Cognitive*

secondary gain where a problem carries a benefit at another level, e.g. smoking may help someone relax. An unconscious secondary gain may override the conscious desire to change. *Neuro-linguistic programming*

self-concept the conscious awareness and understanding we have of ourselves. It roughly corresponds with what we think of when referring to 'I' or 'me'. It informs our actions and perceptions and can be in tune with or at odds with our less conscious experience. *Person-centred*

self-control training is aimed at helping the client with problem behaviour to change their behaviour by initially becoming more aware of the events which immediately precede it. Self-monitoring, such as keeping a daily record, is often used by the client. Eventually the client will be able to identify specific cues and exert self-control when these occur. *Behaviour*

self-realization is the life process by which individuals find meaning and purpose and by which they realize their potential and self. *Psychosynthesis*

self-responsibility accounting for one's own needs and taking the relevant action to meet them. This should not be equated with self-sufficiency since it includes the capacity to receive from others. *Gestalt*

seven-step problem-solving model a sequence of steps used in problem focused counselling which teach clients how to, among other things, identify problems, generate possible solutions to them, put these solutions to the test and evaluate their effectiveness as problem-solving tools. *Problem focused*

skills language consistently using the concept of skills to describe and analyse people's behaviour. Conceptualizing and conversing about client's problems in terms of lifeskills strengths and deficits. *Lifeskills*

snags a type of **procedure** which describes how certain activities or choices seem unavailable to an individual because they may cause guilt or seem forbidden by some unspoken rule which is specific to the person concerned. Achievements may be limited by a fear that they will elicit envy (from others) or guilt (from oneself). *Cognitive-analytic*

social interest the feeling of belonging as an equal and the willingness to cooperate and make a contribution to society. *Adlerian*

submodalities the detailed aspects of the sensory qualities of each of the senses. So, for example, *visual submodalities* include: brightness, colour/black and white, distance, location, focus/fuzzy, two-dimensional or three-dimensional; *auditory submodalities include*: location, volume, tone, pitch, tempo; and *kinaesthetic* (related to body sensations) *submodalities* include: pressure, temperature, texture, location, size. *Neuro-linguistic Programming*

subpersonalities are different parts of the individual with unique feelings, thoughts, behaviours and characteristics, each having its own voice and needs. *Psychosynthesis*

subsuming the personal construct counsellor must be able to see the world as the client sees it – as far as is humanly possible – but also be able to understand the client's world in terms of the theory's set of professional constructs. To empathize is not enough. The counsellor must be able to move beyond the client's experiencing of the world in order to see a way forward *in the client's terms*. *Personal construct*

superego see **ego**.

symbol the best possible way of describing or expressing something relatively unknown. Symbolic thinking is non-linear, complementary to conscious logical and concrete thought, and functions through metaphor, images, etc., which are pregnant with meaning if sometimes enigmatic, e.g. in dreams. *Jungian*

take-away sheets are used in lifeskills counselling during sessions for taking down learnings from the whiteboard. In addition they are used for recording mutually agreed homework assignments. *Lifeskills*

technical eclecticism a therapeutic approach that applies techniques taken from many different psychological theories and systems, without necessarily being concerned with the validity of the theoretical principles that underpin the different approaches from which it takes its techniques. *Multimodal*

teleological purposeful and goal-directed. Adlerians consider that all behaviour has a purpose and to understand behaviour the goal has to be identified. *Adlerian*

the message a summary given by the solution focused counsellor at the end of a session. It may include a compliment and a task for the client to perform. *Solution focused*

theoretical orientation (also known as approach, model, school, brand name) usually refers to any kind of clearly espoused therapeutic identity such as Freudian, Jungian, TA, Gestalt, cognitive, eclectic, etc., but may also refer broadly to humanistic, psychoanalytic, etc. BAC require accredited courses to have an acceptable core theoretical model.

thinking errors also known as 'cognitive distortions', are logical errors based on faulty information processing. These include jumping to conclusions, personalization and all-or-nothing thinking. *Cognitive*

thinking skills are the mental processes through which people can create and influence how they think: for example, perceiving, explaining cause, predicting, and visualizing. *Lifeskills*

total behaviour is a term used in **choice theory** which states that all of our behaviour is 'total behaviour' which is made up of acting, thinking, feelings, and even our physiology – which always accompanies the other three components. Acting and thinking are always under our voluntary control; feelings and physiology can only be changed through changing how we act and think. *Reality*

tracking when tracking, the 'firing order' of the different modalities is noted for a specific problem. Once assessed, the client is instructed to match the firing order of the modalities with a corresponding sequence of modality interventions. *Multimodal*

transference the way we relate to others is based on phantasies which were created as a result of our experiences of people (usually family members) in our past. We interpret every action of the therapist through our phantasies: which derive ultimately from our experiences (real and imaginary and coloured by our emotions, our desires, our wishes) in relation to our parents. Transference refers to this process. As the therapy activates and changes different phantasies about our parents, so the way we perceive a therapist will change. (See also **counter-transference**.) *Kleinian*

transpersonal going beyond the pre-personal and the personal into the realm of mystical experiences. There are a number of different levels of mystical experience, such as the Centaur, the Psychic, the Subtle, the Causal and the Nondual, which have been well explained and described by Ken Wilber. *Primal integration*

transpersonal the realm of human experience which is beyond the personal, everyday and existential awareness. *Psychosynthesis*

traps a type of 'procedure' that describes a vicious circle in which trying to deal with feeling bad about ourselves we think and act in ways that tend to confirm our badness. *Cognitive-analytic*

trauma is the infliction of pain on an organism. Frank Lake has distinguished between four levels of trauma. Each level of trauma produces different effects. The first level may be quite stimulating, and benefit the organism. The second level is harder to overcome, but can be handled effectively and healthily in most cases. The third level produces neurotic defences such as repression, dissociation and splitting. The fourth level is quite unendurable, and produces a turning against the self – a wish to die. *Primal integration*

unconditional positive regard is the accepting or respecting the whole of a person exactly as they are. *Person-centred*

unconditional self-acceptance the concept of never judging or rating oneself on the basis of one's actions or characteristics, the opinions of others or life events. *Rational emotive behaviour*

unconscious is used by psychodynamic counsellors to indicate all those processes of mind which occur outside of consciousness. The assumption that there is an unconscious with its own methods of processing information was imputed by Freud from the reports of his patients describing dreams or from observations of slips of the tongue or from disturbances of affect that were associated with the return of material that Freud proposed had been repressed as a result of trauma. While there is no difficulty in assuming that much of our processing occurs outside of awareness there are great philosophical problems that result from leaping from this to assume that there is a subdivision of mind with its own distinctive methods of processing that in some way knows what to repress. *Freudian*

unfinished business an unmet need does not go away but remains active and demands completion. An accumulation of unmet needs may seriously impair functioning in the present. *Gestalt*

utilization the acceptance of all the behaviours, symptoms, attitudes, and emotional responses of the client, no matter how negative or obstructive they may appear, as assets and resources in the therapy process. *Hypnosis*

'WDEP system' devised by Dr Robert Wubbolding as a way of teaching and counselling with reality therapy. Each of the letters actually contains a cluster of ideas relating to the procedures that lead to change but which can be summarized as: **W** = helping clients determine their *wants*; identify whether they perceive their control as being 'internal' or 'external' to them and to establish a level of commitment to change or for growth. **D** = helping clients to describe what they are *doing*, i.e. their 'total behaviour' including actions, their self-talk and feelings. **E** = helping clients to *evaluate* in other words is what they are doing helping or preventing them from getting what it is that they say they want (via seven kinds of evaluation). **P** = making a *plan* of action that leads to effective change.

working through is the process of testing phantasies against reality, which has to be repeated again and again until we have changed our phantasies to bring them closer into line with reality. *Kleinian*

APPENDIX 1
DIFFERENT PSYCHOTHERAPEUTIC*
ORIENTATIONS

Colin Feltham

T his list is intended to give a flavour of the current range and proliferation of psychotherapies. It must be acknowledged that no attempt has been made to ascertain just how current all these approaches are, although to the best of my knowledge they are all currently being practised. Some may object that certain therapies listed here are merely variants of others (e.g. redecision therapy is a kind of transactional analysis) and might be better described as schools within a particular approach. On the other hand, I have not included, for example, creative novation therapy or other varieties of non-classical behaviour therapy, nor the different schools of Jungian or post-Jungian therapy. Family therapy (and its many variants), group and couple therapy, sex therapy, child psycho-therapy, and so on, have all been omitted. I have not included the many burgeoning forms of brief therapy, such as short-term anxiety-provoking psychotherapy, not to mention different approaches to crisis intervention. Nor have I included all humanistic therapies and complementary or alternative medicine approaches to psychological/emotional/holistic problems or concerns, such as polarity therapy, postural integration, shamanism, est, Alexander Tech-nique, Sufi dancing, acupuncture, homeopathy, Bach flower remedies, and so on. Dianetics (scientology) has been similarly excluded, although many would classify this as therapy. Meditation, yoga, LSD therapy and the many varieties of traditional and non-traditional religious practices have likewise been excluded.

Adlerian Therapy (Individual
  Psychology)
Art Therapy
Behaviour Therapy
Biodynamics
Bioenergetics
Biofeedback
Biosynthesis
Body Psychotherapy

Clinical Theology
Cognitive Analytic Therapy
Cognitive-Behavioural Therapy
Cognitive-Interpersonal Therapy
Cognitive Therapy
Communicative Psychotherapy
Contextual Modular Therapy
Daseinanalyse
Dialogical Psychotherapy

---

* Feltham, C. (1997) *Which Psychotherapy?* London: Sage.

Dramatherapy
Encounter
Existential Therapy
Experiential Psychotherapy
Feminist Therapy
Focused Expressive Psychotherapy
Focusing
Gestalt Therapy
Hypnotherapy
Implosive Therapy
Inner Child Advocacy
Integrative Psychotherapy
Intensive Short-term Dynamic
  Psychotherapy
Interpersonal Psychotherapy
Jungian Analysis (Analytical
  Psychology)
Kleinian Analysis
Lacanian Analysis
Lifeskills Training
Logotherapy
Micropsychoanalysis
Morita Therapy
Motivational Interviewing
Multimodal Therapy
Narrative-Constructivist Therapy
Neuro-Linguistic Programming
Object Relations Therapy

Past Lives Therapy
Personal Construct Therapy
Person-Centred Therapy
Primal Integration
Primal Therapy
Process-Oriented Psychotherapy
Psychoanalysis
Psychoanalytically-Oriented
  Psychotherapy
Psychodrama
Psychosynthesis
Rational Emotive Behaviour
  Therapy
Reality Therapy
Rebirthing
Redecision Therapy
Re-evaluation Counselling
Reichian Therapy (Orgone Therapy)
Rolfing
Single-Session Therapy
Social Therapy
Solution Focused Brief Therapy
Stress Inoculation Training
Systemic Therapy
Transactional Analysis
Transpersonal Therapy
Twelve Steps Therapy
Will Therapy

APPENDIX 2
ISSUES FOR THE CLIENT TO CONSIDER IN COUNSELLING OR PSYCHOTHERAPY

1 Here is a list of topics or questions you may wish to raise when attending your first counselling (assessment) session:

   (a) Check that your counsellor has relevant qualifications and experience in the field of counselling/psychotherapy.

   (b) Ask about the type of approach the counsellor uses, and how it relates to your problem.

   (c) Ask if the counsellor is in supervision (most professional bodies consider supervision to be mandatory; see footnote).

   (d) Ask whether the counsellor or the counselling agency is a member of a professional body and abides by a code of ethics. If possible obtain a copy of the code.

   (e) Discuss your goals/expectations of counselling.

   (f) Ask about the fees if any (if your income is low, check if the counsellor operates on a sliding scale) and discuss the frequency and estimated duration of counselling.

   (g) Arrange regular review sessions with your counsellor to evaluate your progress.

   (h) Do not enter into a long-term counselling contract unless you are satisfied that this is necessary and beneficial to you.

If you do not have a chance to discuss the above points during your first session discuss them at the next possible opportunity.

General issues

2 Counsellor self-disclosure can sometimes be therapeutically useful. However, if the sessions are dominated by the counsellor discussing his/her own problems at length, raise this issue in the counselling session.

3 If at any time you feel discounted, undermined or manipulated within the session, discuss this with the counsellor. It is easier to resolve issues as and when they arise.

4 Do not accept significant gifts from your counsellor. This does not apply to relevant therapeutic material.

5 Do not accept social invitations from your counsellor. For example, dining in a restaurant or going for a drink. However, this does not apply to relevant

therapeutic assignments such as being accompanied by your counsellor into a situation to help you overcome a phobia.

6 If your counsellor proposes a change in venue for the counselling sessions without good reason, do not agree. For example, from a centre to the counsellor's own home.

7 Research has shown that it is not beneficial for clients to have sexual contact with their counsellor. Professional bodies in the field of counselling and psychotherapy consider that it is unethical for counsellors or therapists to engage in sexual activity with current clients.

8 If you have any doubts about the counselling you are receiving, then discuss them with your counsellor. If you are still uncertain, seek advice, perhaps from a friend, your doctor, your local Citizens Advice Bureau, the professional body your counsellor belongs to or the counselling agency that may employ your counsellor.

9 You have the right to terminate counselling whenever you choose.

Footnote: Counselling supervision is a formal arrangement where counsellors discuss their counselling in a confidential setting on a regular basis with one or more professional counsellors.

© 1994, Palmer and Szymanska

AFTERWORD

I hope this book has provided the reader with sufficient information to acquire a basic understanding of the theory and practice of each of the twenty three approaches covered. Appendix 1 highlights some of the different counselling and psychotherapeutic approaches that I initially considered before making the final selection to be included in this introductory text. Inevitably there was insufficient space to incorporate all of them!

In case readers wish to receive therapy or attend a suitable counselling course, I have provided a list of the main British organizations that hold registers of accredited counsellors, chartered counselling psychologists or registered psychotherapists and also recognise relevant therapeutic training programmes or specific training centres. If a reader is interested in making a career in this field of work, it is relatively important when progressing onto advanced training programmes to attend courses that may lead to a qualification recognised by one of these organizations. It is worth noting that in recent years, the advent of professional accreditation or recognition of practitioners has frequently led to employers asking applicants for therapeutic jobs to be accredited or recognized.

If readers wish to give me feedback about this book the address for correspondence, including my email address, is:

Centre for Stress Management
156 Westcombe Hill
London, SE3 7DH
Email: palmer@managingstress.com

Professional bodies

British Association for Counselling
1 Regent Place
Rugby, CV21 2PJ

British Psychological Society
St Andrews House
48 Princess Road East
Leicester, LE1 7DR

United Kingdom Council for Psychotherapy
167-169 Great Portland Street
London, WIN 5FB

INDEX

Page numbers in *italic* refer to figures. Those followed by *g* are glossary references.